T0367845

FADING ECHOES
(Letters of Yesteryears)

R. Garner Brasseur, M.D.

authorHOUSE®

AuthorHouse™
1663 Liberty Drive
Bloomington, IN 47403
www.authorhouse.com
Phone: 1-800-839-8640

Published by AuthorHouse 7/29/2013

ISBN: 978-1-4817-7164-1 (sc)
ISBN: 978-1-4817-7163-4 (e)

3-17-86

Hobbs, New Mexico

Dear Mom,

Well, here comes your birthday again! The years seem somehow to fly, though the minutes, hours and days seem sometimes to drag on interminably. How shall we explain such apparent discrepancy? And what shall we do about it?

As you undoubtedly know, I have been in search of a new area into which I might relocate. I prefer not to have to start up my own practice, as those myriad headaches related to taxes, book-keeping, business, and expensive equipment are cumbersome and thankless in the extreme. Therefore I have been heavily in pursuit of a situation in which I might caste my lot in with an already established physician or group. Failing in that, however, I may yet find it necessary to establish my own practice.

I had some hopes of being able to practice on only a part-time basis, so that I would have more time reading, and limiting, and staring at the stars. I had hoped to go back to school for a few years to improve my literary sense, speaking ability, and writing skills. That plan may now have to be deferred for a couple of years, until these youngsters of ours have all completed their college educations. M.A. is in her first year of

1

college. And RL seems to be getting good grades, now that he is settled down to a married life. RL and TM are expecting my third grandchild sometime in April or may.

This business of life is evasive and troublesome in the extreme. It is so shrouded in darkness and ignorance; and all the pathways toward progress are so encumbered with various obstacles, as to nearly discourage one altogether. Still, what alternatives have we, but to make the most or it as an experience, and to learn from it what we can? And besides, it does seem to be the only game in town. Current events and history indicates that individual man suffers abundantly with a great deal of variation between times and places. It seems to be the case that the burden or human misery can be circumvented and alleviated to a large degree through human agency, subsequent to rational acts and behavior, based in turn upon the accumulation of facts, data, and knowledge. Such an outcome, however, is necessarily dependent upon a measure of good-will and open-minded toleration in a world of prejudice and bigotry. Therefore, is progress slow and fitful.

You too, perhaps - just as I - have some sense of frustration that we are all seem to be inundated by the ignorance and prejudice of our various subcultures and times; and that the limited nature of our individual length of life, experience of life and personal accomplishment of education is such that we can never entirely loosen ourselves from this ancient source of error. Indeed, some never try, nor even consider the possibility of their own prejudice. It is my impression is that our own children are a major contributing force to our personal education and enlightenment, and in making our prejudice visible to us.

We often think of man as that creature, gifted with intelligence. Yet, that intelligence is only relative and is achieved largely through method and purpose - they in turn, being culturally perpetrated through family and community. The evolution of computers and computer technology is beginning to make us aware of the areas of weakness and limitation of human intelligence. Being aware of those limitations, leads us into the possibility of enhancing our intellectual abilities with improved methods and computer technology.

The time, the place, the family, and the circumstances into which we are individually born, greatly influence our opportunity for

2

achievement, and the quality and style of our lives. Even under the most oppressive of circumstances, there seems always, some limited potential of opportunity for the individual of unique strength, intellect, character, outlook or other special gift. In all things, and with all persons, there is the ubiquitous fact of failure, such that a certain minimum of courage and determination are prerequisite to success. Nor is there any certain or unchallenged criteria as to the measure of success.

As I think back upon that family of Brasseur children that moved into a big yellow house on N. Jordan St., in 1942, at Miles City, Montana, I wouldn't have thought that their circumstances and opportunities of life were especially favorable. And yet, compared to the lot of young folks throughout the world at that time, their portion was good. For they enjoyed good health in a community far from the ravishes of a world war. They were too young to be called upon to sacrifice their limbs or risk their lives on the battlefields. They had warm shelter and clothing, as well as adequate educational facilities. Compared to their distant relatives in Russia, Germany, and France, their lot was fortunate at that time in history. And their access to higher education, though economically troublesome, continued then – as now – a realistic option. Certain it is however, that I had no personal intent of attending any classes, beyond the time of my graduation from high school. As it turned out however, the circumstances of my life, my family, and the people of my acquaintance and friendships all conspired - by chance, perhaps - to make it inevitable that my education should continue. Due in part to poor visual acuity caused by high astigmatism, my reading and math skills were poor. The shapes of letters and figures were seen by me as distorted, run together, and difficult to decipher. Naturally, in so far as I knew, that was the way that things were supposed to look. Fortunately, at sometime in high school I obtained a pair of spectacles that gave me pretty good acuity; and reading became a little easier. Eventually, I even came to enjoy it; and it has become one of my favorite pastimes. That is not to say that the technical feat of reading is itself pleasant (as is the chemical and mechanical act of eating nicely cooked meals). But it is the case that one may have or develop an appetite for concepts, ideas, and theories. Somehow, I did. There is no practical method in our society of finding or keeping in touch with such, except through reading.

Perhaps the biggest problem that I have faced over the years is not a paucity of opportunity, but rather, that of finding a lasting contentment once I have arrived anew at any of those bright and promising new-found occupations. I've worked at some 25 or 30 different jobs, and found most of them to be interesting initially, but soon they become sort of routine; and then something else, or some other place seems to attract my interest. And soon I am launched out on some other new course, or in pursuit of some other new truth or ideal. From your point of view, it may well all seem to be erratic and perhaps frustrating to have to witness all of this bumbling about. To be sure, it brings upon my own head a certain quantity of unpleasantness, but that is always diluted out with new - often unrealistic - hopes. And spares me from any prolonged periods of boredom. But you ought not to be surprised that I and other members of the family have a certain tendency to wander about upon the face of the globe, for both sides of the family history give evidence of that over many generations. The Boepple ancestors are probably descended from the Seubi and Alemanni, who occupied the Alsace-Lorraine and Wurttemberg area of central Europe since about 300 AD. After the fall of Napoleon, some of these people emigrated from that area to an area near Odessa, above the Black Sea (about 1816-1817). Dad's ancestors seem probably to have derived from the Walloons, a group related to the Saxons - from an area along the borderlands between France and Belgium. And our Brasseur ancestor came as single young man to the Quebec area of Canada just before the English conquest of New France. One of his descendants, relocated to an area near St. Valerien (about 60 miles to the east of Montreal about 1832) from where the Brasseurs had settled into agriculture just to the southwest of Montreal Island.

There exists the concept of 'roots', as it applies to people and families. As I understand the term, it implies a tendency displayed by some folks to reside permanently in a particular community. A more remote corollary of that notion is that those who move about - for whatever reason - do so because of a certain impropriety in their character. A comforting and self-serving delusion to those who are well-situated economically and socially. The concept, used in that sense, is not one for which I have any use. Plants have their roots in the soil; but people have their roots in their ancestors, and in the traditions of their ancestors. There is no reason to believe that those who wander are more lost than those whose tap-roots have them securely tethered to their fortuitous local sources of wealth.

Does anyone certainly know how to measure and gauge success? Does it arise from virtue, or effort, or chance? Perhaps it is a random gift, or an earned reward? Knotty questions - nichts whar? Though I enjoy wrestling with questions such as these, I don't claim to have their answers. I suspect that you and I and our people have had some measure of success; and that depending upon how we look at the questions, we still retain some measure of success, in the form of courage, industry, and other such virtues. I have been driving back and forth across the United States the past few months, looking for a new place to settle. I have a warm sleeping bag, and sleep on a cot in the pickup camper. You mustn't grieve or worry on my behalf, for I am in good health, and this new wrinkle in the fabric of life causes me no significant suffering or heartache. In truth, there are many things about it that I rather enjoy. It gives me a chance to study the geological formations across the land; and time to think and ponder and to write a little. In truth, it is a whole lot more fun than having to work every day. To be without an income however, is inconvenient. I do have several good job possibilities to investigate and if nothing definite becomes soon available, I may yet simply set up my own office somewhere. Because of the tremendous expense involved in that however, I prefer to avoid it, unless absolutely necessary.

I stopped in to see EVH a few weeks ago, as I was passing through the state of Arizona. He has a handsome bushy beard, but not much hair upon his pate. We embraced and kissed each other upon the cheek, as is the custom between me and my own children. I stayed there two nights and we talked at length. From time to time, I had to close down the conversation, and begin it anew, upon some new trail. For he has a tendency to pass off some of his exotic beliefs as dogmatic truths with a flamboyant take-it-or-leave-it flare. But he remains philosophical and good-natured in the face of all of his current difficulties. One simply has to admire and pay homage to that sort of courage and determination, which keeps him continuously at odds with the IRS. For in this matter of abusive taxes and irresponsible government agents, his cause for concern is well justified. Nor is he simply a tax-evader; for as he points out, the entire constitution is in danger of becoming progressively subverted. He is a patriot; and that he spends a little time in jail from time-to-time, does not prove that his views or his actions are wrong. For all we know, history may yet eventually proclaim him as a hero of his country. He regards himself as a religious sort of guy, and is much attached and loyal to his whole family. That he reaps a certain resentment from his heavy-handed and autocratic methods of dealing with his loved ones does not detract from the fact that he bears them a large measure of good-will and generally has their best interests at heart. His ideas, his conversation, and his behavior throughout his life, are uncommonly idealistic as well exotic. I know of few people that have encouraged and influenced as many lives as has he. If you had the chance this past summer to speak for long with PM, you may have noticed in his attitude and speech, a great deal that gives evidence of EVH's influence upon him. I shall enclose to you a copy of a letter to the editor, recently written by RL. That too, displays the influence of EVH. EVH, like an ancient prophet, continues to harangue and call to repentance, 'publicans and tax collectors' from his base of operations out there in the desert. Though he claims that his efforts are having some affect, I have no way of knowing to what extent that is true; for he too, is, in effect, a political agent, and there seems to be a good deal of propaganda in what he claims and says. He endangers himself somewhat of course by goading the authority, so that he may suddenly one day turn up missing, or be writing to us from the pokey. A great many of the world's great men, and reformers and leaders, have served their time with courage, honor, and distinction, so don't let yourself be unsettled if it comes to that.

Meanwhile, through the years, I too have been continuously at odds with what goes on in this strange and incomprehensible world. And I too have become somewhat of a reformer, though my views and concerns are somewhat at odds with EVH's ideas. Though I had some hopes of getting back to school to reconsider and solidify my views I am nearly broke again; and it is obvious that I will have to slip back into the harness for at least a couple of years until MABC and RL are through college, and to put together a little nest-egg so that I can sit me down by the quiet 'waters of Babylon', after I straighten out my financial affairs.

FADING ECHOES

I don't know if I told you that a few years ago I found a certain foreigner situationally naked and grieving along the roadside of life - because his fondest dreams and hopes in life were slipping from his grasp. Several, even of his own race and country had already passed him by or crossed over to the other side, or merely extended to him their blessing and good wishes. I, being a newcomer and foreigner to this New Mexico area, and unacquainted with its customs, stopped to inquire as to his problem. He had already suffered a great deal in his discouragement, but seemed determined to suffer more; and so, I agreed to encourage and assist him in his self-inflicted course of pain, once he clearly understood that I did not necessarily advocate that course as being worthy of that much suffering. Having thus understood one another, we sent him off to Guadalajara, in the state of Jalisco, in Mexico where he suffered another three years of impoverishment and strain in medical school. He finally obtained his medical degree this past December. He and his wife and their two small children have been staying at our home with us the past several weeks, while he is looking for a job to occupy him in the next three months before he begins his internship in Baltimore, Maryland. He is a bright and interesting young man, and I enjoy having him around. My little difficulties seem like nothing, compared to his.

Perhaps you heard that my wife's oldest sister - RS-H - died a few weeks ago. Mrs. Ny and she were at a dance; and she suddenly died while dancing. It is difficult for me to imagine a better way to go. My wife flew up there for the funeral.

As I am beginning to aspire to be a writer when I grow up, I have recently taken up typing again; and I am gradually getting a little better at it. The main difficulty is that it is more difficult this way to camouflage ones spelling.

Happy birthday.

Love

Your son
Garner Brasseur

3-17-86

3/18/87

Las Vegas, NV

Dear Mom,

As I write you I am sitting here in Caesar's Palace in Las Vegas, Nevada. It is a truly sumptuous place! Of all of these "dens of vice" here in Las Vegas, I find it the most interesting. For I have read a great deal of Roman History and I find that the names of the various conference rooms, as well as the structures, facades, and works of art here - all of these things turn my thoughts towards German and Roman History. Why German History? Because the two histories are intricately bound together. Neither can therefore be comprehended without reference to the other. German peoples were a part of the original peoples involved in the founding of Rome. And throughout her whole history, Rome was forced to struggle against the invasion of the German peoples to the north of the Alps, from the Rhine and Danube River Valleys. Eventually, Rome was conquered, and her territories occupied by Germans Peoples. These Germans in turn were conquered by the civilizing influences which they acquired from the Greek and Roman cultures within that Roman Empire. It was not a matter of merely defeating, and then destroying and looting the Roman Empire, though some of that went on also. Rather, they seem to have had a hankering for the southern climate and the sunshine that bathes those Mediterranean shores. A large proportion of the rest of Europe was a dark and un-cleared forest. In addition to the sunshine and the cleared lands of southern Europe, the Germans also had an eager interest in attaining to a civilized and cultured life style.

Subsequent to the year 98 AD there was only an occasional Roman Emperor that was from Italy. First Spaniards, then a few French, then Illyrians (from what is now Yugoslavia) were it's Emperors. Later, beginning with Valentinian in 364 AD, the people of German origin controlled the western half of the empire first indirectly and then directly. The rank and file of the Roman Legions eventually came to consist of rather few of Italian peoples subsequent to about 200 AD. By the year 350 AD, the whole western half of the Empire had been almost completely taken over by the various Germanic peoples. Though the

Celts had controlled France and Western Europe (known as Gaul), by 250 AD, those lands were, for the most part, in the hands of Germanic peoples. The Franks and the Burgundeans who took control of the areas we now call France and Belgium, were in fact German people. So that what we today call French people, are in fact largely of German origin. They appear in fact to have been derived from the peoples of southwest Germany, namely, the Alemanni, Franks, Saxons, and Subians. These Germanic peoples appear in fact to be those from which we ourselves are derived. Perhaps our direct ancestors were most likely the Seubi and the Alemanni. Dad has told Vic that our particular French origins are from the Walloon tribe out of Belgium, a part of the Saxon group.

I have in the past 4-6 months accumulated about thirty pages of that information. But I need now to rework it into a legible hand or type it. This then is just a brief synopsis for your information, as I don't know just when I might get around to finishing the other. Though the name of Alemanni has persisted since about 250 AD, when they first collided with the Roman Legions on the Rhine frontier, they in fact seem to be derived from the Seubi or vice versa. These Suevi were (at the time of Julius Caesar and Caesar Augustus), situated between the Elbe and the Vistula Rivers. They were a populous and powerful people, divided into many sub-tribes (in the same sense that the American Indians were similarly divided and sub-divided. Complex business, nicts whar?

Back to times more current, though. It appears that an Adam Boepple lived in a small village called Plattenhardt (near Stuttgart) in the state of Wurttemberg of southwest Germany. In 1817, he uprooted what was left of his family and traveled with them down the Danube River to settle in southwest Russia (near Odessa). About 10,000 people from all the many scattered villages of that state made that trip that summer. They were headed with new hope into this Promised Land, where the earth had never previously been touched by a plough share. Unfortunately, they didn't know their history and hence they were doomed to repeat that history. For the territories through which they must pass had been known for a couple hundred years, already, as 'the graveyard of Germans'. About 4,000 of the 10,000 emigrants died en route to south Russia. The evidence suggests that Adam Boepple went on to Elizabeththal in the South Caucus in what is now

Georgia. At least one or some of his sons survived. They wintered in or near Grossliebenthal, about 10 or 12 miles southwest of Odessa, with colonists from their same home state (Wurttemberg), some of whom had settled this area beginning about 1804. In the spring of 1818, after wintering in southern Bessarabia, most of the newcomers remained there or moved on to the north of Odessa, to establish their own new settlements. The survivors of the Boepple family however, seems probably to have remained behind to settle in with those earlier colonists in Bessarabia. For, a generation or two later, Christoph Boepple (your grandfather) seems to have married a woman from the Hoeschlele family (there were two Hoeschele families that were pioneers to Grossliebenthal perhaps about about 1825). Both, however, were from small villages not far from Plattenhardt (where the Adam Boepple group came from).

The parents of your mother, Cristina Fried-Gotz seem to have been derived from the pioneer families (Fried, Gotz, and Mueller) that had established settlement at Borodino in Bessarabia. They, in turn were a part of the 10,000 that came from those Wurttemberg villages in 1817. I had some original difficulty locating Mannsburg (where you say your mother was married). But I discovered it was only a few miles south of Seimeny. In the year of her marriage, a Pastor Beck seems to have served several of these small communities. Whatever little details you provide me helps me fit these things together.

As to Siementhal (Siemeny), where George Boepple was born, I had some difficulty locating it originally. It seems to have been a bit northwest of to Grossliebenthal (10 or 12 miles S.W. of Odessa). Grossliebenthal was an administrative center of the various colonies in Kerson area. Music seems to have been a strong cultural influence among the German peoples, and the Boepples seem to have had their share of musical talent. That he developed those interests and talents, also suggests that he came from a family of tradesmen or merchants, rather than farmers.

Concerning immigration to the USA, a large proportion of those Germans from south Russia converged first upon South Dakota, as did George Boepple. As their kinsmen immigrated through here subsequently, they spread to the north and west to take up homestead properties in the Dakota Territory and subsequently into eastern Montana, and some into Kansas, Nebraska, Oklahoma, and Colorado. By 1920, North Dakota had 70,000 of these German-Russians. South Dakota and Kansas each had 31,000. These peoples clung tightly to their traditions; and were rather clannish. They seldom married outside of their own community and people. That would have been the tendency even when you were married. And it was still true (but, less rigidly) when I married into that Russian German family of Saurs in 1955. Three of my wife's siblings married into a single family (the Huft's). Very few of these Russian-German families had any familial tradition of advanced education. They had a certain pride in their success as farmers and as the progenitors of large families. They seem to have exhibited a sort of anti-intellectual bias. Your own father appears to have been one of the few exceptions to this rule. Though I had never previously given the matter much thought it would appear that George Boepple was a rather remarkable character. Very few from his generation achieved what he did. Music was his avocation, though he became a grain buyer by occupation. We must suppose that he acquired English quickly upon arriving and settling in Tripp, SD, and then devoted himself to a proficiency in English to facilitate his occupation. Towards that end I am given to understand he attended night-school. And later had credentials enough to actually become a music teacher. To change occupations at the age of 45 or 50. Having now first realized all of this; I must acknowledge that I am amazed and proud of his grit; and of the character of which these accomplishments give evidence.

When and if I ever get this little project completed, I shall of course send you a copy. But in the meantime, you can think about this synoptic version and let me know if I seem to have arrived at any obviously erroneous conclusions. And you may have access to some other small details of history which could provide me some extra clues in putting together my final version of family history.

And I realize that your birthday is forthcoming. Though as always, I am short of time, I use your birthday as the occasion to absolutely require of myself that I communicate with you as one person to another. In the realm of ideas and thought, some of which I hope you may find interesting. Perhaps we may uncover and preserve a more comprehensive final historical view of these things.

Have a happy birthday.

Love
Your son
R. Garner Brasseur
[Information updated in 2013]

3/18/87

7 May 1988
Caldwell, Idaho

Dear Mom,

A belated happy birthday; and Mother's Day, too. It reminds me of the many uncomfortable experiences I have had while playing baseball, as a youngster. In taking my turn at batting, the ball often whizzed by my upheld bat before I had a chance to respond. It wasn't that I didn't know the ball was coming; rather, just that the ball arrived … and passed before one had adequate time to decide what to do about it. My batting average seemed to improve, once I figured out that it was best to make up one's mind (to swing, or not to swing) before the pitcher made the pitch. Yet, here, the case is not strictly analogous; and I have not yet figured out how to keep all of these special event days from getting past me. But of course, I don't really have to explain that to you, for you have enough friends and relatives as to make it a certainty, that you are acquainted with the principle. And so it came to pass, that on the very day of your own birthday, my thoughts were centered upon MABC and I was writing a letter to her. For she is away, at college, and away from home for an extended period of time for the first time in her life. And it seems to me that I need to exhort, admonish and encourage her, as a part of her education in order to seed her thought processes with some doubts and a few outrageous ideas - so as to keep her crowded up against the realities of the great unknown world and universe, of which we are a part.

12

FADING ECHOES

For woe be unto those who begin to believe all that they have heard and learned,

As it happens, I never think of MABC, but what I am reminded of you, too - and of your mother. Apparently, my memory banks have got the three of you grouped together somewhere in my cerebral cortex so that the flow of those images and thoughts concerning any one of you, seems to recruit to my conscious being an awareness of the others in that same group. From my point of view you naturally have some things in common, the most obvious being that each is one of a special sequence of three. In so far as I can remember, my mind has always maintained this sense of historical sequence. I think it has become much more pronounced in the past fifteen years since I have acquired an interest in History and in Genealogy. As a youngster, I generally abstained from having my say, but through the years my ability to withhold my opinion has gradually declined. It often brings me additional grief, for it opens more widely the gate to troublesome disagreements; and yet, that is only a way of saying that only those who attempt a thing are subject to failure in that effort. There certainly seems to be some difficulty in the communications between men and women in this world - and not just in our family. For they are reared under entirely different circumstances, and generally have quite different outlooks on life. That, I think, is largely from prejudice that is transmitted to us from cultural circumstance and custom of times past. An influence that we all, as individuals, have difficulty in escaping. And yet, reality is a unity and our individual opinions are mere prejudice, to the degree that they fail to coincide with reality. We are all excusable, of course, for we are mere mortals of a primitive tribe of creatures that is only slowly acquiring some little store of information and habits of the mind such as to enable us to begin to think - and even sometimes act - upon the basis of reason. I was over in Boise a few weeks ago to spend a day in chasing down some family information in the Idaho State Genealogy Library. I stopped in to see your second cousin, Emil Boepple. He is about 67 years of age and a genial sort of fellow, but he and his wife were a little depressed yet, at the death of their only son, who was accidentally killed the early part of this year in a fall of fifteen feet from a construction platform at a mall there in Boise. He landed on his head, and never ever even regained consciousness. He apparently broke his neck in the fall. He was only forty-three years of age. They showed me his picture. He looked to me like Uncle Benny. He was married, and had one boy and one girl. Your cousin, Emil Boepple, also has two daughters. Kind of a small family, compared to the long previous tradition of large families among these German people. He had previously supplied me with some information concerning his branch of the Boepple family and I left with him some additional information that I had recently discovered. When I got home that day I had a letter awaiting me from Mike Rempfer, who is your fourth-cousin-twice-removed, who lives in Santa Fe, NM. He and I have been exchanging information by mail and we now had enough data to trace the family back two more generations and to figure out the point at which these different branches of the family were related. The lineage runs like this:

Gottlieb Boepple (b. 1805)
Married @ Wittenberg, Bessarabia to Salome **Hattig** (b. 1810)
 Christoph Boepple (b. 1838 @ Dennewitz, Bessarabia)
 Married 4 Nov. 1861 to Christine **Hoeschele** (b. ? @
 Teplitz, Bess. d. 15 may 1881 @ Dennewitz)
  George Boepple (1870-1955) born @ Seimental,
  Bess.
  Married @ Mannsberg, Bess. 6 Jan. 1896 to Katherine
  Gotz (1871-1945) born @ Borodino, Bess.

Your grandfather, Christoph Boepple, had five brothers and three sisters. Immanuel was the oldest, born 29 Mar. 1831, in Wittenberg, Bessarabia. The other children all seem to have been born at Dennewitz, Bessarabia. I have them all listed for you upon one of the data sheets I am enclosing to you. I have also listed the spouse of each, except that of Elizabeth, which I have not yet located. I have also listed the children of each, insofar as I have been able to determine at this time, but I do not believe those listings to be complete - the exception being that of Daniel, which I do know to be complete. If you have information that disputes any of that which I have set down on any of the enclosed lists, you might let me know, so that I can make the corrections. On the enclosed map of Bessarabia (which lies between the Pruth River and the Dniester River) you can locate the various communities which are mentioned in that copy of Boepple Family History (which I think originally came from Aunt Ann Schnaidt and/or Aunt Lydia Neuberger). I don't really know where she obtained the information, but I suppose that she might have obtained a lot of it directly from your father, George Boepple, as he apparently lived with them during the last several years of his life. I have heard that Aunt Molly Schutz also corresponded with some of the Boepple relatives that were living in Germany after WW II, but as I have never known of anybody among the relatives who did have a copy of that information, I presume that the information was lost in the settling of her estate after she died. An unfortunate circumstance. These various little villages are not far separated from one another. Wittenberg is only about twenty miles from Dennewitz, and Teplitz is only about six miles from Dennewitz. I have marked in red pencil the various villages that concern our interests.

So far as I know, Christian Boepple and his family (brother to your own Grandfather Christoph Boepple) were the first Boepples to immigrate to this country - in 1876. They apparently settled in or near Freeman, South Dakota, but later moved on into Oklahoma, somewhere between 1900 and 1910. It was one of his sons, Friedrich Boepple, for whom your father worked several years in Covington, Oklahoma. The youngest brother Daniel, brought his family over to the U.S.A. in 1886; and they settled up near Kulm, North Dakota. In the early 1900's they moved down to Hooker, in Texas County of the panhandle of Oklahoma. About ten years later they moved up into southwestern Saskatchewan - a place called maple Creek, not far from Medicine Hat, Alberta. In the early 1930's they settled down not far from Twin Falls, Idaho - a place called Filer. It now appears that the brother Johann George, about twelve years younger than your grandfather Christoph, actually died in 1869, at age 19 - so the children listed as his must actually be those of another George Beopple, probably from the Boepple group centered at Teplitz. The Teplitz and the Dennewitz groups seem to have come from the same family a generation or two earlier, so they are of course related, in any case.

It is a little more difficult to keep track of the female side of the family, since the Genealogic Record is traditionally geared to tabulating and keeping track of the male descendants and the family surname. One then has to locate the name of her spouse, and follow out the line of decent in that family. Among the sisters of your grandfather (Christoph Boepple), Christina was married to Johann George Siegler (This name might easily been altered to Ziegler if they later immigrated to the USA); Catharina was married to Friedrich Weisspfennig; and I have not yet discovered to whom Elizabeth was married. Some, or even all of them may have come to the U.S.A., but I have not yet come across those trails. Perhaps one of George Boepple's cousins (with whom he stayed when he first came to this country) had one of these names; Siegler (Ziegler), or Weisspfennig, or the last name of Elisabeth's husband? You might let me know if those names sound familiar. So far as I know, the older brothers (Immanuel and Gottlieb) did not come to the U.S.A., though I have not yet found any information that definitely establishes that. There was a Christian Fuerst and his wife Rosina Boepple that came to this country in May of 1876, several months before Christian Boepple arrived with his family. They too must have settled (at least temporarily) in or near Freeman, S.D. Rosina Boepple would have been born about 1857 - perhaps a daughter of Immanuel or Gottlieb (?), and if so, a niece to Christian Boepple. I haven't yet learned anything more about them.

Though I have sent out a few letters of inquiry concerning the families of Gotz, Fried, and Mueller - from whom your mother is descended, no information from them has yet returned. I did discover, however, that John Goetz (the brother to your Grandfather Christian Gotz) and his wife (Justine nee Mueller Goetz) are buried in a rural cemetery about ten miles north of Odessa, Washington. John Gotz (1850-1927), and Justine (1855-1924). Do you recall if Justine nee Mueller Gotz was in any way related to the Mueller woman who married H. Fried, and was therefore your grandmother? If that were the case, it would make the finding of that trail a little easier. In any case, don't worry yourself about it, for I will eventually come across that information anyway. The history of these people and their wanderings around the world is interesting; and the genealogical aspect of it serves to give it extra flavor. It is of course, a subject that has no end, for the generation's progress into infinity, both into the past and stretching into the future. Nor is it likely that any records pertaining to our peasant ancestors are yet in existence for any years previous to the seventeenth century. Of course, there are no records that will enable us to trace the genetic and cultural lines of the family into the future. Also, the numbers involved with each succeeding generation soon make the project impossible; and its specific details drifts into something akin to meaningless. At that point, only the general overall picture of Genealogy begins to take on a meaning - and perhaps, a moral. If one considers just the individual, and his two parents etc. (disregarding the siblings altogether - a much more massive number), we see that the 1st generation back has 2 parents; the 2nd generation back contains 4 parents; the 3rd generation back contains 8 parents, etc. In other words, the number doubles in each generation. We might take the number four, to represent the number of generations for each century. In my own case, going back that four generations and one hundred years to 1888, would give me thirty-two direct ancestors in that generation. Going back an additional one hundred years, to 1788, would give me 256 direct ancestors in that generation. The year 1688 shows me to have 4,096 direct ancestors; by 1588 A.D. there are 65,556 ancestors; in 1488 A.D. (just before Columbus discovers America) there are 1,048,576 direct ancestors. Another hundred years brings that number to over 16,000,000, Back in the year 1288 A,D. (when Marco Polo was visiting China), the number of my direct ancestors from that generation is at more than 268,000,000 - the approximate population of the U.S.A. today. That represents a mere twenty-eight generations. The general implication, I think, is that in some very real sense, there is a brotherhood of man. Some of the major socio-economic contest in the world then may be because most folks have not yet troubled themselves to make that estimation of their own lineage; or perhaps because they have been mislead into thinking of themselves in relation to political boundaries of past times. The differences that separate the various opposing camps of mankind are plentiful, but these differences have a whole lot more to do with ideas, beliefs, prejudice, delusions, and misperceptions; than with any actual genetic differences. It is obvious, of course, that the various races of man - black, yellow, red, white - seem to be genetically more different than those with whom we share the same skin color. But even so, it doesn't prove anything more than that these various racial groups lived for many generations, remote and isolated from one another; and separated by geographical barriers and long distances, unmitigated by any such advantage as our currently available modes of easy transportation. It is far and away most likely that these different groups (races) did in fact, have common ancestors prior to their becoming isolated from one another. That they intermarry and that children are regularly produced from those marriages, is fairly strong evidence of that.

Concerning family structure, seen as a group of related individuals succeeding one another, generation after generation, it is obvious that a healthy and vigorous biological strain of physical and intellectual endowment is a fundamental requirement. But since the world is a competitive place, and since man must live by his wits. And since the learning process consumes time; and since that learning process can be greatly enhanced by the accumulation of knowledge that is originally gained to individuals only very slowly. And that body of knowledge only slowly enlarges from the cumulative effort of a great many generations. Therefore, the customs, culture, skills, techniques, information, and the routine of the customary daily life become the critically important factor in determining the survival ability of one group or tribe in its direct and indirect competition with other groups. Health and vigor in the group can then be seen to be but a fundamental prerequisite; while the culturally transmitted customs, habits, system of education, ideas and values become the actual competitive edge that determines survival. As knowledge and technology accumulate, the conditions and circumstances of life change. Tribal, as well as individual customs and habits, have always a certain resistance to change. The very fact indeed, that preserves a habit or custom, be it good or bad. And yet, however valuable that tendency toward unchanging stability, there's another idea somewhere to supersede it. However useful the principle, it must admit of specific compromise in new specific circumstances. So it is that we, in the here-and-now must attempt to gain some sort of knowledge of the past and attempt to project some sort of vision into the future. For we ourselves must somehow bridge the interval. The future must always be dependant upon the past, and the past, to some degree responsible for the future. It seems then that a well balanced relationship to our ancestors of the past requires that we hold them in esteem, without idolizing that past. We must be permissive of some change, even, no doubt, encouraging some change. It behooves us I think, to stay in touch with the facts of the past; and even to recover what we may from the myth that private interests would spin in the name of various vested interests.

The picture I see from the study of History and Family History, is that in the face of great hardships and troubled times, our ancestors have always found the courage and strength of character to quit their past, and to overcome the inertia that tied them to a 'native land' when it became obvious that it no longer served the best interests of themselves and their children. Especially in regards to their children, they seemed fully aware that no one else could be trusted to do that for them. In consequence, they were always upon the newly opening frontiers of life. The state, of course, is always after us to study, to learn of, and to honor their Parthenon of self-serving heroes and saints, but there seems little reason to unduly preoccupy ourselves with the mythical drama of those texts. We have our own martyred ancestors to honor - and their example of action and good-will toward us, their descendants.

In the generations of ancestors from which I am derived, perhaps no generation has had better opportunity than mine, to enjoy good health, benefit from adequate education, and to find time and food for thought. All lives, of course, are tragic in some aspects. Mine too has been troublesome at times. And yet, there always seems to be something of value that we can extract from even those most troublesome aspects. Naturally, folks generally feel more comfortable when their own children and grandchildren see things just as they do; and when they acquire the same beliefs and customs - and the same prejudices. But, the reasons are plentiful and obvious, as to why that can never come about - except, partially. For we ourselves have seen some of the errors and shortcomings of the past, and have tried to correct the effect of these in our own lives, and in the life circumstances of our descendants. We expect and even hope that subsequent generations will see the need and find the method for further necessary change. But you must excuse a part of the previous philosophical paragraphs, mother. I can see that they are wanting, in clarity and conciseness. I find it difficult to resist the temptation, to wrestle with troublesome ideas and concepts - to honor the occasion of your birthday with some sort of a show or parade.

Incidentally, I have enclosed to you a copy of a newspaper notice of the death of Reinhold Boepple, who you and I have previously discussed. It says that his father was John Boepple. On the other hand, if I understand you correctly, Reinhold's mother was Magdalene Boepple (a half-sister to George Boepple). She appears to have been married to her cousin, John Boepple, and Reinhold was their only child. A marriage that didn't last long. It is my understanding that she was then married to Phillip Meissel up near Haliday, ND.

Perhaps I'll get a chance to get up that way for a visit with you sometime within the next few months. Again, my belated best wishes to you for your birthday and for Mothers Day.

With love

your son

Roosevelt Garner Brasseur

7 May 1988

26 March 1989

Caldwell, Idaho 85605

Dear Mom,

Here we are landed once again into the month of March and I wanted to wish you a happy birthday! This letter is begun in Pocatello, Idaho, where I am spending most of this month (and part of next month) working fourteen-hour shifts in an Urgent Care Medical Facility. I get paid by the hour to evaluate the ill and the injured - and those attended by the mere anxiety of a possible medical problem. I treat them and console them in their assorted states of illness, pain, suffering, and grief. They come, bringing their children and, often, their aged parents, for evaluation and recommendations for treatment. Naturally, they have never seen or heard of me, a humble mortal of peasant stock. I am but a figurehead, representative of the healing image of a modern medicine-man. Their coming is in response to commercial publicity, which suggests and acquaints them with the fact that they can be seen here in a short time without the necessity of an appointment. Thus, we see a fairly large proportion of problems in their acute stages - and we, here at the clinic, put forth an effort to solve the problems and get them in and out rapidly. We are generally busy. Even on relatively quiet days, fate seems to decree that patients tend to arrive in clusters, rather than uniformly spaced throughout the fourteen-hour shift, If not seen immediately or very soon upon their arrival, they begin to agitate, complain, and even threaten the poor young ladies who work at the reception desk. Upon occasion one will leave in anger, account of some unavoidable delay - and then not uncommonly vent their hostility in slanderous comments which are not infrequently broadcast upon the grapevine. A fate shared by all health care providers. A sort of democracy, that we share. Nothing so clogs the system as having to process those who are not actually ill, for then the search must be relatively long and labored in order to find something upon them that is treatable - or, to convince them that they don't really require any significant particular treatment at the present time.

I eat my one meal each day after ten o'clock PM, when the shift is over; and return to work each morning prepared to work continuously throughout the entire shift, with no break what-so-ever for food or drink. Though I commonly stop long enough to pee, once or twice during the shift. On most days, there is time between the clusters of patients to do some of the miscellaneous chart work, and to scan some of the assorted textbooks at hand for information pertinent some of the more puzzling diagnostic and treatment problems that continuously arise. In truth, most of those we see would survive without any medical care at all, though the course and severity of many of their ailments can be greatly diminished by relatively early and simple measures available to the field of medicine in our times. Very few arrive with any eye complaints, and when they do, our facility here, is not well equipped to tend to them.

The question might arise, as to what an eye-doctor is doing here in an urgent care center, and practicing general medicine. Part of the answer to that is that I need the money and those who own and manage the facility have some difficulty obtaining physicians to do that work for $52.00 per hour. Perhaps only a slightly higher pay scale than that of, say, a garbage collector in the San Francisco Bay area perhaps, or less. Because I make myself available, the clinic uses my services, for there are some occasional days for which they are unable to obtain any physician at all. And then they can see no patients at all, though the overhead expenses continue to eat into the overall margin of profit - if there is a margin of profit. In any case I am a better general practitioner of medicine now than I was when I entered the general practice of medicine twenty-six years ago. Almost every problem that I see, is something that I have had some personal experience of - an ailment that I, myself, or someone of my own immediate family has owned at some time or another; or a patient from my practice of Ophthalmology - for they have other medical problems in addition to their eye ailments,

We were squeezing by financially in the last few months of 1988 - awaiting the benefit of the arrival of the new telephone book to display my correct phone number and street address. And we were awaiting for the new Medicare Directory to do the same. Lo, and behold, when the telephone directory appeared in Dec., 1969, it turns out that my name, address and phone number are again listed as those of Dr. C___. And, the Medicare Directory has me listed as an Optometrist - the same mistake they made last year! The result is that I don't get many phone calls, nor much work to do in my Caldwell office. I enjoy having all that extra time to read, think, and write - though in truth, it would probably have been better had there been a little more work to occupy my mind. For one's efficiency in work, as well as in the avocations of thought, ideas, and writing, tends to be more efficient and productive when the facets of one's life have a broader scope and more balanced proportion.

In those several months before the end of January of 1989, I managed to get together a bit of genealogy information concerning the Brasseur, and the Boepple families. I am enclosing to you some copy of some of the more recent of that information. I don't usually look at the checkbook balance as it tends to disturb my tranquility when I am reminded of its being so depleted. My wife usually wrangles those books for me in silent forbearance. In the end of January, she suddenly tells me that there is no money with which to pay the bills. The thought of that disturbed my slumber that night. And so, I drove over to Boise the following morning to do some Genealogy research in the library, and to poke about for some part-time work. As it happened, this one particular urgent care center was a man short for the following day. Thereafter, I then worked occasional fourteen-hour shifts for one or the other of the two urgent-care clinics which they operate in Boise. Enough to get the bills paid. Their third such clinic is in Pocatello and the manager there called me in mid-February to see if I might be willing to work in Pocatello in the month of march. The doctor they had been using, had quit to go into private practice. And, so it is that I am working nearly the entire month of March, and a part of April, in Pocatello. I have been getting home for a day or so, once every week or ten days. "make hay while the sun shines", as they say, "so that we can burn it in the moonlight?". The long work hours wear upon my patience, for I am used to the enjoyment of long hours for my private thoughts, and private projects. And yet, there is a certain satisfaction too, in long hours of seeing up to sixty patients per shift of work. Some of them have rather interesting problems. I had never seen a case of scarlet fever - then, one day, I saw three of them. Yes, a sort of satisfaction in doing something quite different for a time - and in going at it intently. And then, with the circumstances of my life again flowing a different course, the notion gradually came upon me that I should take advantage of these new circumstances to free up some extra time - in order to add some depth and put some flesh onto the bare-bones of family history that I have been slowly acquiring. Perhaps I'll put a new set of tires upon the old pick-up, toss a tent and sleeping bag into the rear, and spend a couple of months of the coming summer going through the archives and the graveyards of the Dakotas and into Quebec. I'll chase down some of the descendants of my various ancestors, perhaps - and attempt to gather enough legend and myth to enable me to conjure up some of their historical reality from between the lines. Such at least is the tentative nature of my vague plans.

Meanwhile, I have made application for entrance into Law School, which I would like to begin in January of 1990. However, in truth, it is rather unlikely that I will be accepted, so I shall continue my search, and casting about in various directions in the field of medicine with a sort of general plan to continue working only part-time - enough to earn a regular living income, and spend the rest of my time reading and perhaps even attempt to do some serious writing.

My wife drove up to Portland at the end of February to be of assistance to PM and Shelle at the time of the coming of their third child whose expected date of arrival was right then. Now, a month later, that seventh grandchild is yet unborn, but each passing day would seem to make the event the more inevitably imminent. Meanwhile, my wife has had time visit extensively with all the children and grandchildren and to visit with all of her old friends as far away as even Ashland, As this is PM's thirty-third birthday, I called to talk with him a few hours ago. All but RL's family were over there for the traditional Easter Feast of pizza pie. Shelle had been having a few contractions then, so perhaps the child will yet be born upon its father's own birthday - which would save the expense of an extra birthday party each year.

I write to a great many people, concerning Genealogy information. Hence, there is always a trickle of information coming in from somewhere or another - most of them, distant 'shirt-tail' relatives. The various copy I have enclosed for you is mostly marked so that you see the sources from which It has been derived. I'll continue to send you periodic updates of information as I acquire and continuously update my records of information,

Once more, a happy birthday to you. Perhaps we shall get a chance to get together again somewhere in the next few months.

Love,

Your son

R Garner Brasseur, M.D.

26 March 1989

17 March 1990

Caldwell, Idaho

Dear Mom,

I know I don't write you as often as one might suppose would be best. It is unfair to you, for mothers, I know, are charged with keeping track of their children and in knowing what they are up to. But, on the other hand, when I do write, I expect that you often shake your head in wonder at how it happens that a supposedly well-educated man can be in possession of ideas that seem so far a-field; and on how it is that I manage always to be in some sort of legal or financial strain, since most persons in my profession might seem not to have all of those problems. Under the circumstances, then, you might consider it a mercy that I don't write more often. One of the problems that I have with writing is that I never developed any real proficiency at spelling or at lying. It isn't that I haven't tried, mind you, it is just that I am unpracticed in those arts. I have been known to blurt-out and even to put into writing some of the most awkward truths you can imagine. And it brings me a bit of grief at times. It occurs to me, too, that it might be better, to just remain silent. And I sometimes imagine that I was fairly good at silence in my youth, though that virtue seems to have escaped me, by degree - just as youth itself has done. And I have often repented of silence, too; for it may be that one ought to contest that which is erroneous. In silence one is guilty of another sort lie, as mark Twain says, "the silent lie - the deception which one conveys by simply keeping still, and allowing the truth to remain concealed".

I have been trying a new approach to writing. A form that ends up being a letter-package - rather than a thin letter. The letter-package includes something in the nature of a letter but is packed in with copies of essays, old letters, news clippings, journal articles and genealogy lists. That way, the poor unsuspecting recipient is apt to be so overwhelmed with the sheer volume, as to lose any immediate hope of getting through it all in one sitting. Under that circumstance, he or she may choose to read first some one portion that best suits their interests … may never get around to reading my own strange ideas nor even realize that he hasn't, perhaps.

I have read several times, through Duane's book, *A BRIEF HISTORY OF FAMILY CHAMPIONS; 1909-1989*, and it seems to me nicely done. Certainly more than I have ever accomplished. It is something more, of course, than just a family history; for it gives us some insight to his thought processes and shows us his attempt to grasp the deeper currents that flow, unseen, within a particular family. Currents that suggest somewhat the element of contagiousness of ideas and information from generation to generation, and from one individual to another. It is just the sort of information I am looking for, as I continue my exploration of family history. The names, dates, and the locations of the various families in history are only the skeleton or outline of the family history. For the most part, I suppose, the ideas that dominated the minds and times of the general populace in the areas in which our ancestors lived, were probably the ideas that dominated their minds too. And yet, without some biographical or autobiographical information, that can not be known. As we have recently seen, the minds of the masses of Eastern Europe have suddenly resolved to free themselves from the yoke of Communism. Yet, it seems certain that that resolve has been present there, in the minds of many - and, for many years. It's Victor Hugo's theme, "Greater than the marching of armies, is an idea whose time has come."

It brings to mind a related idea that Duane touches upon, in his book - that one either acts … or is acted upon. History is represented to us as the 'acts-of-men' through time and under the influence of circumstance and chance. At a more fundamental level, however, it seems more properly to represent the 'thoughts-of-men', through time. There was a time in by-gone ages, I suppose, when a man's physical force was a prerequisite to his political force and influence; but one doesn't see that in our times. Except, of course, upon the playgrounds of the schools of elementary education. Power and influence, in our times, seem to accumulate to one mainly through such media as ideas and money; and through association with those that have power, money and influence. We ordinary folk, without inherited title, wealth, nor connections … we have but limited chance to act, to control our own destiny. We are mostly 'acted upon'. Only thought, good-fortune, and the ability to work hard, give us cause for any small hope of owning some control over our own destiny. Most 'fortune' is something other than good-fortune; and long hours of hard work deprive us of the time and energy necessary to direct our lives thoughtfully. Only the potential for (and habit of) thought, gives to us the potential for both attaining and retaining any significant opportunity to act; rather than to be acted upon. Thus, one might suppose, it may be advantageous to continue to cultivate some family tradition of thought - and a penchant to wrestle with ideas.

Pascal says that "thought makes the whole dignity of man; and the endeavor to think well is the basic morality". According to Ben Franklin, "as the happiness or real good of men, consists in right action; and right action cannot be produced without right opinion, it behooves us, above all things in this world, to take care that our opinions of things be according to the nature of things. The foundation of all virtue and happiness is in thinking rightly". Presuming that we are born with normal physical and mental capacity, the most important factor that affects our outlook on life (and our degree of mental attainment) is that of the minds of the men and women who constitute the circle of our family, friends and associates. It is from them - from their demeanor, actions, responses, conversation and writings - that we gather our individual supply of ideas and habits of the mind. Dependent upon that heritage is the variety, veracity, and the breadth of vision that is imparted to us individually. Then, given the luxury of time and permission - and encouragement to growth, it comes about as with "The Chambered Nautilus". "Year after year (proceeds) the silent (mental) toil", to enlarge each successive cell of the ever growing coil. Yearly, leaving behind the narrower view, for one at last so large, as finally to include 'the all'; and "leave behind the outgrown shell, by life's un-resting sea".

Enclosed to you are some genealogic letters that I have written most recently. Still trying to solicit people to send me additional information - on both the Brasseur and the Boepple families. But now, with more emphasis on the biographical aspects, as previously mentioned. I have gotten a-hold of a long list of Brasseur names with addresses, and am putting out about fifty letters among them, hoping it will return to me at least a smattering of information and at least a few contacts that are reasonably knowledgeable and interested in the subject. Some such as may have a small wealth of information about, at least - their own particular branch of the family. If I have any success with that approach, then I shall seek out a similar list of Boepples, and run a similar survey. That would be more complex, however, for I would then need separate lists, for each of the several common variations of the name: Boepple, Bopple, Bepple, and Pepple.

My wife has taken up the custom that you began, of making quilts for each of the individual grandchildren. She left here with the last edition of that artwork, about a week ago to make her spring tour of the households of each of the children. By this time she has already picked up MABC (who currently has about ten days of vacation time between the quarter terms of her schooling). They will probably leave Ashland today, en route to Phoenix. To visit there the remnants of EVH's family. I'll fly down to meet them in Phoenix, on the 27th; and to taka a post-graduate medical refresher course there. I'll probably be home again by April 2nd. By that time, MABC will have returned to Monmouth for her last term; and is supposed to graduate in June. And what will she do then? I don't know that she has any definite plans, about that; or, if she has, she hasn't yet informed me. I think she plans to spend a week in New York City, to visit with one of her best high-school friends, Joy Chan. I am already trying to discourage her from any occult plans she may have of seeking out employment, there. I would rather see her settle somewhere in the rural west - like Idaho, or New Mexico, for example. The decision will ultimately be hers. And it is just as well - perhaps in fact better - that I won't have much say in the matter. One thing certain though, is that she will inexorably be swept from the tender mercies of the care of her fond and aging parents, **"As logs, which on an ocean float/ by chance are into contact brought/ but, tossed about by wind and tide/ together, cannot long abide"**.

I got your check, at Christmas time; and cashed it. And I squandered it all upon myself, for some bit or another of foolishness; though I don't exactly recall what. In any case, the money is gone - and I don't have anything to show for it. But I am hanging on to the measure of good-will which I presume came with the check. And I am returning to you a measure of my own variety of good-will - in honor of your birthday, the 29th of March. Yes, happy birthday! And, "may the menace of the years, yet find us unafraid".

Love to you; and light
Your son,
Roosevelt Garner Brasseur

17 March 1990

September 1998

MUTTER MIR

Nine of twelve conceived were we.
On this I think we can agree.
When mother died aged ninety-two
Her death was greatly overdue.

I saw her last five years ago,
A dearly ruined wreck of woe.
Too punitive for faults she knew.
Sad reward her virtues knew.

She took a swing at me that day,
The reason why, I cannot say.
Might have owed me one I guess.
Perhaps to urge me toward success.

Demented in her final years,
Enough to drive a stone to tears.
Her reign magnificent to us.
Motherhood, her great success.

Admonishing in glance and word,
Exhortatingly her voice we heard.
Encouraged us as best she might,
To go in peace and walk upright.

Just before her great decline,
Eye to eye we spoke our minds.
Conceding each a great unknown.
Signed our truce of flesh and bone.

If there be angels, thou wert mine.
If there be spirits, blest be thine.

If there be honor, courage, grit …
Thou to me embodied it.
RGB

12 September 1998

20 November 1985

7107 Connecticut Avenue

Dear Paul,

Ben Franklin wrote "as the happiness or real good of man consists in right action; and right action cannot be produced without right opinion, it behooves us above all things in this world, to take care that our opinions of things be according to the nature of those things. The foundation of all virtue and happiness is in thinking rightly." He supposes that truth is unitary (i.e. its parts all fit together like the pieces of a jigsaw puzzle). I suspect that it is. I am writing a book entitled *A Unitary Concept of That Which Is*, in which I attempt to delineate my views; and my reason for holding those views.

'That-which-is', simply is; and is independent of our individual opinions of that-which-is. Looked at from that perspective, it seems probable that the fundamental morality consists in our individual upholding of truth. As human morality and the nature of truth would seem to be the main ingredients of what we call 'religion'; then one might say, that there is but one religion. And that every mortal being is under the same obligation, in his relationship to that one religion. An obligation that entails the upholding of personal moral standards, as well as the quest for that truth. As Descartes has said, "he who seeks the truth must – as far as possible – doubt everything".

As to the source of truth, it seems to abide abundantly, in many sources. Each individual finding of a truth, verifies its particular source. Each individual truth is a part of what we call Truth (in its larger overall, and all-inclusive sense) – with a capital T, Truth. The problem concerning individual truths and Truth (overall) which I identify as 'that-which-is', is <u>not</u> that we do not have access to it; but rather that we fail to recognize it. And all, by degree, are remiss in our efforts to recognize it to the fullest of our capacity. The problem it presents us, is much like that of a giant jigsaw puzzle of a zillion parts, whose identifying picture, by design, is hazy, and whose colors are blended and nearly monochromatic. How long each day shall we work at such a forbidding task? Sincere efforts that needs must be voluntary! Can we even control our temper, so as not to, one day, disrupt – in a fit of passion – what little has already been pieced together?

Concerning our quest for the truth(s) – ultimately aimed toward the delineation of that-which-is – our slowly evolving methods of education and our scientific method give evidence of the potential benefit of man's capacity for reason. And I agree with Ethan Allen, that reason is the only true oracle of mankind. Long established religions proclaim each their individual dogma - and authoritative writings alleged to be 'the word of God'. But in my view, these, like all writings are surly authored by mere mortal man, and serve the purposes of an elite ruling faction. That is not to say they have not been of some benefit in the taming of that beast we know as the 'mob', or "The Heavy Bear" in its orgiastic untamed propensity for mayhem and self-destruction. Civilizations of mankind would seem to require some minimum of useful myth along with law and mores, such as to produce the necessary civil deportment that permits of a civilization.

Just as generals, kings, emperors, and lay governors become overly demanding and oppressive of their citizenry, so also do religious 'princes of the church' and popes. Some 'balance of power' between secular and non-secular authority seems generally the better option in that they tend to be restraint upon one another in their contest for supreme control of their populations. In that contest, each is generally inclined to at least some measure of leniency towards their subjective masses with the intent of gaining some measure of support of the masses, as those contesting authorities vie for power. The government of our own nation has recognized the utility of that principle in setting up three competing branches of government. Meanwhile, the commerce of a people tends to evolve in accordance with natural but ill perceived principles. Principles which seem to work most efficiently with but a minimum of regulation by either secular or non-secular ruling authority.

Mark Twain was chiding us when he said "a lie is a poor substitute for a truth – but who has ever invented anything better" (as a substitute for truth). One answer to that – the Roman Catholic Church. For they have very effectively befuddled mankind with half–truths and mysticism for 2000 years. No naked and free-standing lie can withstand the penetrating force of inquiry and time as stoutly as can a half-truth skillfully woven and bonded into the matrix of historical writings with deft deletions and small distortions of the pen. Fortunately, even concrete does eventually weather and wear away. But in this instance – concerning the dubious claims and partial truths of Christianity – we must take pains, that they not be reinforced, now that its 'factuality' is finally beginning to crumble. The religion itself, need not become completely overgrown and lost into history, for it contains a good deal of literary beauty and of value for mankind – as do most other religions. Therefore, like the Chesapeake and Ohio Canal, its ancient intent and function can be lost; yet it might too, be retained and maintained, at a noncommercial status, for the natural truths and beauties that abide along its pathways. Perhaps the U. U. Church does – or shall – function, in just that capacity, in addition to its humanitarian influence in the world.

Best wishes to you and yours.

Sincerely,
Garner Brasseur

20 November 1985

23 December 1985

7107 Connecticut Avenue

Dear Paul,

A couple months ago – in your Sunday oration – you referred to the life of E. E. Cummings. You mentioned that he was raised in the UU tradition; but that he himself never was an active member of any congregation. Where was his commitment to social action? J.S. Mill, for example, had a strong history of social action involvement in England; yet, so far as I know, he never attended any church or congregation. Is there necessarily any consistent relationship between congregational attendance (and membership) for the individual; and ones overt involvement in social concerns? Thus again was precipitated into my mind this question with which I have previously wrestled.

There does seem to be some value in the principle of social action. For without its effect through millennia past, I expect that we should all – or most, at least – remains serfs and slaves, with hours and conditions of labor much less advantageous than those to which we are currently accustomed. And our freedom to choose and to run our own lives should be greatly attenuated.

On the other hand, it is not the case, that we live our lives exempt of coercion; nor that we have any large selection among alternatives from which to choose. And, pragmatically, we commonly labor under a sense of obligation and expectations (to friends and family) to choose an alternative that we may not heartily prefer. Jean Paul Sartre says, "Each time we make a choice, it shapes, limits, and influences the number and direction of our future choices; until finally we checkmate ourselves into an inescapable cubicle of thought and action. We condemn ourselves to live in a world hewn (by ourselves) by the pattern of our past choices". There seems to be an element of truth in that.

That to which we are culturally adapted causes less heat and furor than do new and innovative approaches, actions, responses, and thoughts. This, regardless even, that the new should be an actual improvement or advantageous to each and to all. Yet, change and innovation are inevitable, however slow and obstructed. And individuals commonly do have a good deal more of actual freedom than what they actually ever exercise – in the matter of choice and change in their own lives. In our society, and in this age, we have always ready access to new concepts and ideas – which contain within themselves the potential energy of truth and validity. Just so, as hydrogen or uranium atoms contains each, a store of energy. We needs must but to discover the method of unlocking to ourselves the latent energy within each – and harnessing that energy to a useful and valid purpose.

The concept of congregations and church has been with us for some 2500 years – innovated to us from the Jewish tradition. At its best, it administers to the communal interests and needs of the local folks to encourage a system of values and moral precepts that become duties of the heart, to which men voluntarily subscribe. In the reality of a competitive life, individual men are necessarily alienated one from another to some degree. Yet too, they have in common locally and universally, a great many shared interests, concerns, and needs that gives peoples a basis for a unity of hope and purpose. The harshness of the work-a-day world in a non-utopian society daily calls forth the stark individuality and competitive interest of individual men. One seems to perceive the need, periodically, to repair to his congregation of the larger concerns and fellowship, to maintain a certain balance and psychologically satisfying perspective in ones life. Thus it is, that the concept of congregation – and a fellowship of those of similar beliefs – remains a vital and conspicuous entity in society today. Their beliefs concerning truth, rights, and duties, are tributary to the mainstreams of mores, common law, jurisprudence, and government. Those mainstreams themselves throughout the world, remain diverse and continuously change their courses, as mankind, societies, and civilizations evolve. The diversity in the perception of reality and truth among men is undoubtedly related to the diversity among civilizations. And mankind's ever changing perceptions are derived from the inevitable evolution of society, beliefs, and experience. And the accumulation of knowledge and technology contributes to the continuous change of civilizations.

Many, like myself, drop out of the membership of a congregation into which they were born and raised, because they themselves have adopted new ideas, concerns, and beliefs, which are no longer compatible to the views and practices of their previous congregation. They try another affiliation to which they may be more compatible and may remain there, making a docile contribution of cash. But pressed into an action or a contribution they cannot heartily affirm, they are apt to stray elsewhere once again. After several such moves, they may eventually abandon their search. May merely fellowship with a small group of friends, or family. Or they may fellowship vertically, rather than horizontally, repairing to the writings of men (removed from them in time and place) and themselves perhaps, communicating their own solitary thoughts into writings and to posterity. It must be the case, that every professional minister to a congregation, ultimately recognizes that both the congregation as a whole, and its individual members, have limits beyond which they can not be pressed, in the service of ideology - upon pain and threat of dissent. It only remains then, for them to explore and recognize these limits. But besides ones horizontal interaction in a congregation and community of the here-and-now, one needs must devote himself somewhat to the vertical continuity of reality and the interactions and continuity with times past, present, and future.

Concerning the problem of social action, most discover and recognize that the ways and means of our society are inequitable - and amiss in the qualities of compassion, justice, and brotherhood. A society or system of government, dare not weigh too heavily upon the population, lest it crash from the apathy and loss of support. A great many utopian societies have been seen to not have enjoyed enough facility of adaptation to survive for long. Our government is sufficiently large and heavy as to have acquired a great deal of (the force of) inertia. Individual and small group actions within the state have but little power to influence its course. The ship-of-state responds only to the weight of action of large groups. And it is already overburdened and waterlogged with debt, so that there seems to be a pragmatic limit as to how much more it shall bear in the form of financial burden before the ship-of-state plunges to the bottom. For, while the sum total of a people can support a limited weight of government; a government also cannot support, but a limited portion of those people. Her course can never be ideal, but must always be tempered by the pragmatisms of reality and economic limitations.

Ideas and concepts – more than our meager token involvement in political action – are forces that can sway the course of the ship-of-state (in combination of course with the customary bribery). For ideas can become infectious in proportion epidemic enough to afflict the minds of the many. The force of an idea acting upon the minds of the many, thus produces its action indirectly, and in proportion to its degree of perceptibility. Or, to put it in the words of Victor Hugo, "greater than the marching of armies, is an idea whose time has come." Ideas are the major mechanism for the release and harnessing of the energies of man.

Those who conceive those ideas; and those who dabble with, tinker with, expound upon, and effectively convey those ideas to their fellow man are – by those processes – involved in some form of political action. Though that involvement is indirect, it is of primary significance.

Most men do commonly aim towards some idealistic goal or another, which for the most part, they rarely achieve. Or, having achieved it, they find it to be not at all as satisfying as they imagined. Likewise too, a great many persons have an interest in philosophical questions; and delve into them at a conversational level, only to find themselves entangled with a discouraging 'bag-of-worms'.

The nature of reality of 'that-which-is' (the forms of matter, together with the forms of energy within the universe – and the laws that concern their interrelatedness), is such, that no effect can be achieved, nor goal attained except at the expenditure of a certain cost. And our particular method of achievement or attempt to achieve these goals is commonly encumbered with unanticipated side effects and consequences. We are mere and simple creatures of nature whose ancestors have only recently left their tree nests and cave dwellings to stumble precariously toward the horizon of civilization and understanding. Mankind, as a species, has had no tutor other than experience and verbal intercommunication to facilitate his progress. The individual teeters upon oblivion with each new step. Progressive truths, method, and technology are acquired to our species only slowly and subsequent to the time-consuming exploration of many box canyons and blind-end pathways.

Only in the past few centuries has man begun to recognize the force and benefit to be derived from the development of his capacity to reason; and the effectiveness of a slowly evolving scientific-method. These though, are impeded and slowed by mankind's own cultural debris and redundancies. Languages perhaps, are too ambiguous to allow the mind and the method to evolve freely. The traditional method of education must be reconsidered perhaps; and renovated, for it seems to be counterproductive at many points.

From the earliest of man's drawings and writings, we see the influence of his evolving powers of reason, in its attempt to comprehend the ever mysterious unknown. Within the unknown lies always the potential benefit, as well as the potential dangers which contribute to its sense of the mysterious. Approaching the unknown out of necessity or out of curiosity, we must come prepared to defend ourselves from its dangers. Ones recollection of his personal experience and his second-hand knowledge – (the experience of his family, tribe, and race conveyed to him through language, signs, and demonstrations) – encourage one to anticipate problems and to plan in advance for some actions which might serve to extricate him from unpleasant consequences. Thus one develops a certain sense of probability of things, as a hunter, or explorer, or conquer - which is appropriate to his own time and place of history. The frontiers of theoretical knowledge can be approached with much the same sort of sense-of-probability, at a conceptual level and beyond the first-hand experience of any one man. To apply a method of experimentation beyond the technological capacity of society and civilization of its day.

Speculative ideas do not inevitably bear fruit, but contend with one another for status, even where none in fact be valid. They oft have their appeal and following based upon sophistry; and based upon the rank, prominence, and eloquence, of those that support one, against the other. But, "Our interest should be centered not on the weight of the authority, but on the weight of the argument"

The fatal aspect of the path of pure reason is this. Many theories and hypotheses can be spun on the basis of but a limited number of facts and truths. All, or none of them may be in part, or in some sense correct. To the author of each, or to the discussants, a concept may seem plausible or agreeable at a conversational level; or become so, on the basis of a brief discussion, concerning some one or a few of its objectionable points. And yet, however eloquent and rational a concept may then seem; in fact, far the most of such ideas, once put to the test of rigorous experimentation and observation, are not at all likely to prove useful. Reason, therefore, must always be tempered by pragmatic experience and a cultivated attitude of honest skepticism. The arguments of the theory, and the presumptions upon which it rests, must all be exposed, and tested.

In summary then, both our reasoned conclusions and our limited experience – along with our culturally hereditary stores of knowledge, beliefs, and 'facts', must all be subjected to scrutiny and experimental verification in the real and physical world of "that-which-is". Even that which reason may admit to the charmed status of "possible" – even "probable" – can yet have no validity, except in proportion that it correspond with the reality of 'that-which-is'.

And what does all this have to do with the subject I launched out upon – the church? This, merely. I was brought up in a tradition of regular church and Sunday school attendance, and even attended a church college. I had not yet reason to doubt my limited hand-me-down history of Christian religion, since neither the public school systems nor any of the citizens of the community – to my knowledge – contested that. And even the rougher elements of my community seemed to be connected with some sort of church and religion.

Yet, I never had any genuine and personal verification that the Christian version of religious history was valid. Though the notion of a religious career had once briefly crossed my mind, my natural naivety had not yet become counterbalanced by a proper sense of skepticism. And my subsequent career into the reading of History had not had not yet had its beginning.

Perhaps I had some vague sort of expectation that the fact of its validity would one day crystallize and become to me a certain reality – just as one day, one awakens to find the earth covered with the magic of snow. And for a youngster such as I, all aimed and poised and ready to believe, I don't think it would have taken more than just a small and personal sort of revelation or miracle to solidify my meager foundation in past beliefs. But, the solidifying revelation just didn't make its appearance to me – or if it did, I missed the signal.

Meanwhile, the hours of my life were becoming preoccupied with making a living, struggling through college, being married, raising children, and knocking at the doors of several medical schools for the hope of admission to the even more strenuous challenge of bumbling through to graduation.

At the age of 30 I began the practice of general medicine and surgery with a group of physicians in North Dakota. The young surgeon – perhaps a year or two older than myself – had become party to a Unitarian discussion group in that community recently. He was being chided by some of the other local physicians in the doctor's lounge at the hospital. Alone, but confidently (the nature of surgeons, generally) he answered them and offered some simple questions for them to ponder. I had merely walked in on this, and wasn't a party to the conversation, but I was stunned! I had never previously heard anyone publicly refute the dogma of the Christian faith – nor ever read such questions either. The thought crossed my mind that even the Liberty Bell had cracked, and had never been successfully repaired.

The firmness of my vague religious convictions began to falter. The questions the surgeon had asked were valid. I began to ponder these things in my heart, even as I soon returned to three additional years of medical training. I exempted myself from any further churchly participation other than Sunday service, account of the demands upon my time in consequence of this extra training and study program into which I was now enrolled.

The second year of residency training was not overly strenuous and was one of the first times in my life I read a book which was not required reading. There in Panama was my first exposure to the Spanish and Latin-American culture and Peoples. I was curious about the history of the Spanish influence in Latin America. I found a book by Prescott, *The Conquest of Mexico*, and read it through, hating always to have to put it down. And I was hooked – on books. I have read and studied perhaps 1400 books since then, one thing always leading into something else that excites ones curiosity.

At age 36 my family and I returned to the United States to live. There in southern Oregon I now entered into an Ophthalmology practice. Hesitantly, I consented to attend a church with my spouse, but remained as yet unready to outright admit that I no longer believed in the validity of this religion. Taboo. Still, my disbelief too, was vague. Then it was that I happened upon the skepticisms of Thomas Payne's book, *Common Sense*. And I was a bit ashamed of myself, never to have generated such questions de novo onto myself. In retrospect, they seem like easy questions. I had an inkling then, that I was headed into some philosophical turmoil. My wife had gotten us all signed up for Bible study meetings etc. I never was good at, nor developed any confidence in my ability to deceive; for it has been my conviction that people could somehow see in my face, that which I feel as heat and streams of moisture upon my person. Nor long could I now sit quietly in the midst of piously fraudulent conversation. I needs must at least make an effort to simply head them off with some benign and simple skepticisms. But this group of folks seemed to have a sort of prejudice against skepticism – and a bias that favored the improbable. And though I had regrets about the controversy and the heat that it generated, yet it was apparent this 'illness-of-the-soul' was approaching a point of crisis. Therefore, in the subsequent months, I read and studied and pondered – to be certain of my direction and landmarks in this issue. To paraphrase Xenophon – having then done what I could, I prepared myself to suffer what I must. Next came the confrontation with the saints; the outcome of which was the discontinuation of that particular Bible study group. The parting of our ways was simple enough, but I had now the definite impression of being in exile-from-the-kingdom. And a bit of a chill even in my own home. I made an effort to be patient with my spouse in this matter. I actually thought that by merely pointing out to her the simple logical steps that brought me to my new philosophical position, that she might begin to comprehend and cede its validity. She didn't, though. Seeing that she didn't; and finally concluding that she wouldn't, I ended the discussion by stating bluntly that which I had been trying to say diplomatically. The point found its mark. Her eyelids widened and she let out a bit of a screen as she brought her hand up to her mouth. Up she jumped, ran to the bedroom, and slammed the door. Fleetingly, the thought crossed my mind, that perhaps my visage had suddenly changed from that of Dr. Jekyll, to Mr. Hyde. I slept that night on the couch. For the moaning sound of even only a slight wind generally disturbs my slumber. But I felt a sense of relief, finally now to have acknowledged my doubts. As with an abscessed tooth that has just been extracted, I still had some pain – as well as some relief from it – but I need no longer to fear the surgical event, for it was completed. And I now had reason to hope that it need not be repeated; and that incremental relief of healing would soon be manifest. Surgical care – when successful – usually gives relief quickly. So it was with the incisive approach to this old and trying abscess.

As I withdrew myself from the grasp of Fundamentalist Christianity, my wife became the more firmly entangled with it, taking the children along with her into the 'church family'. It was a problem – as I gradually perceived – in that a large part of ones social life within a community (and of most families that I had known) revolves primarily around church functions. I became a sort of closet father and spouse, and a bit estranged from them. Additionally, of course, the adolescent youth commonly begin to become a bit estranged from parent as they enter the teen-ages of youth. But I expect this philosophical matter contributed somewhat to that.

For the first time, it occurred to me that my own father had probably become similarly a bit estranged from his family over this same religious-philosophical problem. He was by nature a genial person, but as I think of it now, he seems often to have been distant and perhaps a little apathetic. On the other hand, he worked and worried long hours in those 'depression years' to support a family of eleven and was often away for days at a time. Not much opportunity for 'bonding' anyhow. Still, I am left to suppose that he had some notion of the psychodynamics of that religious-philosophical problem that somewhat estranged him from his own family.

It is my impression that for the two years in which we lived in the Catholic village of his nativity, it was his hope and intent to divert us protestant children towards the Catholic faith. In fact, a couple of my sisters did eventually end up in the Catholic fold, in their married years.

I see the Unitarian church as being reasonably well aligned with historical veracity, and compatible to the human needs of modern man in society today. The church and our society have come to have a very social function, in addition to its idealistic and futuristic goals. I am wont to suppose that social interactions between the people of a society can best and most comfortably be maintained when based on truth and valid conceptions of reality. To expect an enlightened and educated people to wink at myths and error, and to bow down to false gods as a condition to the participation in the social functions of life is to ask too much. For many seem to have a native good-will and rustic honesty that does not permit them to be cynical to that degree. The church ought both permit and encourage truth, honesty, progress, and idealism. It might yet seek to retain that from the past, which is useful and beautiful; and yet leave behind – as mere historical artifacts – that which is not.

The Unitarian church has been useful and helpful to me, at a time in my life that I needed it, for an effort of personal growth. It may well have aided me a great deal more, had there been a full-bodied congregation as an alternative in my home community.

Yours truly,

Garner Brasseur

23 December 1985

8 November 1986

Ontario, Oregon

Dear Paul,

We are settling anew, here in Eastern Oregon. Have rented us a large house which seems to be too expensive for anyone to buy. Its owners seem to have concluded (correctly, I think) that it is better to have someone in the house than to leave it unoccupied. Empty houses do seem to fall apart. I started my new practice as we moved into the big house in August. As I was unpacking and shelving my library of music and books, I finally came across some of my surplus of musical gems that I have accumulated to be used as gifts. Among them were a few albums of Handel's, *Messiah* – one of which I am sending to you. Enjoy!

In this town of 9500 people, there is a state and locally supported junior-college. My daughter will be taking her second year college studies there this year. She will live at home. She is the last of our four children, but our three sons have each brought us a grandchild, and new additions are anticipated before Christmas. Two sons live in Portland Oregon – a distance of 375 miles. The third son and his family are now en route to Oregon from New Hampshire, where he has worked at carpentry the past summer. He will now finish up his last year of college at Ashland, Oregon before entering the field of primary education. That puts them 430 miles from us. We are thus, all close enough to see one another upon occasion.

FADING ECHOES

I received your church bulletin. I note some the interesting items on your agenda of activity. And note too, that you yourself will have a year of sabbatical leave. But I was unable to figure out what you will be doing with that time, or where you will be. If you have any cause or interest in doing things here in the Northwest, your family might find it useful or even interesting to drop by and spend some time with us. Ontario, Oregon, of course, is not exactly a cultural center, but it is quiet and pleasant. And our home is large and quite – with a total of four bedrooms and three bathrooms. We are but 55 miles from Boise, Idaho; and there are several colleges within about a 100 mile radius from here. Fairly good library facilities. Our major disadvantage is that if someone should suddenly buy this expensive house, we would have but 30 days notice to relocate. Yet, that hardly seems likely.

Perhaps you remember my telling you of my young friend, Dr. Rosckowoff. He, his wife, and their two children lived with us in Hobbs, New Mexico for some four or six weeks last spring after he graduated from medicals school in Guadalajara Mexico. He has to write exams then, and had plans to do his internship in Baltimore. Of the three exams, he passed two – and will have to take the other this fall, before he can begin that internship. The exams are difficult, since there is a sort of excess of physicians in this country, and there is an effort to begin to exclude foreign trained doctors. Currently, he is working as a Lab Tech in Lubbock, Texas. I expect he will continue into Baltimore after the first of the year.

After departing Washington, DC, just before the New Year, I spent a week at home with children and grandchildren. It is comforting and pleasant to have them about. We partook together, of the fatted calf; and moderately explored the liquid spirits together. And a good time was had by all, as the expression goes. And then, all departed and returned to their self-appointed tasks. And that too, was good.

Not wanting or able to be at the terrible expense of setting up my own practice; and because I had other things that I wanted to do with my life, I began to cast about for other options. Yet, I find satisfaction in my occupation too, and hope to be able to continue to practice at least part-time, for I need to be able to support a family. And I don't anticipate that I am apt to earn a regular income from my other interests.

My interests include history, philosophy, religion, geology, reading, writing, and music. I would like to do some writing and it might be helpful to acquire some proficiency with public speaking. I am interested in pursuing a religion, or philosophical system which is relatively open to ones growth and change – the UU group seems to be that.

Just after the first of the year of 1986, I tossed my cot, my bedroll, and my clothes into the back of my 79 Toyota pickup camper and set out upon a personal odyssey that was to last seven months. After getting my last two children situated into colleges, I had a small residual nest-egg of but several thousand dollars. My wife stayed on in our home, in Hobbs, earning enough at her job, to help with some of the household expenses.

It was obvious to me from the start of my new job search, that we would soon lose our home. For Hobbs, New Mexico, is founded upon oil production, and is currently upon a the 'bust' end of a cycle of its natural history. Few houses are being sold, though offered at what are now bargain price. So long as my nest egg of money would last, that long I had to relocate into another situation where I could earn my living. For the most part, I slept in the pickup, usually parking at a roadside rest area for the night where one may sleep in his vehicle, though it is not permissible to pitch a tent. And there are some well-maintained such rest-areas in the Western states. Most have basic toilet facilities so that wanderers such as I can change clothes and keep clean. Every third or fourth night, I would seek out a relatively inexpensive motel to tidy up my camper shell and luxuriate in a hot shower and its more spacious quarters. I usually had one solid meal a day; and kept a supply of soda-pop, a few bagels, and cream-cheese within the pickup to snack upon. I got home about once a month for two or three days, to launder up my clothes before launching out upon another tack.

Though it is troublesome and in some ways inconvenient not to be earning an income, one could hardly call my little Odyssey a great hardship. At least, nothing about that circumstance bothered me except the necessity to constantly seek out leads and contacts concerning job openings or practices for sale, or opportunities where a new practice might have the chance to thrive. Of course there was always some looming sense of economic desperation about that, and it was distasteful in that it seemed to me somewhat to smack of begging. But there was no choice about its necessity and so I did it – according to my best insights and instincts. And there were always occasional suddenly encouragingly possibilities that roused my spirits and gave me some pleasant hopes.

I have had some vague thoughts for several years concerning the possibility of attending Starr King School in Berkeley. Early in January it occurred to me that I might possibly – right at this time of my disrupted life – accomplish these two objectives together - in this one Odyssey. While researching for leads at the public library, in Long Beach, California, I located information on Starr-King. It was between semesters for the students, and I was therefore able to arrange to speak with Starr King president, Dr. McKeeman. He is a graduate of your own school, in Chicago. I drove to Berkeley that night, and talked with him about 30 minutes the next day. He indicated that the average age of their students was – surprisingly – about forty years. And that they do occasionally accept an older fellow, such as myself, as a student. Within the next 10 days, I submitted the necessary documents along with the application. I then spent the next month or more, seeking and inquiring for just the right work situations somewhere in the Bay Area, where I might work on a part-time basis, while enrolled as a student in Starr-King. I did find a few potential work possibilities that were to be available, perhaps, within a few months. Meanwhile though, I continued my search for work elsewhere, realizing that I might well not be the ideal candidate that Starr King is seeking. I searched in Kansas, Missouri, returned to Maryland, and looked through New Mexico, Oregon, and Washington, in addition to California. Of the few promising work sites that interested me, I set my sights on Las Vegas, New Mexico, and on this place, Ontario, Oregon. Checking them thoroughly, and having heard nothing from Starr-King, I settled here in Oregon with barely enough funds to get a toehold. I opened my office, renting space from the other local ophthalmologist, who was about the age of my oldest son. He was optimistic about the potential for growth here, and was hopeful for some additional income from the rental of his excess of office space.

My overhead expenses are high and I will probably not make a profit the first year. I expected I may have to remain here for a minimum of at least three years in order to catch up on past expenses. By that time, even our youngest child should be through college; and our living expenses at a minimum. If it works out that favorably and if I have been able to accumulate a little nest-egg of cash, I may again be in a position to consider the possibility of seeking admission into Star-King. At the urging of my young associate I have gotten a computer to handle my office business records. He, being familiar with the ways of computer, is getting mine set up to work for me. It has a word processor and a line printer, so that once I become familiar with it, I will be able – with economy of labor and time – to use it also for my various correspondence, and to put into manuscript form, the various essays and treatises that I continue to write upon occasion. And it makes more real the prospect that I may well one day have completed (into manuscript) the two books that I have been writing in the past four years or more.

Such then are my aims and objectives, which may be more optimistic than reality will permit. Only time, my own determination, and the events of coming years will determine the outcome. Rather than three years, it may take four, or five. But what of that? And I'm aware that the aging process reduces my prospects for admission into the postgraduate school programs. It simply is - and I must face the diminishing possibilities along with my declining years. I remain hopeful that I can find a way to get enrolled, once I accomplish the really difficult task; that of resolving my economic problems and becoming financially independent on the basis of part-time work beyond the next 3 to 5 years. But how realistic am I, concerning my own advancing years? I could be through my current 3+ years hitch, and through graduate school by the time I am 60. My own father died at age 80 (of boredom). My own mother is now age 80 – and yet alert healthy.

As to what I might do, should I arrive at age 60 having accomplished these goals, and having completed a three year course of study at Starr-King (or Mead Lombard)? If I have gained sufficient confidence in my ability to speak, I might work as a part-time minister for one of these Western UU informal fellowships; or even perhaps a full-time such assignment. Yet, I should not like to give up entirely the practice of ophthalmology either. And I hope also to find time to read, study, and to write. It comes down, I think, to this: 1) one needs must read and study in quest of Truth (and truths). 2) I write, because I aspire to that as an achievement: and because the process of writing facilitates ones coherence of thought. 3) I am interested in the liberal conception of a congregation as the organizational unit next of importance to that of family. An arrangement based upon the principle of an open-minded good-will fellowship such as that of The Lunar Societies of 17th and 18th centuries in England and France.

But, returning to the subject of my recent seven-month odyssey. I was alone in the Washington, DC area for the 3½ months prior to that. I found it to be an interesting adventure. There were aspects of the experience which I disliked, but the same is true for any other of my life. The poverty of my youth and childhood was a reality that never troubled nor worried me, for my parents worried about that on my behalf.

My recent scrounging about for sustenance was the third time in my adult life that I have been out of work for a prolonged period of time. And I was troubled by its reality even though by this time I have accomplished in my life, much that one needs must accomplish by way of wrenching from life a certain depth of broad experience. But I certainly required yet a way to continue to earn a living.

I have loved, and have been loved and have had the opportunity and good fortune to have achieved more than ever I dreamed possible in my youth. My children are essentially all now grown to adulthood; and I have had the opportunity to contest and grow with them through the years; and to encourage and provide them with adequate educational and cultural opportunities. I travel some too. Though currently broke, I have reason to be optimistic for my own future; as well as for the futures of my children. Throughout my life, I have been acquainted with, and surrounded by – and influenced by – a goodly number of bright, accomplished, and virtuous people; both family and friends. And I have enjoyed generally good health. I have found time to study, reflect, and to formulate my views on the nature of reality. There remains the hope that I may yet find even further opportunity to attain goals and objectives which to me have become meaningful. For all these reasons and more, these months of unemployment were unable to greatly oppress my spirits. Nor was I completely broke or hungry. I was therefore in a position to appreciate and take some little satisfaction in this change of pace; and experience a few things of interest that altered my outlook as a part of my wanderings.

Though I appreciate good company, I also enjoy some occasional solitude – and rarely in my life have had much of that opportunity.

Even those of us whose entire lives are peopled with friends and strong family ties cannot fail to notice that yet, we are in some sense solitary and lonely pilgrims in a strange and alien world. Orphan folks – like Mick Rosckowoff – know it better, of course. I traveled with that perspective in mind. But the orphan is dependent upon strangers for food, shelter, and raiment. I was not. My passage was therefore more akin to that of a free spirit, in its modest self-sufficiency. I passed through the multitudes unseen as an anonymous observer, in my solitary being. Through that orientation I saw things – and aspects of things that I had never previously noticed. I spent many nights and weekends upon the deserts and mountains of Southern California, Arizona, and New Mexico. Especially the Southern California desert and High Plains, are delightful places to be in the winter months. In the rest areas along the roadside, one can read and write in peace and contentment, for in the winter season there are no mosquitoes or other insects to disturb one's thoughts. The other travelers halted there are all 'turned-in' for the night by 10:00 PM. How strange it seems to me, that nearly this entire population is voluntarily evacuated to the world of dreams, in the very hours – 10 PM to 2 AM – that I consider the finest, for reading and writing. A picnic table is my desk; and the local government supplies my light from the nearby street lamp. In my long experience, I have never seen so much as an argument to disrupt the tranquility of one of these rest areas, though I have later read of the occurrence of a couple of robberies. Rare enough to be considered 'statistically insignificant'. I stayed two days at one such rest area, living out of the back my old pickup and at a concrete picnic table. My attention was drawn to a handsome young woman who approached every car that arrived, offering to wash their windows for a one dollar donation. Only myself, and a Navajo Indian in a broken down pickup, did she exclude from her solicitations. Only the circumstances of us two perhaps, did she regard as more desperate than her own.

I have stopped here and there, to visit with old friends and acquaintances. I was able to locate my deceased father's brother, from whom nothing had been heard for several years. We thought that perhaps he had died. But he was hale and hearty at age 83 – and bright as he sobered up. I spent some time with each of my brothers; and had some long strait talks with each. One brother and I took some days to investigate Central Oregon's geology; and later, a similar four-day trip to look at the geology of central Idaho. Besides Taos, Ruidoso, and Silver City, I found another old and backward town in New Mexico – Las Vegas – where to be was like traveling back 75 years into the past. I spent many weekends reading and writing to my hearts content. I spent three or four days with my family – and their families – at a mountain camp near Yellowstone Park. A reunion meeting of all of the descendents of my wife's mother whose age is 84 this year, a group of about 200.

She had 11 children. There are 44 grandchildren, 66 great-grandchildren, and already three of her fourth-generation descendents. 124 in all! In so far as I can gather from what I read, the Native American Indians never had a reproductive rate anywhere nearly approaching that. That reproductive differential between the races, and the fact of high susceptibility to disease carried by a white man (and white man's own high resistance to those same diseases) doomed the Native American Indian to a rather minority status. Indeed, many tribes were completely eradicated. They had some attrition to warfare too, but that seemed not to have been a major factor.

Have you read, *The Children of Sanchez*, by Oscar Lewis? I would be glad to make you a gift of an extra copy that I have. An interesting book that deals with the depressive sociological circumstances of the Hispanic Mexicans that escape continuously into our country in the dark of night, across the Rio Grande, as aliens. Poor devils. I offer you as a suggestion, something I would personally enjoy doing myself – if I had a sabbatical leave, with job assurance to return to. I would merely extend my taste for experience of the wandering life. January, February, and March are excellent and beautiful months to be in the desert states of Arizona and Southern California; but a little too cold to be able to count on being comfortable in New Mexico. One might take the time, to live and travel from a small motor home, among the various roadside rest areas and park areas designated as 'national monuments'. In places such as these, one would encounter many of the aliens and assorted poor folks who were nearly out of money - and nearly out of hope. There too, in the southwest, abide a great number of Native American Indians – who are also somewhat dispossessed and impoverished. One could read and study about these people, and their interesting history; while at the time, encountering and extending ones personal experience of them. I have a number of books concerning their history. Such a project might have any number of possible variations that one could choose, to serve his own interest educationally. And one can rent cheaply – sometimes even borrow a motor home for the winter 'off-season', so that living expenses could be moderately low. And one would be again surprised at the population of stars in the night sky. Too, the desert itself has an oft-acknowledged reputation of encouragement and transcendent renewal for the casual wayfarer who might expose ones self to its quiet influence. That can happen even while intellectually probing the complexities of its geology.

But it's late, and my writing is becoming illegible. And though I intended to write more, it can wait for another chapter. Let me know whatever plans you may have for your recess from Silver Spring – and where I might write you.

Best wishes to you and your family,

Garner Brasseur, MD

11-8-1986

5-18-1988

Caldwell, Idaho

Dear Paul,

Here am I, in rural America, where news and updated information reaches me as rapidly as it did when I resided on Connecticut Avenue, in our nation's capital. The larger cities of the world are no longer dependant upon the rural areas as a constant source from which to replenish their ever diminishing numbers; for in the past two hundred years the control of epidemic disease has been so successful, that even city populations more than replenish their own numbers. In the two week interval, since I received your letter, my conscious and subconscious processes have been preoccupied in tendering to you a reasonable and timely response. My thesis - and not mine, alone — is that the storm-clouds of a new and potentially terrible epidemic are upon the horizon; and that the threat is a great deal more serious than what we are generally led to believe. My ideas, concerns, thoughts, reflections and research for current relevant information have been simmering to completion; but this day, as I approached the typewriter to lay it out, the mail arrived, and with it, *The Uniter*, from your own congregation. I am sorry to have missed your comments, concerning 'channeling', a concept which I had not previously encountered. Of course, I will also miss the re-enactment of your conversation with Emerson, whose writings have long intrigued me. That Stephen Kendrick "was right - sort of", heightens one's anticipation for the re-enactment. We can't avoid dealing with subjects concerning which there is a great deal of uncertainty. It is a bit more frustrating undoubtedly, to end up leaving a subject gracefully undecided, than to end up at some certainty. For in the throws of uncertainty one must ever be prepared, to 'tap-dance' in the face of every confrontation. I read 'Paul's Piece', concerning the Golden Rule; and it recalled to mind the quotation from Confucianism which is related to, but not the same thing as the Golden Rule. It has been called the Silver Rule. The Golden Rule and the Silver Rule, when combined with yet a third rule — The Iron Rule (do not allow others to do unto you, what you would not do unto them) — provide a more realistic basis for the government of conduct of mankind, in my opinion.

There are enough problems in the day-to-day existence and in the rearing and education of one's family, that it is difficult at the grass-roots level, in our nation to mobilize even concern, for problems seemingly so remote, complex, and vague as AIDS. The prevalence of the disease seems to be low in Idaho. I am told there are only two or three cases in our town of 18,000 population. Chatting with a local physician, I enquired of him concerning any recent specific technical information he might have, concerning the AIDS virus. He didn't recall having seen much information on that subject. I had the impression that he might be suspicious of me, a newcomer, that I should inquire. The hospital and the local physicians are very much caught up in the potential medical-legal aspects of the disease, for even merely testing patients for the disease is fraught with so much legal danger as to frighten any prudent being. But, as for the disease itself, few, I think have much considered that as a realistic possibility that might afflict them, personally. You might then ask, "Well, who then is concerning themselves about the realities of this potential problem if not the Medical Profession?" The answer to that is, The Public Health System, of which there are representative departments at federal, state, county, and community levels. They collect, tabulate, collate and attempt to deduce reasonable and probable interpretations as to the nature and epidemiologic character of disease in the communities to which they are responsible. They make that information available to all licensed physicians.

In fact, they mail that information regularly to physicians weather they do or do not request it. By tradition, they are thought of as being involved with 'preventative health measures'. That approach to medical care is unquestionably the most important form of health care available to the citizens of a nation. Even in this age, it is probably the only form of health care available to the majority of citizens of most nations of the world. A large expenditure of public funds goes into the operations of the public health system, but to do without its services would be far more costly. By no means, are the public health systems of third world nations as active and effective as that by which we are served, here in the U.S. The World Health Organization (WHO) coordinates an effort to enhance the effectiveness of public health throughout the world, by expropriating information, methods, medical materials, and even personnel – from the technically and economically advanced nations of the world to those which are more impoverished. This, in order to maintain some minimum standard of care, within the limits of their budget. A benefit to all parties.

Every epidemic disease has its own particular history. No two diseases run the same course or have the same effect upon the populations which they afflict. Perhaps all have points of similarity as to communicability, signs and symptoms, mode of contagion, intermediary hosts, reservoir of disease for future contagion, etc. such that much of what is learned from one disease, can often be useful to the identification and control of another. All arise at some particular point in history and out of some peculiar circumstance of living conditions. Some of those diseases seem to disappear, and are never again heard from; or perhaps, they merely change their form and are no longer recognizable as they were. Dengue Fever seems to have been first reported in about 1779. Tuberculosis seems to have been an ancient disease that disappeared, then suddenly reappeared in the seventeenth century and has only recently been controlled, Poliomyelitis seems to have first appeared about 1840, Influenza seems to be an ancient disease whose genetic structure changes so frequently, that its course through history is difficult to trace. Its yearly outbreaks commonly bring about a highly prevalent but mild cluster of respiratory symptoms. Occasionally, as in 1918-1919, it brings a severe and lethal pandemic, having killed 20,000,000 people on that occasion (world wide figure). AIDS seems to have first appeared in 1981. I have read what seemed to be wild allegations to the effect that the disease was actually created in the laboratory; but now, even a recent article in Scientific American seems to leave that open as a possibility. In any case, AIDS is a new disease, and it is potentially so threatening a public health menace, that very large sums of money are being requisitioned and approved by the National Institute of Health to expedite research into its structure, its mode of operation and in search of some mode of effective treatment and control. Indeed, they are concerned! No disease process has ever previously been investigated so expeditiously or intently, nor at so great an expenditure. As I mentioned to you in previous communication, though the subject of AIDS comes up not infrequently within the hospital, it largely concerns procedure, policy, patient rights and the enforcing of valid sterile precautions. Though there are vague hopes that we will get to the bottom of this problem, the hope for an immunizing serum seems beclouded by the fact that the AIDS virus particle is highly mutagenic — the same problem we have always had with the Influenza virus. By the time the vaccine becomes available, the virus particle has changed its structure. I have neither heard of nor read of what the long-term potential prospects for the health of the nation might be, in the event that some break-through is not forthcoming. It seems certain however, that it is being discussed in more private circles. It is not in the interests of the officials in charge to encourage a stampede (from irrational panic), for that too would be a public health problem. And in point of fact, no epidemic disease is ever decidedly predictable in its course; least of all, this one called AIDS, partially because of its remarkable capacity to change its structure, and also because we have had no previous experience with this creature. There are two especially troublesome factors concerning AIDS, which we need to keep in mind; first, here is a disease with a long incubation period of up to five or ten years! Secondly, we do not actually know the prevalence of AIDS at this time. Only recently have accurate tests become available, by which we can determine whether one has been infected with the AIDS virus. Only those are being tested, in whom the disease is suspected. If we are considering AIDS to be a communicable disease, it seems reasonable that we should know which of those among us already is infected with the virus, for they are the ones from whom we should protect ourselves. We have some vague assurances that communicability is low. Consider though, that we keep getting the bad news a bit at a time, so that the matter of 'low communicability' may be a soft fact, subject to revision. Originally AIDS was said to be a disease of homosexual males — a comforting delusion to us puritans. It appears to be much more prevalent among IV drug users. In Africa, where the disease is said to have originated, the disease now shows about an equal prevalence between male and female, especially in heterosexually active young adults. There was repeated assurance to the physicians, of the safety of blood products from contamination with AIDS virus. A great many patients and their physicians have been badly disappointed to have discovered otherwise. U.S. NEWS & WORLD REPORT of may 16, 1988, page 10, informs us that the Surgeon general of the United States will soon be mailing an eight-page report on AIDS to every household in the country. I look forward to receiving my copy. The difficulty with facts though, is that they may be interpreted in different ways. And even facts must change when superseded by new facts. Additionally, the AIDS virus itself may change before the postman delivers to us the data.

FADING ECHOES

Consider now the consequences once one has become infected with the AIDS virus. That, alone, should be enough to unsettle one's equanimity. The original cautious projection was that the disease would prove to be fatal to perhaps twenty or thirty percent of those who acquired it. That figure has been incrementally adjusted upward; and at this time, some are beginning to suggest — tentatively — that the disease is one hundred percent fatal! The number of deaths in this country from Influenza was 18,500 in 1957. By comparison, the number of deaths reported from AIDS was only 15,000 for 1986. A not terribly high figure in a population of 255,000,000 - but that comparison is deceptive. For, all of the deaths attributed to Influenza were visible and accounted for within several weeks of the time that the individuals were infected with the Influenza virus; whereas, very few (or perhaps, none) of the individuals who were infected with the AIDS virus in that year actually died that year. The AIDS related deaths will be strung out over the next five to ten years. Only then will one be able to tabulate those deaths and compare them to the deaths attributable to the 1986 Influenza Epidemic. There is also the matter of year-to-year variation in contagiousness. For Influenza, from 1% to 30% of a population is infected every year. That variation presumably related to the rapid genetic variation of the virus year-to-year. Presumably, every person who acquired an Influenza infection in 1957 was accounted for, and the ratio of deaths to reported cases is low — I don't have the figure. Say, perhaps less than one death per one hundred thousand. Who has ever seen an epidemic disease that killed one thousand persons per one thousand cases? Perhaps there is no such fatal a disease, but AIDS could well prove itself to be the champion, even if the mortality rate does turn out to be less than one hundred percent. Actually, several epidemic diseases have approached one hundred percent mortality under certain unique circumstances in the course of their particular history. Bubonic Plague was very nearly that fatal at several points in the history of that disease. The same has been intermittently true concerning Measles and Smallpox in the past two or three thousand years. When the 'Sweating Disease' suddenly appeared in England, in the 1485's it is reported to have killed 99 of every one hundred who contracted the disease — and rapidly — within twenty four hours; we don't know the causative agent of that disease, perhaps it was an early variant form of Typhus. At the turn of the century Yellow Fever was equally as devastating, upon those working at the digging of the Panama Canal; but the U.S. Army Medical Corps, fresh from victory over malaria in Havana, were called in, established the cause and controlled the epidemic in an astonishingly short period of time. And why should the Army be concerning itself with epidemic disease? Throughout history, epidemic disease has had a larger influence than has the actual fighting of battles, as to the outcome of warfare. Napoleon was the first to recognize and take advantage of that truth, and his military success is largely attributable to his enforcement of vaccination and the simple personal hygiene and sanitary conditions of the camp environment. Even so, his Grand Army was eventually destroyed by epidemic Typhus and Typhoid fever, when standards of hygiene deteriorated in their hurried exodus from Russia.

I offer you a few references, upon which I base my information:

- McNeill, William H.; *Plagues and People*
- Zinsser, Hans; *Rats, Lice and History*
- Henderson, Donald A., M.D.; "Smallpox - Epitaph for a Killer?"; *National Geographic;* Dec. 1978
- I've forgotten the name; an excellent article concerning bubonic plague; *National Geographic*; May 1988
- Gallo, Robert C.; "The AIDS Virus"; *Scientific American;* Jan. 1987. And "part one of same"; *Scientific American;* Dec, 1986.
- "Science and the Citizen"; *Scientific American*; Jan. 1987; concerning the AIDS Pandemic; pages 58-59
- Swenson, Robert; "Plagues, History and AIDS"; *The American Scholar;* Spring, 1988.

Enclosed copy of College of Idaho '*Coyote*'"; April 25, 1988.

I have no great sympathy for the causes of the homosexual community. It seems to me that the interests of the wantonly homosexual run counter to those of the heterosexual and family oriented. But they intermingle largely unseen within the general population in such a way as to make it seem likely that the epidemic may well spill over into the general population. But as the homosexual community seems to be the primary harbinger and transmitter of AIDS it might be prudent to maintain a certain distance of separation between the two populations. Caution suggests that the homosexual might well generally be excluded from the teaching profession; and from any occupation wherein they are given custody of children and young adults. As ideas too are 'communicable' neither am I enthusiastic that the religious Fundamentalists are individually involved in public teaching. Yet I would not so much as trouble myself to cast a public vote against them, for they do have a strong family orientation, and people seem able to move into, and out from Fundamentalism. I see sexuality, however, as so potent a force and apparently so easily subject to perversities, that it seems folly to expose our youth to that potential influence, at the very time in their lives when they are most ripe to the influence of that perversion. But that is a long and fascinating subject — and I shall have to explore it by essay on another occasion. Here, my main point about homosexuals is that they seem to have been one of the primary agents in the early dissemination of the AIDS virus in the early stages of its epidemic history. And they continue to be one of the primary 'at risk' groups; and to the degree that one mingles with them — even in the non-sexual aspects of their lives, one escalates the risk to himself and his family of contracting infection with the AIDS virus through mechanisms not yet foreseen. A possibly irreversible and fatal incident. This, especially as the prevalence of AIDS increases.

We might consider how AIDS compares to Tuberculosis as a slow progressive communicable disease. Tuberculosis is a bacterial disease, transmitted to the individual in many ways both directly and indirectly: from contaminated foods - most commonly milk, from inadequate cleanliness, from body wastes. From kissing, across the tonsils into the intestinal and respiratory tracts. And through coughing and respiratory aerosols, across an incidental skin break, and perhaps occasionally transmitted sexually. Laws were passed to prohibit spitting on sidewalks. The course of the disease was slow and progressive in the individual, so that there were many opportunities for the infection to be transmitted long before being diagnosed. But Tb disease has been greatly on the decline in this country since the mid-1950s, though the incidence was as high as 85% percent in some age groups, and the death rate as high as three hundred per 100,000 population. It regularly accounted for as many as 3,500,000 deaths per year, world wide. In this country it was considered necessary to survey the entire population in order to identify and isolate and treat the infectious cases; and there was annual retesting. Among those who contracted the disease, only a small proportion died — most went onto a spontaneous recovery, though many relapsed back into active cases. The high prevalence of the disease (when it was a major health problem in this country) was undoubtedly related to the lengthy duration of the illness in the individual, so that people were repeatedly exposed to the organism. Fortunately, the recovered cases developed a degree of immunity against re-infection. Concerning AIDS virus, we are confronted with the possibility of repeated re-exposure to the disease, for there has been no effort, nor is there currently any intent for testing of the entire population. Currently, we have only projected estimates as to the actual prevalence of AIDS in the population at large. Considering the high rate of death (approaching 100%?), we might be justified in doubting the pronouncement that AIDS "is not highly communicable", especially, as the prevalence of the disease rises. Another reason to consider a survey of the entire population. In regards to Smallpox (see ref. list), it may be well for us to reverse the method — by taking something we have learned from AIDS, and to apply that lesson in dealing with the potential threat from recurrent epidemic disaster at the hands of Smallpox. You will note that the article suggests that Smallpox has been completely eradicated in the world — a cheerful idea; but permit me to retain some little doubt. I asked my sons and daughters-in-law to be certain that my grandchildren had all been vaccinated (against Smallpox) regardless that the prevailing medical opinion was that it was no longer deemed necessary. For in the past twenty-five hundred years, Smallpox has reared its ugly head repeatedly. And on several of those occasions, there seems to have been doubt that mankind would escape extinction. And there have been many occasions — in the new world — when entire tribes have been on the verge of extinction from a single passage of a Smallpox epidemic through their company. Let but a generation or two pass without immunologic experience of that disease, and then the stage is set for a new — and an old lesson. But where will smallpox come from, if it has been eradicated?

Why - out of nowhere, like it always has! These pronouncements of having destroyed a thing as immortal as Smallpox? Hubris and vanity. If nothing else, it is a fact that the virus still abides in bacteriological laboratories in Russia; and in other nations of the world. And the lesson from AIDS is that it might indeed escape from the laboratory, as did AIDS (?). Alternatively, of course, it could be released — intentionally - when the time is ripe. A biological warfare. Next, in asking about in the medical community, I discovered that not only is the Smallpox vaccine no longer being advocated, but that the vaccine is no longer even available! Paul, I swear it is true. And the military no longer vaccinates the soldiers of our highly touted military corps. Why trouble to even put them into snappy uniforms, if they are but destined to tread the path of Napoleon's Grand Army? But hold. More recently I have heard that the military is reconsidering the idea of reverting to the previous requirement of vaccination for all military personnel. One related bit of information is recently available to us from an experience that is unique to the State of Idaho. This past year, we have experienced an epidemic of Whooping Cough in Idaho. The only state in the nation in which this occurred; and the only such epidemic of Whooping Cough in the nation in several years. It seems that the State of Idaho had been supplying that vaccine — free - to the medical practitioners so that the expense of the immunization would prohibit no-one from receiving that protection. There was a law-suit or two over some 'reactions' to the immune vaccine. That, of course, raised the price of the vaccine. Noting that Whooping Cough no longer seemed to be much of a public health problem anyhow; the legislators failed to allocate funds for the vaccine; and a great many of the 'at risk' age groups in consequence, failed to obtain the immunization. I have forgotten the Latin expression that the Lawyers use — that means something like, "the thing speaks for itself". I have never been involved in the fighting of a forest fire, but a brother of mine has told me of some of his experiences in that line. Ordinarily, a fire will spread by continuity, as we have all seen, at some time or another; but it is common for a hot fire to leap across a road or a wide cleared swath when there was hope that its progress might be halted. When a fire gets big enough, and hot enough, in a dry forest, on a hot summer day, it may dramatically change its mode of spread, by 'topping out'. Apparently, the wind and the combination of heating factors in the timber toward which the fire is advancing, are great enough that it pre-heats and volatilizes enough of the combustible materials in advance of the flame. A whole large area of many acres will then suddenly explode into flame in one grand burst. A terrible thing for those unlucky enough to be there at the time. Epidemic disease can sometimes behave comparatively to that. The Bubonic Plague has done that on some occasions. Ordinarily the disease would spread up a limb from the site of the flea-bite, into the lymph nodes and the organism would proliferate so rapidly as to clog major vessels of the circulatory system to cause a rapid death. But in an occasional case, a few organisms would get past the lymph nodes early, and into the pulmonary system, where they produced a form of pneumonia. Then, the spread of the disease was no longer dependant upon the bite of a flea to inoculate the organism into further individuals. For then the disease could spread from person-to-person on the misty spray of a cough. A very efficient mechanism; and the whole pattern of that disease was now altered for the remainder of this local epidemic. And that episode of wild-fire ceased only when there were no further surviving potential victims.

Consider another viral disease. Chicken Pox. I vaguely recall reading an article in *Pediatrics Clinics of North America,* when I was a medical student. The article dealt with the high communicability of the disease in a pediatrics ward. The lesson was that there seemed hardly any way to prevent contagion to other children on the ward who had not previously had chicken pox. Even keeping them in isolation and using mask, gown, and gloves, failed to prevent the disease from spreading. The virus, of course, is shed from the skin lesions, from the naso-pharynx in the cough, and is present in the excreta. It seemed somehow to travel through the heating and ventilation ducts of the ward. The viruses are small particles, and they find a way to travel; apparently wafted upon the gentlest of drafts to their destination. Surely the AIDS virus will travel also, once brushed free from a stain of blood or saliva, or from a faint fecal-smear, unnoticed upon a bed-cloth. Then it is a question of how intact and how effective is the primary defense mechanism of the individual to whom this challenge has been presented — unbenounced to his awareness. And it is a question of whether the AIDS virus will find a combination within its repertoire of changeability that <u>will</u> find a way to get past the primary line of defense of the individual — and the species. Presumably also, the AIDS diseased patient will shed progressively greater quantities of virus as he becomes progressively more ill. An additional factor, separate and above that of prevalence of the disease.

In any disease-causing infectious agent, it is somewhat advantageous for the organism or virus particle to moderate in severity toward its host by causing a prolonged disease, rather than a severe illness that causes rapid death. For with the death of the host goes the loss of the meal-ticket and the free ride. Once situated comfortably in the host, then generation-after-generation of causative agent has a long period of time during which it has many repeated opportunities to transmit its infective particles to other individuals of the society in which its host mingles. Malaria is a good example of a disease causing agent that has accomplished that. Typhus is another. When Typhus first appeared in Europe, in the sixteenth century it was a severe and fulminating illness. As mentioned earlier, 'The Sweating Disease' may have been an early form of the Typhus. In addition to being rapidly fatal to the individual (killing at times 99 of every hundred it touched), it was highly contagious, killing from thirty to ninety percent of those in any community through which the epidemic passed. But gradually, through scores of years, its severity moderated, until finally, in some local areas such as Eastern Europe, the disease lives on in a low grade chronic form. The people who live in the area have gradually acquired a genetic and an individual resistance to the disease, such that they have only mild symptoms when they individually contract the disease. The virus-like agents of Typhus situate themselves deep into body tissues such as bone marrow (true also of AIDS virus, according to a recent article in *Science News*) and abide there — never being completely eradicated. The body louse and the tick have intermittent occasion to pick up the agent while feeding; and then, to pass it on, at a subsequent feeding. The rat, too, is a reservoir of the Typhus agent — so that the rat-flea can also transmit the disease. In the fifteenth and the sixteenth centuries, those eastern European countries — particularly Hungary, Rumania, and Silesia - began to acquire a reputation as 'the graveyard of Germans'. On more than one occasion, a German Army would invade into those areas, only to find themselves soon defeated — upon occasion, without even having engaged the enemy troops. Defeated … by disease. By Typhus, with some assistance too, from Dysentery. The German solders, their individual immune systems unacquainted with the Typhus agent became deathly ill and died, or retreated to safety, if they were fortunate, "And the might of the Gentile unsmote by the sword/ Hath melted like snow, in the glance of the Lord …" In WW-I, Typhus broke out early along the whole eastern European front. The Germans were cautious. The Russian Army was ravished by disease; and they quit the war early, thereby releasing the German troops to fight elsewhere. Silesia had no defense, but the Austrian troops would not invade. For a little bombing and shelling had diminished Silesia's standards of cleanliness and Typhus was again there in epidemic form. Naturally, there was some Typhus among the German troops too but they had a scientific medical corps, and they kept the monster contained with delousing, isolation of the ill, and the best possible standards of cleanliness. But they dared not to transfer those German troops from the eastern to the western front, for they knew that it would mean the defeat of their own army — by Typhus. The disease still lingers and smolders there in Eastern Europe. In fact, there is a pocket of a variant of that same disease in New York — where it is known as Brill's Disease — apparently brought in by some immigrants from Hungary. Does all this business about Typhus have any bearing on AIDS? It may well. No one has proved it yet, though. It took many scores of years of experience and many deaths to deduce the cause of what is finally known about Typhus. Perhaps we would be well advised to presume that AIDS is every bit as elusive, as dangerous, and as protean as is Typhus. The body louse, the fly, the tick, the cockroach and perhaps even the particular mosquito that was chased off of its last feeding site before it had its fill — and has now penetrated one's own hide. All of these, and more, seem to me to be potential intermediaries and mechanisms for the spread of this contagion. Many diseases that afflict mankind are shared in common with birds, rats, swine, ground rodents etc. And the ticks, lice and fleas seem often willing to intermediate the disease. The pool of contagion from AIDS could thus be vastly expanded, making it potentially dangerous even to be in the fields of the great out-of-doors. But these are only possibilities, and I don't wish to start a panic. And yet, however unlikely they seem, history has already established such things as these as possibilities. In our times, it is inevitable that there must be an official public policy concerning any threat to the public health, of such potential magnitude as is AIDS. And that policy must be based upon, at least, the most dangerous and the most definitely known epidemiological facts of that disease. For, that policy dare not be a sham policy; but must, in fact, embody measures that reflect our experience of past epidemics. Furthermore, the policy must include a program of some kind to 'attack' the invading agent, by throwing money and an appropriate army against the invading agent. That policy must be made known to the public, and periodic optimistic updated information released to the public. Along with the good news ... to give the public a timely opportunity for the release of bad news — in small, bite-size increments which the public will tolerate without going into a 'crazy' panic. For a stampede is dangerous — in addition to being useless against disease. And public officials are in danger of being thrown out, if the public loses its confidence in the government. There is also the danger of economic depression, aggravated by the economic death of individuals - if people become so fearful as to change their liberal habits of unnecessary spending. In general then, I believe that we do well to place some confidence in a public policy which is likely to result in some remnant of survivors. And if you and I wish to be a part of that remnant, along with our children and grandchildren, it is best for us to adhere to a rational policy. It is best, in fact, for us to adhere to the spirit ... of that policy; and enforce unto ourselves a policy even perhaps more strenuous than the official policy. The enclosed college newspaper is an example of the type of information which I most commonly encounter — policy, rules and regulations; rather than technical information. I expect that institutions and organizations are well advised to adopt some such policy — not only for legal protection of their own organization; but also to maintain a high level of awareness of the problem among their own members. Again, one must be mindful that estimated figures as to the prevalence of AIDS are <u>only</u> an estimate. There are widely different estimates coming from different sources. The highest figures I have seen, suggest there may be 1,500,000 cases in the U.S.A. by 1991; currently there are said to be perhaps 10,000,000 world-wide. Cause enough to take it very seriously. Remember too, that no individual can tell you where nor how he actually contracted his case of AIDS infection. If the individual has had a blood transfusion or has been injecting drugs, the investigator who is interviewing will assuredly attribute the infection to that; but in any particular case, who is to say that he did not, in fact, acquire it by inhalation or ingestion etc?

Peace attend thee.

R. Garner Brasseur, M.D.

18 May 1988

3 Sept 1984

Hobbs, NM

Dear Nephew RAK,

In the contest of life, be it recreational or in deadly earnest, a general principle is always to catch your opponent slightly off-balance – if that be possible. In a sense, we are forced into the same tactic with our family and friends, in our efforts to encourage them to make their lives what best they can. This, because man's nature is such that he learns best when he has a sudden shock or a rude setback. Or perhaps when having pushed ahead upon some genetically inherited course, he suddenly begins to recognize a measure of doubt and uncertainty concerning the earning of his livelihood.

I saw you at that point of uncertainty in August of 1984, and would not wish to be guilty of neglecting my duty to gently prolong your moment of doubt and confusion. If you have any notion of wanting to work at a career more challenging, interesting and, and economically promising, then do so quickly, before the urge leaves you.

There are two distinguishing characteristics of my wife's family. First, they all have a strong native intellect along with strong personal character. Secondly, they have almost all neglected to develop that intellectual potential into advanced education. Only the lack of a formal education prevents them from becoming what ever they might wish to be. Nor is the possibility of obtaining that education, by any means beyond their grasp.

I was pleased a year or two ago when my son informed me that RJK had gone back to college. I wasn't surprised to hear he had some problems with some of the courses, because the first year is always the most difficult. On top of that, of course, he was single. And all those hormones raging through a young man's veins with no outlet are a great obstacle to meditation and concentration. Being married now, one would expect he might find the continuation of his education less of a problem. Married men and older men generally do better at college course work then the young and single.

I myself was never a good student, and never wanted to go to college – or high school even, for that matter. Various subtle pressures upon my life were such however, that it became inescapable. And I had a difficult time adjusting to college. But I was married before I completed my second year of college, and the course of study after that seemed less troublesome. It may be the case though, that the courses only seemed less troublesome compared with being married and raising a family on the side - ha. I was age 36 when I finished my training, with youngsters ranging from ages 1 to 14 years of age.

I have a brother about three years older than myself that left home at the age of 14. Then, when he was age 27 or 28, he developed a sudden passion for an education. He arranged for and passed his GED equivalency test and then went on to college at Missoula. He became a good student – still is. He graduated from the U of Montana the year after I did; and then went on to get a masters degree before he began teaching literature, first in high school and then over at Wenatchee Junior college in Washington. He has subsequently gone into farming, but he loves to read and write; and we exchange ideas and notes frequently. He is trying to coach me into becoming a better writer.

So, anyhow, Ron, if you want to do something else for a living, why then, give it a try. You would make a fine teacher or engineer (or whatever else you wish to be). Take a couple of evening courses at the college to get your feet wet. If you find it to your liking, you can go at it more energetically next year.

Your Uncle,

R. Garner Brasseur, M.D.

3 Sept 1984

Oct 16, 1985
Chevy Chase, Maryland

Dear Nephew TWS,

Just a note to let you know that I wasn't pulling your leg - when we last talked together in Billings. I do agree however, that what I suggested to you - about attending medical school in Mexico, beginning sometime within the next six or 12 months - would be a rather uncommon suggestion to one of your age, who probably never considered such a thing realistically. But, what of that? That so few would even consider it, makes it the more probable that you could succeed. If you find yourself unemployed and are looking for a way to earn a living - what I have suggested, would fill that requirements. There would be difficulties and obstacles; but those more than offset by the accomplishment, and the secondary benefits. So also is it difficult to climb a mountain - and I think you might be surprised at how few who might actually ever have climbed one.

To reiterate what I already told you - for it may well be, that you have doubts as to its veracity. As you already have an undergraduate degree, I would think it is entirely possible that you could gain an acceptance into medical school at Guadalajara. It is a private school; and perhaps the best medical school in Mexico. They have always a good number of US citizens enrolled there; and a good number of physicians in this country are graduates of that medical school. I am a bit acquainted with the school, and with the situation down there because of a young man - Mick Rosckowff - currently enrolled there; and who is due to complete his medical school education there at the end of December 1985. He was a foundling of Chinese-Russian ancestors; born and partially educated in Peru. He then attended school beyond the eighth grade in the USA under the auspices of various cultural exchange programs; and became a US citizen by naturalization after he completed high school. As he had no family, he had to earn his way through college. He then worked a few years to earn enough to begin medical school in Mexico; but he couldn't afford to continue after the first year. I met him three years ago, in a state of despair of ever being able to continue his medical education because of having been unable to save enough money in the intervening 2 ½ years. Though orphaned, it was his vague understanding that his Chinese mother was Jewish - thus he thought of himself, and listed himself, as of the Jewish faith. Perhaps that is part of the reason that he was unable to enlist help in finding funds enough to return to school? I was impressed by his fortitude and strength of character. Therefore, I befriended him and encouraged him to continue his education. He and his small family stayed with us for brief periods of time on more that one occasion. I helped him find information for arranging to obtain federal loan money; have also cosigned some bank notes for him. And have personally advanced him some funds. He is now, almost over the last hurdle, and will probably not require much additional assistance from me.

But nephew, what is all of this to you? Only this: it is a specific example of what I have suggested to you as indeed being a feasible educational opportunity for yourself - and not merely rhetoric. Furthermore, besides the offer to you of my own assistance in helping you to find the necessary financial sources for such an undertaking, I believe that you can count upon the experience, advice, and assistance of Mick Rosckowff in guiding you through the intimidating obstacles of admission, should you decide to follow such a course.

I also need to reassure you once again, that the opportunity is entirely feasible on an economic basis. In the first place, you are not an orphan; and there is reason to suppose that your own family would not be adverse to such an undertaking. Though they are not wealthy, you would probably find that they might skimp and pinch to lend you some little assistance - without even being asked, for they seem to be of a generous nature.

Secondly, medical students by law are entitled to $5000 annually of guaranteed student loans - and at a low rate of interest beginning only when the course of study is completed.

Third, you may well already possess assets such as partial ownership in a home, which you could liquidate in order to further your education. One ought not wince at such a possibility, since it would merely represent a reinvestment from material things, into your own skills, ability, and earning potential. An actual improvement in the mode of investment.

Fourth, there are probably other federal and state loan and grant funds for which you would be eligible, other than The Guaranteed Student Loans.

Fifth, there are always funds available to you through private banks. These are best avoided for as long as possible - and may not ever be required at all - because of the high rates of interest. Even so, were it necessary, you need have no fear of these, since you're increased earning power would enable you to repay them.

One other thing of which I should inform you will, is that you may well - as a resident of the state of Washington – be able to transfer into the University of Washington Medical School after successfully completing the first year or two years of training in Guadalajara.

I am convinced from what I know of you, nephew, that your strength of character, integrity, and background of education and training are adequate to accomplish such a thing as I have suggested to you. One could well suppose that your wife has enough optimism and native cheerfulness to be able to endure your undertaking such a program. Young middle-aged folks such as yourself, snug and secure in their accustomed occupation, would be generally unapt to consider such a radical change in occupation and way of life. It seems to have been your good fortune to have become dislodged from the complacency of your accustomed occupation. Only that fall from complacency I think, is what opens you, in any sense, to such a change in the direction of your life. In such a situation, rather than grasping for something meaner or mediocre, you might, alternatively, fetch – from within yourself – that potential to acquire higher skill and useful arts. My only intent, is that the opportunity not be passed by unrecognized by you.

If you are, even a little bit interested in considering this possibility, then let me know. I would then have Mick Rosckowff send you all the pertinent information and application forms for the Guadalajara school. He and I could then give you further additional advice on how to proceed. Meanwhile, you – of course – may not be interested in the least. And that too is perfectly all right, for it is not as though I am requesting you to head in this or any other particular direction.

I am currently working in Washington DC, where I've been living the life of a hermit during my nonworking hours in a big empty house as I proceed into to ever uncertain future which will determine the course of my ongoing career.

Peace and plenty be your share

Your Uncle,

R. Garner Brasseur, M.D.

Oct 16, 1985

4/20/86

[Most of this day at EVH's home in Mesa, AZ.]

Up at 10:00 AM. Fry up a batch of eggs and toast for EVH and myself for breakfast. He and I then walked a mile in the sun with our shirts off. I got a slight sunburn on my shoulders. Talked a few minutes with his son, Mal to indicate to him that I thought EVH's interest in Constitutional Law was good, but that I thought that his religious ideas are bigoted and eccentric. Mal seems to be taking some interest in constitutional work, too.

Talked a bit with A.G. - an industrious and fine young man, studying music in college. He was age 23 last week. I gave him a ten dollar bill, and a one dollar silver certificate. He intends to go to Washington State when his school is out to work for his Uncle DFB on the farm this summer.

Fluff is out of town on a camping trip this weekend. I saw Dolly and her friend, Tom. Dolly also studies music at the U of Arizona - a sophomore.

I spend a few hours reading some of EVH's literature, including rescissional briefs of social security, driver's license, etc. Some seem to me a bit erroneous, but they have excellent sections of historical information and valid argumentation. In my secular view, they seem too heavily laced with all sorts of Biblical quotations, religious historical data, and bigoted assertions that diminish one's estimate of their overall value and credibility. And they are voluminous.

His conversation to me seems overly dogmatic and assertive. He quotes a good deal of scripture, but more often merely mentions the relevant verses - name of book and verse - often stringing three to six or more together perhaps to give the rhetorical impression that everyone surely ought to be immediately and intimately acquainted from memory with such. He surely knows however that such is not the case, and I presume he wishes thereby merely to silence one's dissent by shaming them with their own ignorance. That he himself can actually recite more than just a few of these verses seems doubtful. I interrupt his rhetoric upon occasion, when he halts to take a breath of air. But my interjections and questions have no power to end his diatribe or alter their content. He is in a preaching mode, and nothing he says is open for discussion or ripe for reconsideration. It as though he regards himself as the instrument of Yahweh's pronouncements and has infallibly captured His intent and design. Though he refers often to a great deal of what is actually pseudo-history, he never offers to divulge any references for his authority, other than those that are alleged specifically to be biblical. He has large flow charts of historical scheme upon his wall - specifically concerning only biblical history. As though biblical history were all there were of history. One of these charts in pictorial outline form simply displays arrows of movements of the so-called 'ten-lost-tribes', eastward from Palestine; then indicating an eastwardly arrow curving northeasterly upwards indicating a flow of peoples to the east of the Black Sea. And the pointing then towards a westerly course into Europe. It is as though he seems to have forgotten that the historical past was peopled with the movements of hundreds or thousands of tribes, most of which were entirely distinct and separate from the Jewish tribes. [I say 'forgotten' because I know him to have been unusually well read through many previous years.] Presumably then, it is his current view that all of the tribes that swept into Europe from the

Steppes of Asia, were in fact derived from the lost ten-tribes-of-Israel. Not likely! Certainly, among the histories I have read, none suggest any such thing. Such however is the assertive and audacious nature of our fundamentalist 'scholars', that they postulate as valid, that which pleases their preconceptions and 'hand-me-down' religious myths.

Because of EVH's currently held narrow religious/historical conceptions, I was rather curious to know what he actually reads on these matters. And so I scanned and read through some of his assorted copies of literature. A retired Lt. Col. from the Korean War era; that now lives in St. Louis. He cites military data supposedly from 'inside-sources'. But, of course, he can't reveal his sources etc. He adds to these, his interpretations and speculations, as though his ex-military title guaranteed the pre- eminence of his deductions. Another of EVH's sources: one robust and smiling Nord Davis Jr. seems to be a self-styled fundamentalist author and news monger - after the style of Garner Ted Armstrong's *"Plain Truth"*. He is fairly newsy, and does have some seemingly valid angles on the perverse nature of government; but he conglomerates his political insights along with his fundamentalist view of history. And postulates apocalyptic expectations derived from ambiguous personal and religious 'revelations'. And he tunes in regularly some sort of 'freeman' tax-rebel (Scott?) out of the San Francisco area. What EVH sets out to unravel, is reworked again into something of a new and obscure conjecture.

I am then told of George Washington's 'famous vision' (news to me) and I was unable to find reference to the source, wherein he is alleged to have reported of seeing simultaneous (?) visions of three great American War struggles. He (Nord Davis, Jr.) assures us that the first two "have come to pass, exactly as detailed in the vision". And now the third great struggle is imminently upon us, says he. The first two times of trouble were the Revolutionary War (already in process at the time of said vision) and the Civil War. But why no vision of WW-I, WW-II, or the great depression, or of Korea or Vietnam?

And in any case, what do dreams reveal to us, but just mostly unremembered fragments, images, and symbols. And in what way have these supposed G.W. 'visions' enabled us to prepare for, or to resolve the conflicts and threats? Yes, what then was the purpose of the 'visions'? And from whence derived? Indeed, what reason is there to believe that he (George Washington) ever actually had any such 'vision'? A 'vision' that might seem to have more of the character of the mystical pseudo-meaningful religious lore and myth. 'Visions' that add nothing to the historic stature of G.W, and supplies us no useful information. More likely, they are of the nature of folklore myth which tends to precipitate about heroic historical figures and is seized upon and embellished subsequent to the death of Geo. Wash. 'Attributed to' the now defenseless G.W. to give the thing credence.

My report would have to suggest that the religious views of EVH (at this stage of his life) were more than just a little bigoted. So too was his patriotism a bit tarnished in that he coupled it with his apocalyptic religious leanings. And he displayed to me not a shred of redeeming modesty or the tiniest uncertainty in the views he expressed - concerning these things unknowable.

The Jews alone, are the source of our problems in this world!? Upon my inquiry, he informs me that he can tell when a man has Jewish beliefs, simply by his physiognomy? (large nose, bucket lower lip, etc). Apparently no discarding of ones Jewish belief can redeem the Jew - presumably a miracle can't either. Negroes, American Indians, (and all other such) as well as all that are of mixed breed are not (in his view) entitled to have standing as American citizens. They have not any capacity for understanding scripture. They have no valid 'breath-of-life' such as to make them 'immortal souls'. Have not 'initiative' and are stupid. He himself - and his wife and children - are of the pure and unmixed blood that establishes them (not the Jews) as the true "Chosen People". He is willing to accede that same preferred status to me and my Aryan spouse (and our children), but he insists that PM's and JRO's children are 'bastardized' Mongols (because begotten from women outside of the pure Aryan stock. They ought to have taken women that are blue-eyed and blond. Curiously, even though in his view, lineage and Genealogy are the limiting and determining factors through which alone God's moral virtue and redeeming grace may flow; yet, he actually (so far as I can discern, from what he says) has no specific information as to his own genealogy, nor that of his wife. Nor has he ever concerned himself to seek and record such data. He seems simply to presume that the pattern of his mental speculations and conclusions is prima facia evidence of its own validity - simply, perhaps, because he knows himself to be pious and sober. And because of the consistency of his bigotries, one with another. And he takes it as obvious - from his Caucasian characteristics - that nowhere in his ancestral lineage (of say, perhaps three or four hundred generations) is there any direct or indirect compromise of the purity of his racial strain. Again, his knowledge of the unknowable is absolute, all-encompassing, and certain. No factual history, nor documents, seems able to cause him to acknowledge any degree whatever, of any uncertainty of his assertions, one must suppose.

Or, perhaps, these wild assertions are more of the nature of his low regard for my limited personal intelligence. The beauty of his views on constitutional law, government, bureaucracy; and of inherent rights and freedom of the individual, is that these things too, are internally consistent in their ideation; and compatible logically with one another. Furthermore, the authority of government can be said to derive - correctly, in my view - from the natural sovereignty of the each individual among mankind, over whom that any government presides - if by their consent. And that the government of the United States is, in theory - by virtue of the Constitution and the Bill of Rights - constrained by, 1st) the sovereignty of its individual men; and 2nd) by the sovereignty of individual state legislations, from the working of injustices against the natural rights, prerogatives, and freedoms of its any individual citizen. And in this matter - most importantly - individual sovereignty stands alone and upon its own force of authority and merit. It rests upon a logical philosophical principle; from and pertaining to the natural man, whom we perceive - and with whom we deal - in our familiar and daily trek, through the waking world of 'that-which-is'. The question of whether there be; or not be a Deity - natural or supernatural - is entirely irrelevant; and preferably ignored, as concerns the concept of government.

It appears to me that EVH's current concept of religious veracity is enough radically bigoted and apocalyptic as to be incomprehensible. For his religious views are built upon dogmatic authoritative assertions which he expects to be accepted without the exercise of reason, on the part of the mass of its slavish subscribers.

Yet, those religious views would appear to be completely <u>detachable from his view of theory of government</u> and the proper source of its base of authority and legitimacy. His views of government authority and political action are predicated upon an enlightened exercise of the rational intellect of its individual citizens, who individually comprehend the rationally correct source of their government's authority, and who individually act upon their individually reserved rights and prerogative (secured to them by The Constitution and Bill of Rights) to preserve continuously, their natural rights and freedom, against even their own primary government; and against foreign governments which would threaten their own voluntary government – a factor of secondary importance.

Thus it is that though I was disallowed from having any significant voice in our conversation; yet, from what EVH said, and from what he had written, and from reprints of writing which he seems to hold in high esteem – I was enabled to get a picture of his thoughts, beliefs, concepts, and motivations; and derive some clues as to the sources of his views.

RGB

4/20/86

━━━■◆■━━━

Having visited now for hours with EVH I am left with the impression that his natural studiousness has taken a turn into some odd directions. He is hypomanic and very talkative. I can hardly get a word in so as to slow him down a bit. Having later then taken my leave from him, I needs must then debrief myself (in writing) of some of the content of his rhetoric so as to ponder the nature of his mental state. He is not currently employed, and we know that he is terminally ill from metastatic cancer. Subsequent medical reports indicate that he will have had some scattered vascular insult to at least his cerebellum and that there has been some widening of his cerebral sulci and ventricles. Consistent with early dementia. And the examining neurologist on the basis of interview also suggests that he may be demented.

Generalized illnesses do predispose to various organ failures, including that of the CNS. A fluctuating delirium may well be a part of this, along with exaggerated tendencies to paranoia and delusional states. That, as well as a loosening of any even slight natural tendency towards ones native underlying bipolar status.

I well recall my own unpleasant fluctuating difficulty in thinking, and in being prepossessed with disturbing delusions which I could not shake during a few weeks of my nearly terminal illness in 1996. With recovery and restoration to health, one can hopefully expect also a restoration of normal mental status.

None of what I am pointing out is being said as though to belittle or in an accusatory sense. Each evidence of sign and symptom is merely being identified so as to establish and assure myself as to a valid and proper diagnoses. Thus to explain the probable cause of his progressing mental deterioration. We can thus be aware that a disease process rather than just some perversity of character is the cause of his present psychic instability. We continue to admire the strength of his character and the intellectual achievement he attained as a younger man and in good health. And continue to be grateful to him for the important positive influence he exerted on the course of our own lives through many earlier years of his energetic life.

Peace Thee Attend EVHB

Friend, physician, patriot.
Virtuous son; and ancestor.
Lived full his life
In cheerful optimism.
Met life's obstacles with a will.
His word and deed inspired us
- does so yet.
We loved him well.

R.G. Brasseur, MD
1988

- Addendum Perspective -

[I was to discover sometime later that brother VBB had also been in communication with brother EVH. And he seems to have been as much alarmed by EVH's progressive psychic disintegration as was I. He took the time and made the effort to confront EVH in writing with the hope of encouraging EVH to get a hold of himself and to reign in some of the extremities of his thought and futile writhing 'like a devil in holy water'.]

Jan. 7. 1986

To EVH:

Some of your thoughts are very complex and "off the wall". No, you do not "snow" me with unbelievable material. You do Scare me, though, as I am concerned for your future and that of your family. Where do you think all of this will finally lead? I have no quarrel with honest disagreement with the Law, that's a citizen's right, and the Courts are the proper place to settle these differences. The strength of our Republic lies in free speech and the Courts of Law. If you wish to pursue grievances in the Courts the remainder of your life, you're free to do so, at your option. However, it seems to me the way you're doing it will probably not make you a nickel. Why don't you get a Law degree and plead others' grievances for a fee? You surely have seen by now that there are enough people out there with grievances of one kind or another in this most litigious country on earth or in history. Enough of a discontented population who are financially willing and able to compensate you for your time, and simultaneously you could get in a few licks of your own. But the part that bothers me is that you've become (or maybe always were) too strongly prejudiced against those persons of Jewish persuasion, as though the whole fault lies with them, the so-called Zionists. That's not rational, old boy. Not all bankers, attorneys, judges, and government pen-pushers are Jewish, and certainly the majority of the Laws of this country were not written by Jews. But then who's to deny that the Laws of Moses, the Ten Commandments, came through the Jews; or that Christ was born a Jew, or that the Bible acknowledges that the Jews are God's chosen people? How can you say on the one hand that you accept the Ten Commandments and the teachings of Christ, then on the other hand condemn the people who brought you these … hypocritical? Not a very consistent way to look at things - shouldn't allow your prejudices to destroy your objectively. That is, if you have grievances about some part of the laws of this country, then work to correct the fault, but don't stew in hatred toward some imaginary group of enemies such as the Jews. What Jews have you known personally who were so hateful or a part of any grand conspiracy? I've known Jewish people all of my life and even have a few Jewish friends and neighbors and have found no fault with them that was not purely personal, the same as one would find in a Mormon, a Catholic, a Protestant, or Buddhist. Most are just struggling along to make ends meet and raise their little families and have a peaceful life, and pay their taxes, before they reel off this mortal coil. So, for yourself and for those simple souls around you, lay off this prejudice, put it to rest. Don't let these worms gnaw you from within.

As far us going to Western Montana to "live off the land", perhaps your long stay there in Phoenix has made you forget how cold it is in Montana, and how much snow they get there. The average growth season is something like 130 days - about four months; the rest of the year it's blanketed under snow. About all you can farm is cabbages, kale, and barley. The whole population there in the Western part lives on government subsidies of one kind or another, or on unemployment benefits, or disability, food stamps, free cheese, and welfare. Even the people who <u>own</u> their own land can't make a living. So you wouldn't be "living on the land", you'd be <u>dying</u> on the land. Or freezing on the land. And since nobody much can make a living there now with the timber industry dead, you and/or Betty couldn't find work. What few jobs are there are taken by the natives. For companionship you'd have all the freeloaders, drugstore cowboys, and assorted crazies. Plus don't forget that Andre and Adrienne have scholarships to go to the Univ. of Arizona, not to the Univ. of Montana - so you'd either have to forego their further education or leave them behind in Arizona. Plus

Betty would have to give up a good-paying job there in Phoenix so you would have no income. Thus you would lose your independence to pursue your legal cases and you personally would no doubt have to get out and use some elbow grease to keep from starving. Also where it's cold like that you need a lot of money to keep the house warm, at least nine months of the years and have to buy a lot of warm clothing and keep your car winterized, etc. Living in Montana takes a different kind of person and more effort than laying around in the sun in Arizona, wondering when it will get cool enough to go for a little walk in the evening. So don't expend too much time in fixing up any trucks or getting building materials to go to Montana. Besides, if you want to go to Montana sometime in the summer when it's warm just to see the country again and dream dreams, they already have all those things like trucks and tools there; and don't need any more from Arizona - you can buy or steal the stuff when you get there - ha! After all, Montana isn't some 'new wilderness' or Shangri-La where you can just go there and everything is for the taking. It's been pretty well settled and owned for a hundred years y'know. It's pretty in the summertime and the fishing is good then in the mountains; and in the Fall you might be able to shoot some game if you have a good eye, good gun, and a license; but the rest of the year it just lays there under cold and snow and nothing much moves. People just come out of their hovels to pick up their government checks and cheese and get some groceries. Not very adventurous, all in all.

So, EVH, it looks to me like you're turning into a little bundle of prejudices and pipe-dreams and it's hard for me to find a common footing to talk to you about real things and real ideas that might pan out. I liked you better when you were in Chicago, and Miles City, and Hamilton, and Idaho Falls, and Spokane. You were real then, had good aspirations, worked hard, tried to give good advice, and listened, at least nominally, to what people were saying. Since this Richland thing though you've changed a lot and right now it looks like you're in over your head and off somewhere in left field. Nothing more to it that that. Happened to Dad, too, and who knows might be part and parcel in some way or another of the whole family. Everybody needs a little squaring off from time to time but if he doesn't listen to his friends and family then who will he listen to? – some "voice from above"? Even that's not too bad unless you start answering back.

Your brother

VBB

Jan. 7, 1986

2/14/88

Caldwell, Idaho

Dear EVH,

I was awakened this morning about 5:00 A.M., on account of the delivery of a new-born child. RL and TM Brasseur's second son had arrived, down there in Ashland, Oregon. No name has yet been assigned to him; and in consequence of that, the little rascal is probably not yet well oriented as to what direction he should follow in the course and purpose of his life.

Nor is it an easy matter for a parent to determine precisely just what name is apt to accomplish that. Those names of course tend to be laden with all sorts of expectations, implications, hopes, and historical references. I did resist the temptation to suggest a name — not an easy temptation for one to resist. I wish I had thought to warn my spouse from that trap, before she journeyed down there a couple of days ago. She plans to stay down there to help them out for ten days or so, perhaps; before returning to the more hopeless task of getting me straightened out. But we can be sure the child will get a name, ere long – and a social security number, too, undoubtedly. And then we sages of the older generation can page the family and historical archives, to attempt to divine the meaning of it all.

Enclosed for your personal records are various photostatic photos, family documents, and genealogy lists which I have recently compiled – concerning both the Brasseur and Boepple families. Please feel at liberty to correct and supply the missing information. I am researching information that will possibly enable me to extend the Boepple line of ancestors back to about 1750. In fact I think that I already have most of those names and dates, but there is still a little information that is wanting; so, I'11 not put that together until I have adequate documentation. But, to extend the Brasseur line beyond about 1825 promises to be a whole lot more difficult - largely because I don't read nor understand French. It may be the case that you know or have access to some of the information which is wanting - as you can see from the charts.

You know, of course, that I have been shifting about, like a Mexican jumping-bean in the dance of life, as one might say. It is not an easy dance, for there is no set pattern to the steps. It has something of the imperative of the saber-dance, for one must always exercise a little caution, as to where to place ones foot next. And place it one must! Then too, I am but an auslander here, in a land that is overpopulated with physicians, and especially with eye surgeons. Und, Ich Wollen Deutch Bleiben. The docs all have at least an externally pleasant demeanor, however; and they are willing to smile and to shake ones hand. But doubts and questions seem always to crop-up in my increasingly skeptical grey-matter. "Is the lion smiling, when he bares his teeth?" "Why does the limp paw seem so chilly?" "Dare I at his bidding, proceed him through the doorway?; or must I protect my backside?" But it must be admitted that they are reasonable in their bland friendliness, after all;

for they never know — either — when they might be confronting their own assassin. In truth, I think, there is a lot of intended goodness, kindness, and virtue within them, individually; but their systems of government torment them into a chronic state of frenzy — by abusing their individual sovereignty and their intellect, and wrenching their painful joints upon the 'cross-of-gold', and threatening always economically to impale their dear families, in lieu of a generous contribution of tax dollars. No wonder the poor devils cringe and slink. No wonder their genial gestures often seem half-hearted. For one might squeeze their painful knuckles too tightly; or pat the tender skin of their recently flogged back.

I had some hopes that I might come down to see you, but I don't yet have much to do here, and so it is difficult for me to get away. If I were a busy practitioner though, this is about the time that I would choose for such a trip. For this is the finest time of the year to be in Arizona and southern Calif. I remember with fondness my several sojourns through there in 1986. I visited and stayed at your place a couple of times in that season of my life; but mostly, I slept in my pickup, alongside the road. And it was good for a season to be a nomad, and a solitary wanderer in the deserts of this earth. But that chapter ended, and I passed on to other forms of futility. And I still haven't decided what I should do when I grow up, but they tell me I have several bright and promising grandchildren. So, perhaps I'll consult with them from time to time, about goals and directions; and about what things in life might be worth doing. And, perhaps one day I shall be civilized; and neat, and clean, and well-advised. And wouldn't your mother be surprised! (those last two sentences, by way of paraphrase from a record album of Irish ditties that I once heard from your collection). There was another time in my life, when your own vision and courage; and goal-directed exertions and exhortations to me greatly influenced the momentum and course of my life. I am grateful that you troubled yourself to encourage me along. For it was a good education, and we had some uniquely fine seasons of hope and great expectations. Yes, and even some small measure of transient prosperity. "Failure is not fatal, and success is not permanent." I remember it being said then, that the benefits of one's education were transient, and that one would have to retool in, perhaps, some ten or fifteen years. It seems to me that I have been having to retool continuously. But, perhaps I misunderstood the meaning of the expression. I expect that what was implied, was that one might be well advised to switch into another occupation, for in that interval of time, society may well have squeezed both the glory and adventure from one's chosen field — as well as the financial reward.

I hear from VBB occasionally, though his hand-writing is difficult to decipher. He will probably be back in the U.S.A. before long to begin a new pilgrimage concerning where to settle and what to do. I hear from Duane occasionally, too. Farming seems another plight laden with difficulties, largely through the agency of meddlesome government. The poor devils can't make a decent living from their hours of hopeful labor in the dirt; yet, neither can they find a way to get out of it. In short, they have the tiger by the tail. It hardly seems now worth the effort of having gotten into it in the first place.

I hear that your family is to have a get-together in March. Be sure to leave the porch-light on, for, as I recall your address is a little hard to find. I presume that young GJB will be going back up to Alaska after a little holiday. Let me enclose to you the name of Lea Bryan (840 Hilltop Drive; Palmer, Alaska, 99645). She is a daughter to your Uncle Herman, and she is terribly interested in family connections. She and I have exchanged letters a couple of times. There is every indication that she may energetically pursue the genealogy of the Brasseur family, thereby sparing me some of that labor. So, ask your youngsters to look her up, as I am sure she would be delighted. And, Alaska being an expensive place to live, family connections there could prove economically advantageous.

But, I must get this out to you before your birthday, and get on with my other projects.

Your brother,
R. Garner Brasseur

2/14/88

2/1/82

Hobbs, NM

Dear DFB,

Thanks for your commentary on my spiral notebook of miscellaneous ideas. What you had to say concerning 'good humor' seems close to the central core of what it is that turns writing into reading. And also what it is that turns life into living. It is related to "wa", (from *Shogun*) - harmony and balance.

Sorry you didn't get a chance to come down to New Mexico. As you indicate, it is a terribly long distance. We often travel up to 900 miles per day by car when we have to make those long trips. But then our travels are usually under compulsion. And it is tiring to be so inactive all day long.

Perhaps we might arrange to get together for a couple of days at some point half way between here and there - like in Nevada or Utah.

Or, we might fly up there for a medical meeting sometime, and arrange a couple of extra days for some time at the beach. It would be a good thing especially while the kids are still young.

I have been intending to write you, but got tangled up with those books you gave me (two of them were looong). Concerning the story of the Sioux, *Hanta Yo*. The history that she enumerates is not greatly different than what I had come to suppose. That is to say, that they had migrated to the western plains from a more easterly woodlands area. Dr. DuBose tells me they originally lived in the east, got pushed westward, lost another round to the Mohicans and were forced even further westward. Then when smallpox and other epidemics decimated the then Plains Indians, they were able to cross the Missouri and claim those lands. And that they were constantly on the move; constantly changing their customs and living habits as circumstances changed. I am surprised at the apparently small number of their offspring per parent. Are not we also a migratory people?

In retrospect, I am surprised at how little I had ever come to know about these Indians, considering that there were always Indian tribes and peoples about us wherever we lived in Dakota and Montana. As children, we heard whisperings and rumors about them (they eat dogs; they steal; etc.). But it is as though our society (of whites) simply looked through them, pretending they didn't exist. But one must suppose they had a similar distain for us.

I especially enjoyed *Shogun*. Both *Hanta Yo* and *Shogun* had elements of style that were simple and effective for the conveyance of information in a straightforward and unencumbered manner. The mechanism that I have reference to is that of the stated but unquoted statements and observations interspersed with lines of conversation (in quotes) between the various characters of the plot. It surely is not a newly created device?, and it must be the case that I have just only now noticed it. It is precisely these unstated (rather, unquoted) statements and comments – the internal dialog – which is the better and truest part of every person. And interspersing this material with external behavior and spoken dialog gives to the material of a novel a quality of stereoscopic-like reality.

Concerning *Hanta Yo*, one might guess it was written by an

Americanized woman from the way she touched upon the subject of the romantic feelings of the Indian women. It didn't quite ring true of what I conceive to be characteristic of the cultural outlook of the Native American Indian woman.

It is my guess that there are two basic modes of internal (psychological) activity when two people interact (or when one person interacts with others). The first mode is one of simple internal perceptions of vague and varying emotional tone (such, for example, as the seven emotions listed in *Shogun*: hate, adoration, joy, anxiety, anger, grief, fear). The other mode is simply the analytical state of mind (varying from simple to sophisticated; from moment to moment, and somewhat unique from one individual to another). The Japanese samurai were wisely cautioned to hold back the inclination to these seven emotions, presumably to replace it with analytical and attentive thought.

If one were therefore to write a dialog between, for example, Uncle August and Aunt Lydia, the external dialog of the uncle would have to be countered by a considerable volume of his unspoken and internal dialog. At least, that is my opinion, as he seems to me to have been a rather rational and thoughtful person.

In your own story, *It Was Written*, you did use a lot of external dialog, but I don't recall that you used this other device, the unspoken internal dialog. That is the mechanism that would uniquely delineate the special and interesting characteristics and motives of each character. And where the whites interacted with the Indian, you could easily expand (with this device) upon the nature of and the un-resolvability of their philosophical cross-currents. You have spoken of images and I was impressed by those you portrayed. I recall the rain and rivulets beginning to flow down the incline, carrying a bolus of mud to a point, and the stream then diverting itself around the bolus. You have portrayed the lonesome feeling of squatting on ones heels watching tumbleweeds misbehave. And the landmark images of a riverboat … a big rock … and the muddy Knife River etc. Thus it seems to me that your story possesses the essential components of an interesting book, but that you might take more time to expand upon these things. Allowing each character to put forth directly and indirectly his impressions and ideas to do contest with those put forth by each of the other characters. Or indicating how ones emotional state has led his external manifestations down some rabbit trail and up against a cactus bush.

That big rock. That muddy river. The misplaced riverboat. Each suggests a moral message that some of your characters may comprehend (or mis-comprehend); and that even the reader retains as he follows the narrative of the action.

Its true that that I have had no formal training in writing. Nor have I had any training or experience with the analysis of literature such as one might receive in a Humanities course. But still, I hope that my comments don't strike you as overly elementary. I have the impression that you are intending yet for another draft of your book.

After we left Washington State in November, following that (practical joke they call a) trial proceeding, we stopped in southern Oregon to visit Bill W___. His oldest son just graduated last spring from Linfield College. That boy (Bud W___) is JRO's age and they were classmates in Ashland. Bud thinks his name isn't formal enough – and sometimes jokingly tells people his name is "Buderick". Bud is a personable and bright fellow, and was planning on going into a seminary. I have the impression that his dad would prefer to see him do something more useful with his talents. Also, their second son, Roy, one year older than RL is also enrolled at San Jose Bible College.

Anyhow, I told Bill that I wasn't all pleased about RL being in Bible School, and that I was writing to him to encourage him to get into something useful. Bill asked me to send him a copy of the letter for his two sons to read. As I know both of these two boys fairly well, it is in fact, just the same letter I would write to each of them personally if I had the time. I needed the exercise of wrestling with those ideas and clearing my thoughts enough to put them on paper. I asked Bill W___ to forward that letter copy on to you after he and his sons had read it, as I thought you might wish to peruse it and might yourself have some comments upon the problems with which it deals. Something to chew upon.

I take note of your suggestions for the general improvement of the quality of my several poems. I find poetry to be difficult. As with music, I have no training in literary forms either; I only know what is pleasing to my rustic perceptions. Actually, I don't believe it would be accurate for me to imply that I have a large appetite for poetry. But, there are some poems that I have read, that I treasure for one reason or another. So much so, that I have taken the trouble to memorize about thirty of them over the past several years. Most, among these, I like for their philosophical content, or for the story they tell, and for their elegance of phrasing.

I have read but perhaps a dozen books of poetry. Only occasionally do I come across a poem that seems to connect to my sympathies and outlook; and that poem, I mark for re-reading. Most of what I read in poetry seems to miss me widely, and I have trouble maintaining enough interest even to get through a first reading. Some of it is in archaic lingo that I cannot comprehend - a foreign language to me. It seems to me somehow that wisdom, wit, and humor are somewhat enhanced by well chosen phrases in poetic form. That emotional subjects are more easily and more deeply broached in the formality of the poetic mode, since they otherwise tend to be blurted out, sob-like, in embarrassingly incoherent phrases.

I have made attempt to write an occasional poem. A time consuming task, which does not come out even to my own satisfaction. I find that I am most apt to get started on such a task when I am in a state of emotional chaos; and about some philosophical problem; or about some protest I have churning within myself. Such things as Hawthorne might label as 'bosom serpents'. And once started, the intent seems never to let me off the hook until I have brought it to at least a tentative conclusion. Perhaps someday I will begin to get a feel for it. But I do find it a difficult thing. If this were not the case, why is it that I see so little poetry that I consider to be even worth the trouble of wrestling? And look at the small (tiny) volume of extant poetry compared to other forms of writing.

"Rhymes the rudders are of verses by which like ships they steer their courses". Certainly the ideal and classic expectation one has of a poem, is the rhyming characteristic. And the first poems to which I was ever exposed (in the second grade of school) did fit this model. I see that since at least the time of Whitman, many poets write some or much poetry in defiance of this maxim. And yet, it seems to me that any non-rhyming poem, no matter how well written, would be even a little better, had its author brought it up to meet the rhyming standard. On the other hand, many discussions of poetry have rightfully pointed out the stiffening effect that this 'requirement' imposes upon their verse, at least on verse written in the English Language.

M.A. is now age 14. One of her school friends is a little Mexican girl who just turned 15. One of their customs concerning the maturing daughter is a day of celebration to honor that child and the coming-of-age event. They fill that day with religious and secular events. The girl had a dozen maids-of-honor, with each an escort of the male gender to attend these events with her. In the morning it was 'Holy Mass' and a reaffirmation of baptismal vows. This was followed by a big luncheon reception. And in the evening there was a grand-ball with live music, dancing, drinks, and food. These events are all attended by the child's family, relatives, and friends, as well as by the attendants and escorts and the parents thereof. So far as I know, the parents foot the bill for the whole celebration. And for all I know, may have to pay 'indulgences' to the priests besides. It must have cost them a minimum of perhaps two or three thousand dollars. The mother of the girl even made all of the gowns for the daughter and for the maids-of-honor.

M.A. was invited to be one of the maids-of-honor and thusly had a chance to become aware and more accepting of folks with other religions and customs outside of her own fundamentalist associations. The spouse and I attended the evening dance which ended about midnight. Most of the people there were of 'Hispanic' origins and they had a Mexican dance band with mariachi music. Mexican and Latin rhythms and song in Spanish. It was too noisy for conversation so I danced most of the evening. The two-step and the waltz were nice but the samba was hands down favorite. It was an unusual opportunity to 'let-go' - to stomp about, and holler, and act a little crazy. I had thought I might take a drink with a bit of Tequila in it to ease me through the evening, but it wasn't necessary. The general excitement along with the delightful music and rhythms was more than enough.

The young folks certainly appeared have had fun, and it was obvious the adults did. I expect that 15 year old celebrant will probably long recall that day set aside in her honor. I am undecided about the cost to value ratio, but those that paid the bills will have to decide that for themselves. It has been my experience that those parties are always the most enjoyable where the kids are invited to take part in the festivities along with the adults. The adult-only parties seem to me generally to be too tense and political.

You may have heard that PM got married to girl named Dianne just before Christmas. And so PM, Dianne, JRO, and RL all came down together in JRO's 1972 Luv pickup for the holiday season. It was nice to have them about for a few days.

We expect to be in Orlando, Florida March 14-20. The wife and M.A. will be able to while-away their hours in Disney World while I am attending meetings. Are you awfully busy at that time of year? If not, you might consider bringing your family down for a few days. Eastern Airline has some good package plans on their flights. And lodging accommodations are costing us but seventy dollars a day. We could suffice with sandwiches part of the time. We would have some evenings to chat and compare notes after the youngsters have tucked-in for the night. Or, more likely while they were taking in the Disney World attractions.

Your brother,
R. Garner Brasseur

2/1/82

1/16/83

Hobbs, NM

Dear DFB,

Enclosed please find prescriptions for the three medications you requested. Back problems are troublesome to more people than perhaps any other ailment aside from headaches. And the cost, around the world for the diagnosis, treatment, medications, disability payments, loss of wages, etc. is perhaps not exceeded by any disease or ailment whatsoever. Insofar as I can determine, no back problems are ever cured to the point of full rehabilitation. For the most part, 'what-has-been' is 'what-shall-be', concerning back disorders. Those people who suffer back disorders are up against an iron-clad reality, and they must make their peace with the limitations imposed by that reality. Their life style must change to within a more restricted set of activities. Failing to recognize this while recuperating from the first round commonly assures them a second reminder … and a third …

One learns from experience to avoid lifting and whatever such things aggravate the back problem. One must then learn from trial and error just which bending, flexing, and strengthening exercises alleviate the pain. Medicines are perhaps equally important, along with rest and to non-lifting in expedition of ones recovery from recurrence.

Advise your youngsters against heavy lifting. The vertebral structures simply will not withstand repeated insult without showing its results in progressive degenerative change. Stretching, bending, and flexing exercises to maintain strength and stability are good, but not the lifting of unduly heavy materials. Perhaps a man ought not lift ever, more than (say) one half his own weight. This is an important and relevant message that ought perhaps be impressed upon our youngsters.

As a lad and as a young man, I took a certain pride in my physical strength and agility despite the wont of evidence that I was in any way significantly above average. I was often willing (though not enthusiastic) to involve myself in the lifting of heavy objects such as rocks, refrigerators, pianos etc. I still find myself unintentionally challenged to some such lifting tasks on rare occasion, but studiously find ways to avoid them. When foresight does not save me, I can frequently escaped by jokingly referring to 'my bad back'. But it is no joke, and my inner being is deadly serious about the matter.

An amusing little poem by Sarah Cleghorn:
"The golf links lie so near the mill
That almost every day
The laboring children can look out
And see the men at play."

Regarding your request to peruse a copy of one or the other of my daily log journals. I often wonder if they are worth the daily effort. I can make some copy for your perusal.

In truth, I expect that most people like you and me who find and enjoy some little time to work out our ideas and thoughts in writing, rarely actually find the time to write their book, or even put order into their scattered writings. Whatever they have written is passed over, even by their families at the time of 'the settling of the estate' and relegated to the junk heap or the flame. Of even our own family members, we generally know but very little; such as how old they were (at death); where they were born; what they did for a living; who they married; who were their children; a few of their eccentric habits and thoughts; that they were regarded as religious (or not); when they died; and where they were buried. Such things are of interesting to me also, for they do give at least some insight as to what folks were like - especially when we recall also some of our conversations with them. Far more interesting to me however, are the specific things that they may have thought, their essay opinions of this and that, the philosophical questions with which their lives forced them to wrestle; their tentative conclusions; how their outlook changed over the years (and why); the things and beliefs that they held dear, etc. But do we ever discover such things? If not, why?

I have one copy of a letter that dad wrote to his children concerning a problem that greatly disturbed him. I was touched by its gentle tone and it recalls to me the many times he disagreed with me in this same quiet sort of way. Actually, he had only started to write the letter but never got far into its text before he gave it up and left it forever unfinished, six years before his death. Dad once told me that he had taken the time to write a number of essays when he was younger; and that he still had these writings about the house somewhere. If such is the case, I can only presume they were destroyed after he died. I don't think PP would let such papers pass through his fingers and into destruction. In fact, the one letter that I have was given to be by PP because he knew that I would be interested to have it.

Do you not think it strange that things should be this way? Do you not think it likely that one day your descendants and mine may wonder too about us and what we thought? Not only is it probable that I (and you too) may never get our notes organized, but likewise these journals and papers will likely also disappear into the flame and rubbish heaps of time. Perhaps then, it may be useful and interesting for you and me to exchange copies of our journals, essays, etc. To assure us access to them later in the event of fire; and to assure that copies might be available to our children at our demise. As you have suggested, they might at least be interesting familial documents.

Presently, of course, I am far too occupied in working and making a living; and in various interactions and communications with my immediate family to be able to find time to organize any writing project. But I have vague hopes that I may be able to find such time in perhaps ten years when the kids are all out and settled into their own lives and families. In the meanwhile, it seems I am not uncommonly under pressure to write them letters to admonish, exhort, and encourage them to think, to learn, to progress, and to transcend.

Of course, I understand that I myself am the chief beneficiary of these words and letters and essays that I write to them. For they are a large part of the stimulus that I receive to keep me at this ongoing task of soul-searching and pondering the mysteries of life and the vast socio-economic constraints upon our ongoing existence.

The youngsters have cost me a fair chunk of change in the past few years, but I feel fortunate to be in a position to be of some little help to them economically as well as rhetorically. And right now the economy, even here in Hobbs America is not good. Nor to me, do prospects for economic recovery in this nation seem optimistic for the near future. Our society is one of consumers, a large proportion now unable to consume up to their usual expectations account of being unemployed. Some form of chaos or civil war seems to be a possible consequence of such a situation. Civil wars being bloody things, it would not be surprising to see our legislators opt for some sort of external war in preference to that.

PM is working full time with computer development at the technician level. He is putting in long hours of even his personal time into this work in order to learn from it all that he can. He has tentative plans for returning to school next fall to pick up his engineering degree so that he can work at the design and concept level in computer intelligence systems. He and JRO and RL were all home for several days at Christmas time.

JRO is in his 3rd year of Electrical Engineering at Portland State, and plans to be in school through the summer, and then to graduate in the spring of (George Orwell's?) 1984. I think PM may have gotten him interested in computer field also.

RL spent a couple of months wandering about Europe and got back home in early October. I had a chance (after 20 years) to talk to him for an extended period of time when we spent three days together at a hunting camp in the Guadeloupe Mountains 150 west of here. Neither he nor I do any hunting, but it was a nice trip just being out in the wilderness and living around the campfire with a few hunters of my acquaintance. Like so many other men of the Brasseur line, RL seems uncertain, and reluctant about getting started in school. I charged his brothers to use their influence to prod him out of that Bible School and into something serious. They all three drove back to California together. RL is still looking but I expect that he will probably enroll at Fresno State College for the second semester, towards the end of January. A large part of his reluctance seems to be related to a lack of self-confidence. But he won't fail for want of intellectual gift; his main problem will be self-discipline - the most difficult of disciplines.

M.A. is in the 10th grade and is doing well. She studies regularly on a day-to-day basis, but seems to have great difficulty organizing an approach to any long term projects. I have started early and put the word out to her, that I am not wanting to have her attending any Bible College. And I plan to repeat that message to her often.

We have launched a small discussion group that my friends call the 'Lunar Society'. By no means is it a new idea of course, but certainly a worth while effort. Addison and Steele of *The Tattler* belonged to one such. James Watt belonged to one that concentrated upon applied science. Ben Franklin belonged to one. I am sure that there must be hundreds of such groups. We meet once every three or four weeks to sip together a little wine and spend the evening discussing books and ideas. I always look forward to the occasions.

Best wishes to you and yours for the New Year.

Sincerely yours,

Garner Brasseur

1/16/83

3/2/83

Hobbs, NM

Dear DFB,

Your recent correspondence with EVHB was interesting and informative. I could almost feel the sweat in your analytical presentation as you touched upon specific points and issues, one after another, in order to elucidate and tie together your concepts. Tedious work; and of benefit (to you - though not necessarily to EVH) in that it clarifies to yourself many things that have perhaps vaguely annoyed you over the years. Matters and issues that perhaps you never previously took time to resolve within your own mind.

Perhaps in fact, EVH did actually read your letter (though evidence in his response leaves some room for doubt). It is even possible that he pondered what you said. Certainly you touched a nerve that he noticed when you mentioned his financial arrangement with his mother. He might have, and undoubtedly could have written you a prolix and philosophical response; but you would have been none the more satisfied with it than with the abrupt reply that you actually received. For his journal ledgers never seem to tally, despite an abundance of cryptic and disordered entries.

In the same way, I too wrote him a long letter, outlining to him my views on the problems he and I have had (in December 1979). His first complaint was that "the letter was so long" - an observation that jarred my bone marrow, yet properly prepared me for his eventual response. For the first time in my life, I had a sudden insight into the meaning of that poem by Lewis Carroll that runs:

> "Beware the Jabberwock my son!
> The jaws that bite,
> The claws that catch!
> Beware the Jubjub bird, and shun
> The furious Bandersnatch."

Before EVH contacted you, he called me (and VBB, before that) in search of an immediate transfusion of money. Since I received your letter, he called again (a week or ten days ago) saying that he had been evicted from his office. I truly did not – nor do now have any funds give or to lend him. Had I such funds, I would not have sent him any. For I have already once tried to 'save him' – yet left him only bitter and economically unregenerate. He has had other saviors besides myself; and may even yet have other prospective saviors for future events. I fear he may never learn that a man must eventually save himself.

EVH has enough gifts and training to enable him to make a living. He certainly has a capacity for rote learning and he has the temperament and euphoria of an evangelist. As long as I can remember, he has always had everyone within shouting distance whipped up into a frenzy. In my case, perhaps I truly needed at one time in my life to have him beating his wings, stirring the dust, and tossing lightning bolts about. When he and I have been planted, I hope the sites are remote from each other, lest the refuge of 'eternal rest' might otherwise be meaningless.

But I wish him no ill. I only have become aware that I have been unable to deal with him on a rational basis. Perhaps just a matter of how honest a desperate man can be?

I do not recall him as being much taken with religious ideation as a young man. My estimation is that he began perhaps to involve himself in that theme at about the same time as he began to become an income tax protestor 'freeman' – just before or about the time he left Spokane for the Tri-Cities. I perceive the two themes as being intertwined in the evolution of his thought. Even as his personal beliefs were evolving, he expounded each with an iron-clad certainty. "Frequently wrong, but never in doubt", is the expression that comes to mind.

Through it all, EVH has meant something to me through these many years. I am sorry to see him pinched financially, but he continues to manufacture much of his own difficulty as he rails to no effect against the IRS and ever present inequities of the political and legal systems. It is my guess that even now, he is going through far more money than we can imagine. I greatly fear however, that if he continues to rail against the system, the IRS may get him tossed into prison for a couple of years. Having been convicted, he will automatically lose his license to practice medicine and will indeed then face a stark and difficult world. By then, his family will have gone and he will be alone at nearly sixty years of age. It seems an evil time to have to have to begin anew.

FADING ECHOES

I get an uneasy feeling when I talk with EVH for long. He rambles on about his court victories and against the IRS. But that seems unlikely, and he does not offer to substantiate his claims. His perception of 'victories' seem to me to have various aspects of defeats. I am loath to question what he sees as evidence for his claims. For his reasoning does not fly straight, nor swiftly to the point. He confabulates dubious and shameful statistics with which he insults my intelligence. He misinterprets documents. He will not follow an accounting ledger, but only wants to know final net figures which he promptly disbelieves and then forgets. He seems as though to believe that the Constitution and the Bill of Rights were inscribed upon the back surface of the stone tablets that Moses presented as the Ten Commandment; and that both surfaces were inscribed by the finger of God. He points me clear and lucid prophesy from that clearest of books called *Revelations*, and he ducks around behind the skirt of God when I doubt him whatsoever. When I indicate that my religion disagrees with his, he tries to make me feel bad, by 'feeling-sorry-for-me' and by labeling me with names like 'Secular Humanist' or 'Gentile'.

Clearly, EVH and I have become separated by a great chasm of thought. Though I occasionally see him (the last time, a couple of years ago) and oftener hear from him via telephone, it leaves me oft with that distant and 'de-ja-vu' sort of feeling. It has that dream-like quality even at the very moment of its actuality. It is as though while we walk along in conversation (Jabberwok) that we are in parallel but separate worlds; visible to one another and taking turns alternately at speaking. Yet, there seems no unifying reality between our separate perceptive worlds of experience. He dominates the conversation, but at each change of speaker, the one stops, as at an intersection, to allow the other to proceed across the grain of progression, each time but narrowly missing a collision. There is thesis and antithesis, but they are sterile - never culminating in a joint conclusion. I probe his psyche, trying to engage his thought for some point where he has a doubt; but I am unable to 'hook' him at any specific instance, for the whole of his understanding is in generalities. He seems unwilling or unable to concede to any doubts (except, of course, in general terms). Nor can I comprehend any of his iron-clad certainties.

I am enclosing copies of a couple letters I have written to my sons, JRO and RL. You will note that in each, I have enclosed a few remarks concerning their Uncle EVH. Both of these boys, as well as PM, were with us in the Tri-Cities. During those two years we wrangled often with EVH and the vortex of complexities that he continuously generates. Each of these three sons was personally involved in several aspects of our business arrangements and the complications thereof. Each labored and was personally burned, at least a little, in one way or another. Always little lessons for one to absorb.

Despite the financial setbacks and the personal affronts we each endured as a result of that prolonged encounter with EVH, we all gained some useful experience. We were all exposed to many problems and complications of business, P.R., of real estate, of law, of economics, etc. For there was endless conversation, discussion, argument, phone calls, and philosophical speculations. No matter that the human tendency and circumstance is usually such as to consider things from a detached and utopian point of view. The true moral good of it all, was the pragmatic result, which did not fail to touch us all. Nor did it fail to affect my circumstance - of which these sons were fully aware. Neither did it fail to deliver its brutal reality upon their Uncle EVH - whose course they continue to follow with awe and wonder. These sons did, and continue to see, touch, taste, and feel the physical reality of the consequences of all of that trouble which we encountered in the Tri-Cities. They ponder no mere rhetoric.

Throughout it all, I have had to call upon each of these sons for some assistance, and understanding. They have lived (for at least a short time) in the home of their Uncle EVH and thus become somewhat acquainted with a man whose form of insanity is, after all, somewhat different in nature than is that possessed by their own father. And perhaps it has taught them to be forgiving. Although I have tried to point out to them the nature of his madness and the fact of his delusions in that it fails to come to grips with reality; yet I have specifically avoided stirring their anger against him. They each still drop in to see him occasionally. I hope that they can develop a sympathy and a sense of understanding for the weakness possessed even by sometimes strong and valiant men.

Over the years, the little fellows continue to mature and my influence with them declines. They have seen their father change not only physically, but also philosophically, in his concepts, in his habits, and customs. I hope that they begin to see, as I (tentatively) believe, that even as mankind has evolved into a human species, so also must men individually evolve and change under the tutorship of the lessons of reality.

Enclosed is a book I want you to have. It contains the short story, *A man Called Horse*, which I enjoyed. It also has other stories that I liked; the setting of some of these are around Miles City. You may be acquainted with some of the stories, or even with the author?

I have recently been reading *Godel, Escher and Bach* by D. Hofstadter, which we are to discuss in our Lunar Society Meeting. It is interestingly filled with concepts and ideas that revolve around mathematics and number theory. It deals with computer concepts and artificial intelligence. Few books have ever vexed me so! I have been at it two or three months and am yet but halfway through. Despite the difficulty, it deals with just the sort of thing that I feel I must yet attempt to comprehend. If you get into a bookstore, browse through it. I think you might enjoy it. Since you have a better math background that I, you would undoubtedly have an easier time with it.

The wife, daughter, and I are headed to Miami, Florida. We leave this Friday (March 4th) and return on Monday the 14th. The family will vacation, while I earn my fifty credit hours of study for the year. It will certainly be no vacation for me, but it will be a welcome change of pace.

Best regards to you and yours.

Sincerely yours,

R. Garner Brasseur

P.S.: Concerning EVH being evicted from his office? I heard yesterday that the so-called closure of his office was but a false alarm. Yet, he must see the fatal day to be impending - that he would jump to such a conclusion just because the door was stuck.

RGB

3/2/83

– <u>Addendum Perspective</u> –

[I am aware that that since at least 1978 EVH may well have already been experiencing some problems in consequence of metastatic cancer. I recall from that year a conversation in which he made mention of having already then some difficulty in initiating urination. Resorting to the tactic of getting into tub of water to get things started. We know that he had cerebral problems including metastasis in at least final few years of his unfortunately short life]

13 May 1984

Hobbs, NM

Dear DFB,

The newspaper reporter was interviewing a few of the local people on the street, to get brief opinions for his column. His question this week was "Which would you say is the greatest shortcoming of the American public - apathy or ignorance?" The first man he interviewed responded, "I don't know, and I don't give a damn!"

If I had known that you and your family were thinking of coming down for a visit at the Christmas/New Year season I would have encouraged you to do so. That is usually one of the quietest periods of the year for me, as few choose that season for elective surgery. Nor do many come into the office in that holiday season, unless for acutely painful problems or sudden worrisome visual deterioration.

All of our kids were home including JRO, with his wife. They had good rates and flew into Albuquerque for about $100 each. The wife borrowed a passenger van and met them all up there on the night of the 23rd. There would have been enough room for your family, too. They all departed from the Midland airport on 3 January. Airplane rates went up shortly after that - as is usually the case after the first of the year.

I think you would have been reasonably comfortable (psychologically as well as physically) since our arrangements are informal. We usually aim to have a supper meal together and some of the folks have a late breakfast together, if they happen to be wandering into the kitchen at the same time. I don't usually eat breakfast or lunch, being content with one square meal at supper time, and a bowl of cold cereal just before I go to bed somewhere between 2:00 and 4:00 in the morning. Those that hunger in between are free to scrounge up whatever they want in the kitchen.

There is the sense of having wasted valuable time and a vague 'hung-over' feeling that I experience from sleeping too late into the morning. Therefore, even on weekends and holidays, it is my custom to arise not later than 9:00 a.m., dress quickly and then leave the house to see a few people at the office and make rounds at the hospital. Even in the occasional event that I have no patients to see, I still go through the routine of being regularly at those appointed places, at times which are characteristic for me. For I have a vague notion that referring doctors and patients gradually become aware of that pattern of availability, so that it tends to bring in a few patients that I otherwise might not get to see. Just as important is that, the ceremonial performance of visiting the widowed, the poor, and the orphans, fulfills some vague sense of duty which is somehow deeply permeated into my psyche. It keeps me circulating for that ritual period of time, within my society. Having fulfilled the duty of public accessibility, I can then feel free to withdraw to the privacy of my own life to read and wrestle with ideas, and to listen to music. And I am generally able to siesta for an hour in the afternoon.

My time of departure for my morning circuit coincides roughly with the time that others in the family depart on Sundays for Sunday school and church. Perhaps that is a coincidence. Yet, I rather think it may have a history, and that I may have used it originally as somewhat of a pretext of partial excuse for absenting myself from churchly functions. Having then once forged that separation, the pattern persists for other useful reasons, and because it has come to have an additional twist of philosophic irony. For while others parade out to religious services with their little Christian airs of slight superiority, I see in my own aberrant pattern, something akin to transcendentalism. For while they hear sermons and talks about kindness and visits to shut-ins, the widowed, poor, and the sick, I myself am actively attending to those very things.

Where they pray the Deity for healing and courage to the ill, I myself move as if in answer to prayers and by virtue of study, work, experience, and availability, am among those most humanly able to accomplish some of those things.

I visit patients at their homes (under some circumstances, at the nursing homes, meet them at the clinic outside of working hours, and visit them in the hospital). Few doctors, especially the specialists, will submit to that without a certain fuss. Yet, I am comfortable with it - perhaps partly because I know I am not required to do these things. But, perhaps that makes it easier to humble oneself. In the face of a necessity and requirement to do these things, I suspect that ones pride might then be in the way.

The white scrub-suit attire traditionally characteristic of the doctor image has, I think, become in fact more specifically associated with the image of the doctor in training, and has been overdone and overly familiar through T.V. exposure. The Marcus Welby image was not specifically associated with the wearing of white attire. His home-spun pragmatism and wisdom as portrayed during the season of his popularity on T.V. is an image that I think still lingers in the minds of the doctoring public; and is there closely allied with the old time 'doc'. His function is partly priestly, partly physician. That way, he covers all of the bases. It is difficult to doubt his advise concerning Folgers coffee (or whatever) even years now after his T.V. program series has ended. I suspect he was too uninvolved with romantic intrigue to titillate T.V. viewers of today. Yet, he lives on in memories, having been incorporated vaguely into the gestalt patterns of some as something familiar to which even they can return in times of deep and personal illness. Though I never watched perhaps, even a single complete show of the Marcus Welby series, I had recurrent glimpses of it over the years. He had somewhat the image of a prophet. His advice was like a proverb - "short sentences drawn from large experience." Such is the image that I prefer and perhaps even strive for.

You are aware that our upbringing was humble and earthy. Even as school boys, we circulated among the rougher elements within our communities - those of our generation as well the adult generations. As newspaper-boys, we trod the main streets with the tough kids of the community. And it was nothing to me to be in and out of all of the bars on Main Street several times a day. We wandered easily through the back rooms of card-playing gamblers. I yet recall the solemnity of those smoked-filled cathedrals with cones of light from overhead green shades which pierced the smoke to illuminate the green flannel-covered card-tables. Sober studious faces gathered there about those tables to ponder their prospects. Occasionally I might sell there a newspaper for a nickel even while many dollars were at stake upon the tables. I had been given the impression that even Grant's Pool Hall was at least a little bit disreputable, though I did occasionally stop by there for what was a generous serving of a strawberry milk-shake at a cost of 10 cents. And on a half dozen occasions, I was even tempted into shelling out a dime to play a game of pool with a buddy.

In the bar, I watched with awe as someone placed quarter after quarter into a machine and pulled the handle that generally sent that modest fortune away into eternity. Occasionally someone would even feed one of those machines with silver dollars. I tried to adjust myself to that point of view, so as to comprehend the difference in our economic status, but my progress was slow. On rare occasions, I witnessed a payout to one of the depositors and once drew some hasty conclusions that gobbled up a day's wages of several nickels that left me sorrowfully re-examining those notions. The concept of probabilities began to cross my mind. I was about nine years of age when I first came into contact with all of this. In addition to disreputable saloons and gambling dens, I soon heard rumors about even such a thing as a house of prostitution and its forbidden location. Later, as a high school student and working at a drugstore, I occasionally stopped by there to deliver medications. I felt small and experienced a bit of anxiety just being present in such a forbidden place. I was aware in a vague sense of what went on there. But the girls there were pleasantly friendly and they gave the lad a tip.

Simply to be an observer and alone to wander through this other world, left me in eternal wonder, yet I never was in any way involved with any of it except - as it were - as a passer-by and spectator; or more accurately, as one obliged within a system and required to interact impersonally, as an agent. And when the preacher spoke of sin, I had come to have some vague notions of what it was that he meant, and to which parts of town they particularly had reference. Yet, I had never witnessed personally anything or any act that I might regard as a specific example of this particular sort of 'sin'. Most of the action there would have occurred at hours when I was asleep.

As a youngster it began to dawn upon me that there were divergent versions of historical reality.

There was a mystical history which we encountered rhetorically in Sunday school and church. Rhetoric suggested it to have been inhabited with, cherubs, winged angels, miracles, robed and haloed saints, and grungy sinners - and a mighty … but currently inactive God. A God, who like Santa Claus, was making a list (for future reference) of who was naughty and who was nice. This mystical history seemed to be centered upon rather ancient times and far away places that remained static. We of the here-and-now had only word-of-mouth information - but no personal experience of it. There seemed an implication that we and our own times were unreal and entirely unimportant. Implied that some obscure history of a miniscule portion of the world's huge population, in a miniscule of obscure times past was the only true reality. And that it, alone, was worthy of our contemplation and analysis. We youngsters supposed a certain reality to that version even yet on Mondays and diminishingly on through the week-days.

On the other hand, there was the history we derived from our American schoolrooms and textbooks which were filled with the specific goings-on of ordinary persons, of nations, and of war. It was one of a dynamic past, contiguous with current events. An immediate past of which I and my own clan were a part. And I was decidedly a part of that moving and ongoing history that clearly burst along with ourselves into a new future at every new dawn. The retrograde horizons of that secular past sort of dimmed and vanished into a fog of history beyond somewhere between 1776 and 1492. God, heaven and immortality seemed greatly atrophied and mostly detached from the here and now of this version of history. How this all related to past biblical history was entirely vague to me, though seemingly crystal clear to the clergy, or at least they gave us that impression. How were these two views to be reconciled? Alternatives that I could not truly integrate.

My own view and personal experience affirmed that my life was bound up about the essential realities of the here and now, and of a life which was based in the home surrounded by family and extended family. No evidence here of cherubs, winged angels, nor haloed saints that I could clearly distinguish from sinners. My world was a place to sleep, 3 meals a day, and a pattern of life that suggested I was to abide a long while in the public schools, advancing year after year to a higher grade. And its everyday reality demonstrated that I was free to wander into a dark and troubled side of life as a servant or agent, at 'respectable hours' to earn some little income. But home and in bed by 9:00 PM.

From what I could discern from within the life of my family, I must presume that I was destined ultimately to metamorphose into mere mortal adulthood. Surely, the reality of my personal experience of that world could not escape my notice. Existential reality of the here and now.

What vague deportments and accomplishments in life were expected of me? I am to get an education. I am to graduate. I am to get a summer job. I am to do my share around the home and not cause trouble. It is okay to have a girlfriend. Somehow, I am to find 'an occupation' to earn a living; and some day, perhaps, to have a family of my own. I am to avoid bad habits such as cursing, drinking, smoking, and partying. I am to obey rules of the home and of the school and of society. I am not to spend more than what I make - and I ought to save some. I am to present myself clean and well dressed. I am to make some effort to make people proud of me - or at least not ashamed of me. So, one needs must strive and exert himself and be the kind of person he is informally expected to be, with some minimum of knowledge, occupational skill, a scheme of values, and hopes of achievement. Or, one could be a failure, and disappear from the presence of family and friends. Perhaps even from their memory. So long as we continue to strain upon the course before us within the fetters of our own limited imaginations, we hear the cheers and encouragement of our loved ones, church folks, and of teachers. When we stumble or give up hope (and quit the race) we perceive a hush - a loud hush. And we sense the stadium as emptying of disappointed spectators. ("Well you better mind your parents/ And your teachers fond and dear/ And cherish them that loves you/ And dry the orphan's tear ...")

It was only later in my life - perhaps into my teens - before I began progressively to ask myself questions, to think for myself, and to doubt. My education was basically that of simply attending school and obtaining the basic tools of learning and of self expression. I certainly had no concept whatever of where I was going, nor exactly why. Yet, forever, by custom of habit I was advancing, progressing, clearing hurdles, and preparing for tests. I rarely had a time of my own, or a place of my own, or a firm view to affirm. Parents, preachers, teachers, custom, and law; all contributed to the push for getting through school. All were authoritative, and there seemed little alternative to the general direction of ones life.

We come to have visual impressions of the various environments through which we pass in the course of our every day life. The open meadow, the doctor's office, the hospital, the grocery store, the pharmacy, the saloon, the barber shop, the home, the school room, and the church. We also come to have distinct olfactory impression of each that, in itself, would identify each separate environment to our awareness.

I have been acquainted with the mystical property of perfume and of burning incense throughout my life. I always perhaps regarded it as one of life's stranger vanities. I had often experienced vivid feelings precipitated by various subtle odors. I have upon occasion been momentarily overwhelmed and in awe by chance encounter with a potent symphony of smell, as in coming into the home during the preparation of an exquisite meal while fortuitously in possession of a large appetite; or at party or dance in the presence of womenfolk who - for some unfathomable reason - have dabbed themselves with perfume. From some rare occasions I even recall the mystic influence of incense. And there have also been offensive odors that have affected me powerfully, such as that of decayed flesh or rotten eggs. I read and studied concerning odors and became intellectually acquainted with the psychology of its workings and its power of making vivid impressions upon the mind. Still, even though I at one time used after-shave lotion to cool my face, I have generally always regarded the intentional use of vivid odors as feminine, and beneath the dignity of a man.

While cooling my heels one autumn day in a small country courthouse in 1981, I happened upon another perspective concerning odors. Bad odors are a vivid offense by definition. To my mind, the habit of cleanliness which we acquired was partly the process of eliminating our own mortal odors. Through the years, it became apparent that one had often to take special pains to eliminate bad odors, such as brushing and flossing one's teeth, and occasionally even brushing the tongue. For one would not wish to offend the women-folk of his acquaintance anymore than he enjoyed dealing with offensive women, knowing how ones own malodorousness would reduce ones esteem at the very moment one is wanting to enhance his impression on that present company.

While in the hallway of the courthouse, I passed an attorney who reeked of perfume to the extent that it sharply caught my attention and centered it upon him. He was not a handsome young man, but dressed well. It occurred to me that I had been favorably impressed by him despite a variety of factors that would otherwise have left me with the opposite response to that person. Why had he impressed me so positively, I asked myself? Clearly, it was the affect of the perfume.

In retrospect, I then perceive that I had been thus strongly impressed by the pheromones of perfume. Not only might an outside opinion toward oneself fail to be diminished by mere personal cleanliness, but that same opinion may in fact be positively enhanced with the essence of a fragrance. Why does it matter if people be negatively, neutrally, or positively affected by our person? Because the rewards for which we strive in life are more easily obtained when we positively influence those about us. Perfume, perhaps, a supplement to a smile and civil decency such as might ingratiate us to those who might reward us with their friendship, accessibility, votes, business, and confidence. Thus did I acquire the custom for the use of a smattering of cologne. Usually a musk scent and costing me $6 to $9 for four ounces. A bottle of which lasts perhaps a month or 6 weeks. I vaguely supposed this to have positively influenced my practice at some subtle level. It seems to me that fragrance makes my patients more affable? That it makes them just a little more alert and present in the here and now, so that the necessary testing can be accomplished with greater ease and facility. One might even suppose that the impression might subtly influence them in favor of returning again at subsequent occasion. Subliminal advertising, as it were.

My experience of having worked at many jobs in the course of my life was more or less a continuation of the same process of schooling and acquiring new interests. Having once learned a particular job, one might move on to another job where there were additional things forever to be learned, and of which to gain experience. I was predisposed to an informal learning of ever new things, acquiring new skills through activity, as opposed to the didactics of studying and reading. As a youngster I enjoyed playing sports and rarely listened even to the radio. Of course, we had no T.V. and our home never had a phonograph. Somehow, in church and school, I learned to love music and song. Once learned, song and music seems to stay with one forever, sort of as the payment for the effort. And that particular wealth can never be spent out - it remains with one always. Neither is it taxable.

It occurs to me, DFB, that I have never seen you tuned into a radio or apparently listening to any musical records. But surely you must enjoy a preference for some form of music. I really don't know of anyone that doesn't make at least some little effort to listen to music from time to time. I have about 800 records and perhaps 50 tapes, that include folk music, western music and blue-grass, classical music, operas, oratorios, and even some religious music. From time to time, I search among them and find something I have never closely listened to, but just in parts. A thing that happens, because I tend to order and receive my musical records and purchases of 8 to 20 at a time, and select out that which most pleases me - thereafter neglecting the other portion. Then, upon occasion, I come across one of these neglected discs while in the mood for diversion to something new; and find myself pleasantly surprised. Just the other day, I put on a record *TeDeum* by Bizet, and found it to be hauntingly lovely. I may go sometimes for a week or more without intentionally listening to any music; and without realizing how much it adds to the quality of my life, until I again one evening redirect my attention to the music. Upon listening again, I feel renewed and wonder myself as to why the interval of neglect. RL and JRO have indicated that they think music to be one of the most independently powerful influences in their lives. My own experience with music does not greatly contradict that opinion. It is poetry of sorts, but infinitely more familiar to us. So familiar to us, and so continuously so over the years of our lives, that it has become bound to the variations of the emotional aspects of our lives. Thus, the particular composition or category of compositions of music, upon being heard again after even a long interval, will rekindle in one many of the emotional tones and sensations that we experienced at the time of our lives when we first became attracted to that music. Words said to music seem to have the power to endure within our memories as phrases and verses, in perfect sequence, doubly fixed there - as it were - by the influence of both verbal concept and a pattern of sequence and relatedness to melodic strain. For our custom of lyrics tends toward idealized concepts and idealized heroic saga of events. Yet, even wordless and nonsense syllables once coupled to music have much the same staying power in our minds.

Feats of memory are accomplished with poetic jingles and with lyric voices. Surely, crash courses could be taught in subjects that required learning of, and familiarization with names and classifications such as biology, zoology, anatomy, historical sequences, etc.

Throughout history, perhaps many lives have been lived with but minimal experience of music. The European-Western developments in music, especially over the past 4 or 5 hundred years, seem to me to have been rapid and profound, giving us nearly everything in the way of instrumentation and musical form that make music what it is for me. My experience with it (as a listener) is wide and there are few categories of music that I do not enjoy. Some, though, I have found more or less uninteresting or even gratingly unpleasant. Especially such as the professional and sensuous music of modern vintage, or dance band music of the Tommy Dorsey era, or jazz, blues and rock, and hard rock. Nor is there much in the aged motets and plain song that I can take seriously. Yet, somehow, even much of this I have mentioned I could tolerate to the point that I could enjoy dancing to it; for it permits some wild and outlandish steps and motions, which we need not seriously own up to once the dance is over.

I grew up with 3 kinds of music, which all seemed therefore to be a very intimate part of my nature. These were church music, western or blue- grass type music, and the secular traditional folk music. My interest from there has continuously spread, and I actively search for new and interesting music just as I seek to become acquainted with poetry, good literature, and new concepts. I even heard some oriental music that I have liked, despite the profound difference of texture that it displays from what our western tradition offers. With an increased exposure, I believe, I would learn to like it more.

There is some music that for me, brings pure joy and euphoria. Music that is a healing balm to my spirits in times of anguish. It is music - to me, the listener - that comforts, restores, and rehabilitates. Living with music through the years, I think has enabled my nervous system habitually to resonate in harmony or with its euphoric qualities. So much so, that my own system, in becoming undone through the stresses of the day, quickly renews itself to the lure of musical raptures. "Music hath charms to calm the savage breast". However much I am personally attuned to music, I have doubts that the 'beasts of the fields pay any much heed to it. There are those who claim that plants are responsive to music, but I remain skeptical on that matter.

I enclose to you a listing of some of the music I found most enriching. Some of it I much admired from the first hearing (i.e., *The 1812 Overture*) while some I only gradually learned to appreciate through a number of hearings intermittently over the years (such as the Berlioz *Symphony Fantastique*).

I was especially interested in what you have to say about music and of your experience with it. For I gather your experience of music is rather different than mine and I am curious as to why. Additionally, if you have failed to develop a taste for music, then you are unnecessarily depriving yourself of one of the finer things in life.

Is there something in our familial background that predisposes us to the hope and often even the effort of trying to get social and economic problems ironed out, and to set things right and upon an equal and fair basis? The reality is that of a 'dog-eat-dog' world. The German and the French people of our ancestors were basically derived from a common stock, though separated geographically, then politically on the basis of the religious issue that fractured the Holy Roman Empire. Thus, in our historical background, there is a generic predisposition of people groping for the ever elusive truth and freedom. And those same European people have had some propensity toward a tradition of formal education that keeps alive the historic deeds and tales of valor perpetrated always to right some previous wrongs. There is a strong history of revolutions stemming at least from the time of Cromwell through the American and the French revolutions. But those things ought not affect those of our particular family more than other families from the same areas and tradition. It must be the case that it is culturally derived to us through an unconscious predisposition within family members. The seed of cynicism and skepticism is seen and perpetuated from father to son or grandson. Then, perhaps a generation arises in which there is relatively a small amount of external resistance to the maintenance of health and life, such that there is an increase of free time, energy of life, and access to ideas such as to allow loose the tendency to ferment various form of social revolution. One or two generations of a family develop inter-relationships between them such as to directly and indirectly encourage and enhance among themselves this tendency toward doubt and skepticism - this tendency to brood deeply and inquire among themselves, first - and then within their separate communities. It is difficult for me to grasp. Perhaps the most conspicuous examples of it that we might be aware of are those of the Rockefeller and Kennedy families. Families, much provided for against the physical wants and demands of life, and nested together about the dinner table, with conversation and discussions of history, politics, and intrigue and with encouragement offered from parents and from one another to get a grasp on reality and to be competitors in an intellectual world. Backed by intellectual family cultural tradition and economic wherewithal they were provided with good educations and attained a good measure of success in boosting one another along into offices of political power and influence. But behind their achievement and primary to it, there had to have been fermenting the familial tradition of 'will to power' localized within a brood of siblings within a whole generation or two.

I mention this now as I specifically notice the notebook containing my various communications to Norte Vista Medical Center, and its various personnel for the past 3 years that I have been here. Hardly a period of 2 or 3 months go by but what I have had to write them somewhat about this problem or that problem, or an incident that I didn't like, or to give them a bit of a cut for some shortsighted policy, etc. But there seems never much response to my missiles. It must mean that they have ideas of their own. I expect then, that they are probably getting a little weary of hearing from me. And now I am into it with a group of the same sort of people acting as officers of the hospital executive committee concerning some hospital policies whose boundaries I have unwittingly transgressed. Infringement having been discovered, they expected me to 'kow-tow' as is the usual custom. But, no! I had to make their lives hard and difficult by writing them one of those homely philosophical letters that makes them ponder whether they are dealing here with a lunatic or (what makes them really worry) possibly some sort of prophet (out here on the desert and all) that lives on milk and on honey imported from some bee pasture up in Washington State. As with that allegory of Socrates - these guys might be likened onto the state that holds the office, money, and power; while I might be likened onto the horsefly who's buzzing keeps them agitated and active, rather than comfortably indolent. Actually, I would kind of like to rest my wings too, but that leaves me vulnerable to their zillion policies which threaten forever to crush one.

Thus you see, I would seem to have a lot in common with brother EVH in this ongoing wrangling on all sides with various inter-related communities. The nature of my own predicament is much the same, only different in specifics of detail and scope of operation. Perhaps I too am at times tilting at windmills?

Our family moved about (uncommon in those days) and I was forever a stranger in someone else's territory. Hoping to establish something akin to 'squatter's rights'. And the land itself, as well as the peoples thereof, was always a potential source of trouble and contest. Even just to walk in the country had its small danger on account of snakes and the possibility of acquiring 'Tick fever'; and was uncomfortable on account of extremes of heat and cold. About the city there were always tough guys and bullies to violate the peace and wanting to give one trouble and anxieties - though in the presence of adults, no such injustice transpired. Perhaps that is part of the reason we aspired to be adults - to get beyond the stage of adolescent contentiousness. But also, because our own parents and teachers also (unknowingly) brought upon us an occasional injustice that hurt our feelings. And so, we longed to be free of them too, and to be our own adults and be free of all injustice. Yes, supposing that as adults we were apt to be less subject to injustices - hah.

Through it all, I am surprised at how accidental it is, that we as adults have the specific occupations that we did finally acquire. The children of farmers and ranchers of course, were very likely to have inherited that same occupation themselves. But we children of the city, had no such certain passage to our life's work. As youngsters though, it really was not a thing that we ever much thought about or could grasp, as it was simply too far into the future to comprehend realistically. We thought easily about what we might do after supper or sometimes about the weekend. Sometimes we even thought about the upcoming Christmas or summer vacation, but we never would have thought about what we would do 2 years or more from now, for though that was not as far removed as eternity, still, it was very far removed indeed. I did not want to have to go to school, for there were many things about it I did not like. Yet, there was no other place for me - no alternative. I knew not how to escape the expectation of my family and friends, and therefore eventually even found myself in college, wrestling with courses which I felt were far beyond my humble capacity. Then, I found to my surprise, that I could cope with it and even found some subject materials such as psychology and biology more or less interesting in themselves.

Our basic educational system in this country is really quite satisfactory - as it seems to me. Certainly its teachings are limited, as well as more or less filled with a certain amount of American propaganda and the religious prejudice. Beyond the age of puberty, of course, a certain proportion of the students began to lose their tractability to schooling, due to high concentrations of hormones that rattled their frames and made them restless, irritable, and feeling profoundly unfulfilled. It becomes impractical then to keep them in school on account of the troubles that they tend to foment. By then, they had their basic intellectual tools. And a need to continue to learn at a different pace, or after an interval of a few years abroad or in the military. Whether or not they used their tools to progress intellectually, and to gain in wisdom and stature, depends upon the self-motivation and the encouragement they receive from their family and associates. Public libraries abound and are accessible to all who wish to use them. Even better, used book stores are everywhere and a plethora of good reading (along with the mass of junk) is there to be found inexpensively.

As one ages, his experiences and range of association with people of various odd and unusual tendencies is such that one begins to drift from the simplistic concepts and vague ideals of youth. The government and religious organizations tend to propagate things like nationalism, high degrees of patriotism, 'kow-towing' to judges, all encompassing religious concepts, myths, etc. Many, however, find opportunity for escape and to ponder new ideas and concepts. Not perhaps easily, however, unless one owns a sense of skepticism and is possessed of the habit of reading and wrestling with new concepts and ideas. The perpetual rereading of one's limited old ideas is, of course, intellectual death.

In 1968, at the age of 35, I first took time out from a lifetime of school preparation and lessons, to read something on my own initiative. I will never forget the book, for I still count it among the most interesting that I have read. That book was *The Conquest of Mexico*, by William Prescott. *The Conquest of Peru* was but a continuation of the same history in the same excellent and informative style. And that, followed by *A Crossbowman's Story* (Exploration of the Amazon by Pizzaro people). I still keep an extra copy of these works on hand to recommend, and to loan out to anyone that might be interested. Besides the story narrative itself, one can see between the lines, the various religious and political forces behind the history and the ruthless blunderings to which the Conquistadores indulged themselves in blind self-serving. That history was alive with specific events and the details thereof that made them vivid and lively. They justified their actions on religious grounds and brought with them monks and priests to strengthen and perpetrate that delusion which contributed so greatly to their near invincibility. Here, in these books, was an alternative approach to history; something other than that of the generalizations in the textbooks that we studied for history in schools. I was perhaps as surprised at these historical facts as were those conquistadores who encountered and recorded them. Since that time, I have read a considerable volume of history from non-textbooks and I find that those historical facts considerably change the complexion of the glossy generalizations that we learned in school.

I recently took off a week from work to attend some post-graduate education courses in the land of Florida. The family spent their time seeing the sights, while I spent my time in lectures. I had the time to read a few books; *Space* by Michener and two books by Albert Camus, *The Plague* and *The Stranger*.

Space was an interesting historical novel though rather prolix with an apparent rigor of form - a form probably developed by the author and used repeatedly in the writing of his many books. Such a form, and the facility to mold and reshape some historical facts could conceivably enable one to write many such books. Yet, that would be a harsh judgment for me to make of Michener, since I have really only read one other of his books - *The Fires of Spring* (perhaps an autobiographical historical novel). I own several of his books that I have not yet begun - perhaps because of their forbidding size.

I was impressed by Albert Camus' books. *The Plague* was fascinating. It appears to be based upon historical incident that is filled with philosophical speculation and introspective detail. *The Stranger* was a unique story built upon introspective detail of the life of the young man who is a victim of the historical circumstances of his own life. Our hero is a murderer, and yet in a deeper sense, is also the victim of a complex and guilt-laden society. He struggles to comprehend what is happening and why. He is on trial for the murder, and receives the death sentence. But not so much because of the murder; rather, because his understanding of life and the institutions of civilization are unique and fervent and because he has no family or social ties to much befriend him. He finds himself defenseless against the system which must grind and feed upon the bones of a certain number of victims with regularity.

In *The Stranger*, the life of the hero is preoccupied with the necessities of life. He has obtained the rudiments of a grade school (?) education before having to leave school in order to work for a living. Though he is apparently healthy, the work of life and the care of his mother have occupied his energy and time, leaving him with no excess of funds or any but the simple diversions of life. Besides having no free time, he also has no place of solitude or a room of his own (until the jail cell, quite recently).

His rudimentary education has served him moderately well, considering the background of his time and place of history. He has been a dependable and competent employee. He has analyzed some of the concepts of his race and found himself personally out of tune with these. He is trapped in the harness of work, at a scale of pay inadequate to stimulate his imagination to any real hope of improvement. He is further trapped into life by his natural passions and needs. Many, in his corner of the world are even less fortunate than he. He at least has developed his own thoughts and an internal life of contemplation.

Perhaps nothing stimulates a man's thought and rational processes like a personal experience of injustice. Particularly, when one suffers as the result of the system of justice within one's own culture.

Our man is indicted for murder, and finds himself in jail for long periods of time awaiting trial, leaving him plenty of time to think and ponder.

Presuming a healthy intellect; and presuming one's experience of and acquaintances with life are such as to make one skeptical of the rampant confusion and propaganda within one's society; then given the stimulus (a experience of injustice), the time and the solitude (both provided by time in jail), the vagueness of one's thoughts and concepts is very apt to become more crisp and delineate. Within the city especially, our lives are tuned to a certain constant view of things that gets us by from day to day. We have transient insights of vague overviews in moments between our constant goings and comings, but usually find not time enough to wrestle them into a coherent view of 'the-nature-of-reality'.

So it is with geology. It is always with us and recognized at some rudimentary level (as rock, or hill, or rivers, etc.), but rarely dealt with by the common citizen. Its facts, though, are always present for us to ascertain, should we wish to do so. One must see from different points of view and combine these views for a comprehensive concept of geology and the workings thereof. With experience, one can begin to 'see' geological processes from the patterns in geologic formations.

Once we become interested in ideas, concepts, philosophy, truth, justice, etc., our basic urge of expression may drift toward poetry. Our overly vague and general beliefs we might wish to thresh out and set down in brief illuminating line and stanza. Thus to precipitate our vague and cloudy notions, our incomplete beliefs, and our disconnected ideas into clear and expressible precepts and doctrines. Ideas compressed and readily retrievable to our minds; and against which we can easily inspect our course and plan our next and immediate progress - as a traveler has immediate access to his current and accurate road map. We want a view of reality consistent with both our negative and positive experiences of life. Remembrances experienced with the whole of our being, both conceptually and physically. And immediately available for our goal oriented direction, and even when currently far from immediate access to our books and journals. One would wish to own a valid comprehensible and expressible view, as well as a realistic and probable approach to the problems and questions of life in general. One's philosophical being might prefer that one's verbal message and the message of his deeds perhaps to say something like "here it is, and all organized for you, so that you may verify its certainty." Poetry, though, seems to me the ultimate and purest form of expression. Poetry, with its concise illuminating and clever arrangements of sounds and phrases, embodying lucid thought. And all logically interlocked and held together within a purity of something akin to a crystalline form. Few perhaps ever find time and talent for the poem. Yet, prose too is poetry, though of a lesser variety of compacted form. Valued less too, perhaps. Yet, the story and the essay too, can be studiously infused with value and worth by the gifted wordsmith. Skillfully done, they too are forms that can reveal wisdom and probe at the embers of truth. Perhaps ones initial organizing skills evolve with practice and onto progressively purer form.

<hr />

I recall Solzhenitsyn's *Gulag Archipelago* and other stories of inquisition; and I am impressed perpetually at the manner in which a brutal and evil system detains so often the most innocent (along with the hardened criminal); and tortures them into exotic confessions of evil and wrongdoing. Few have the courage of conviction to stand up against the prolonged expectation of confession. All are heavily imbued with so vague a sense of guilt, that once they ascertain what the interrogators wish by way of confession, they promptly 'repent' and everyone (themselves included?) feels better - even though the confession be entirely factitious. Folks come to believe a great deal about themselves that is not entirely valid.

The ability to think and conceptualize has only slowly evolved in mankind over hundreds of years. A concept may be entirely useful and perhaps necessary for a time in the evolution of a man or the race of men, and yet later becomes an encumbrance to progress and best dispensed with. So it was with our flights to the moon, the first stage rockets were large and powerful - they were necessary for lift-off. Yet, once they had served that function it was necessary to eject and be free of them, and to operate from the power of another system and unencumbered by the dead weight of the previous motive force.

I was reading *The Trial,* by Franz Kafka, and as I was feeling my way along the strange impressions it imparts, I perceived a certain familiarity about it. Its style reminded me at once, both of *Alice in Wonderland* and of the writings of James Thurber. For its outlook and tone of concepts seems rather odd and always slightly enigmatic. The story unfolds, concerning a rather strange and doubtful legal system which ensnares citizen "K" abruptly in legal proceedings - the ins and outs of which are mysterious and inaccessible to both the story characters, and to us, the readers. In particular, I was drawn to the story because of its general reference to the ubiquitous 'they' the accusers (who are never identified), or 'the system' of the court which can never be delineated and whose responsible representatives can never be ascertained. It seems to be some secondary sort of legal system apart from the courthouse, state, and federal system. The apartments for the housing of the functionary officers, judges, and inter-related attorneys are more or less unbelievable as described - improbably housed in the attics of buildings. Yet, despite the fact that they are unbelievable, yet the charlatans within the plot work their legalistic terror upon the lives of our 'hero'.

It brings to my mind the many conversations that I have had with EVH, wherein he raves about 'those bastards' and the schemes 'they' have for burdening our lives with their absurd legalistic tamperings. Citizens subject to continuous unreasonable (unconstitutional in our case) summons, hearings, etc., where the evidence is controversial and the outcome seems not to depend much upon the innocent 'accused' who is centered there in the spotlight in the midst of the vague proceedings. Rather, we quickly get the feeling of all manner of backstage rumblings and whispers which are scattered about in the encircling darkness. And we are left to suppose that these unknowable irrelevancies are the matters that actually influence our case. Explains a functionary menial of our 'authority' within this shady court, "we must distinguish between two things: what is written in the law, and what I have discovered through personal experience. It is, of course, laid down on the one hand that the innocent shall be acquitted; but it is not acknowledged on the other hand, that the judges are open to influence. Now, my experience is diametrically opposed to that. I have not met one case of definite acquittal and I have met many cases of influential intervention."

So to has my experience with the law and legal system (even here in free Amerika), so often left me dumbfounded and in awe of its workings.

There are other sources of legalistic grief to confront one in addition to the IRS, and I have been astonished through the years at how many have worked their threats and extortions against even a naïve innocent such as myself. The IRS in our culture has its cryptic workings in much the same way as those described by Kafka in his book. The thing about the IRS in particular (but by no means unique to it) is that it comes to confront one abruptly in the guise of 'justice', accusing one of being guilty of some sort of injustice against what is actually an incomprehensible and voluminous code of law. We are amazed to find that the supposedly deeply knowing and authoritative writings accuse us of some flagrantly hideous dealings or improprieties of accounting. The intricacy of the rules that we have transgressed are beyond our grasp of comprehension; and the specific law itself, as a distant star of dense magnitude in some minor constellation itself, whose configuration is news to us. And we are further apprised of a fundamental legalistic truth, which in fact is among the most obvious of untruths - that ignorance of the law is no valid excuse for the transgression of tax law. The sudden shock and interruption of our previous continuous life is enough to throw a spasm into one's coronary circulation. Still, one yet has no option other than to face the mysterious proceedings. Inevitably, our prejudiced and unfounded respect for the law and authority is such, that we waste the reserve of our energy, time, and wealth under the delusion that there is some mistake here, and that we can explain and justify our alleged 'transgression' upon some logical basis, and thereby absolve ourselves of guilt. Though true in theory, it is in reality an exercise in futility. When the court of the IRS discovers that we have actual savings and the potential to make payments, its judgment is inevitably that we shall be found guilty, and that we shall pay. An occasional exception to these truths is permitted to reside in the annals, in order to burden the innocent unnecessarily with false hope and as rhetorical 'evidence' of the respectability of this variety of 'justice'.

Thus it is that I, of course, agree with my brother EVH; that in theory, men ought to agitate against an injustice so absurd. Yet, I believe he exceeds the limits of what is expected of an honest man in exposing the corruption of a system. But the thing most apt eventually to topple such injustice, is its own progressive injustice. And in all probability, it will then inevitably be replaced only by a new system of injustice, perhaps initially more lenient only by virtue of its youth. With time, it too shall also become a more formidable system of injustice.

Meanwhile, there is in fact some beauty in life which we might strive to appreciate. "Consider the lilies of the field ..." Here find enclosed a copy of an essay on pragmatism by William James which I regard as philosophically important. Does it have major flaws that you can point out? Also enclosed is a list of some of the books which have most impressed me as worthy of being read. I am sending copies of these to my sons and hoping to encourage them to reciprocate in kind.

I have recently enjoyed the book by Maclean, *A River Runs Through It*. He has an easy and interesting style of writing.

One of the most interesting books I have read, however, is by Andrew Garcia entitled *Tough Trip Through Paradise*. As a historical document of time and place in history, I think it is nearly the equal of

Thucydides or of Caesar's *War Commentaries*. I have been developing an interest in the history of the American West and especially of the Native American Indian culture. That history has been in danger of being obscured here in this country as much as it has been by the hand of the Spanish in Central and South America. I recently made the acquaintance of a purebred Cheyenne Indian who has become a physician and is soon to join our clinic medical staff. He has wrestled with reality and seems to have good insight. I talked with him at length for a couple of hours the other evening and I think that I may be able to wrangle from him some insight to the Indian ways of looking at things. I hope to be able to encourage him to join our discussion group.

I shall also send you a couple of paperback books in a package separate from this letter.

Your brother,
R. Garner Brasseur

13 May 1984

12/09/85

7107 Connecticut Avenue

Dear DFB,

My employment circumstances here in the D.C. area have not been satisfactory. I therefore plan to leave here Friday, Dec. 27th. It will take me 2 or 3 days to drive back to Hobbs. My spouse seems to have all our children and their families committed to being in Hobbs for Christmas and New Years. My friend, Mick Rosckowff will graduate from medical school in Guadalajara on Dec. 13th; and I expect he will be with us there in Hobbs over the holidays also.

I have been living here alone in this big house on Connecticut here in Chevy Chase for the past three months and have made a dozen weekend trips to the mountains of West Virginia etc. A lovely time of year, and I have enjoyed the solitude. But I find that I am beginning to talk to myself; and so I had better head back to family again before the habit gets too firm.

After the first of the year, I shall probably head west, into California to seek employment. I have enclosed some copies of notes and letters for you to read and save for me.

Greetings to your people.

Your brother

R. Garner Brasseur

12/09/85

10/03/87

Ontario, Oregon

Dear DFB,

While working on my genealogy notebook a few days ago, I notice that your birthday has recently passed. It is not likely that you made a big thing or it. Like me, perhaps, you would prefer that such milestones went unnoticed, but I am using that occasion to satisfy my own interests - that of getting back in touch with you. So, a happy birthday to you.

I got your letter about a year ago. An interesting discussion concerning a video movie, *Plenty*, as I recall. And now that both your sons are gone, I suppose that you are called upon to write more letters that usual. And we have now in common the circumstance of finding ourselves without children in the home. I miss seeing mine of course, but the pace of life seems smoother. And my own experience is that writing is a far better mode of communication than conversation in any case; so that only an occasional physical interaction seems to suffice. That is not to say that they actually write much, but the medium is such that I can actually get said (written) to them, what it is that I want to say.

The past summer, I returned to Miles City to the 35th high school class reunion. While on that trip I finally got around to reading that book you sent me, *Little Big man*. A great book, and loaded with humor. We watched the video film movie of *Little Big man* at home, a couple of weeks subsequently. As M.A. and her friends were wanting me to watch a movie with them one night, I consented to that one. Perhaps henceforth, when the kids are home, one might make an effort to prepare in advance some quality movies, to incite their interest in themes that are interesting and worthy of subsequent discussion. You might perhaps be willing to supply me a list of some that you have found interesting?

About this time last year, VBB and I drove out into mountainous central Idaho, to observe the geological features of the land. We poked about in some streams looking for interesting rocks and for gold. Rocks are plentiful. And we got into discussions on a great many things. In consequence we exchanged a few letters. I'll get some of the legible one's together and send them to you under separate cover for your interest. As you know, VBB has now left Yakima and gone over to Hawaii. I haven't seen EVH for a year and a half, but he occasionally calls. He claims to be euphoric concerning his remarkable recovery from cancer (?) and his progressive restoration to health and vitality, in consequence of eating smashed vegetables etc. But we all know the rate of discount exchange on such currency as that? In Billings (in July) I stopped in several times to see sister ALKE and Carl E. ALKE was just home from gall bladder surgery and making slow recovery. CE was abed and out of commission with a herniated disc. The circumstances enabled me to talk separately with each, for quite a while. I saw nephew MK and JK only briefly. MK is an interesting conversationalist, and has had a few interesting shocks from reality. I should like to get a chance to talk to him at greater length sometime.

My own life here is chaotic, and my economic survival remains in doubt. Since the first of the year I have been working part-time in Caldwell, Idaho (32 miles distant) and here in Ontario. Local medical politics, intrigue, and the economic plight of the nation all contribute to the uncertainty of my situation here. I believe we shall soon move on over to Caldwell - a little larger town than Ontario. Meanwhile, I am not yet overly busy. When not busy, one is tempted to push himself into make-work. But I can't find just cause for faith in that, despite the impulse. Perhaps I'll pretend that I am off at some important 'meeting', or sneak off into the desert or the mountains for a few days or a week. Perhaps I could talk you into joining me? We might retreat to an area where we would have access to a hot springs. We could hike, take rock samples, cogitate on cloud formations, discuss some books and movies, nap for spells, and read a little. If interested, let me know and we might work something out.

Your brother,
R. Garner Brasseur

10/03/87

11/20/87

Caldwell, Idaho

Dear DFB,

Enclosed are some copies of letters and essays which you may find interesting. All of them studied or written by myself, in my ongoing attempt to figure out the nature of reality, and to see my way towards some specific truths.

Creationism, though silly, is a big issue in our times. The article enclosed covers the ground quite succinctly. It behooves us, and the young folks, to know the issues. And ponder as to the integrity of the information upon which they are based.

I am especially fond of the chapter, "Aims and Objectives" (from J. N. Parkinson's book) because it deals with a critically important subject - especially for folks our age - yet its humor gives the article charm and makes it eminently readable.

Continental drift has indeed been fairly well validated; and that, only during our own life-time. A recent article in <u>Scientific American</u> points out an identity between the Wallowa/Seven Devils formation of Idaho and the Austrian Alps, indicating that they both originated at the same time and same area. Does it sound fantastic? You can look it up in your local library in <u>Scientific American</u>, Oct. or Nov. issue of 1987.

I enjoyed my recent visit with you. We will be gone to Portland for Thanksgiving weekend.

Your brother,
R. Garner Brasseur

11/20/87

1988?

Dear DFB,

Yes, I have gotten your recent letters, notes and a couple of books; and a vague rough reckoning suggests to me, that I am about three down, to you. On the other hand, you are about to enter an exceedingly busy series of months which is apt to slacken your production of correspondence and may well enable me catch up on mine. I received the book you sent, *Wir Wollen Deutsche Bleiben*. The spirit of Russian nationalism attempted to eradicate the German colonists to Russia; as well as the history of those people. Those Germans that subsequently immigrated to America from Russia (not wishing to be thought of as Russian) played down, ignored and almost forgot about that fact of their own race and family history. That whole history came close to being lost. But in about 1962 or 1963, this book that you sent - and three or four others in the same vein - suddenly became available. The result was that it sparked a sudden interest in that history, in this country. The American Historical Society of Germans From Russia (HSGR) was then formed. Societies and groups interested in the subject have cropped up all over the west and mid-west. Its members have busied themselves collecting records and documents from family attics and from the memories of all the old timers; as well as the pertinent books and documents from all over Russia and Germany. They produce a couple of publications annually, into which a host of individuals contributes each, the specific information to which he by chance has access through their family records and diaries. A good deal of information is thus gradually becoming available. Those who can read German are translating many informative books and genealogical lists into English. I see a couple of titles that may well provide me some specific information I seek concerning the Boepple and related families of our ancestors. In looking at some ship lists from those journals, I see that George Boepple and his wife, Catherine (he age 28, she age 27) along with one year old Bertha, departed Liverpool aboard the S.S.Parisian, on Nov. 15, 1898, and arrived in Halifax on Nov. 28. Another list tells me that a Lydia Boepple age 19, from the village of Kulm, in Bessarabia, arrived in New York, aboard the S.S. Kaiser Wilhelm II, on May 20, 1903. Her destination - Ritzville, Washington. But, I don't believe she ever made it out to Washington. It happens that Lydia (Boepple) Neuberger was baptized on Sept. 30, 1903; and another Lydia Boepple (presumably this one from Bessarabia) was one of her sponsors at that ceremony. She would be the half-sister to George Boepple. She must have met Johann Hildebrandt there, in or near Tripp, SD, and married him shortly thereafter. Presumably there are some Boepple family connections from Kulm, Bessarabia as well as in Mannsburg, Bessarabia. I shall enclose to you a map of the lower part of Bessarabia (bounded on the west by the Pruth River, on the east by the Dneister River, and on the south by the Black Sea and the delta of the Danube River). There one can locate all of these Bessarabian villages where most of our German Russian ancestors lived. I'll underscore them in red - Teplitz, Dennewitz, Mannsburg, Seimenthal (Seimeny), Olgenthal, Gnadenthal and possibly Kulm.

I found some notes in one or my journals that says Uncle August's father and brother had gone to Crimea. There, they rented lands to farm. There his father's first wife must have died. They took what was left of their families and belongings, and returned to Germany, from whence shortly thereafter, they immigrated to North Dakota. It is my understanding, that Uncle August is the second child from his father's second wife, born in Mannhaven, ND. This information from Uncle August, when they visited us in Kennewick, in 1979. I note too, that Aunt and Uncle rented farms around Hazen, Beulah, and Goldendale etc. until they were first able to secure their own land in about 1946. It certainly is possible that some of Uncle August's uncles did go further into the Volga settlements also. There were some Boepples that settled far to the east, a place called Elizabeththal, not far to the west from the Caspian Sea. The book you sent was informative especially concerning the first wave of German immigrants to the Volga. They represent the third wave of immigration into Russia - mostly from the northern lowlands of Germany. Among our own German ancestors, the Boepples, at least, seem to have come from the southern highlands of Germany, and they represent the fourth wave of that immigration. many of them had planned to go all the way to the Elizabethal area (thought by them to be "the place of final refuge prior to the-second-coming") and some few of them did make it that far. But they were so decimated by disease and death, as they came down the Danube River, that most stayed right there in Bessarabia, after they were finally released from the quarantine station there at Ismal near the Danube delta. Some of them went just across the Dneister River into the Odessa area, and the Beresan Valley settlements. Jakob Saur (Sauer) settled into a Pietistic Religious settlement, which they called Hoffnungstal. You will see a community of this same name in Bessarabia, too. It was a daughter settlement to the original Hoffnungstal... and rather exclusive as to whom they would allow among their settlers. The Bessarabians had the advantage of having been annexed by Romania in 1918, sparing them a lot of turmoil from the Russian Revolution animosity, as well as sparing them from the great famines. A 1940 treaty between Hitler and Russia, allowed Russia to regain Bessarabia, provided they allow all its people of German origin to return to Germany, if they so wished. Many of them did so - perhaps most of them. Certainly, those who did not own large pieces of land, I suppose. They had no reason to expect that the Russians would treat them well. The section that speaks of the German invasion in that book you sent is speaking of those colonies just across the Dneister River, which includes the village of the Saur people. Those relatives of hers that remained behind are scattered all over the Urals, Siberia and some have finally gotten back into Germany. George Boepple's brothers, Emanuel and Daniel apparently went over into Germany held territory in 1940, as did his half-sisters, Catherine and Marie. AL and mother tell me that Aunt Molly used to correspond with them, after WW-II. Isn't it a curious thing? Until five or ten years ago, I was never really aware that our ancestors had come out of Russia for that matter, nor that most of the German people in the Dakotas, Neb, Kansas, Colorado and the western states had come from those Russian colonies of Germans. Most of them in your area are out of the Volga area, with smaller proportions from the Black Sea and Bessarabian areas. This whole Treasure Valley and the Twin Falls area also have a great many of these German people. They were prolific. It seems to me that half the people in this nation must be at least part German in ancestry. It is difficult to know what the situation is in Russia, in regards to their ethnic origin, but looking at the pictures in the news magazines, the purely Russian-Slav peoples, according to the demographic maps, seem to be congregated up around Moscow. I have never seen any book or article that has worked out or even suggested this theme, but I have almost come to the conclusion that most of the Caucasian world is dominated - in numbers - by people with at least some German blood in their veins. If you were to scan the list of German family names that appear in these GRHS journals and the reference books which deal with the subject, you would be surprised at how many of those names can be found here in western USA. Recalling the names of former classmates that I came across this past summer, in Miles City, it seems to me that half of them were German. It is also the case that many of those Germans who eventually immigrated into Russia, did so after first sojourning two or three generations in Poland, Latvian areas, or the lowlands of eastern Prussia (Pomerania). There, many of them acquired modifications to their names, such as to give them a Slavic character. I cannot tell you the ethnic origin of Harold Kransky's parents, but I would guess there is a 50/50 probability that the name comes from people of that Russian-German stock. I recall that mom had a very best friend whose last was Krankoski - or some such thing. I am sure that you remember the name, too. I don't remember the people, though. I was too young at the time, perhaps. I always sort of presumed that they must have been Slavic people, but I am now more suspicious that they were actually - you guessed it, German.

Concerning the flyer you sent on Palatine genealogy; it seems to hold promise of being a good source, provided one can actually trace a part of his roots into that area. But, I have not yet found any of ours that do so. It may be that Uncle August's do? The Palatinate lies immediately west of Wurttemberg from whence the Boepples, Hoescheles, and Saurs derived. I am suspicious that the Gotz people came into Bessarabia via a sojourn in Poland. That, mere speculation so far.

I have studied your comments and am still pondering what, if anything, to do about those financial matters which you mentioned. Perhaps I shall discuss it with PP, as you mentioned. My whole current situation is besieged with so many uncertainties at the present, as to make almost any additional initiative dubious. There is a great deal of crowding and competition in the field of Ophthalmology. And me, on shank's mare.

FADING ECHOES

Because of their human interest value, and because you are already acquainted with most of the earlier information, I will enclose to you the more recent information concerning Mick Rosckowff copy from one of my notebooks. And I remind you, that his natural parents escaped eastward out of Asia to immigrate into Peru. His father was Russian, his mother Chinese. I had never previously heard of any similar such escape route being used by others; and political-geographic difficulties make it seem improbable to me. Yet it seems indeed, to have been done not infrequently. Enclosed is an interesting article from The ARSGR journal that explains some of the wheres, whys, and hows. The very people, who are the subject of this article, may even have been involved in abetting the passage of Mick's father across the river. Though the father is said to have been Russian, he is actually more likely to have been a German-Russian. Since the letters which I sent to Mick never came back to me, I presume he received them. But no reply. I was impressed with the deftness of those banking people at locating folks who owe them big chunks of money! When they were pressuring me for payment on Mick's note a few months ago, they didn't say if they had lost track of him again, or if he was still in Laredo, Texas. Finding him still broke; I suspect that they thought it would simply be more expedient to pressure the co-signing doctor (me) into settling the thing. They even turned up this additional former spouse of Mick's and presumably tried to put the touch on her (a Pediatrician) for the cash. And what am I to think about this additional family of Mick's? I confess that I hadn't suspected any such thing. And yet, it is consistent with the condition of mortality. Whatever life he had previously, he must have been somewhat discontent with it. A common thing, after all, but not a thing that most are apt to take pride in. Not surprising therefore, that he did not convey any such information to me. To do so, could hardly have been expected by him to increase the probability of soliciting my assistance to his cause. Men, who conceive themselves as failures, not uncommonly go away, leaving their family behind. Many of them never return. As was common in this country, during the depression years. Some of them wander the remainder of their lives. Others create for themselves a new life elsewhere, if they have enough residual courage and energy. That sense of failure in the face of life's difficulties gives a man bad feelings, sometimes referred to - interestingly - as impotence.

I read that excerpt from *The Honey Badger*. A lucid account of what one can anticipate from metastatic prostate cancer. VBB says that the fact of our brother having developed prostate cancer gives us an increased probability of developing the same - by a factor of 2+, above the rest of the male population. Therefore, one ought be checked for it annually. Usually, by the time it can be detected by palpation, it has already metastasized. The only probable way to pick it up early, is with an ultrasound device. You would have to call your local Radiologist to enquire if he has that equipment. If not, you might go to a somewhat larger medical facility to enquire into it. In so far as dad is concerned, I think we can reasonably dismiss as a possibility that he had prostate cancer. For he seems to have had neither signs nor symptoms of metastatic disease in all of those years after 1950 - a long time! As I recall, it is the case however, that our grandfather, George Boepple had that problem, and died of it. From what I hear, I presume that EVH will soon depart in similar fashion. I wrote to him a few days past, in salutation of all of his fine qualities and bravery in the face of an absurd world.

I stopped in to Marysville in March of 1986, to locate Uncle Louis; and I spent a day and a night with him. On the occasion of our get together, it has sort of been his custom to fill the air with conversation. As we walk along, he stops at each different type of tree to enquire if I know its Latin scientific name. If I should know the English name, he then gives me the Latin name; if I know neither, he gives me both. He seems to be knowledgeable on a lot of different topics and subjects that he plans to cover, in order to make me heir to the nuggets and pearls of insight that he has acquired through the years. Often as though to inquire of me, if my general experience of a thing is not quite similar to his own. And so the conversation drifts down one valley, over a ridge and maybe a box-canyon, to return again to the main stream of conversation. And the main stream itself tends to meander broadly across the valley of his view of history with a slow and easy majesty. One can but estimate the intensity of effort required, to continuously articulate the flow of thought, and to order that thought into a progressing and orderly theme, paragraph by paragraph. One senses the adrenalin surge of such effort as a sort of vague anxiety and dryness of ones speaking parts. The speaker's awareness of the external is diminished in proportion to his heightened awareness of his own memories and thought processes. And the listener may be required to be watchful of the speaker's safety, as they cross the intersection together.

On one of those diversionary topics, Uncle L. mentioned to me some of his friends; and some of his girl-friends of recent years. I recognized the name of one as being a distant cousin from the Boepple people. He indicated that he was still active and able, in his male capacity. Mortal man has a psychic being, which possesses his consciousness during every waking hour of his existence. More, there is a vast reservoir of subconscious material that lies directly beneath that. The heat and pressure from external and internal sources, both of our planet, and of man are such that those drives, questions, doubts, currents, eddy currents, passions, ambiguities, ghosts, ideals, fears, hopes, and aspirations are forever threatening to erupt into the psychic consciousness of the moment. To change that content just a little, or a lot. The principles of psychological reality undoubtedly apply uniformly to the entire race - and the interactions between the esthetic spirit and the material aspects of each being are the common reality. Yet, each individual's situation is unique in regards to his mental-intellectual composition, and habits of the mind; as well as his special situation as to met and unmet needs at any moment. Thus, no two people can ever be quite exactly like one another. Like the myriads of planets that are undoubtedly scattered throughout the universe, no two, even of the same species shall ever be identical. And each shall be forever continuously evolving. The external reality of our planet earth is forever in a state of flux in regard to its weather and cloud formation, its seasons, and its individual geology. Its appearance is continuously variable, just as is a man's psychic content. An earthquake here, a volcanic eruption there, and a meteoric impact somewhere else... These effects constituting, along with weather patterns and the actions of life, a sum total of the explanation of each sequential moment by moment change. As man has absolute needs and requirements as to water, food, oxygen, shelter, and excretory functions, it is not surprising that these needs dominate his consciousness - each in its moment of urgency crowding away all of his other concerns. Once resolved, or sated, then, some other passion, desire, wish, need… takes foremost place in one's psychic awareness.

And a man's being has many facets, so that except for those needs essential to his absolute homeostasis, his wishes, desires, and drives can be played off against one another; **and against time and promise**. Society accomplishes this regularly with its citizens and prisoners, directly and indirectly compelling the local organization, the family and the individual to become censor of the self. Thus, overt compliance is required, upon pain of penalty. Yet the willful individual and the irrepressible impulse continue, through anonymity and cover of darkness – always at a certain risk and cost. Societies support and maintain a great many illusions and delusions in attempt to solicit the voluntary compliance of the individual. A spoonful of sugar to help the medicine go down, as it were. And an armed guard, where those measures alone are wanting in effectiveness. Beyond anonymity and the shade of night, the private mental life of the individual remains inscrutable.

I once read of how some surplus military airplanes were used to investigate various weather phenomena, subsequent to WW II. One was flown by a test pilot directly into a large and towering thunderhead cloud upon a certain warm summer afternoon. There was a brief and terrible wrenching of the aircraft. Then, like the man on the strawberry roan, he found himself taking the-great-sky-dive, but already separated from his mount. Fortunately, he was harnessed into his parachute. Though bereft of his plane and adrift within the cloud, he dare not pull the rip-cord until he could get free of the cloud, fearing that the fabric of the parachute might be ripped to shreds. Powerful updrafts alternated with downdrafts in that evolving storm that constituted that thunderhead cloud. The pilot was up, down, and all around in that cloud for an hour or more before he finally dropped out of the bottom of it, opened the parachute and came to earth. A uniquely amazing and true adventure that stunned my imagination when I came across it casually tucked away in a little book about the weather. That was some ten or fifteen years ago, but I have thought about that story hundreds of times in the interim, and often told the story to others. Since that time, I never see a cloud or experience the weather but what I am tempted to speculate about its past, present, and future. I wish I had made a copy of the story, for its marvelous uniqueness and power to incite the imagination seem to make it a candidate for my accumulating collection which I call, *A More Recent Testament*. I'm sure I still have the source book, and when I come across it again I'll send you a copy. I remind you of the story so that I can invoke its image to your mind, as I continue just a few more comments on the matter of human sexuality.

But before re-entering that jungle, let me remind you of yet another story whose image rooted firmly in my mind about thirty years ago, at the time when you and I were both attending classes at the University of Mont. Though an ancient story, I had never previously heard it. And it was you, in fact, who told me the story of the 'the riddle of the sphinx' - (What animal walks on four legs in the morning, on two legs at mid-day, and three legs in the evening?). You might be surprised at how few people I encounter, who have ever heard of it. If it were to be found in the Bible, I suspect that it might rank among those best known.

If one were to raise a newborn male Chimp, pup, goat, or colt in isolation from any sensual experience whatsoever, concerning the sexuality of its species; still, I suspect that upon reaching its adult state, it would have no difficulty in knowing how to perform the essential feat of copulation when presented with the female of its species, in appropriate season. The same, I suspect, is true of Homo sapiens. For the same types of hormones that transform those other mammals into their adult form, also ripen and kindle the interest - and enlighten the human creature with a certain minimum of genetically derived sexual know-how (instinct). And yet, while the other male creatures flow easily into their adult sexuality with seemingly no incidence of sexual perversion (in so far as I am aware), the same cannot be said, in regards to Homo sapiens. I suspect however, that the incidence of perversion may well vary from one tribe to another, and comparing the various civilizations. That may well have something to do with the magnitude of ambiguities and social complexities which each generates as a by-product of its civilization and civilizing processes with which its youth must wrestle en route to adulthood. It is also true that the individual of our species may well continue to learn at a steady clip for many years into its adult life. Some, apparently, even on into advanced years of age. This, being less the case in any other species. Thus it is that late adolescence brings the maturing individual or our species into the Fires-of-Spring - a profoundly troubling time. For the natural animal channels of its sexual expression (in the human species) are uniquely stifled and re-directed by the social order of one's particular family and tribe; even while those very pressures are simultaneously kindled to ever higher levels of intensity. And at this stage in their adolescent lives, society and their own families do take notice or them (rites of puberty). As in our own society there seems a certain contest and competition between the various elements of society for the capture of the adolescent interest, time, and loyalty. That, in addition to the inescapable attraction between the sexes. Cults and causes compete for the energies and loyalty of youthful adolescence.

Man has a certain capacity for rational thought and there is nothing intrinsic to his being that prevents his will and intent from following his line of reason. Yet, the race is not far advanced in the acquisition of facts and knowledge upon which reason can grasp for leverage. The larger problem however, is that the various elements of societies are all at cross-purposes to one another. There seems too to be some as yet unresolved cultural neglect in the method and habit of reason. As though some key concepts were yet missing, such as might enable reason to run with precision and regular dependability. Though reason gives promise of being man's best light (considering the achievement of science and the scientific method) yet, the matter is hotly contested. Reason is a word that is often mentioned in our society, and all seem able to apply it to some parts of their thought and conversation, and to some sequence in their necessary functioning within society. It is obviously an ideal to which many aspire - a good sign, surely - and yet, it seems somehow neglected. The way of reason is a long and arduous journey, compared to the quick-fix of certitude-of-belief. And the tradition of authoritarianism is deeply entrenched into the customs and rituals of the species. Thus, the energy of youth is drawn off, into the various cross-purposes of society; and the early two-legged phase of their being finds them predisposed to aim themselves at those great thunderclouds. Very educational to those who survive it. The parents, in particular - and the educational system in general – need to encourage our youth to at least stay harnessed into the parachute, and to avoid the larger thunderclouds.

Physiologically, one's normal sexual functioning is not required to the maintenance of the individuals' homeostasis. That is to say, it is not essential to the continued existence of that individual's animal being. Yet, the sexual drive is a force to be reckoned with, and susceptible to being harnessed to potentially useful purpose – as is a dammed river. Useful to the taming and control of human motivation and behavior such as might be beneficial to the evolving of a civilization.

What then would have been the motive source from which civilizations and the man-made wonders of the world might have derived? From hunger or thirst, perhaps? But there is not enough elasticity in the supply mechanisms, and the margin of safety is too critical. We might consider the sheer restless physical strength and vitality of youth, but it seems not to offer promise of adequate subtlety and susceptibility to direction. The driving potential of reason? – too slow to evolve and too late to mature in the individual. Curiosity as to the ever mystic unknown? – tied to the limitations of reason.

Superstitions, and their evolving religions seem well situated to dominate the imaginations of the multitude when bonded to the motivational essence of sexuality. Especially in the absence of information, knowledge, and mature reason. Thus it is that religions arise into every evolving civilization.

Religions seem suited as a mechanism for accumulating the energy of sexuality, restless physicality, the sating of curiosity, and misguidance of reason into self-serving purpose and power as civilizations arise. And dissipating it into channels that build and drive religion and civilization.

It might fairly be said, that human sexuality and restless physicality have been harnessed and exploited, so that like the water supply of a city, it runs restrained and unseen throughout the community under a great head of pressure, to sometimes useful purposes in a society. Basic principles of human nature, being diverted to a civilizing purpose. Yet, it remains as sexual energy and restless physicality in the course of its distribution and having been restrained, though then channeled under a pressurized system and distributed toward the enhancement of other aspects modern and civilized personhood.

But this channeling of human sexuality into purposes useful to government and religion may bring about a certain amount of chaos when it escapes confinement - into counterproductive purpose. May contribute to some unanticipated perverse sexual manifestations of a society and into the lives of individual citizens.

Before arriving, to its civilizing purposes it may occasionally burst from its channel at any number of connecting joints and fittings, turning loose that sexual energy into un-natural unexpected behavior. While utilizing restless physicality into field work and the building of pyramids.

Under that head of pressure the psycho-sexual component of the individual is susceptible to an unhealthy enlargement - and a major preoccupation to the mind especially among adolescent and young adults. For it is among the adolescent and young adults of most societies where the obstruction impinges most severely upon the natural channels of expression of that sexual energy. At the same time, our society is selling and encouraging every form of deviant sexual allurement and interest, which our youth cannot escape. Were our educational methods successful in diverting that accumulating psycho-sexual energy into constructive channels toward the enhancement of the individual mental and intellectual processes, it might cause no significant problem. But our educational system has no such precision. Thus, those psycho-sexually generated pressures are readily susceptible to diversion into unusual and unnatural sexual practices, sometimes known as perversions.

The civilizing process brings with it culturally derived mores, regulations, rules, legal codes, customs, taboos, and superstitions. All of this with considerable variation from one tribe to another.

What is being suggested is that something as useful as civil decency may have been nudged along by the restraints imposed by evolving civilizations (restraints upon the energy of sexuality, and restless physicality). Those restraints along with mankind's natural curiosity and the capacity for reason have contributed to the evolving of civilizations. And that the civilizing process brings with it the possibility for individuals of the species to concomitantly become something more than mere consecutive reproductive units endlessly from one generation to the next. Mere mortal man thus enabled to the possibilities of becoming tradesmen, artists, and professionals of the various specialties required by advancing civilizations. And attaining unto something more than a meager time-consuming hand-to-mouth existence.

For that matter, it is well to keep in mind, that the socially sanctioned (religious-political) destinations to which that energy had been diverted is often also of sometimes questionable value; and not infrequently detrimental. In any case, all societies seem to have their share of devious sexual waywardness - though it is generally recognized to be unacceptable, and carries with it some certain risk of penalty, however widespread and common. And, not uncommonly, there are special occasions in the calendar year for temporary reprieve from constraints, wherein the taboos are lifted and the citizens of that society are given tacit permission to indulge themselves in lewd deportment - and free of penalty. They may protect their individual identity and reputation by wearing costumes and masks; or under cover of darkness; or under the protective aura of alcohol or other drugs; or under the pretense of religious ecstasy. Then, having had opportunity for a lusty satiation, the Mardi Gras ends. The slaves and citizens alike, then all return satiated into the harness of the work-a-day-world, but with the comforting certainty that Mardi Gras shall come again as certainly as shall another good Friday.

In the case of war, however dangerous and difficult, one of the spurs to battle and victory has generally been the promise of the conqueror's right to rape and plunder - a right commonly extended to each and every warrior. So far as I know, war is still generally like that, except that it is fitted up with a more decorous appearance - account of the close coverage by TV cameras and newspaper reporters. Too, it must be admitted that the U.S.A. has more or less stood the warrior's license upon its head, so that the whole business of war seems to have become somewhat more schizophrenic in our own times.

Whence comes the power peculiar to the sexual drive? Unlike the simpler passions such as anger, fear or hate, it is not derived from purely mental processes. Rather, it is strongly reinforced by long-acting internally generated hormones - most especially in young adults.

Titillation and specific meditation, seem certainly to enhance the storm of that passion. Mankind has a cultural tradition of thousands of years of intentionally enhancing and exploiting that passion to all manner of various purposes. And in that process mankind has probably slowly accumulated some genetic traits that reinforce the production and force of that hormonal influence.

One may suspect that few give much thought to the question of whether a man can control his own performance. The female of the species and, perhaps, most men, might well suppose in the affirmative. But that belief is a mere prejudice in my view, for such evidence with which I am acquainted, suggests otherwise. It is true, that those hormonal-autonomic powers can be enhanced and diminished by intentions previously mentioned. We exclude from consideration here, those pathological disease states which absolutely preclude that possibility in specific individuals, such as organic disease problems. The question does not arise concerning the female. On the other hand, nothing could be more obvious than that the female can potentially as much effectively enhance a man's power to arise to an occasion, as can that man himself. The psycho part of psycho-sexual. It does 'take two to tango'. That, at least is the theoretical aspect of the matter. Her difficulty in this matter is that such topics are generally taboo and isolated from discussion between male and female. A subject allied much closer to emotion than reason.

It is worth noting, that in Jane Goodall's book, *In the Shadow of man*, she gives us her observations of the habits and customs of the Chimpanzees. She notes, specifically, that there seems to be very little that one might liken onto the sexual taboos of the human species. The female will accept a male only at a particular time in her cycle. Then, she seems to be generally provocative to most of the males in her band. The male appetite seems to be in response to visual and olfactory signals, generated by the female. The male interest in that business seems not to have a significant subterranean depth, nor force of current such as to make of their sexual interest an overpowering preoccupation to their minds. Being called to the opportunity, they by no means pass it up, but the response is straightforward and without ritual, ceremony, or lingering at the task. The essay by J. Huxley, *On Bird Mind*, informs us that the case is quite different concerning birds. Such evidence as there is then, is at least compatible to what I am suggesting. That the human species has a culturally evolved preoccupation with sex. And that certain consequences inevitably follow, both advantageous and disadvantageous. The essay on *Elephant Intelligence* suggests that those critters, like man, have come at least a few steps down the path in emphasizing sexuality. The chimps though, seem not to have done so.

One might recall that of all creatures, the chimpanzee is genetically the most nearly related to Homo sapiens. The evidence supporting this is sketched out in an essay which I sent you a couple of months ago, *The Creationists.*

A few months ago, a cardiovascular surgeon at Loma Linda Medical School transplanted the heart of a baboon into a child. The patient didn't long survive. It may the case that she might not have done much better, even with the heart of a Chimpanzee. And yet, if there were even the remotest hope of her survival with a non-human heart, even that chance was doomed by selecting a baboon heart, rather than a chimp heart. Not only is that true in theory, but the accumulated experience with all sorts of tissue transplants has already demonstrated its validity. That particular medical school is a Seventh Day Adventist institution, and the surgeon involved was of the SDA persuasion. When asked why he had not used a chimp heart - it being nearest man on the evolutionary tree - his response was that he didn't believe in the theory of evolution.

I recall to your attention the thought experiments of Albert Einstein, wherein he contemplates the notion of relativity. An odd notion at that time. He envisioned for example, a person enclosed within an elevator that accelerates upward. It not only moves upward at "X" feet per second, but it increases that speed continuously, at a rate of (say) "Y" feet per second, in each subsequent second. Acceleration=distance/sec./sec. Envisioning himself alternatingly as both passenger, and then again as stationary observer, he contemplates how he might perceive the experience differently in each of those two situations. The observer would perceive it as commonplace acceleration, but the passenger would perceive it as - interestingly - gravity! This concept of relativity is so widely applicable to every aspect of our lives in this century, that few realize the difficulty of its acceptance, or how very recently it was even conceived.

We now might contemplate a similar sort of thought experiment regarding the Chimpanzee. What would happen if we were to experiment with the sex life of a certain small tribe of them. Might an experiment, for example, progressively, slowly, and consistently obstruct the currently normal channels and modes of its expression in Chimps - to see if it causes them to accumulate any increasing stores of psycho-sexual anxiety (unattached psychic energy) which might then be siphoned-off to enhance their learning of a set of customs and rituals of sexual behavior.

The fact is that our nation has attained unto a certain status of what we might call an advanced and civilized nation. And our citizens have each, perhaps, acquired some of the graces, refinements, tastes, interests, skills and incisive perceptiveness such as to have transformed them into civilized beings of variable degree.

To put it into the obverse connotation, it can also be said that we are yet primitive barbarians to some variable degree. In any case, nobody is ashamed of his civilized attainment - nor need be - though each, no doubt, has had cause to blush at the revelation of his whatever backwardness. Most people, responding to the civilizing influence, are able and do take steps to enlarge their horizons and acquire personal skills and qualities during at least some period of their lives, yet there is certainly a tendency for folks to get mired down with the ambiguities and wayward pressures of sexuality.

It is a common thing for people to scrimp and struggle long and energetically, in order to acquire or achieve things of very little value to themselves and of no use to almost anyone they know. Consider the case of a young man who aspires to be an airplane pilot - a reasonable objective if he has some use for that experience - such for example as to design and build better airplanes, or because he wants a good paying job, such as to assure him an income adequate to enable him to pursue his personal interest in archeology etc. True, the owning of a handsome uniform will be a comforting flattery for him. But, just to be a pilot? There is no point in flying unless one has somewhere to go. And if all one is then to do, is to fly others where they must

138

go, then one is really not much more than a chauffeur. And most any occupation can be similarly analyzed to similar effect. In the end all one can reasonably ask of his job, is that it provide him with an adequate and regular income, honestly derived - so that he can raise his family and live a comfortable and orderly life if he so chooses. So it is with sexuality, too; and in this matter, one might do well, to recall that its ground-state valence in Chimps is low indeed (see Goodall's book). For Homo sapiens to have elevated its energy state, by fitting it up with ritual and ceremony excites ones admiration for the genius of our remote ancestors - especially so, since it seems at the same time that they have gotten some useful work from the system - toward the civilization of the species. But the point is that we do well to keep that aspect of our lives in a stable balance and proportion, with the other aspects of our mortal being. Yes, work it into ones life so as to derive from it some of the ecstasies, joys, pleasures and satisfactions that it can provide. But take the time and make the effort to keep it in balance and in harmony with the other aspects of ones civilized and transcendent being. For the point of civilization is not to take a mere lowly motive and transform it into super-sex; but rather, to take the lowly creature (Homo sap.) and give him the opportunity and the method to explore and develop other aspects of his innate potential. It may be the case that as our race and individuals in increasing numbers achieve and aspire to valid mortal and esthetic values - that the gods themselves may reform in their deportment and attitude toward mankind. I think that history already gives some evidence of that. Religion is beginning to behave less menacingly.

We are well advised, I think, to devote more attention to the multiple aspects of our being. To grasp what we can (conceptually) and to make ourselves useful and productive in this world. To strive to know ourselves as best we can; to develop our interest concerning the world about us; to raise up and seek out kin and kindred beings with whom we may communicate; and to devote ourselves to the task of (one of my favorite expressions - from Ben Franklin) aliening our opinion of reality, with the facts of that reality. Why so?

Recall the little essay chapter by C. N. Parkinson, Aims and Objectives, which I sent you. I suspect that not before we are a long way

R. GARNER BRASSEUR, M.D.

past the midpoint of our years, do we ever get around to considering what those aims and objectives ought to be. To improve our own lot and circumstances in life certainly seem as though it might reasonably be one of those objectives; and to aid and encourage our dependants to do the same, another. Assuredly, we do well to exercise and explore the physical aspects of our being. But the great unknown aspect of being, lies in the mental and rational aspect of our being. Here, but little has been achieved – and the whole destiny of mankind is yet to be determined … by the revelations which it has yet to deliver.

I would deem the quest for valid information and knowledge (such as to facilitate our powers of reason) to be the most esteemed and worthy of our mere mortal goals and objectives. Always on a <u>search for meaning</u>. And a primary aim – to live a peaceful, healthy, and well balanced life.

Nothing could be more obvious to us from our personal experience of life, than that we are continuously called upon to play an assortment of roles in the course of our lives. We are stuck with some certain minimum number of roles, no matter how simple a life style we assume. The process is precisely the same as that of portraying a role in a dramatic production. The more entirely and unselfconsciously we give of our efforts, the more convincing its effect. Each successful performance improves our facility. Each role enlarges our repertoire. The larger the repertoire, the more adaptable one becomes in a society that – indeed – does play the roles game. Often one can defend oneself, or improve ones status by the skillful playing of the roles; and a facility to switch, rapidly and convincingly, from one role to another – as a truck driver is proficient in his occupation by his ability to transit skillfully through the gear box to maintain his maximum mechanical advantage when negotiating a hill.

All of our roles; all of our interests; all of our insights and comprehension of various truths and realities; all of our cultural tastes; all of our skills and self-discipline; all of our organizing skills; all of our productive and reproductive capacity – together – constitute the sum total of the <u>facets of our own being</u>. Our ability to surround ourselves with loyal and genial associates, friends, family, relatives, and neighbors – all further enhances our own position and enlarges our potential for

140

achievement of our private agenda of what we consider to be worthy objectives.

And for warding off the influence of individuals and organizations who would wish to dominate our lives with their private agendas - generally only for the sake of their own advantage. But in any event, to our own detriment; and to the detriment of those ideas, ideals, and values which we hold most dear. In our dealings with persons and causes, always cautious of <u>covert intent</u> in hiding - behind the façade of noble intentions.

As to your sons attending "Wazoo", I would suppose those deaths among their young friends may bring them some deep thoughts and help to keep them in touch with reality. I gather that you keep in touch with them regularly. Should you have cause to cash in your chips early, I would be glad to keep in touch with them to find out where they are going, and why - and to encourage them to maintain a taste for ironic humor, a respectable skepticism, and an awareness of their family traditions. This, knowing that you would do the same on my behalf.

One of the difficulties in our society is that of keeping in touch with our youth, particularly in the age years of about 14 through the early twenties. I think it has been more of a problem in the past fifty years or more, than it was previously; the reason for it undoubtedly related to the quickened pace of life brought about in response to the advances in science and technology. For along with the intended benison, comes also some problems and disadvantage - most of them having sociological implications. For whatever reason, we tend to recognize and acknowledge these problems only belatedly, after they have already stirred up considerable difficulty in our lives.

Though the individuals of the species have inherited the capacity for intelligent thought and behavior for at least thousands of years, few historically have ever had or taken the time to explore and develop that potential which they possess. Rather, the whole cultural and traditional structure has been dogmatic and authoritarian. Each age and generation seems to have brought forth a few who have given themselves to some degree to the cultivation of the intellect, though it seems commonly to have stirred controversy and trouble. It still does so, but technology derived from science seems to have acknowledged the issue; and given some hope of survival to those whose unwanted ideas challenge the establishment. The struggle and contest within society persists, but is more like guerilla warfare, there being some difficulty in deciding who is on which side. In our own times, there was some vague notion that one's peers among his schoolmates were a vital and dependable relationship, though from its beginning it has been rather counterproductive.

Before that, was the idea of nationalism, above all loyalties; and before that, the idea of a fixed and authoritarian religious creed. Despite the comings and goings or those fashions however, the ancient significance of familial ties has been irrepressible. Along with it, another ancient concept has been slowly evolving and gaining momentum despite being repeatedly and continuously distorted, by way of opposition to its force – the idea of a man's right and responsibility to seek and enquire after truth; and to be guided in his own self-discipline, in accordance with his own best lights.

Among men, there has always been this thing we call charisma and personality. There is no way to estimate its significant incidence even in our own land, and in our times. Historically, it seems unlikely ever to have been encouraged; except among the elite. The concept of the thing has lagged amazingly far behind the actuality of the item itself. The majority ever to have possessed the quality, seem to have acquired it more by emulation, than by studied analysis. Among its qualities is that of a certain unflappable self-confidence. When this thing - charisma - begins to appear among an oppressed people; and when conjoined to this notion of personal responsibility to one's best lights, the inevitable consequence is conflict with the powers that be.

During the time of our own lives, in this country, the individual personality has been an eminently permissible thing; and since - perhaps - the end of W.W.II, has even been encouraged. *The Virginian* still sits upon my bookshelf unread; but it sits among those that I definitely intend to read, for in my view, the romanticized cowboy image is the personification of these ideals, as discussed here. And, what a powerful and enduring image it is! The curious thing - and a matter of perceptual genius on the part of those who handle that image in their creative works is the ambiguous status of the cowboy's religion. But I don't want to get into that subject any further, until I have had a chance to complete the reading of the book; and some commentary concerning the cowboy image.

I definitely plan to see that musical concerning the story of Chas. Russell's life. One of my favorite musical productions is the one called *Oklahoma*. I have seen it at least a dozen times in the past twenty years; and I hope to be able to see it several times again. There was another, called *Texas*, first produced about five years ago, which I have not yet seen though I have been told that it is nearly as good as *Oklahoma*.

But what I started out to say is that this idea of an individual persona for each individual, seems to be a generally useful concept. For in identifying one's own self-image and character as unique, the automatic implication is that each is entitled to differ, as he sees fit to do so. It somewhat disturbs the authoritarian structure of society and family and brings about a continuous reactive interaction between individuals and groups. But in the long run, it seems a much more practical basis of association than the authoritative ultimatum. That it brings us into some conflict with our own children, is not necessarily all that bad – providing that we have enough curiosity, flexibility, and intent to deal with those issues upon a rational basis. The give and take aspect of those confrontations gives us also, thinks I, a broader understanding and respect for one another. In the long view, of course, we have no ultimate use for the personality, and needs must depart from it, as well as from the mortal flesh. And in departing, the only thing of any consequence is the amount of truth that we have comprehended and endorsed to those within the sphere of our influence; and the inspiration which their memory of us has given them, to live a well-proportioned life of self-discipline; so as to enable them to see farther and more clearly than ourselves.

There is just this one other idea that I needs must touch upon in the conclusion of this note. And I hope to work it over a little more definitively, later. You no doubt remember John Galt, from Ayn Rand's, *Atlas Shrugged*, and why he seemed as though content to work at a lowly occupation. I am pretty much convinced that that is the impasse at which we have arrived in our own society; and that my own age, occupation, and circumstance in life is such that there is little point in straining energetically against a current that makes it impossible to gain those our particular objectives. The more so, since my own objectives have changed gradually over the past ten years or more. Hence, the quandary over what to do about those financial matters you mentioned in your letter.

I am reading *Winter Brothers*. It seems an odd perspective from which to write. The man, Swan, seems to have much the same sort of interests that I have; and I enjoy a well written dairy, in which to follow the workings of a man's mind. Yet, I would be surprised if it were a widely read book. His other book, *The House of Sky*, I had started reading, and then got caught up in some other project and never got back to it. I'll hunt it down and get back to it when I finish this one.

Your brother
Garner Brasseur

1988?

Sept. 3, 1988

Caldwell, Idaho

Dear DFB,

Just a note here, along with the enclosures, to give you some idea of what is going on in my life. The four children and the six grandchildren were all here together at our home for a couple of days before we drove out together to Montana for the family reunion of the Saur people. That, a three day affair at a Bible camp facility near Livingston. Then we stopped in Billings a couple of days. I saw AL and CE, MK and JK and Joyce and Johnnie Schlecht. My spouse then went into the Dakotas, but I returned to the west, bringing PM and his family with me in the pickup. We visited mom one afternoon - she seems to be doing well. We stayed overnight with PP and D. Then south on Hwy 95 to camp out one night near the 'Heaven's Gate' where we viewed the 'Seven Devils' mountain formation - a remarkable view. And we stopped to soak in a mountain creek at Bonneville camping area (near Lohman, Idaho), which was comfortably heated by a hot springs.

At this time, my spouse, PM, and M.A. have driven down to Phoenix; and I have the satisfaction of living as a domesticated hermit for a week.

Mars is bright and red in the southeast beginning early each evening. Jupiter follows it by about two or three hours. It is the first time I have ever seen mars - the brightest it has been in seventeen years (says *Sky and Telescope*).

Your brother
R. Garner Brasseur

Sept. 3, 1988

- <u>Addendum Perspective</u> -

[In these intervening years 1989-1996 I was preoccupied with full time work, and ongoing search for a more permanent work location. At the same time I was becoming preoccupied with the genealogy project that took me often into New England, New France and into mid-America's farm states. Then again settled into a steady job 1991-1998, I had opportunity nearly every year to stop by at the farm a couple days at a time, a couple times each year. There DFB had been accumulating for my perusal some numerous articles and books to occupy my days as I enjoyed the comforts and use of the bunkhouse. At mealtimes and in the evenings we then had time to discuss the materials at hand and to watch some thought provoking movies for further discussion.

DFB and I were both enrolled in college at the Univ. of Montana in 1957 and 1958. Beginning then, and ever subsequently, he had been nudging me to try my hand at writing. And even more so since he became aware about 1975 that I had been keeping a journal for many years. Just as EVH had been urging me along into the highly improbable notion of gaining acceptance into medical school; here now I had DFB nudging me along to yet another career for which I had no training and which struck me as being quite unrealistic.]

1989-1996

December 1996

Las Vegas, NM

[I had continued to gain in strength as I slowly recovered from major surgery 7 months ago. I had no realistic prospects for having thus recovered from liver cancer, but having done so; I was determined now to promptly get on with the various writing projects that had been accumulating to my intentions before the development of that recent illness]

———⊰•⊱———

Dear DFB,

I have gotten myself worked up into a sort of tizzy this day. I have just gotten this new word processor, and have spent this whole day and evening putting it together, scanning the instructions, and now trying to actually make it perform in a civilized manner. And the above sentence is the first fruit of about 10 hours of frustration. Though it seems like a terrible expenditure of time for so small an output, there still remains hope. What is lost on the merry-go-round, one hopes always to be able to pick up on the swings … as the expression goes. In any case, I have a great many projects that I needs must get after via the printed page, and it is becoming obvious that this accursed machine is not going to accommodate to my wishes and idiosyncrasies. So, this business of accommodation would seem to fall upon my shoulders.

As I continued to recover from recent surgery, I started back to work the 20th of November. Working 20 hours per week, two ten-hour days. In the last few days of 1996 and early days of 1997, Bayloo and I took a trip into Texas. A big state and a lot of driving. There, I chased down some information concerning some of the Boepple people. We stopped in to have dinner with Mitch and Molly Boepple at Ganado, TX. I was especially interested in this particular group because his Grandfather, John Boepple (cousin to George Boepple) seems to have been a particularly much traveled and diversified fellow (information enclosed). Only recently have I finally gotten both the Brasseur and the Boepple manuscripts up to date with the bits and scraps of information gathered in the past couple of years. Which is why I am now getting hot about getting after some of my other projects. The next project that I must get into manuscript form is that of my autobiographical family recollections. I have now got about 140 hand written pages of that text done and maybe yet another 50 or more pages to completion.

In San Antonio I managed to locate Mick Rosckowff - of whom I have written you on previous occasions over the years. My curiosity got the best of me, and I just had to find out the rest of the story. I need yet to set down my impressions and analysis of that meeting.

I was reviewing this essay by Albert Camus, *The Myth of Sisyphus* - a little obtuse, but rather interesting. He says living is never easy, and that suicide is not worth the trouble. (Suicide is of interest to me because we have to deal with it as an issue so commonly among the psychiatric patients.) He says the suicidal person has come to a point of despair; and that the alternative is merely that of coming to recognize the absurdity of this world. This of course, excluding those who are in terminal painful and hopeless illness.

> Metaphysical the honor
> Accrued to patient men.
> Endure this world's absurdities
> Again yet again
>
> To seek and advocate for light
> With Sisyphusian cheer
> The soul's symbolic blood is wept
> For causes quite unclear."
>
> RGB

I picked up a copy of *LILA*, by Robert Pirsig - the same fellow who wrote, *Zen, And the Art of Motorcycle Repair*. But I am thinking that perhaps I happened to have the book because you, DFB, gave it to me. In any case, I wanted you to know that I thought it was an important book. It seems to me that what he has to say about Value=Quality and about Dynamic vs. Static is something of the nature of a breakthrough, to the field of Philosophy. I am going to have to study it through again.

Perhaps we should discuss it sometime. And here is a copy of the poem that I sent in this year to The North American Poetry Contest. I have-not heard yet if they are going to publish it for me:

Sufficient well unto themselves
The troubles of each hour,
Yet crowded too by waking dreams
Into one's sleepy bower.

I lay me down to rest at night
From thoughts so unresolved
Where merciful enfolding sleep
Dismembers and absolves.

Downcast to the archetypes,
Fragmented shards of care.
Mid Freudian theme in Vulcan stream
Are sent to simmer there.

Till sudden thrust to consciousness
In black of quiet night
Disturb the peaceful slumber
With urgent thoughts a-flight.

Evasive rays of insight
Tempt the foggy mind.
Shall I arrest and ponder this
New meaning to divine?

I needs must act if I would grasp
Ephemera sink and fade.
Affix them firmly, yet while fresh,
Onto the written page.

Sweet repose abandon,
Creations of my night to stalk.

FADING ECHOES

Their parts defy adjoinment
Of splicing pen and thought.

Beyond the now-horizon
Elusive promise lead,
To worlds I fain would conquer
With heroic thought and deed.

Dreams which luminate the night,
All dissipate at dawn.
The troubles of each passing day
Evolve and linger on.

In endless cycle seek repose,
To futile dreams enthrall.
Where dreams disturb the quiet rest;
Again to wake us after all.

RGB

———◆◆———

I am delayed in my intended response to your letter in large part because of your fervent message concerning health maintenance. In addition to this written document, I recall that we discussed this general subject in our visits during the past year. And I vividly recall that you introduced me one by one to the various herbs, extracts, and supplements to which you have had recourse in recent years. When you had completed your presentation, I was a little astounded at the number of bottles that stood arrayed upon your table top. I have no cause to doubt that you are sincere in what you advocate; nor that you have been remiss in your effort to validate your views with an honest research. I appreciate and am touched by your concern to offer to me your best advice from your most recent tentative conclusions in this matter of health maintenance. And I philosophically agree with you about the fundamental importance of maintaining a healthy life style and an adequate nutritious diet. Based on what you showed me, and considering my limited knowledge of the specific active ingredients of those substances, I have at this time no cause to impugn the potential benefits to our systems of any one of them. Neither do I disregard your personal testimony as to the benefits of any one of them specifically. It is on the basis of such personal testimonies that we can begin to evaluate the potential benefit of any such substances. But a thorough scientific evaluation is a complex and time consuming business; and we are best advised to defer our final judgment, nor confer our final validation until our information is complete. However – since our lives are short and the tedious process of full validation is long, there is nothing to prevent our personal experimentation with these various substances, in the hope that one or the other may convey to us such benefit as we require. Provided, of course, that there is adequate empirical evidence and testimonial experience to reasonably assure that the substances are not known to be dangerous.

And so, the problem with the use of these substances being based on testimonial is that when it comes to checking these things out, our research is, of necessity, limited indeed … Limited, in fact, to other testimonials; because the scientific and definitive information is nowhere available. Has not yet been completed … often, perhaps not yet even begun. Pragmatically, the other main problem that I have with testimonial recommendations is that there are so many of them, and one's time is so limited that there simply is not time enough to permit a perusal of the testimonials – themselves, each, a somewhat dubious source.

Having reviewed and reflected upon my own views concerning cancer, it is my tentative view that the major causes of cancer are primarily: 1) cigarette smoke, 2) cosmic radiation, and 3) dietary. There are other causes, including harsh chemicals and radiation from radioactive elements of our earthly environment, but items 1 and 2 each constitute about 30% of the cause. Each of them is within our individual ability to control or limit. Dietary factors pertaining to our general health may also eventually be within our ability to control, but what we know about them is only of a general nature – too much fatty food and too much alcohol are certainly a part of that. As far as I know, the eating of sugar does not cause diabetes. What you have said about the weakening of individual immune systems certainly increases our susceptibility to all of the above causes of cancer … as is clearly evident from our experience of AIDS.

It would be erroneous to say that the treatment of cancer by surgery, radiation, and chemicals is not advancing. A part of that advancement has to do with gradually discovering which of the three is the most effective for any specific type of cancer. Another has to do with the slow development of more effective and less traumatic procedures; and with the development of more effective chemicals. No one denies that fortifying the immune system will also be very beneficial to the treatment of cancer - another approach that is slow in developing. Once I have concocted the 'divine elixir', that too, may be beneficial. But we are a primitive and only slowly developing species of creatures; so all of these things will take time. The Sept 1996 issue of <u>Scientific American</u> is devoted to the subject of cancer. I am enclosing to you some copy of a couple of those articles for your perusal.

Dr. Whitager seems to be fudging at the game he has invented specifically to "wow" us pilgrims. It isn't outright lying, just a sort of slight-of-hand operation. *WHAT HE WOULD DO IF HE HAD CANCER.* He cleverly selects an irrelevant case in order to demonstrate what seems very unlikely to be true if he were to select a more realistic example. He proposes unto himself the situation in which he has a proven case of lung cancer … the very worst and most hopeless of all the malignancies. It generally manifests itself suddenly - although it most probably been present and worsening for quite some while. When once it has become detected it is usually so far advanced that nothing at all (that any therapy can actually benefit) has any chance whatever of arresting the problem … or, of even retarding its inevitable and speedy march to resolution (in death). We can see then, how this evasive maneuver might seem to support his radical skepticism concerning a generality of hopelessness for all forms of cancer whatsoever - since it applies already to the full thirty percent of all cancer (which is lung cancer). In the case of lung cancer, I suppose that I myself would do much as he suggests he would do - since the well recognized and nearly always hopeless outcome is usually always the same. Supposing however that newly evolving techniques and medication were soon to demonstrate that we could now effect a 50% five-year-survival rate. That sort of scenario, for example, has already come to pass concerning some forms of leukemia. Or, supposing that Dr. W's annual sigmoidoscopy exam had, this year, demonstrated an early and histological proven colon cancer. I don't believe that he would resort to the multitude of herbs and supplements as his only reasonable recourse.

But the matter of health maintenance is a subject quite apart from that of cancer treatment; though it seems to me that our state of information concerning both is rather nothing more than in its beginning stages. However, the matter of health maintenance is a lifelong project which we each must face. Yet, it seems to me that our individuality in the matter of digestion and assimilation of nutrients is so prominent a factor that only the most general of guiding principles would seem to apply. So our situations are such, perhaps, that we needs must each be personally involved in a certain amount of dietary experimentation - for which the only reasonable guides would seem to be the various testimonials that come our way. That, coupled with our individual digestive experiences, reported to us by our innards subsequent to our every experimentation. Coupled with that, there is in fact at least a little firm factual information for our guidance, such as the things that have been discovered pertaining to vitamins, essential proteins, and trace minerals, for example. Said information having been only recently acquired by our struggling race of creatures - within only the past 150 years, more or less. A further evidence of just how primitive our species of creatures truly is. I believe that I do vaguely recall having given you some information concerning this material you call 'prostata'. And that I happened across that information not long after I had become aware of this new prescription medication, 'Proscar'. I have never used either of them ... but I am beginning to think that perhaps the time in now about ripe for a beginning trial of one of those. So, I'll borrow back from you that recommendation for 'Prostata'.

I read your *Code of the Plains Indian*, which is not far off the mark of my own vague view on this subject. As you have indicated, it is also transcendentalist. And as I lay dying some 10 months ago, I was in no way tempted to abandon that code in favor of the Roman prejudice. But to speak of that reminds me that I am living on borrowed time;

and that I had best get to cracking on these projects that I had hoped to complete - and get on to the exploration of some of the others that continue to tempt me. My life - its direction, aspirations and meager little accomplishments - has certainly turned out a great deal differently than I would ever have anticipated. As it seems to me, the influence of, and interactions with my four brothers - yourself, EVH, VBB, and PP - loom as certainly among the most positive and (taken together) continuously guiding influences of my entire life. Each of you contributing to me something of his own particular genius and outlook. Exhortation, encouragement, admonishment, and interaction - it seems all to have flowed so inevitably. Including always into our communion, great thoughts and ideas, great music, great literature, and the remembrance of great minds and our own worthy friends and teachers.

> ["And Little Orphan Annie says that when the blaze is blue/ and when the lamp wick sputters and the wind goes 'woo-o'/ And you can hear the crickets stop and the moon is gray/ and the lightnin' bugs and dew is all squinched away/ Well then you better mind your parents; and your teachers fond and dear/ And cherish them that loves you/ And dry the orphans tear/ And help the poor and needy ones 'ats gathered all about...]

Ah, yes ... we five idealists. Regularly and fortuitously humbled by the harsh realities of life, and the grim necessity of wrangling a living. Yet, "clinging desperately to some rag of honor" ... as Stevenson has put it. "And gentlemen of England now abed, shall think themselves accursed they were not here. And hold their manhood's cheap whiles any speak, that fought with us ... upon St.Crispin's Day." (Shakespeare). And so I speak of these impressions now, remembering that in the final extremity, I may not again have the energy nor opportunity to do so.

I spoke with RL and TM a few days ago. It seems that about the first of April they expect to be adding a set of twins to their present family of six children. And MABC informs me that she and BC are expecting a child in about 6-7 months. She further indicates that they will be going down into Mexico about Feb.7th - to do some missionary type of work at 'the orphanatorio'. Into Baja ... about 40 miles south of the border; and 40 miles east of Ensenada.

Best wishes to you and yours. I look forward to the possibility of visiting you again in the coming summer.

Love

your brother

R. Garner Brasseur

Dec? 1996

March 2005

- Addendum Perspective -

[Since the 26th I have been pondering and putting together my notes concerning this problem, to clarify to myself what I think is going on here.

Because of my professional and personal experience with just such personal problems as are confronting TMB, and because DFB and G are so concerned and seemingly so uncertain as to how to proceed to protect TMB's best interests, I verbalized a tentative plan as we discussed the issues one by one on Saturday the 26th. As they had seemed on the 26th to accede to what I suggested, I then ponder the situation and complete a note of analysis to myself on Sunday the 27th.

In order to avoid any misunderstanding with them concerning my suggestions, it seemed to me advisable to write out my view of the essential nature of the problem for clarification to them, to myself, and for TMB's councilor. If TMB is going to have his problems resolved, it appears to me that it needs must be through the professional path and agencies with which he is already reluctantly engaged, and to get at it promptly.]

Dated 29 March 2005

From the cabin of Tumbling B Farm
North of Ephrata, Washington

To whom it may concern: Re: TMB

I write as a friend and relative of the family of TMB to inform you that in my professional opinion, TMB's current life situation makes him a danger to his own life and a danger to lives of others. I have been employed as a physician with the state psychiatric hospital in Las Vegas, New Mexico from 1991 through 1999, and served as a staff member of admitting and treatment teams to their psychiatric units throughout that time. Though I have been acquainted with TMB throughout his life, my main source of information concerning his current life crisis is from his mother and father who are gravely concerned for his best interests and well-being: information that is supplemented by my phone conversation with TMB on the evening of 27 March 2003. I have been in close contact with his parents on a regular basis for many years and through them, have followed TMB's progress in the ups and downs of his life since his early childhood.

TMB was raised on a farm near Ephrata, WA where he attended public schools, maintaining an excellent scholastic record all through high school. He subsequently obtained bachelors and masters degrees in Engineering at WSU in Pullman, Washington. The past nine years he has been employed as a locomotive engineer and trainman with the BNSF Railway out of Spokane and Wenatchee. His parents are both college educated, sober, honest, and hard working folks who still operate their own farm. Parents who gave due thought, time, and attention to the rearing and training of their two sons. TMB's two daughters have and continue often to spend days to a week at a time with TMB's parents on the farm.

I am aware that the seven year old marriage of TMB and B has been a stormy saga often troubled with threats of divorce and interrupted five or six times by court ordered restraining orders against TMB account of allegations of domestic threat and violence. It is my understanding that both TMB and B___ have histories of alcohol abuse, and I am told that she has abused herself with other substances as well. Their individual problems - let alone their combined problems - seem not to bode well for much hope of domestic tranquility in their marriage. In fact, they are currently involved in divorce proceedings which she has initiated. I am told that there is also a current court ordered restraining order against TMB. And yet, despite that order, they still socially communicate by phone and not infrequently get together for brief interludes. Does a restraining order permit that? Even more strangely, TMB and B___ are said yet maintain considerable affection for one another. I must suppose that to be more of the nature of a co-dependence in their individual psychopathologies. One might suppose that TMB is a little confused to be sometimes encouraged in his affections towards B___ while yet she maintains a restraining order and divorce proceedings against him.

The current status of the divorce proceedings as well as the long history of repeated court interventions into their marriage suggest that B___ may well have just cause to fear domestic violence even while yet owning some measure of affection for TMB.

Though TMB is big, powerful, and handsome, he is shy and socially inhibited by nature. B___, by contrast, is very talkative and socially uninhibited, and a physically attractive specimen of womanhood. Both of his parents inform me that TMB is very much opposed to the divorce, and is reticent to any arrangement that might constrain his access to the affections of his daughters. I am told (and TMB does not deny) that he is very depressed about the many current family and economic threats to his well-being. Even in my only brief phone conversation with TMB, he does not deny that he has been very agitated and depressed for a least the past month. Does not deny that he recently made an attempt to asphyxiate himself with the carbon monoxide fumes of his motor vehicle. His supportive mother, who is in close communication with TMB by telephone and frequent visitation, indicates that he sometimes approaches a vegetative state immersed totally beneath his bed covers for unusually long periods of time. And my impression from my phone call to TMB is that he is courting the loss of his job and income by dint of his neglect of the expectations and demands of his employment.

I have discussed TMB's problems with his concerned parents and they seem to agree: that TMB ought to be admitted to a psychiatric ward, either voluntarily, or on an involuntary basis for diagnoses and initiation of such treatment plans as might be in order to attempt a rehabilitation from his current situational crisis and the complex of his self-defeating and long established pattern of his dysfunctional life style. As you might suppose however, TMB is very opposed to either admitting to, or submitting to treatment of his problems.

Of course, our primary concern for TMB revolves about his suicidal ideation and his recent attempt at suicide. But his problems of substance abuse as well as the self-defeating pattern of his life and marriage seem surely in need of rehabilitation. Also, given the fact of his determined opposition to his wife's insistence upon divorce and the history of his impulsive violence under the influence of alcohol, there may also be cause for concern to the possibility of further violence to her in the heat of passion as she toys with his affections and obstructs his access to the affections of his children.

Concerning B___, it may help you to be informed that she is the product of a broken family which is dysfunctional on the basis of alcoholism; and that B___ was previously married and has two other children from that marriage who are in the custody of their father. She has a long history of alcohol and other substance of abuse for which she has previously had treatment with subsequent relapse. Though her intelligence seems average, her education is rather limited. It is my impression that she has characterological trait disorders which include; Narcissism, Hysteria, and Passive-Aggressiveness.

Information from TMB's children suggests the State of Washington's Children's Services might be well advised to investigate the quality of the parenting to which TMB's children are subjected while in the custody of the mother. She is said to pop OTC medications and chase it with Vodka fairly commonly in the evening. I am told that TMB seems reluctant to make any such allegations against B___ for possible fear that it might compromise his chances of reconciliation with B___.

Neglect, perhaps, though I have no information to suggest that the children might be physically or verbally abused.

Thank you for your attention to the above information.

Sincerely,

R. Garner Brasseur, MD

Dated 29 March 2005

March 31st 2005

PART TWO. Re: TMB's Problems;

Several days ago (Monday the 28th?)I wrote the first draft of a letter concerning "TMB's Problems", but I have had no hankering to be in any way involved with the problem except in so far as I believed that DFB and G___ were interested in what advice I might offer on how to proceed so as to facilitate a resolution to TMB's problems. In the several days prior to that, I had listened to the details of the problem from them and we had discussed it for several hours. The evening of Monday, March 28, as I was pondering the implications of my newly acquired information, G___ came to the bunkhouse and handed me the phone. It was live, with TMB at the other end – not wanting to speak with me. But he calmed down quickly and we talked about twenty minutes. In that time I was able to gather a little additional information from him and discuss with him my major concerns of the consequences he was confronting unless he faces up to his problems with will and determination to confront his problems and to act on his own behalf.

That evening of Monday the 28th I compose a first draft of a letter to advise TMB be hospitalized account of his being suicidal. Next day (Tuesday the 29th) I do the final draft of the letter re: TMB. I gave the letter for their approval to his parents … for them to read and contemplate. I was not wanting to rush them to this definitive step. The next morning – then having their tacit approval – I and they signed the letter and DFB took it to the mail-box that same morning of the 30th.

In the early hours of that evening of the 30th, there is a flurry of phone calls to and concerning TMB. Overhearing this, it begins to dawn on me that I have not been fully informed of all that has transpired since I gave them my final draft of the letter for their perusal just after mid-day the 29th.

Having written the final draft of letter on Tuesday the 29th, I had given the letter to DFB and G___ for their perusal and contemplation, indicating that if they were agreeable to the details of the plan, we would send the letter to the counselor the following morning of Wednesday the 30th. For threats of suicide are not to be taken lightly.

The letter was upon the breakfast table and ready for signature on the morning of Wednesday the 30th. They indicated to me their assent and I signed it, placed it in the envelope, and handed it over to DFB for placement in the postal box out front on that same day.

But that same evening of the 30th I was hearing things that made me suspect they had NOT mailed the letter. A vague and eerie suspicion then crossed my mind as I seemed to have the notion that she was intending (allegedly) to then take the letter with her to Spokane when she drives up there the following day, Thursday the 31st. And I recalled then a comment which she made the night before (Tuesday the 29th) as I was deeply in thought on another aspect of TMB's problems. A comment which I ignored at that time - doubting the implication of what I only vaguely thought I had heard. In the evening of this day (Wednesday the 30th), I had cause to try to remember that comment. Meanwhile, I had told DFB that I thought the letter ought to have gone out by postal service this very day (Wednesday the 30th), after I had signed it. He had seemed to agree and promptly sealed the envelope and then went out to put the letter in the mail-box. But, did he in fact do so? And if so, is it not possible that either he or she went out later to retrieve it before the arrival of the postman?

I have been aware that there is a court order of restrain prohibiting TMB from contacting his spouse. It now begins to dawn on me that on the evening of Monday the 28th, G___ called the wife of TMB and warned her: 1) to give up seeing and encouraging TMB, and 2) to insist that B___ not call 911 on TMB again. I am sure that DFB must have known this too. In fact, I had given this information little attention, as I had been so distracted by other aspects of TMB's problems. And I presumed that certainly the court ordered restraining order was not being disregarded.

In fact though, the unlikely truth was that both DFB and G___ are complicit to the fact that the judge's restraining order was regularly being obviated by TMB. What G___ has told the wife of TMB involves her unwittingly in a cover-up to a 'Contempt of Court' conspiracy. It would appear that both DFB and G___ are allowing TMB to manipulate and involve them in his risky self-defeating misbehavior. With good intentions undoubtedly - however ill-advised. Who among us would not desire to save an errant son from the consequences of the son's own folly. Just so do we permit children to journey through the storybook fairy-lands of pleasant delusions.

These new insights began to coagulate into my consciousness after supper the evening of March 30. DFB was talking about how most of this day had for him been expended on phone calls concerning TMB's problems. (How so?, for I thought that the course of events had been set by the written letter I presumed to have gone into the mail earlier on this very day.) But this evening of the 30th, further phone calls were arriving. DFB and G___ had been trying last night (Wednesday the 29th) and all today (without success) to reach TMB by phone. And now, there is a call from TMB indicating (new information to me) that last evening (the 29th) TMB had been picked up and jailed when his wife's neighbor had called 911 to report that TMB was face to face with B___ at her apartment - in defiance of the restraining order. And then a part of today's events (perhaps late this afternoon?) includes the fact of TMB's release today (the 30th) from jail on $5,000.00 bail. Where did he get the bail money? Something fishy about DFB's story that Barbara's attorney sister had arranged it. I took my leave early from DFB and G___ this evening and returned to the bunk-house to try to put all of these unlikely things together into something comprehensible. As I write this, it now dawns upon me that the bail money had to have been provided by DFB and G___. I presume DFB told me this fib of its origin to protect himself from my censure, as I had just finished (that evening of the 30th) confronting G___ about the apparent reality that they were allowing themselves to be manipulated. It is probably also the case that the bail was actually $50,000.00 and that the $5,000.00 they paid is a non-refundable amount that is paid to the bail company.

The other item of interest is that G___ was furious at the wife of TMB for having called 911 last evening (Wednesday). However, in reality, it turns out that Barbara had been cowed by G___'s previous intimidating call on this matter; and that it wasn't TMB's wife who called 911. Rather, it was the wife's neighbor who made the call. One is left to suppose that the wife was clever enough to live within the letter of her promise (but not its spirit) by making previous arrangement with the neighbor to make the call if TMB were to have showed up at her door - as he did the 29th.

That evening of Thursday the 30th, arrives now a call from TMB (now out on bail) who has been told (by whom?) that a psych-swat team is en route to pick him up (or perhaps at least only to interrogate him?). He is in a panic, wanting his mother to call them off as he says he has to go to work this night. So, on the one hand, they themselves seem to have bailed TMB out: but now on the other hand, appear to have arranged for the psych-swat team to take him to the psych ward? Am I to suppose that TMB supposes his mother has control over this psych-swat team? Seemingly she does? Here yet still another reversal in their dilemma of how to handle this difficult situation!! I confront G___ with this question but get no answer. Who would have informed TMB to expect their arrival? Next thing I know, G___ is off to make this call of intervention - (as it seems to me, though I didn't actually overhear the substance of the call). In a mere minute or two, she comes back to the supper table to report that the psych-swat team can't get out to TMB's place because the road is blocked with a big boulder account of some road work being done out there??. Am I to suppose that there is only one route out to his apartment? And that everybody else living out near him is cut off from access to their homes? I am ashamed to admit that I was tempted to believe there could be at least some little truth in this story.

I am left to suppose that DFB and G___ did indeed arrange today for the psych-swat team to contact TMB, and that because of that, she is in a position to drop her intention of this afternoon's calls in order to accede to the manipulations of the characterological foibles of the son.

This whole business, something of the nature of a storm of erratic and counterproductive lightning, thunder, rain, and violent air currents. They would seem to be isolating TMB from the potentially benevolent consequences of a reality that might otherwise prove to be his salvation in this crises.

RGB

March–April 2005

3 February 1976

Ashland, Oregon

Dear VBB,

Enclosed please find two copies of IRS form 2120.

I am recently saddened by the death of a good friend, Nick D. I don't really have that many, and can hardly spare one.

> As logs that on an ocean float
> By chance are into contact brought,
> But, tossed about by wind and tide
> Together, cannot long abide.
>
> So, wives, sons, kinsman, riches, all
> What ere own we fondly call –
> Obtained, possessed, enjoyed today
> Tomorrow, all are snatched away.
>
> Since none can nature's course elude
> Why, or their doom, in sorrow brood?
> > From the Ramayana (Hindu writings)

We are going down to Death Valley for about a week during spring vacation. Other than that, no immediate plans have yet materialized.

Thanks for taking care of the paperwork on the trust fund.

Sincerely yours,
Garner Brasseur

3 February 1976

18 November 1977

Ashland, Oregon

Dear VBB,

Have not heard from you or about you for a long while, but I presume you are alive and well and still living in Yakima. We were in Yakima in August for the wedding of a niece. I tried to look you up, but you must have been out of town on vacation.

Enclosed you will find my $600 check for the Brasseur retirement fund. We are trying to get all of our obligations and payments out of the way before we find ourselves 'short', following that spending mania entitled 'Christmas'.

We are going to Portland tomorrow for the opera. And then next week we're going to Richland to see son PM, and brother EVH and family over Thanksgiving holiday.

I was going to launch into a discussion of some of the good books I have been reading and of the music I have been hearing. But it dawned upon me that if I commit myself thusly on paper, it might be relatively easy for someone later to have me committed. Additionally, I would have no way to sense when I might be nearing a touchy subject – and thereby unwittingly offend someone's feelings. So, I'll restrain myself until next week when I'll have both PM and EVH to walk and talk to death.

Son JRO (finished high school last spring) still lives with us and has been doing some day labor for Harry and David's. He has been into a lot of boyish mischief the past couple of years, and so I have frequent opportunity to preach to him and talk his ears off, but it is about as satisfying as talking to a post. He doesn't seem to have much enthusiasm for talking – or listening either. But the paying of fines and suffering the 'payoffs' of cause and effect relationships of life is beginning to jar his lethargic soul, I believe. He is toying already with the idea of going back to school, as though he seems already a bit adverse to the rigors of manual labor. But I note that he still has a few more practical exams to endure before his inner man fully and desperately grasps the harsher realities of life. So I need to encourage him out of the nest and into some living arrangements with some of his friends and buddies; so that he might personally experience what happens to friends and friendships under financial and unformulated socio-economic stresses. And also, he must yet buy his own car with insurance, payments, gas, repair bills, dead-battery-on-cold-mornings etc. Only then is he apt to begin to understand why every scratch, wrinkle, flat tire, cracked window causes his father to moan and redden – as though to personally feel the car's pain. He does!

RL is a sophomore this year. He is just a little taller than JRO and I, and he has much bigger feet then either of us. It looks as though we may get to be as large as PM. He has built his own room in the garage this past year and bunks out there with his dog. He keeps himself busy with photograph enlargements, model ships, and airplanes, war–games, etc. It is difficult to extract any much conversation from him but he doesn't seem to get in much trouble, so I only rarely get a chance to exhort him.

M.A. (age 8) was upset about not getting to see Yvette this past summer and is already trying to extort promises from me toward that end for this coming summer. She is in the fifth grade and also takes lessons in piano, violin, and gymnastics. And she still finds time to assault my eardrums periodically. Her conversation is full of news, secondhand and sometimes garbled. Sometimes I think I could get more accurate information from a news program. And she has questions without end; but they are strung together so closely, that one would be hard-pressed to find a space or time for the answers.

I still work Monday, Wednesday, and Friday. At the end of January, My spouse and I are going to be gone for two weeks to Florida, then Mexico. I am thinking about the possibility of taking a year off beginning this summer – to travel, watch the night skies, read, and write. [In retrospect, I can't conceive or how that would have been economically possible.]

Best wishes to you and your children.

Love,
Garner Brasseur

18 November 1977

June 2010

- Addendum Perspective -

[Through the years subsequent to my high school graduation it was necessary to write an occasional letter to either brothers EVH or VBB; perhaps an occasional letter to the parents, also. They would have been brief letters with information about who is doing what, why, and where. Information to coordinate our plans for work and schooling etc. They would have been handwritten. The most nearly permanent address we had in those times would have been that of sister ALKC's home in Miles City, Montana. There, in her attic or in her basement would accumulate our little troves of a few old letters, books, articles of clothing, and a scant few photographs as we wandered about the country in search of employment and attending various schools of higher education.

ALKC and HK separated somewhere about 1970, and as they sold their home, it would have been necessary for them to discard our accumulated debris along with their own accumulated 'stuff' as they vacated their home. Thus, little if any of our accumulated writings and documents of those early years would have survived to us.

Once married, however, there is a new beginning to one's accumulations. I accumulated mostly books, and recorded music. Beginning about 1968 I became progressively engrossed in reading and study. Progressively less reading of text books, and ever more of history, philosophy, astronomy, geology, etc.

After years of schooling, reading, and study it seemed to become necessary for me organize my thoughts, reflections, ideas, and beliefs. Thus with my career of writing, which had already begun in the early 1970's. After the tribulations of my sojourn into the Tri-Cities, I enjoyed 4 1/2 years of relative economic tranquility, which left me greater leisure for the pursuit of reading and writing. And there was then some necessity to correspond with my children, who were beginning to face the world on their own.

I was then a sort of professional vagabond several years, in search of a nitch where I might earn a steady and certain income. There was time and opportunity in that slack season of years to spend time in communication with my brothers. We made a few trips together; and explored philosophy, religion, geography, geology, and literature. And we discovered that we knew ever so little about our roots and ancestors. In part, perhaps, it was because we ourselves were then in the process of becoming ancestors, that I soon found myself preoccupied with genealogy - a large project that can lead one on endlessly, with a little information here, and promising lead there.

The long and the short of it is that I have gradually become ever more obsessed with study, reading, and writing concerning all these things. The reading is interesting, and the conversations are stimulating, but only by writing can I thoroughly explore and settle unto myself some tentative answers to the problems, complexities, and uncertainties that ever confront me. Dialog. The dialog with oneself seems of limited benefit unless it be self enforced by the writing of one's thoughts which one can then compare to one another for reflective scrutiny so as to urge them into a state of reasonable compatibility to one another. **Dialectic** is stated to be the art of reasoning or disputing correctly or soundly. In one's writing, one can reason and dispute with oneself. But there does seem to be some advantage in the batting about of ideas with a thoughtful and analytic correspondent.

The larger part of my written dialectic of correspondence has been with brothers VBB and DFB]

9 June 2010

Nov 6, 1986

Ashland, Oregon

Dear VBB,

Enclosed you will find a number of essays, concerning things which we recently discussed. They are numbered in a sequence which seems to me relatively logical, on a subject continuum. I have also enclosed for you a couple of books. The book by Ayn Rand concerns a subject we discussed in the past summer. The other - by Mueller - is one of the few history books, of which I am aware, that is not in some way tainted with a great much of Christian bias.

You and I have had similar and uncommonly wide experience of life; supplemented by the opportunity and the will to read, such as greatly to expand our experience of life. We have enough in common by way of experience, to enable us to communicate advantageously, concerning our differences in views and the interpretations of reality that we do not share. [A month earlier, VBB and I had spent three days together exploring the geology of central Idaho; and discussing a great deal of history and philosophy] I greatly enjoyed our outing. The weather and un-crowded circumstances were ideal for our purposes. I have spent some time studying the rocks I brought back with me. That, and the reading preparation concerning the geology of the area are far the most educational aspects of the trip. Only the reality of being there however, produces the motivation and interest required to examine the facts and the samples; and improves the detail and proportion of our personal psychological maps of the area.

By way of conversation, it was pleasant to conjure up the old impressions; and to try to evaluate them more critically through the haze of past years, and layers of encrusted subsequent experience. I am still pinned-down to the specimen board of life; but wriggling yet to free myself from the, seemingly real, pins and barbs. Some few, of course, hold flesh and bone; those, perhaps, I must continue to endure. Those that hold only the ethereal mind and spirit though - these I may yet elude. Our lot in life has been relatively good; and at our age our children having reached adulthood and completed their educations, we may each yet have a span of unclaimed remaining years of life - to spend off in leisurely options of our own choosing. Yes, an interesting possibility, though I don't yet know if I will be able to pull it off. And so, we considered some of the vague possibilities that might hold our interest, while also giving us a measure of satisfaction. Such possibilities as: sailing, sky-piloting, happy-island hopping, writing, politicking etc. To think of them, is one order of their reality; to speak of them is, perhaps one order of magnitude nearer; but to act in that direction, brings it closer to reality. But, is it worth doing? Does it have pragmatic value? Those are the things to consider. We yet may have time and energy enough in this world and universe to accomplish some of what we wish. The benign and worthwhile plan, however and the will to expend the time and energy to its service, seems to be wanting. The will and the energy may yet come forth in yet unborn ideas, perhaps.

Our ideas concerning the probability for the future of the practice of medicine and surgery were similar. It has become a giant lottery system, made expensive by the exploitation of lawyers and insurance companies. Public Health Medicine, alone, circumvents far the majority of the potential disease and sufferings of mankind. It, alone, would suffice to insure the general health of a nation; and does so in perhaps most of the nations of the world. The elderly ill need not live forever, though most seem a bit unwilling to give life up even when its quality has significantly deteriorated. I am personally a little fearful about the possibility of having no available escape from some of the wretchedness such as I have seen borne by some of the elderly.

In addition to the benefits of Public Health Measures, a minimalist approach to medical care might require a few surgeons to remove the occasional inflamed appendix and gall-bladder. Peptic ulcer disease is almost out of fashion, and nearing extinction. Many people seem content in any case, to figure out their own problems, by discussing its symptoms with their peers; and deciding their own course of treatment with over-the-counter medicines. And many of the medicines available in our times, are effective. Ultrasound, CAT-scans and MRI-scans improve and give better diagnostic information, such as to greatly facilitate previously difficult diagnostic problems. The sum of it all, is that the country can get by with far fewer physicians; and that hospitals - which are seeing progressively shortening the average length of hospital stay - may be adequate in lesser numbers and spaced at far greater intervals.

We in America, have yet the traditional regard for the puritan work ethic. There was a time - but a hundred years ago - when most of the energy for farm and factory production was supplied by man and beast. Steam engines, gasoline engines, and electrical power have greatly diminished the need for the physical exertions of man and animal. The working man's hours have diminished from ninety to forty hours of work per week - in some industries, down to thirty-six hours. Tractors and other power equipment on the farms; and chemical fertilizers have greatly increased the productive capacity of the fields, and decreased the man-hours of work, so that relatively little human labor is required to feed the population. Men and women otherwise unemployed, have been taken up into clerical occupations of bookkeeping, to supply documents to several tiers of government overseers of private business. The governments hire, each, a similar squad of clerks who pretend to process the documents for validity. Still other ranks of persons are set above us in government agencies to administer the rules and codes of their departments, to citizens and businesses that stand in their lines awaiting licenses, renewals, and authorizations. And, despite all of the make-work, many are unemployed. The nation is fitted up with a host of additional agencies that dispense welfare to citizens in the form of food-stamps, rent-subsidies and checks. And yet another army of clerks is required in the management and tabulations of the flow of credit and checks; which might be deleted by returning to the use of a valid currency. Because of the government's gigantic expenditure of the GNP being so large a proportion - perhaps 50% or 60% - there is no probable way for that to happen. No way, that is, short of biting the bullet, and annually reducing the federal and state government's payroll; and the governmentally supported welfare and retirement programs. No one is apt to be launched into a political career from such an austerity platform as that. Nor will the legislators merely abdicate power by failing to appropriate funds the government agencies and social action programs. And the gigantic bank loans to third world countries - which are guaranteed for repayment by the USA government – will never be repaid. The American taxpayer (the forgotten man) shall therefore, unknowingly, be required to pay it. A great many Americans are now unemployed and disenchanted with their lot in life. The great dream of upward mobility and prosperity of economic enterprise has eluded them. They each are isolated in their frustration and discontent, feeling themselves to be individually (at least, in part) at fault for their own achievement or failure – for each is privately aware of his own shortcomings and missed opportunities. It would be better, were they to perceive it as a failure in governmental policy and practice, for then there might be some rethinking as to the limits of Governmental expenditure. In our complicated society, the ego perceives it as an insult to accept employment at the minimum wage scale, unless there is definite and imminent prospect of receiving a wage increase. And to accept the minimum wage, is to nearly exclude oneself from the probability of locating a better offer. The lot of the self-employed is scarcely better, despite the occasional exception, for their average success is but marginal. A great many fail. Failing not merely to make a profit, but losing also their investment of funds and energy, and many even forced into the indignity of bankruptcy proceedings – and from there, merely relegated to the ranks of the unemployed.

It may be the case that people ought not to expect so much from life in the form of material compensation, benefits, and great expectations; but neither ought governmental largess unnecessarily expend the private income. The political system itself, and the propaganda of the educational system are largely responsible for perpetrating the utopian expectation of great success; even at the same time that they vilify personal financial independence. And individuals, of course, are also at fault for the uncritical acceptance of all of this double-talk. In general, one might suppose that all would be better advised than to seek material prosperity as their primary source of satisfaction in life. Better, a balance and harmony of other interests and concerns.

I look forward to the opportunity to examine Toynbee, subsequent to our discussion of history. Besides the ancient and medieval Historians themselves, I have found several modern historians to be excellent, including: Wm. Prescott, Harold Lamb, max Dimont, Henri Pirenne,

Herbert Mueller, and Jacob Burckhardt. The ancients have the vital advantage (as historical sources of information) of writing about events in, and near in time to their own lives. They represent our only source materials of their respective periods of history. To read them is to put one in a position to be able to evaluate the encyclopedic, political-philosophical works of the more modern historians. You may recall that I am specifically preoccupied with the effect which epidemic disease has had in shaping (or deforming) the political world, as it has evolved to our times. Hans Zinser, in *Rats, Lice is History*, and Wm. McNeill, in *Plagues and Peoples*, speak to that theme only in very recent times. Concerning epidemic disease, its vast direct effect with each sweeping episode; and its indirect demoralizing effect upon the remnant populations, has perhaps had more to do with religious and political consequences than any other single agent cause.

The tenuous balance that man has maintained (passively, until the past century) with disease seems to be causally related to the distribution and energies or men in their respective societies throughout out historical times and locations. Paleontology and Archeology suggest that perhaps man and his ancestral forms first appeared in Africa; but that civilizations of peoples first arose in the Tigris-Euphrates Valley. In the Shanidar Cave Site on the Upper Zab River - and spilling over into the surrounding lowlands - is a continuous archeological record of the remains and artifacts of primitive man, dating from close to 100,000 years ago. There one can follow the step-by-step evolution of his tools, utensils, crafts, and structures progressively down river and merging into the sites of the earliest villages of civilization. Civilizations of the Nile, Indus, and Yangtze Rivers may well all have had the origin of their civilizations beginning soon after that of the Tigres-Euphrates, and in parallel stages of development. For it seems probable that curious and adventuresome bands of men have ranged widely since times far in advance of what might be designated as civilizations.

The host of disease that abides in the south and middle portions of Africa is so manifold; and so intricately adapted to the exploitations of the loop-holes of mankind's natural defense mechanisms as to suggest that here, indeed, mankind has had its most prolonged and continuous exposure to disease. Only such a prolonged exposure and interaction seem likely to have evolved the variety and subtleties of disease patterns; and inter-connections of the life cycles of these intermediary hosts of diseases, such as to weave and interconnect that cycle effectively between man and the life cycles of other species of creatures which serve as its various intermediary hosts. Often, even, there is a third species in which a disease may linger innocuously, serving there as a reservoir of that disease, between its epidemic manifestation in mankind. man, the Tsetse Fly and Ungulates, for example, are locked into such a pattern of disease with African Sleeping Sickness, as is greatly advantageous to the survival of the Ungulates, against the depredations of man-the-hunter; but which is so disadvantageous to the survival of man, as to keep him only precariously situated upon the margins of the territory which is favorable to the life cycle of the Tsetse Fly. In any case, the general effect of extensive disease in Africa, was to decrease the health and vigor of mankind there, throughout the centuries of the history of mankind. Groups of men migrating northward against a generally negative disease gradient, would be serendipitously endowed with a greater vigor and energy, in consequence of a relative freedom from the disease they unknowingly left behind them, in the ancient provinces of their ancestors. A more vigorous people had a greater probability of evolving into cultural patterns of higher civilization, which were not incompatible with their own dormant and unutilized genetic potential. There is no reason to suspect that man has - even yet - realized but a fraction of his human potential to think and reason, and to accomplish technological wonders. And to move forward scientifically and morally. Meanwhile, Africa remains a dark continent, only recently explored. And its ancient and intricate disease patterns still threaten men who tread there, despite immunization precautions and the gradual improvement of the treatment of those diseases. We, in America live in a healthy climate, relatively free from disease. Yet, when we travel away from our immediate local area, even within this land, we pit ourselves against always some positive disease gradient. Coming into contact with diseases previously unknown to us, or immunologically disremembered, we have a propensity to become ill - noted most commonly in our children, whose immune systems do not yet have a complete adult repertoire of experience to combat these diseases with either general or specific responses.

In our various conversations, we discussed the obvious fact that people are able to hold various beliefs and opinions that are contradictory to one another, within the individual's aggregate of concepts. It seems doubtful however, that the individuals themselves are aware of their individual contradictions. For the cultural transmission of information continuously feeds us with all sorts of complex ideas and beliefs. Notions which are conceptually taxing to the young and only slowly evolving intellect. They learn what they must, or can, at a superficial level, but rarely learn anything comprehensively. When and if that capacity arises, it is rarely before young adulthood - and usually in but limited fields of interest, specific to each individual's needs, purposes, and interests. Most commonly relevant to an anticipated occupation. Busy thereafter, throughout their short lives, in raising a family and making a living, few have time for any analysis at all - let alone comparative and critical analysis of all that they have learned, heard, and read.

You and I have a certain objective experience of life, which we share in common; in consequence of our common background and education. When you think of that experience, I am sure that you realize that our experience of life confirms to us that there is no such thing as a 'supernatural'. For alone, the natural causes, relationships, processes, and events encompass the whole of our personal experience of life. If such a system (comprising the supernatural) truly exists, it simply is not a part of the universe to which we have access. Nor could it in any way reach into our natural universe to disrupt any natural cause, relationship, process, or event. For to set anything of the natural order of things askew, would be to disrupt all - like a gigantic domino push-over display. No, it cannot be! As short and limited as are our lives, we know that in general the things of our universe are explicable. And we know it even more certainly when we look about us at the humor and the pathos from the humbug and ignorance that infests our world - related to people and their cloudy ideas, and unfounded beliefs. But not related to any irregularities or malfunction of the laws of nature and relationships of the natural world.

Though our understanding of individual events, causes, relationships, and processes is slow in accumulating, still we (as individuals and as a race of creatures) make some average daily increment of progress. The art of magic is seen to have its roots in previously shrouded technology. The inventive genius of technology advances and progressively reveals the anatomy and process of previously un-comprehended natural phenomena. Miracles atrophy as valid explanation of anything whatsoever in the natural universe. Indeed, the whole of scientific and technological progress of the past two hundred years suggests that the concept of the miracle, has been a distinct detriment and obstacle to the progress of mankind throughout its existence. As to the myths and remembrances of alleged ancient miracles, it must be understood that memories are faulty, and that a primitive and simple people are easily deceived. And that mere reports of miracles are not, in fact, themselves miracles - any more than an idea of a tree (or even a picture of one) is, in itself, a tree.

I have included to you an essay on Semantics, as it pertains to the nature of the difficulties that arise to obstruct communications. The communications between you and me were relatively unencumbered, except for one topic - pertaining to the essential truth of the Christian Religion. I doubt though, that any other religion would cause us any such difficulty. I was about to enumerate the specific issues that I have with the Christian View of the J.C.; and with the beliefs of the Christian religion. But there was a vague sense of turbulence of air and earth that disrupted our ideas und conversation at that point, as we were descending into the Miniature Grand Canyon, to the north of Mt. Borah. Perhaps it was an aftershock of the 1983 earthquake.

For my own enlightenment and for your perusal, I proceed to list some objections to the myths of J.C. and Christianity which are currently compatible to my evolving views;

- Many of his saying predate him.
- He is burdened with duty, and amiss in the quality of spontaneous joy of life.
- He has no wife nor children of his own - a great and fundamental weakness in his own education. Siddhartha Guttama was much better qualified in this.

- He has no apparent respect for wealth or personal accomplishment. More especially in the case of wealth, he has an absolute distain for it. A harsh and unreasonable view. I think Parkinson gives a better appraisal - 'making a fortune is a more harmless activity than many people imagine'.

- He has no earthly social action program for the relief of the poor, enslaved, and down-trodden masses (unless, indeed, he is of the warrior messiah tradition). None other than that of his own personal mission and out-reach.

- His own disciples seem not to have understood him. Not a good recommendation for him as a teacher.

- He failed to leave us a self written record of his views, aims, and objectives - thus assuring that he would not only be misunderstood but widely misunderstood.

- Especially the Roman Christians, seem to have the impression that he was a mama's boy, and obliged to do as his mother says.

- Nowhere does J.C. say or imply that a man needs and may befit from some formal education concerning such things as the three R's. The implication then, is that pure ignorance, and willingness to believe simply what one is told, has moral and intellectual superiority over an attempt to learn. His example on this issue is in fact doubly to be faulted. For on the one hand it is implied that he himself neither had, nor needed any education. Whereas probability and currently evolving evidence seem to suggest that he was very probably educated by the Essenes. Additionally, that impression of his approval of intentional neglect of education encourages people into intellectual indolence.

- His alleged sayings are more or less ambiguous. Nor is he by any means the first sage to teach in parables.

- He is not the first messiah to appear among the Jewish people - nor the last.

- The religion of J.C. was Judaism, not Christianity. As to the person of J.C., the documents (such as they are) are sufficiently ambiguous to support either view; the peaceful, or the warrior messiah.

- The divinity, death, nor resurrection of a man/God is by no means an innovation of the religion concerning J.C.
- So also, concerning the virgin birth, the star-of-the-east, the wise men, the cross etc.
- My keenest and most distinct objection is the 'Jesus is God' concept. For there is no record of him having made any such claim. A remarkable fact. One that suggests that at least some of the lines represented as being quotations from J.C. could be authentic - whether or not he was the originator and author of those lines. It further suggests that there was an absolute limit beyond which the early church fathers were reluctant to transgress, in self-serving purpose.
- The philosophical view of reality as is implied by the Christian non-Aryan viewpoint, suggests that there is both a natural and a supernatural order of things. I cannot agree to that proposal, because the natural world would, of necessity, be unable to function in the face of interference and disruption from sporadic and random intrusions of supernatural phenomena.

At our time in history, most of our 'knowledge' concerning J.C. is controversial. It is known however, that **the Aryan concept (the non-deity of J.C.) was the prevailing view among the original Christians, in the first centuries of their history.** The opposing view seems to have originated with the Pauline groups of Christian converts in Asia-minor. Among folks who had no direct connection or personal acquaintance with the historical J.C. or his relatives and friends in his native Palestine. Paul's interpretation soon became theological and enveloped in Greek mysticism and Greek sophist logic. The head office in Jerusalem put Paul on notice that he had better reign-in, and stick with the standard version of their Christian-Jewish Sect, as well as with the standard operating procedure. But Paul's own version; and his own method was enough successful for him in Asia-minor, that he couldn't find the heart to abandon it. Later, he returned to Jerusalem with the assignments of the votes of the stock-holders of his teeming multitudes of converts in Asia-minor. Perhaps he felt that he was now in a position to force the powers in Rome to compromise to his views and methods. But he completely lost his head when they put him on trial as he appealed for a judgment to Rome. He had the misfortune to arrive there and still be awaiting that trial when Rome burned (and Nero fiddled). In consequence of that fire, the Christians are said to have been accused and persecuted. Paul was beheaded (about A.D.64).

Not long after that, the first of the N.T. Gospels was written in about AD 71 - the Gospel of Mark. It is a document pregnant with significant and highly political overtones. The troublesome Jews are made to appear guilty of the death of their own messiah. And the Romans are made to appear to have no blood on their hands, concerning that affair. The Jews are thus made to appear to have richly deserved the destruction of Jerusalem, which was completed in A.D.70. And Paul's converted multitudes of the-peaceful-messiah persuasion could then be accommodated marginally into the graces of Rome as Christians - instead of as a Jewish-Christian Sect. Though still somewhat irritating, they might be held in check, and perhaps gradually rehabilitated through the offices of the original religion of Rome. Meanwhile, Rome had her hands full with continuous rebellion in Palestine; and on the frontiers of the empire.

Here in Rome is where J.C. was probably deified. For the Romans were long accustomed to the habit of flattering their emperors by voting to them the status of Deity. The Roman Christians had gradually become a cohesive and assertive group of Romans who perhaps felt constrained to bestow nothing inferior by way of title for the man - J.C. - in the myth at the center of their religious ceremonies, whom they honored.

The common man would hardly dare approach so august a personage as a king or an emperor. The thought of it would fill the soul with 'fear and trembling' lest in so rude a condition the common citizen might somehow inadvertently offend. And then possibly hear an utterance such as that which we hear from the Red Queen of *Alice in Wonderland*, "Off with their heads". Much safer to make ones supplication through some intermediary acquaintance with someone who has 'influence' with the Majestic One. J.C. comes to mind. The Romans have devised even one additional degree of remote safeness in Mother Mary. They go farther, with even a more remote access through any one of a multitude of 'saints'.

Diocletian was emperor 285-305 AD. He de-centralized the empire and Rome ceased to be the empirical city. The Senatorial Families, having become nearly impotent of power previously, now lost even the appearance of having any authority - except for their continued authority in matters of purely local government. One might say that Rome was decidedly into a decline - except that the Christian Church was decidedly on the upward slope of its growth of authority and power. And it became the acknowledged center of a vast and growing body of believers, ordained into congregations in towns and cities scattered diffusely throughout the empire. It was in this third century AD that the Senatorial Class of Roman citizens were, by degree, high-handedly eliminated from all posts of administrative importance in the Roman Empire. The senators became church prelates increasingly now - a trend that seems to have begun at least as early as 210 AD. Voltaire says that Diocletian protected the Christians for 18 years. That only in later years, was Diocletian induced by Gallerius to persecute the Christians.

Diocletian divided the empire into more than a hundred provinces, organized into thirteen Dioceses. (Does the word 'diocese' originate from Diocletian's name?). Just so also (as a shadow of a government) was the Christian Church organized and housed into each of the diocese and provincial cities and towns. However, the supreme authority of the church organization continued to be Rome; whereas the authority of the Empire was split between four associate Augusti and Caesars located in four widely scattered cities within the empire: Nicomedia, Alexandria, Milan, and Treves.

Diocletian and Maxiomian eventually retired as the Augusti. The two Caesars, Constantine's father and Gallerius became now the two new Augusta; and two new Caesars were appointed: 1.) Severus and 2.) Maximinus Daia.

When Diocletian and his three associate rulers did retire in 305 AD, Constantine was specifically disbarred as a candidate for appointment to any of those positions of authority; whereupon, he proceeded to usurp all of the empire's authority into his own hands by right of conquest, as it were. The mechanisms through which he was able to effect that reunification were these: first, as second in command to the Roman army in Gaul, Constantine fell heir to its command when his father – its commander – suddenly died in 306 AD. Secondly, utilizing the concept and example of the unified church, he seems to have struck up a political agreement with the church officials, where-by the secular and the non-secular would mutually support one another, in their respective spheres of authority. That Constantine ever became a Christian, except perhaps on his death-bed, (where he had not the residual wit or strength to resist the passive act of baptism) is a very dubious improbability. An exaggerated fiction at best!

Never-the-less, Constantine did traffic with the church prelates as a 'councilor' to church policy, in the interests of unity within the Empire. His opinion and vote at the church council meetings, was more than equal to that of a bishop's. And that (not holy) alliance between church and state, not only exempted the church from any further state-directed recriminations, but also, in effect, made Christianity sort of a semi-official religion in the empire.

The Roman delegates to the Prelate meeting in Nicea dis-invited the majority of the prelates because they were known to be of the Aryan persuasion (the non-deity concept of J.C.). Privately, they next convinced Constantine to side with the Roman View on this issue, though his personal opinion was said by some, to be more in alignment with the Aryan View. We don't know the nature of the trade-off that secured Constantine's support to the Roman delegation, but the final outcome made the dominant Aryan View a heresy. Even so, Constantine was to be greatly disappointed with the quality of the unity for which he had hoped in consequence of his secular agreements with that Christian Religion. Though not now the official view, the Arian View continued to dominate throughout the empire – except in the Roman Provinces. The church was fractured over the issue. The Roman policy of relentless war and politics only finally secured a general submission to the non-Aryan (Roman) View (even in the western part of the empire) subsequent to the conquests of Charlemagne, some five hundred years later.

The whole official history of the Christian religion, is a willful and shameless disjunction with historical veracity, consequent to a heavy-handed policy enforced through centuries of non-humanitarian persecution of dissenters who were labeled as heretics.

Consider the ignorance and the uncritical gullibility of the early Christian world. The gospels were alleged and believed to have been written by the original apostles of J.C. Albert Schweitzer points out that not until the mid-1800's did anyone question that fact. The Germans scholars then, initiated an honest critical method of analysis and comparison of the gospel texts. It culminated in the publications of C.H. Weisse, in 1836 and 1856, indicating that the first Gospel to have been written was that of Mark, in about 71 AD. But that even Mark was not the work of an eyewitness, nor even one who had an opportunity to question eyewitnesses thoroughly and carefully. Nor even of deriving assistance from inquirers who - on their part - had made a connected study of the subject, with a view to filling up the gaps and placing each part into its correct position chronologically in history. The other gospels - appearing even later - have derived a good part of their content from Mark. So far as I know, most Biblical Scholars will now generally concede these things to be correct, though they don't generally advertise it. For their business is generally more concerned with the elicitation of faith, rather than with the conveyance of facts or clarification of myths.

All beliefs - religious, cultic, and secular - seem mighty real to those who hold them; most especially so to those who have involved themselves in the selling of those ideas. As in the fable of *The Man Who Believed His Own Tale*, they tend finally to be convinced by a story merely because it <u>seems</u> to be convincing to others. Only objective scrutiny gradually makes the seeming reality of unfounded beliefs appear dubious. A great number of fads, frenzies, crazes, and delusions have thus come - and mostly gone. That is to say, psychic phenomena. Such for example as: recurrent hysterical diseases, witchcraft, mob frenzies, human leopards, Mississippi Bubble-like schemes, and electromagnetically induced psychic phenomena. Magic has often every appearance of the miraculous, and vexes even its doubters by the force of its appearances. And the uncritical masses of the world continue to be led and misled by mere rhetoric and appearances,

I remind you that no historical document from the secular world is found to substantiate the existence of J.C. And the four gospels themselves, are not written as an enquiry into historical validity, but they seem more <u>intended to obscure</u> and distort some underlying legends and perhaps some actual written documents that may have been in existence in those times. We don't know exactly how many earlier and more original gospels than the Roman versions have been driven out of existence; as with Gresham's Law, "bad money drives out good money". Voltaire indicates there may have been some thirty such gospels. Matthew and Luke were not written until somewhere about 80-85 AD. John perhaps, about 100 A.D. It does seem probable though, that some such person as J.C. did indeed exist, and may have come down in legendary form with highly exaggerated details. More likely, is that the characters of several memorable heroic personalities and legends have gradually commingled in the vague recollections of the 'mass mind' of successive generations to produce the delusion of a 'historical figure' into a hero for the times. Considering the influence of a legend about J.C. - and the religions that have been created from that legend - it seems a shame that there is no way of penetrating through the historical fog, and into whatever facts comprised its actual history. "Myths are public dreams; dreams are private myths."

There seems little doubt, that the Palestinian Jewish notion of the ever expected messiah, was that of a strong-armed militant conqueror whose orientation was directed merely to the hopes of a less oppressive government. The Maccabees 166-143 BC played out that role by way of demonstration.

The peaceful concept of the messiah, was more akin to the views of the Diaspora Jewish people - those involved in social niceties, such as to expedite and promote the flow of commerce throughout the known world, where commerce was their major occupation. It is also obvious that whatever the beliefs of the early Christians may have been - and that seems destined to remain unknown - subsequent Christian concepts and beliefs were greatly altered. For the earliest Christians were, in fact, but a new sect within the Jewish Religion. And they were head-quartered in Jerusalem. The vital core of that sect probably perished along with the fall and destruction of Jerusalem in 70 A.D. Time and talk seem rapidly to have altered the legends to suit the needs and purposes of the many and rapidly sub-dividing groups that claim, (each) the events of that legend as the source of their diverging authority and energy. It seems not improbable that any real J.C. was more closely related to the militant and rebellious element in the long repressed and violent Jewish Homeland. J.C. is said, in fact, to have begun his career in Galilee, from whence the most militant faction of Jews was derived. Though present day Christians are strongly biased so as to interpret the gospels as though J.C. were of the peaceful variety; yet, those gospels are sufficiently vague so as to easily admit of another interpretation - that of a warrior messiah.

My primary interest in all of this religious, political, psychological, and philosophical business, is that I see the subjects as being indeed pertinent to the proper living of our lives. For throughout the whole confused morass of material, there are scattered ideas, concepts, ideals, principles, and nubbins of truth that are relevant to the ordering and balance of our yet disordered lives. The technological and scientific advances of the world have made good progress - though only in the past two hundred years. But the other aspects: religious, political, psychological, and philosophical are greatly retarded in their progress. Though we have expensive school facilities and personnel, and though the mechanisms in this country for getting people into schools is good, yet, the progress in getting people to make a personal exertion to learn is limited by the prevailing schizophrenia of firmly entrenched superfluous beliefs and superstition. There is a great battle for the minds of men; and for their loyalties (to say nothing of their votes, tithes, and tax dollars) between national, personal, and a host of religious and cultish interests, scattered throughout the country - scattered throughout the world.

I don't believe that the whip or the sword has ever proved itself to be an effective or efficient mechanism for getting people to give up one prejudice, in favor of another prejudice. (Might force the bending of the knee, even while the intangible thought remains inscrutable in the deep caves of ones thought.)

Rhetoric is effective, however; and so is brainwashing. The Catholics indicate - on the basis of long and extensive experience - that the minds of children are much more malleable to religious indoctrination than are those of adults, and that once a system of beliefs and practices is fixed into their young minds, it is not likely ever to be rooted out completely. Though there seem to be conditions and circumstances that bring about some exceptions to that, there are few that would argue with its general validity. Even those who themselves are exceptions to the fact, would not deny the general validity of the method. The Romans from the time of the republic, and their second king (Numa) have methodically improved that mechanism and its procedures, to enhance its efficiency. Polybius thought it (the Roman religious indoctrination) to be the most important aspect of Roman culture; and the root source of their national unity, which made them essentially invincible in war - though they might occasionally lose a battle. That determined policy from the experience of Rome, is continued directly into the Roman Catholic Church, through the centuries and up to present day. The principles of the method were undoubtedly stumbled upon, one by one, long before they were woven into an overall policy. The Jewish religion too - and probably independently - discovered much the same method, and indoctrinated their own people with a sense of national unity. All successful religions have subsequently done so. And through the centuries they have each learned something from one another so as to continue to improve their empirical methods.

The Roman Empire ceased to conquer further territory subsequent to the time of Justinian; and its own territories have themselves been invaded by barbarians. The Roman Culture however, and the Roman Religion have continued to conquer and subject the minds of those who came into the Empire as its conquerors; and to have a large say - directly and indirectly - in the governing of those people; and of the multitude of the subsequently conquered peoples of the new world. The ideas and beliefs themselves (of the original pre-Christian Roman Religion) were long ago restructured and replaced by those abstracted from Jewish and Greek influences, but the structure and organization of the church remained Roman.

Our own Germanic ancestors, coming into the Roman Empire as barbarian conquerors were required to accept the Roman Religion. They were not especially disagreeable to that requirement, having no formal nor structured religion of their own; and knowing that a mere formal obeisance could not change their personal inner convictions

- if they had any at that time in the history of the tribe. Such was the structure and organization however, of the Roman Church; and so advanced and steady in the method of the conquest of minds, that subsequent generations of the tribal youth, exposed to Roman rhetoric, Roman culture, Roman myths, and the organizing congregations, became quickly more familiar with these, than with the particulars of the vague and unwritten customs and beliefs of their own personal ancient ancestors. Then, the organized Roman methods simply reinterpreted and recorded the pagan myths and Deities into forms and connotations compatible to the new Roman Religion, and annexed them into the Roman Catholic Faith.

The Protestant Faiths, of course, are no more than modified versions of the Roman Religion, cast anew into the various emerging national molds.

Through the centuries, the main objection to The Church has been its greed for wealth and power. Yet it is that very wealth and power that enable its ongoing existence. But the Church's adamant resistance to reason and science has been a debit to the civilizations under its influence. Unfortunately for the church, mankind has had a slowly evolving curiosity, and a ponderous instinct for truth; combined with a will to progress technologically, scientifically, and intellectually. Here arises the impasse; and the current difficulty, concerning the traditional Christian Religions

As yet, only a small percentage of men have anything like a more-or-less well-rounded education, combined with a will to grow in wisdom and in stature. Failing to evolve and progress, their passions and superstitions predispose them to unwholesome fads, and precipitate them into unruly mobs - dangerous to themselves and to one another. Though mandatory education has some potential to lead the peoples of a nation on to truth and enlightenment, the educational system is not only overly expensive; but also hamstrung in its ability to achieve this. Its efforts to teach science, culture, truth, and to improve the powers of reason by the exercise of that facility, are combated and counteracted by the traditional religions (and various cults of teen-age thuggary). The Christian Church, having distorted truth and misrepresented the facts of history, continues to impede progress, lest this condition of the state of affairs become obvious to all. And a good many of the school teachers are unwitting double agents to the educational process. Nor will individual preaching men relinquish the power and source of income they hold over their congregations, and in their communities.

My interest in the Unitarian Church is this: it is the one denomination sprung from the Judeo-Christian tradition that seems most capable to relinquish progressively, the untruths and half-truths of its heritage; and to allow and encourage its members to seek truth in schools, in libraries, in book stores, in nature - wherever truth can be found. This, while yet striving to apprehend and retain the vital and good things that congregations can do to strengthen families and promote a sense of community and brotherhood among men; and to promote cultural growth. And yet to maintain a vital congregation with humanitarian concerns, as a useful and cohesive force within the community. And to give ritual and symbolic expression to man's ideas, hopes, fears, and concerns.

So, while I cannot in good conscience, continue to lend my support to the traditional Christian Religion, still, I see the congregation concept as a useful and important force in the community. Therefore, I am interested in maintaining a connection with the Unitarians in my life of study and work.

There seems a great deal of pragmatic value to be abstracted from the experience of synagogues, congregations, rituals, and symbolism. Culturally, it can be said that congregations have a solid historical tradition in regards to music and art. They seem almost deprived however, concerning interest and exposure to science and literature.

In truth it must be said, that the Christian Church is capable of change; and it has changed continuously throughout its history. But having once more obtained a monopoly status, the nature of its change became again ever more radical and oppressive, until the time of martin Luther. His was by no means the first attempt as at a separatist movement; but because his was supported by the German Principalities in a move of identity with the German nationalist awakening, he obtained the support and protection that spared his group from extinction. Its general result however, was the same as all dissent against Catholicism - the death and slaughter of thousands of innocent people, culminating in the Thirty years war, a century later. The success of the Protestant Reformation was, perhaps of only secondary importance to the invention of the printing press - in the encouragement of the common man in learning to read. Reading, is as important to education, as is public health to the general health of the masses of mankind. Equally important, as a by-product of the reformation, was the consequent splintering of the whole religious establishment. Only that has finally brought about a measure of religious toleration. And even the Catholic Church was forced into a reform of many of its evils. If the Christian Religion is to evolve into something of continued usefulness, it must - I think - put itself back on the road to alignment with historical veracity; and begin to acknowledge the mythical aspect of that which they have traditionally believed. Only that might end the continuous telling of old fables; and the continuous inventing of new misinformation, intended to cover-up or bolster the old deceits. For the enlightened layman must get tired of having to pretend to believe the old faith. Nor is it likely that even the well-read preacher does not begin to doubt a goodly amount of what he has been preaching - some of them end up having a preference for selling cars etc. And even the relatively uneducated of the congregation, good-naturedly string along without overly much actual belief in the old truths either; as they are ever more preoccupied with the secular aspects of their lives. So that in Christian congregations, the whole mechanism of communication is stressed and strained by the want of honest communication. Mainly the women and children are generally credulous enough to accept it piously, and the church seems to hold its parishioners mainly through it workings upon them, and by <u>the significant advantage of having positioned itself as a predominant center of social interaction in their communities</u>. And the children, maturing, (in their embarrassment) tend simply to fall away, rather than to fully acknowledge or confront the hypocrisy of the ritual sham.

The least that will suffice, I think, is to cease emphasizing or trying to reinforce the "J.C. is God" myth, and let the natural force of Aryanism reassert itself in accordance with the principles of a humanistic psychology ("Know then thyself, presume not God to scan/ The proper study of mankind, is man …" - from Pope's *Essay on man*. And the churches need not ardently confess nor acknowledge the past errors of the church, for those would then be forgotten by-and-by - along with old misconceptions of history. The hysteria of the alter-call participants could then be replaced by small-group therapy, using the syntax of transactional analysis, so as to give these disturbed people a vocabulary and experience in its use, such as to enable them to formulate the nature of their psychological stress, and encourage them to find some insight into their being, such as might improve character and interpersonal relationships within the ranks of mankind - and with reality. What we need to honor and cherish in not a particular religion which we somehow inherited; but rather, wisdom, Truth, and truths.

As to how we should order our lives, so as to remain more or less financially independent as we mature - that is difficult to know. To say that it were knowable, is to imply that things are economically predictable on the basis of naturally functioning economic law and order, in our times. I do not believe that to be the case. For in the free market, there is so much hedging, guessing, second guessing, stock manipulation - and so many groups with (not of their own) money for leveraged power speculations; and so much that goes on, based upon inside information and 'toxic assets' scams, as to make it highly improbable that my own limited assets for the investment pit would produce any significant income to me. The continuous interference of the government with the economy, by its random, frequent policy changes, only further assures that the economic future is, in fact, unpredictable in these times.

My own situation is such that were I to acquire any material assets, they are much apt to be confiscated through 'claims', equity courts and the increased probability of malpractice claims in a progressively litigious society. Based on the turbulence of my past experience therefore, I am not overly concerned to acquire any much home equity, nor cars, bank accounts, or investments - for such as these, are quite apt to cause one grief and assure of harassment. That it is so, does not cause me any particular discouragement for I am fully content to work; at something or another - at least on a part-time basis - for the rest of my life. Should I earn some little profit, I'll take the cash or coin and use it - along with part-time work - for a hand-to-mouth subsistence existence. Thus one may escape the continuous preoccupation of the mind with economic concern; leaving the mind free, for matters in life that are intrinsically more interesting. It may be the case that your economic situation; and relative freedom from tax claims and judgments is enough more optimistic than mine, so that you can play your hand differently. I know that you don't count on it absolutely, though, for you already know how these spurious and expensive legal claims can suddenly materialize out of nowhere, as it were.

It turns out VBB, that your have a folksy and easy going outlook on life; and are well-read enough, that you might probably be able to get into politics, if you had a mind to do so. You might not enjoy it though, for the voters and lobbyists seem largely intent on pressuring and tempting the office holder as a tool for their private interests; and might give a man no rest. Still, with a little practice, one might be able to figure out a way to handle that - particularly if one had no fervent desire for so much as even a second term-of-office. And what politician ever went hungry? Surprisingly few of them seem even ever to get shot or hung.

Whatever else you do, you really ought to try your hand at writing, for you have a definite flare with words. And your experience of life is broad enough and tinted with enough modest success in the face of great enough improbability, so as to give your tales an interesting color, with need for hardly any varnish at all. But the best reason for writing is simply that of communication. As a medium for the conveyance of ideas it exceeds the simple dialog, or impromptu rhetoric. Best of all, I believe, the process of writing facilitates clear thinking. Though we get a few words with our children through the years, it is not at all certain that they penetrate well; or that those words re-crystallize (in their minds) into anything similar to what we had intended. Even when they are looking directly at you, you can't really be sure you have their attention. To write them of your ideas and experiences leaves them a record of potential future interest to them - in addition to its value for both them and you in the here and now. Though they may not hear what you say, they are likely to read what you write. And they, themselves will choose a time to read it - or to re-read it - when they are ready to give it their full attention. And the example of your effort is by no means apt to be insignificant. That, is challenge and response. An example that could become a tradition in your family for generations, for all you know. And an example in the exercise and practice of clear thinking.

I was amazed to read that the crust of the earth is composed of:

46% Oxygen by weight	91.97% by volume
27% Silicone by weight	0.8% by volume
8% Aluminum by weight	0.77% by volume

The rock we brought back from our recent trip had many interesting features, some of which we discussed when we first examined them up at Stanly. And I do think there are at least a couple of flakes of gold in those shaggy quartz-seam fragments.

Out of space; out of time; this letter overdue; other projects etc.

Your brother,

Garner Brasseur

Nov 6, 1986

January 22, 1987

Ontario, Oregon

Dear VBB,

I've been getting your interesting and thought provoking communications and since I know that your 51st birthday is on Feb. 11th, I thought that I might use that event as the circumstance that now absolutely requires me to write you again. For I have been procrastinating already too long in my intent to do so.

After we returned from our central Idaho trip in October, my reading began to center upon another area of cryptic history. Namely, that of the origin of the Seubi and Alemanni - the German people from whom our mother is descended. They settled on the east of the Rhine, upon the headwaters of the Danube. The territory was conquered centuries later by Charlemagne and evolved into a number of small states and principalities, one of which was Swabia - the local region from which mother's ancestors seem to have come. The same area from which my wife's ancestors seem to have derived. The name changed to Wurttemberg, but the boundaries of the territory changed very little. Stuttgart remains its principle city; and Wurttemberg remains as one of the states that constitute modern Germany.

Pinned down as I am, to this location where I am trying to make a living, my access to adequate library facility is limited. And therefore I have at my disposal only a few remnant skeletal remains of raw information upon which to conjecture the history and family ties that bring us into contact with our ancestors at the headwaters of the Rhine and the Danube. Having more interest in the subject than I have of accumulated definite facts, I found myself writing a sort of legend of history to fit the facts that I do have. And I accumulated a dozen or more pages in November and December. Then I found that I was sort of half-intending to tie together and finish the three or four different writings I had done, into a unified whole, so that I might give a copy of it to each of my children at Christmas time when they were all home for the holiday. And of course, I was going to send you a copy too. But I didn't get the rewriting done; and so there it sits in my notebook - awaiting another burst of creative energy - and time. But I'll send you a chapter from a book that deals with the Swabian Expedition to south Russia; and some diary entries of a couple of people who may have made that trip as shipmates of your very own ancestors. Later, I'll send you a copy of my completed essay on the subject, along with a map or two. And in a subsequent intended effort, I shall use my legendary history as a guide and stimulus to research the subject, and fill it out with more specific and more factual details. Sufficient to say for now, that the ancestors of George Boepple's father came from the village of Plattenhardt in Wurttemberg. As you can see from the map, that is only about a dozen kilometers south of Stuttgardt. His mother's ancestry is either from the village of Gerlinger or Kaltental, to the west and the south of Stuttgart, respectively.

I am sorry to have missed that TV program on Geology that you mentioned; for those pictorial things coupled with reading and our own very limited experience, are the things that begin to give us a grasp of the immensity and bursts of almost unimaginable energy that have shaped our western landscapes. Even the immanently slower processes of wind and water erosion are, in fact, a dynamic process that we mere mortals fail to see - because of the very transient nature of our individual being.

I am enclosing some National Geographic articles pertaining to geology and its processes. The great bone-yard of northeastern Nebraska in most probably from one of Yellowstone's great blow-offs. Eastern Montana (Ekalaka, the Pine Hills, etc.) and Colorado and Wyoming all have had similar catastrophic episodes of great dying of fauna. For every similar site of bone diggings, perhaps a hundred remain yet undiscovered. There are two other similar known giant calderas in the U.S., both of which I visited in the past year. One is the Jemez Mts., to the northwest of Santa Fe, New Mexico; the other near Lake Mono, north of Bishop, California. As with your own Mt. Ste. Hélène's, the great bulk of the ash-fall is somewhat to the east - depending on the precise direction of the westerly wind at the time of the event. The Italian winds must have been out of the north east on the occasion of the burial of Pompeii. And compared to the giant calderas, Vesuvius too was a small event.

I liked your letter to the editor. But, of course you know that the editor only writes to fill up a space, hoping to touch upon a subject with enough charge so as to catch the eye of the maximum number of readers. And if he can get any letters in response … well, that is so much glory and fan-mail. Some few responses like yours, the editor finds informative perhaps. These he can use as a basis for further editorials, when he has more space to fill on another occasion. The Medicare problem, of course, touches almost everyone directly or indirectly, sooner or later. The current bureaucratic gimmick in our area is this: they are sending out 'inspection teams' to the nursing homes concerning certification for payment by Medicare. The teams are turning up all kinds of vague 'evil' and 'disqualifying details' and facts. (Did you know that a patient discovered to have bedsores is considered to be a 'civil offense' for which the nursing home is subject to fine? That a janitorial closet found unlocked at any time is 'disqualifying'? That any bruise on any patient is evidence of physical abuse? That any patient found with any medicine whatsoever in the room is a dangerously disqualifying event? Not even may they have Aspergum, eye drops, nor Tums, etc.). The game of course is this: the government wants to spend less on Welfare, Medicare, and social services. This they hope to accomplish by disqualifying and fining the nursing homes. But of course, they will end up paying what they 'save' by spending out that same money - and more - to the 'inspection teams'. I'll leave you to guess as to the training and background of the individual members of the inspection team. But, the theme is ubiquitous, old, and tired.

PM and Shelle brought us a forth grandchild, François, on 11/16/86. JRO and MSRB presented us a fifth grandchild, Tristan Isabelle, on 11/22/86. All were here in Ontario for Christmas, except JRO and family.

I am reading Toynbee's book, *A Study of History*. It is an unusual history book. While it may be widely quoted, I can't believe that many have actually read it through, for it is very long, philosophical, and chock-full of those long precariously balanced German-like sentences. The author refers to historical events without stating any history; presuming apparently, that the reader of the book is already well-read concerning the whole historical record of the world. Not even all of college level history instructors and professors are apt to have that broad a background in history! His analysis and generalizing view of history overall, civilization by civilization, is certainly interesting and useful. Yet, he made generalizations and drew conclusions, many of which I could not agree to. Though he freely cites the historical evils of Christianity, one can see that he is unable to skate free of his personal bias that certifies Christianity above all other of the 'higher religions'. But I have yet another 200 pages to read in that 500 page volume. Perhaps he shall draw it all out into a clearly discernable pattern, and end up with a palatable and balanced perspective; and a set of conclusions that seem probable, and that square with reality, ?Quien sabe? At the present stage of my life, I have no qualms about letting my family in on my evolving impressions of life, religion, philosophy etc., for if they develop some interest in these things that lie upon the conceptual frontiers of mankind's realities of the future, it may broaden their view and may help them to shake free of some of the ignorance and prejudice that acts as a drag upon the progress of individual men - and upon mankind. Though it be the customary situation for the older generation to become salt-encrusted pillars, from this looking-backwardness, we need to ask ourselves to what degree this is beneficial, either to ourselves, to our children, or to posterity. The young, particularly - and ourselves, too - have need to exercise some restraint against the urge to run with open throttle on the down-hill grades. But we might do well to be up there with them, so that they may benefit from our experience - by calling their attention to the signal indications and forewarning them of the particularly troublesome curves ahead. Pilots, as it were. Now, though I haven't found much chance to converse with them on esoterics against the customary mundane grain of conversation; yet one may write to them, for they are apt to give that material their attention - at a proper context of time that is appropriate to their mood. And, by way of conversation, I do not hesitate to modestly interject my views, when-so-ever the natural conversation drifts upon the questions pertaining to Faith, Truth, Belief, Sin, Right vs. wrong, Good vs. Evil, etc.; with the hope thereby, that their various faiths and beliefs do not become too arrogantly situated within their psychic structures and mechanisms. And they ought also to be questioned, so that they can retrospectively brood upon the unsatisfactory nature of their own answers, too - as well as the answers of their ancestors. And it seems worthwhile to point out to them, that their own sense of morals, values, and ethical principles do not seem to produce between us any very significant disparity of social conduct. Nor do they escape awareness from my example, that I am at odds with the Judo-Christian tradition of belief into which they were conceived and raised - just as was I, too. For, like my father, a brother and others I have known and admired, I too have given up most of the proscribed rituals of my inherited religion, as much as that is possible without being overly offensive and obnoxious. That simple passive resistance is intended as a landmark and beacon unto them, that I no longer buy that product. For the most part we pass through this world unnoticed. Our children though, they watch us - perhaps even more than do our parents. And what we do, and what we don't do seems to have a greater impression upon them than what we say. Perhaps that is because the symbolism of acts is perceived gestalt-like, within their psyches, while the spoken word and idea can be so easily misperceived – and often not perceived at all. For, with words, one must have their full attention in order to *get* the words and ideas even superficially lodged into their perceptive apparatus. And the 'distance' between individuals and generations – of the meaning of words, expressions and concepts – is so prone to variation, that we often needs must ingeniously repeat ourselves in several different modes of expression, in order to effect an accurate communication. But the written word – if we can learn to express ourselves well – may have a better chance of getting a message transmitted, because they can read it at a time of their choosing; and later re-read to clarify to themselves. Just so, in fact, as you and I do when reading – more, when studying a book. "What was that?", we say to ourselves, as we start the sentence over again.

There are those who maintain that the mass of mankind is the better off, for having some sort of a religious myth, to which they are taught some fealty. A religion with a virtuous hero, concerning whose example they are regularly exhorted; and encouraged to emulate in virtue and piety. But it has never been shown to be the case that those (religious parables from 'canonized' writings) are more effective as learning and teaching devices than are secular parables (such as Aesop's Fables, Hans Christian Anderson's, or the fables of James Thurber). It does seem to be the case that the sturdy youth are so naturally subject to the temptations of novelty, passions, lust, desire, and greed, as to make them vulnerable to downfall from disease and accident – unless they be disciplined, circumspect and restrained. And since they cannot be policed upon a continuous basis, the most probable of efficient restraints is self-restraint. And the most efficient of disciplines, is self-discipline. And every society has its code of conduct that governs a reciprocity of generally acceptable and peaceful relationships between its members and generations. They also have ceremonious occasions that bind together, the members of a society; and still additional ceremonies for its sub-societies. A slow and halting progress from vague intuitive perception, to bumbling and advancing powers of reason, to crude technology, and finally an advancing scientific method – all made possible through a culturally transmitted tradition of education – has fostered the advancement of society. Religions, in general, have not favored nor enhanced that progress. Most commonly, they have set themselves against it.

No one has ever been able to demonstrate that religion has any effect in enabling any person to communicate with the Deity; or that through religion, the Deity communicates with man. The main benefit of religion to man is largely in proportion as it encourages man to treat with one another humanely, and to effect a general sort of detente between its individual members. When people treat of one another humanely - i.e. as one human being compassionate to the condition and circumstance of other human beings (because, as a human being, he can comprehend human weakness, error, stupidity, and superstition), they are relatively well dealt with. To the extent that a religion might encourage that, it is of some potential use, and of value to the requirements of living - and to the quality of life. But humanitarianism derives from human beings, and is therefore not a very palatable concept to most religions of the Judo-Christian variety, even though it is the very quality of redeeming virtue that best sustains their religions, and most touches the individuals among their varied memberships. It is when people treat of one another condescendingly arrogate as though they themselves were God, or Demigod, or as the appointed agent of God, that things are relatively bad, and times evil (for a people who are subjected to that religion). The same for a state, acting in the name of that religion.

As to the question of good or evil, here again is a slippery piece of soap - difficult to take hold of. There is reason for a good deal of misunderstanding concerning those terms, for they have an ancient history, have had heavy usage, and have acquired quite a number of meanings - with a host of annotations and connotations. As we probe through the various layers of the etymology of the words, it seems there is plenty of reason for the de-facto ambiguity which surrounds their usage in our time. They are drummed at us so early, so often and so emphatically, that they acquire for us a connotation quite specific and apart from their ambiguous historical usage. And so it is, that without troubling ourselves about definitions and history, we sort of come to believe that we know what we are talking about when we speak of good an evil. But do we? Unless we specifically re-define their usage into current idioms, the terms 'good' and 'evil' refer themselves back specifically to an ancient age, where demons and angels were commonly believed to be as real in their embodiment as are tigers and elephants. To be sure, especially the fundamentalist religions are still caught up in these ancient concepts, to some degree; and their members believe in it to some degree, too - at least on Sundays, and on Wednesday nights. Mark Twain has commented upon how commonly good intentions bring forth an evil result and evil side-effect. And conversely, how often too, a selfish or evil design or intent brings with is some unexpected good or beneficial side-effect. But in any case, if we wish to consider the good and evil lodged within the framework of mortal man, we do well to re-consider and define more specifically what precisely we mean by these things. I suspect that what is actually meant, is that we mortals display in our behavior, a certain want of proportion in the balance of our lives. Thus, a thing like lust which is certainly a very great good; in that it brings to us some of the better things of life: like children, moments of ecstasy, times of contented release, and relaxation. But is also apt to bring us a great deal of agony, pain, and misery. These things in proportion to the balance and direction that we give to lust, through restraint and self-discipline; and in accordance with the principles of order and proportion.

In the musical production of *The Man of La Mancha*, Don Quixote asks, "Is it more reasonable to see life as it is? Or, is it more reasonable to see life as it ought to be?" Certainly a mature insight into life has to encompass both views. How shall we gauge and measure ideas, concepts, theories and points of view; to put them into perspective with reality? We have no hope of an answer, except through our whatever capacity and powers of reason, I rank man's capacity to reason, as foremost among his redeeming features. Through the exercise of reason, one can organize and transcend from one level of understanding, to a higher level. But, of course, one can reason to good, or to evil intentions. As Socrates pointed out, one can reason to support distorted sophisms, merely in attempt to exalt in victory. Yet, along with Socrates, I conceive of reason as - by nature - being goal directed. Specifically oriented toward the detection of truths; and Truth. In that sense, it is intricately akin to virtue and morality. For reason to arrive at erroneous conclusion, is to defeat itself. Error is arrived upon, as a conclusion, by an incompletion of its task; account of inaccurate data, or account of a weak and poorly exercised capacity of reason. The regular and conscientious exercise of the powers of reason, when coupled with study; with research; with memory; and with internal reflection, can become a progressively powerful tool, enabling one to find answers to the riddles of reality, and the interrelatedness of truths and Truth. And so, along with Ethan Allen, I regard <u>reason</u> as <u>man's only true oracle</u>.

Suppose a man argue with us, in attempt to show us the futility of reason. His entire effort must be founded upon reason, and his efforts thereby give evidence contrary to the theme of his argument. Suppose again, that a man proclaim Religion "X" or sacred book "Y" as the foundation and oracle of Truth. He can not even begin his argument, except he begin and proceed on the basis of some form of reason. He believes such and so because … (reason). Or, he claims to have spoken with the Deity, and concludes (again, reason) that he must accept … (whatever).

Though it be true that Reason has not yet taken mankind as a whole to any lengths, still, it is as yet in its primitive stages of development among the likes of mankind. Neither has the principle of flight taken us yet, to but the first tottering steps, even in our own planetary system. But the prospects for both have a long history since their initial conception in the minds of men. And both have shown steady and encouraging prospects. Reason oft reveals a truth; and oft exposes an untruth. The distinctions between the valid and the in-valid come but slowly and gradually as our enlarging experience and advancing powers of rational thought increase.

And as you and I, and the likes of men, become practiced in these things, we hopefully anticipate that accumulating truths will gradually coagulate into a valid conception of the nature of reality. A hopeful prospect to some yet distant future. Retarded always by the reality that not all men reason equally well, for in this, as in all things, men are assuredly not equal. And among those equally gifted by birth, not all practice with equal diligence to develop their powers. Nor are all equally motivated. Not all - if any - have as yet much of any access to reliable facts and data. Few can escape the gravity of their early learned prejudice; and that gravity tends always to bend and distort light waves of truth. Distorted truths make poor material for the operations of reason. No wonder then, that reason has not yet taken us farther. Yet, it seems to me that mankind is making progress toward truth; and toward the alignment of the opinions of men - with reality.

So it is that reason has led to the sciences, which in turn have led to applied technology. Many now have begun to understand that the world is round, rather than flat. Many have begun to understand that neither the earth, nor even the sun is the center of the universe, despite the resistance of religion, and the flat earth society. And surely it seems to yourself, as it seems to me, that we ourselves too, make progress in our understanding from day to day. For why else do we discard what we thought yesterday, on the basis of our experience, and under the influence of new facts and new theories - and the contemplation thereof? These new facts, ideas, and concepts, give us reason to accept the new - and always tentative conclusions. And by experience, we accept the new so assuredly, that we but rarely have need to revert to the old concepts, now that we are shed free of them. But reason still permits of the occasional reclamation of something of valid utility from the past, when reason and experience again make that appear reasonable. But generally it seems to us that what we accepted yesterday is less near the truth, than what we today are considering. And the moral quality of reason is such, that we generally harbor compassionate understanding for the error of the past times and persons.

The rational mind, based upon the impressions it receives from its always limited perspective, forms mental habits which thereafter determine - intuitively? - what it further will or will not accept freely. And yet, rarely do we see an individual who, under some circumstances, cannot be induced to reconsider, as an aside, the soundness of some one or another of his limiting rational structure and apparatus. Zoroaster, Buddha, Emerson, Thoreau, Gandhi, Socrates, Diogenes, Jesus, Galileo, Einstein, Schweitzer, Paine, Ethan Alien, Mark Twain - all are examples of men who have opened up their mental perceptions onto new perspectives and broader horizons of comprehension. To honor them, and to retain their idealized images symbolically, seems to help us to open up our own minds; and encourages us to take that next step in the process of our own enlightenment - and to transcend. But, to worship them, is to stymie transcendence - and to destroy the spirit of their efforts and intents.

The condition of mortality is such, that we do, in fact, act upon the basis of belief and faith, in a great deal of that which we individually undertake. And those acts are conditioned and supported by habit and experience; and reinforced to us by custom and by the example and precedent of the individuals of our society. For what we know - absolutely - is far too limited to initiate in us any much premature and innovative action. But when we can garner adequate reason for the compelling and direction of our acts and behavior, we do not hesitate to use that for a basis of our action - even though the action be a variation from our customarily expected response to a challenge or a specific situation. In short, we do acquire an ability to respond rationally in this world - and that is probably true of almost every person. I point that out because I do not believe that it is commonly recognized to be the case. In this world where ignorance and superstition seem to reign supreme, many go into a fit of fear and trembling at the very suggestion that they consider a thing from a rational point of view. As though it were an entirely foreign and novel possibility - possibly even 'sinful'. And still, in all, the world is a complex place; and the span of life and the energy of life are limited. The puzzles that we encounter therefore as we bumble through the slime and ooze of life, are far in excess of our individual probability of solving any but a small fraction. Even of those we recognize and understand as being puzzles, often seem to make of man's intellect a mere joke. We are therefore commonly obliged to (condemned to) act upon the basis of incomplete information, knowledge, and thought. In faith, therefore, we are tempted to follow the crowd; heed the advice of family and friends; and act upon but vague impressions of our past experience. But while I concede that belief and faith are present and to some degree necessary to us all - still, they are tired horses, and greatly overworked.

I awoke at 7:15 A.M. on 12/10/1986, having dreamed this excellent and ingenious mystery story; and which at the same time, endowed me with an enlightened perception of the whole universe. It was so clearly obvious and unforgettable, that I hardly wanted to rouse myself. And so I sat there on the edge of the bed, in the darkness for a minute;

debating myself, as to whether I should arise now, to sketch down the details and outline of my story and enlightenment. Yet it seemed so clear, complete, and distinct a story, that I didn't want to risk falling back to sleep; fearing from past experience, that I might not recover the story upon awakening. For I have missed enlightenment on several previous similar occasions from just that same careless procrastination. Therefore did I arise; and began to write. But I was disappointed. For, though I truly believed in the exquisite excellence of this story; and had complete confidence in my grasp of its details, its course, and the moral of its message, yet, I could hardly have been more wrong. I was pleased only in this - that I had made an appropriate and honest effort to capture the essence of this enlightenment. Otherwise, I might now be unjustly reviling myself for missing 'that, to which I had been called'. And, even as I bent myself to the necessary task, the details of that grand illusion receded ever before me, as a mirage. "Hath melted like snow, in the glance of the Lord".

Such though, is the nature of the confidence that we place in our beliefs. Our certainty of their validity is nearly iron clad. So much so, that they hardly seem in need of our personal inquiry, as to their veracity - having come to us as they have, seemingly as from the great mystical beyond. Yet, once inquired into, so as to enable us to delineate their specifics, and the compatibility of their parts to one another; then, the delusional nature of their being becomes apparent, and often tends to leave us willing to toil more honestly - toward some shreds of truth. I suspect that in the past two thousand years, the attitude of our culture has conditioned us to accept belief and faith as the ultimate refuge against the embarrassing inquiry from those about us; and as adequate justification to ourselves for our 'sin of omission' of rational thought. Because it is closely related to this subject, I have included to you a copy of my *The Genesis of A Delusion*, written earlier; and based upon a real life experience which I had about fifteen years ago. It likewise indicates that, like pricked balloons, these beliefs, faiths, delusions … are fragile; and tend easily to rupture, when subjected to a sharp and rigorous probing. But supposing some don't? well, that too is acceptable. For it is our hope, that not all of what seems to constitute reality, shall be proven absolutely erroneous.

FADING ECHOES

I was over in Caldwell recently, making some tentative arrangements to begin practicing there, perhaps a day or two each week. I made it a point to attend medical staff meeting, during the lunch hour at this HCA affiliated hospital. It happened that the hospital administrator and the comptroller delivered their annual message concerning the current economic state of the hospital, and its prospects for the coming year. I could give you some of the details, but you are already aware of the governmental bureaucratic strategy; and that no relief is apt to be forthcoming to an alienated group who believe - like Xenephon's 10,000 - that "having done what they could, they (are) prepared to suffer what they must".

Concerning Ayn Rand and *The Virtue of Selfishness*, the essential point she makes is that the individual <u>must</u> be accorded the freedom to honestly acquire unto himself; and to look after ones own best interests, regardless that such acquirements may be mislabeled as selfish. For that, is the essence of freedom. <u>Unless</u> we insist that freedom be accorded to: Ayn Rand, and to each of her story characters, and to each of our friends and relatives, and to our follow citizens, then, we ourselves, have <u>no basis</u> whatsoever <u>for any</u> personal <u>freedom</u>. Nor then, do your children. The whole matter revolves around the very central issue of the Constitution of the United States of America (if you will pardon me for sounding so sanctimoniously patriotic). That issue: whence derives the proper and legitimate authority for the governing of a people? I believe it can only arise from the voluntary consent of that people. What think ye?

All that your letter said and implied about the adverse benefits of unbridled and relentlessly pursued selfishness is obviously the case. But then again, everyone does have, or acquires: family, friends, associates, fellow citizens, and connecting links throughout society. So that one is not apt to come across any real-life characters of absolute individual selfishness. The nearest case we are acquainted with is that of E. Scrooge, in Dickens' novel; and even that is but a story of the erosion of selfishness. And so selfishness and generosity are, in fact, the two obverse sides of the one coin. Each is good or bad in proportion to the situation and the particular circumstances of the individual case, and instance.

California has thousands of earthquake shocks yearly, of which about 500 are energetic enough to be noticed; and they have about one yearly, that is more or less of major importance. But overall, the danger from that to your person, is considerably less than that from your fellow citizens. Bishop, CA just had a big shake-up the past spring, so may not be due for a big one again for a long while. But, on the other hand, it is intimately close to the Long Valley Caldera, so who can say? For a place to live 'the quiet life' without too much severe weather, perhaps the central valley is the best, except for the delta area of Sacramento, Stockton etc. For there they are subject to springtime flooding. Actually, almost everyplace in California, is nice, and if I were to find a town there that I especially liked, and where I could make a good living, I certainly wouldn't be intimidated against living there on account of some occasional local natural disaster. Just don't plant yourself directly astride one of the obviously major fault lines, nor at the bottom of a dry wash.

If you catch up with Uncle Louis, out there in Marysville, give him my warmest regards. I always liked him. Why shouldn't I - he was always kind to me.

Sincerely yours,
your brother,
R. Garner Brasseur

January 22, 1987

5/13/87

Dear VBB,

I am in receipt of your recent letter packet which arrived just as I was writing a long overdue letter to son, JRO. It took me a couple hours to get through your letter and then to skim through about half of the other enclosures. Then I pressed on to continue my letter and packet to JRO, as I was already late for his 28th birthday. Next then, a similar project to PM in remembrance of his even further overdue birthday - he was age 31 on march 26th. Yes, my wife and I did travel up to Coeur d'Alene, for mom's 81st birthday. She seems to be getting along reasonably well, and making progress against the disabling effects of polymyalgia rheumatica; and of the troublesome side-effects of the prednisone which is used to suppress the inflammatory response. She is on the Humulin type of insulin, which she injects into her abdominal wall without difficulty. She also has a glucometer with which she tests her blood sugar. Naturally, she is a little frustrated and perplexed by all of these things. The pain, the disability, the disease concepts with which she must wrestle and somehow translate into aliquots of exercise, calories of food types and units of insulin. Perhaps PP shall yet be able to impart to her some of his capacity to find wonder and satisfaction in the intricacy of all those little details. She doesn't like pain though, nor disability - insofar as I can tell - and she has a lot to say about that; hoping, perhaps, that we might just happen to know where 'the healing fountain' or 'river of youth' might be.

Mother, D., PP, spouse and I ate out at the waterfront. Then, the spouse and I stayed the night with mom at C.d.A., and departed for home about 4;00 p.m. the next day. While there we went through some of the old family pictures and I brought some back with me - from which I made some Photostatic copy enlargements. I have enclosed some for you.

I had intended for you to keep those books I sent you, including the one by Muller; for I buy these up inexpensively in order to be able to give them out to those I find who may be interested in them. And there is always the vague hope that you might put them down somewhere, where your youngsters might perchance see and be tempted to read them.

I was most pleased to receive from you, copies of those letters you had gotten from dad. Of course, you are right about the business of taking sides in those parental disagreements of which we are ill informed and to which we were not party, for it seems prudent to remain impartial. And the other part - about there being fault and guilt on either side - is also correct. Yet, psychologically, it is far more interesting and instructive to see it from both sides - though in a spirit of good will to each. "By ironically qualifying triumphs, and reverently qualifying failures, we may get both a richer appreciation of the poetry and drama of history, and a clearer understanding of the facts. We hope to be at once more humane and more realistic; more generous in our sympathies and more sober in our judgments". The mortal condition is not, after all, an easy lot to have to bear, for either parent; neither is it for ourselves. Understood in that light, I don't think that they themselves would object to our learning from their experience, even that which they themselves might not have perceived. Reading through those letters of dad but once, I was impressed that he had acquired a system of values based so firmly on land and family unity. Values perhaps akin to those of the French Canadian farm family of his ancestors. Those values, and that style of life perhaps not much different than that of the Russian-German farm family as it existed in south Russia at the turn of the century; and as it existed on the Great Plains states and provinces, just before he was born, and at the time and in the area where he lived out most all of his life. No wonder that he felt more or less comfortable living and working in the presence of all those German people of those small towns in North Dakota. One might suppose, in fact, that in the early years of his career, he had - in a sense - transcended his any tribal antipathies, while yet remaining true to its ideals. That, much in the same way as a country lad goes off to become a priest or a physician, then returns to his own people with a sort of higher understanding; to observe and serve these same people. For though his being French among a German people, yet his personal affability overcame those linguistic and nationalistic prejudices. He was even almost at the point of transcending beyond the narrowness of religious variations. All of the up-and-coming ideas and young men of the rural ND community came regularly through the barber shop. But even apart from that, barbering was a respectable and profitable trade to those who had just the right touch and were able to communicate with the people they served. The great depression, and the safety razor dealt an almost fatal blow to barbering as an elite business - just as medicine is about to be sheared of a great deal of its elite aspect.

Like yourself, I too was surprised and interested by dad's comments concerning the Germans and George Boepple - our grandfather. It is probably the closest thing we shall ever have to a character analysis from an eye-witness source. I had already recently come to the conclusion that

George Boepple was more-or-less a remarkable person, as to energy, determination, ambition, and achievement. Then came your letter with at least some evidence that tends to further substantiate that impression. I enclose to you a copy of my letter to mom in which I make mention of this to her. In retrospect of course, that is obvious - in comparing grandfather to his people and his times. I remember him as an alert and genial old man, but I don't recall ever having had a conversation with him. Of course, he died when I was only 20 ears of age - before I had ever had a conversation with anybody. Partly because of his unusually small stature, I envision him in his younger days as being somewhat like AG Brasseur, the son of your brother, EVH. Vital, virtuous, idealistic, self-disciplined, musically accomplished and determined to meet the world on its own terms. I don't believe that George Boepple was ever a farmer, nor raised upon a farm. I rather suspect that his father, Christoph, was a village merchant or artisan by the time he arrived in Mannsburg. Probably involved in the grain business, as was grandfather. Farming was not perhaps an essentially better life, nor more prosperous or certain than that of commerce. And the mental lives of farmers had most characteristically been a bit narrow. The Russian-German farmers who immigrated to this country were very similar in their customs and rural preferences to the French-Canadians described in the recent article that you sent me. They were not quite as closely tied to their church, however. The habit of periodically protesting against religion was already theirs when they left Wurttemberg, in 1817. To be a Protestant preacher in the German colonies of south Russia was not an especially rewarding occupation. Though the farmers there became for a while generally prosperous, their preachers were generally not well paid, well listened to, nor idolized. These German colonists had schools too, which were likewise not well attended. They were good farmers and knew how to care for livestock, but one is left with the impression that they had a sort of general aversion to school learning. That attitude among them still prevails to this day. That it is genetic, seems not likely. But culturally, it was deeply ingrained in their life-style; and their clannishness was further reinforced upon them by the hostility of Russian Nationalism when they sojourned near the waters of the Black Sea, especially in the last half of the 19th Century.

Of all of those 300,000 Russian-born-Germans who immigrated to the USA, precious few of those of the first generation ever took the time and effort to study or read anything at all. They preferred to remain in their small communities, and to continue all of their old customs, and to retain their own language. Certainly, that would be an understandable tendency, but realistically, they needs must also assimilate into the new and evolving American frontier. Your mother was somewhat a radical, in marrying outside of the German community. A radical predisposition that appears to have been imparted to her by her father – George Beopple. Few, other than George Boepple (of the first generation immigrants) ever studied or read to improve themselves, or took the trouble to become proficient in the new language. George Boepple was eccentric enough as to move on from his grain-man occupation to qualify as an educator at fifty plus years of age. Few rural families had members that accomplished such a thing as that, even in the second generation.

As for what I heard previously concerning Grandfather Boepple – that he loved to watch western movies; and that he was wont to became so caught up in the action as to hoot and holler there in the theatre – it may be true, but it may be that he was only 'puttin the folks on' a little. In any case, it wasn't that aspect of his character that most accurately defines to us the penetrating influence of his genius and determination; nor the unique and personal view of life which he owned. One wonders, in fact, if George Boepple did not have some influence on the adult outlook and character of Joe Brasseur, despite Joe Brasseur's letter which implies that he merely endured George Boepple's efforts. This evangelical zeal and passion for influencing friends and family, by the constant bombardment with letters, quotations, recitations, readings; and the conveyance of operational concepts, ideas, ideals, and a calling into question this and that. I discovered a trace of that within myself some fifteen years ago. And I have often wondered where it had come from, and why it should afflict me. Again, I suspect, a trait transmitted culturally, through example within a family. Perhaps it might be more accurately expressed by putting it another way. There are a number of passions to which mankind is subject. Among these are lust, hate, greed, power etc. Each can be nurtured and cultivated into a thing of gigantic and grotesque proportions, such as to totally possess and destroy its owner, or consume his life in a frenzy of monomania. Each, on the other hand, with a balance of its potential to drive and to satisfy, might conceivably be integrated so as to broaden one's grasp of reality and to live a more nearly fulfilled life. And by the example and teachings and influence of that life, to encourage others to do likewise. A sort of physical transcendence - as described - but one that does not preclude a sort of spiritual component; and a goal. Curiosity and the will to know are among those passions to which man is subject. Some few have consumed their lives in that passion, as a sort of monomania - though many seem not much troubled by any excess of curiosity. Curiosity is perhaps the most useful of passions, when pursued in moderation, for it is the potential cure for ignorance.

Though I would congratulate George Boepple for exercising his passion for knowing, truth, and wisdom, I would not wish to imply that it was absent or deficient in GF Xavier Brasseur. For he led an active and enterprising life, which suggests that thought and ideas were not strangers to his gray matter, and that he was able to couple his thought to productive activity. There arises the question as to whether the Germans or the French have the more strength of character and intellect; but, it is a poor question because, in the first place, no one has ever been able to demonstrate that there is any significant difference among the races of mankind, as to native capacity for the exercise of the power of the mind.

Still, of course, it may be the case that the French farming families that settled into Canada were more heavily drawn from the far western provinces of France, where dwelt a heavier proportion of those with Celtic ancestors. But human nature, being what it is, we can be sure that there were no residual islands of pure Celts, beyond the first few generations after they were depopulated by epidemic disease and over-run by German invaders - the Burgundians and the Franks. It is the case that culturally and scholastically, France developed earlier than did Germany, but, what of that? For the peoples of Germany have certainly made their intellectual contributions. As to this willingness to learn, affability to new ideas, and propensity to take pleasure from wrestling with ideas and concepts: the appearance, development, and perpetration of that in an individual, a family, and a race, seems to me to be an important factor in the transition from the barbaric to the civilized state of existence. Pascal put it nicely, "Thought makes the whole dignity of man; and the endeavor to think well is the basic morality". I don't believe that one can accurately pinpoint the time in my own life when that passion began to work upon me. As you see, I can not accurately locate it in the family either, nor in the Franco-German Race, nor in mankind as a whole. It seems to be a slow and insidious thing, somehow expedited by adequate example, perhaps - and by habits perpetrated within the mini-culture of family-life or friendships. In-so-far as we know, all peoples seem to have the genetic capacity to be outstanding in their intellectual achievement. The crucial element in the case of each would seem to be that of a culturally and commonly transmitted tradition and expectation. One that is handed down from one generation, to the next. Obviously, even then, the social and economic circumstances must be permissive; and a resource of knowledge, available to those who have such inclination and tradition. In Western Europe, that resource for open-minded scholasticism dried up and all but ceased to exist for many centuries - a big factor in the nearly impenetrable darkness of the 'dark ages'.

Julian "The Apostate" was emperor 360-364 AD, - the last of but few scholarly rulers of the western portion of the empire. The church thereafter severely constricted and controlled open-mindedness in all fields of endeavor. Ancius Boetheus (480-524), was a private scholar and a citizen of Rome. His translations of what we now consider as "the classical Greek manuscripts" preserved to us the Greek wisdom which was finally resurrected to us again in the renaissance. As a non-Christian advisor to King Theodoric, he was trapped into admitting that Aryanism seemed a more probable possibility than the Roman and opposing view of Christianity. Such was the influence of the Roman Church already at that time, that Boetheus was cast into prison, and eventually put to death for refusing to change his opinion. Already at that time, books and heretics were being burned to rid the world of ideas which contradicted the tomes of myth which the Roman Church was in the process of generating. The Benedictine monks made themselves official curators of what the church would admit of, as worthy knowledge - under license of the church hierarchy. For six hundred years (550-1150) the Benedictines 'educated' some *95%* of the few learned persons in Europe. The Merovingian kings were reduced to the expedient of using exclusively ecclesiastic men as the functionaries of their administration as no one else could read or write in Latin - the only universal tongue in the realm. In Europe, the non-ecclesiastical stimulus to knowledge and culture first appeared in southern France. In the meanwhile - while Europe was mired in the darkness of religious myth - the followers of Mohammed made way in their religious system for scholarship, religious freedom, and intellectual advancement. The intellectual stimulus proceeded out of Persia, as that conquered culture infiltrated, and then dominated that very religion through which they had been conquered. The intellectual and cultural influences of the Jewish Diaspora also blossomed under that religious toleration.

But let me digress for a moment, to say something more about the Brasseur family. It has been said that Philomena (Brin) Brasseur was from a higher status of family connections than was Xavier. Whoever said so may well have had specific resource to information such as to support that conclusion. If so, it may well have some bearing on the matter of cultural transmission of the learning habit. Though high schools were being established all over the state of North Dakota at the turn of the century, I don't believe that more than, perhaps, 5 or 10% of those eligible to attend ever actually graduated at that time. And of those that did, only a small proportion went on to college. But now, suddenly, the younger part of the Brasseur family - from Leah on down (except for Mary Ann) seem to have been under some sort of pressure and influence to obtain a high school education. And then to attend college also. Why? Perhaps the Catholic priests encouraged it among the children of their more well-to-do parishioners, seeing that some Catholic influence among the teachers of the newly organizing school systems would be some benefit to the church. Or, perhaps, it was a man's way of expressing that he had 'arrived' - economically - and that he too had some transcending cultural objectives that tickled his fancy. And by that time - say 1912 - Xavier would have been fifty years of age, and his financial circumstances fairly comfortable - such, at least, is my understanding. Yet, not a single line was penned by him, nor quoted of him, such as to give us any definite clue as to his intellectual interests. Though our father escaped the education which was intended for him, yet Leah, Louis and Herman all went on even into college. About Anthony, mother says he only went to a 'barber college'. I wouldn't conceive of that as being a course of more than a few months in length. Leah may even have an old trunk or suitcase full of old letters, photos, records, documents, and clippings that would answer many of those question and more.

I happened upon a section in a book, *The Medieval World* by Friedrick Hear - the chapter, "Courtly Love and Courtly Literature". It describes the secular awakening in southern France, in the twelfth century AD. Here, round about the area or Poitiers, was the beginning and development of the customs, habits, ideals, and patterns of life that led to the romantic and courtly ideals that were soon to characterize courts of the kings and princes of all Europe. Its influence continues to the present time, and even into our very own lives. Here, Queen Eleanor and her gang of lovely ladies developed and practiced the art of romantic titillation and amore. Here, they worked out the rules of a Code of Love - by trial and error, undoubtedly; but it was considered and codified on a rational and intellectual basis too. Here was developed a romantic literature and the romantic ballad. And it came to pass, that in late June of every year, the young and wealthy princesses from all of southern France would gather here. The princes too, of course, made their annual appearance. Here they would display their strength and skill at the games of war, while the eligible young ladies would "oooo" and "ahh" appropriately from the stands. Here a maiden could learn to sedately catch the eye or an eligible young swain, and learn how then to entice him in graceful steps to glide through a hoop - perhaps even through the eye of a needle, if she were skillful and clever enough. And in the end, she might even land him for her very own, and properly disciplined to trot gracefully, and to rein dependably to the left or right, with but the gentlest pressure upon his neck. And the young knight of depressed economic circumstances, might find and win here, a lovely princess fortuitously endowed with estate such as to make her a prize from any point of view. As for the social hurdles he must pass en route to the prize, there was certain to be titillation and gamesmanship enough to make it interesting. "The essence of love, as taught at Poitiers, was not the indulgence of uncontrollable passion, but the molding of a man's passion by a man's lady."

Therein is the connection between France and amore, of which we are all vaguely aware. I was especially interested in that history, because I am aware that the cult of romantic love has strongly influenced me from the early years of my life. I dare say that the western movie is very heavily laced with that same theme. I was again reminded in this of Heinrich Schliemann, who as a mere lad was outcast into the world and left to his own devices. This concept of romantic love obviously and powerfully affected his life, too. Shortly before finding himself alone in this cruel world he had - from afar - 'fallen in love' with a girl of about his own age - eight or nine years of age, say. He would catch sight of her occasionally, and she would return the visual favor. She would occasionally come into the store, where he worked long hard hours through difficult years. Their occasional exchange of glances was enough to suggest a hint of promise to romantic connection that might ultimately bring them together. He carried within always, the image and ideal of this maiden. It inspired him through the drudgery or his days, and on to the additional effort of self-discipline into self-education. He eventually became a linguist, a scholar, and a businessman. Having acquired his first million dollars, he returned to his homeland, in search of this girl. This man you will recall, is best known as an archeologist, and for his finding of the lost city of Troy. You can see how the story demonstrates that molding of a passion into a driving force and motivation in the private life of a man. One who has not personally experienced this sort of thing might easily doubt its validity. And I have no way of knowing how common this sort of thing is, to the experience of men in our society. I am tempted to believe, however, that it is very common indeed. If so, here then we have another passion - and in no way especially diminished as a source of pleasure - and turned into a powerful civilizing motive.

Now, concerning the article which you sent me, by Judd Dougherty - Re: Marx, Dewey etc. - let me say that I was flabbergasted. I have both Marx and Dewey upon my book shelves, but I haven't yet gotten around to reading them. I doubt though that either is apt to be more lucid in his own writings, than is Dougherty, in giving us his thumbnail sketch of each. Each appears to have contributed some few key points in a process that seems to be slowly evolving toward a rational and philosophic sort of religion. But how are we to explain the unlikely appearance of an article such as this one? This man is obviously writing on behalf of the Catholic Church. In fact, as the Dean of Philosophy in a Catholic university I should think that he has risked his job; and that, perhaps, his claim to sanity may be contested. Perhaps - confined for life to an ivory tower - he has lost his pragmatic perspective imagining finally, some such simplicity as, "only truths and Truth matter, after all". Or, perhaps he sees that all the clergy themselves do finally acknowledge these things - at least to themselves. What shall be the outcome to Dougherty of having written such an essay? But, perhaps Dougherty has died - and left the article to be published upon that occasion. Surely, that is the answer?

Wm. James and Dewey are closely linked. I have enclosed to you an essay concerning my thoughts upon an essay that was written by Joseph Wood Krutch. It deals with Wm. James' pragmatism - and so I will say no more about that here. This article by Dougherty now touches down in perfect sequence behind my own essay, and upon the very subject with which I was destined next to wrestle. For you to have just now put it into my hands has spared me a heavy task that might easily have taken me a year or more of effort and time - to wrangle from the original writings of Dewey, on my own. What Dewey says - about the churches having distorted moral faith, into a speculative faith in the hereafter - fits closely with my own personal impression. And though stated well, needs yet to be stated a little clearer, perhaps. I haven't yet figured out how, though. I agree too, as Dewey says, that it must finally be admitted - that "there is but one method for ascertaining fact and truth; it is that conveyed by the word 'scientific' in its most general and generous sense."

My own religious inclinations and musings have led me closer to a familial type of piety; one that acknowledges the spiritual link of generation to generation. It includes the concepts of obligation, duty, honor, reciprocity, error, pardon, and primacy of truth and Truth. It includes the use of symbolism, ceremony, commemoration, celebration and festive occasion. It does not exclude the possibility of there being a single Deity within the universe - or within ourselves. It gives primacy to the family, which earns its own blessing in the production of offspring; and in proportion as its members learn to cherish, love, honor, and respect one another. The familial relationship between a man and his spouse does not require the ratification of the state. Nor ought we to encourage that to become a fixed rule by custom or law: for the natural perversities of the state will then do their utmost to make of it a privilege, rather than a right. Though the spiritual principle of that religion must of necessity, operate upon the products of genetic reality, (since it cannot operate upon hypothetical beings) its cultural-spiritual aspect is its most important link, or connection between individuals. That same cultural-spiritual bond is also extensible to one's extended family, adopted family, family of friends, residents of one's neighborhood and community, mankind in general, all creatures, all forms of life, etc … Such bonds are susceptible to strain and rupture - and to renewal. Because of the reality of the limitation of our physical extensibility, our time, and our energy of life; therefore, in general, our interactions and physical ministrations are centered upon those near at hand. ("The ways of shining heaven are far / Turn thou, ah turn / To things yet near / Turn to thy earthly home oh friend / And try to do thy duty here.") For the same reason, and because the bonds of kinship are not infrequently replaced by some animosities; therefore 'The Golden Rule' is not applicable between one's self and all of mankind. The Golden Rule can however be made more useful by combining it with 'The Silver Rule' and the 'Iron Rule'. Certainly good-will between men is an ideal to strive for, in place of animosity. For, as Dewey puts it. "The things in civilization that we most prize are not of ourselves. They exist by the grace of the doings and sufferings of the continuous human community, in which we are a link". In addition to plain curiosity, something perhaps of that feeling is what excites my interest in history - and in family history. I have been reading *The Ancient City*, by Fustel de Coulanges (a classic study of the religious and civil institutions of ancient Greece and Rome). It turns out that the ancient religions of these peoples - perhaps of all peoples - were, in fact, a familial religion. The Chinese, of course, we know had strong leanings toward such a familial piety. As communities of unrelated families began to congeal, there developed some general forms and rituals pertaining to the evolution of generic community deities - the basis of their common laws, customs, and common cause; and from which was derived their sense of community unity and loyalty. In other words, it appears that their most ancient religion may have been familial, arising spontaneously and gradually out of the familial experience of companionship, love, common sympathies, and human pathos. The pragmatic and unifying force of that religion was only later - and gradually - perceived. Then it was, presumably, that religious forms, beliefs, and practices were designed and manipulated intentionally - to subdue the individual will of the many, and utilize the consent, will, and energy of the masses of men into useful public purposes, voting - with their arms - against the will of all of the hostile forces of the world - both man's and nature's. There is a poem which I have on my list of 'things I wish to submit to memory'. Few, in this country, get through the requirements of high school English without coming across it - *"The Jabberwok"*. Does it say something; or does it not? And there is a short, one-page article, written in the form of a political speech - filled with patriotic eloquence. As one reads it or has it read to him, it does tend to pump his veins full of patriotic fervor; yet, on analysis, it actually fails to make even a single complete statement. I wish I had kept a copy of it - for reference. Anyhow, I thought of these two items as I read the essay on education by Albert Szent-Gyorgyi that you recently sent; and the copy by C.S. Lewis. Albert S-G is undoubtedly correct in what he says about education; and the mind not being a vessel of infinite capacity. And he does (or would, I think) acknowledge that any and every education requires that strength of memory. Needs must be stimulated by some sort of memory exercise. For one needs the facility of memory; and one must have some not insignificant minimum recollection of facts in order to have access (via memory) to new information and old information. Too, just as a stomach or a bladder can increase its capacity by physiological necessity; so also with memory. So it is a question then, of what to put into to the memory banks, how to accomplish that effectively, and to what purpose. Merlin was attempting to badger Hot Spur, telling him menacingly, "I can summon the very devils from Hades". Says Hot

Spur, "So can I. So can any man. But when we so summon them, will they answer?!" That is what we needs must consider. Will it answer - to useful, timely, or worthwhile purpose? That judgment, preferably, before we put the information into memory.

Another obvious question whose answer is often far from obvious. What, if anything, is being said in an allegory, a parable, a sentence, a paragraph ...? The question is particularly relevant concerning the ubiquitous allegory and allegorical parable. Is there a culture - anywhere - that has neglected to use allegories and parables in its archives of wisdom, in its rhetoric, in its political discussions, or even in its routine communications of every day life? It must be rare. I bring the question up, because it pertains to what I have to say concerning C.S. Lewis. I do believe that his (non-science fiction) writings are fairly laden with allegories and allegorical parables. As we discussed on previous occasions, both of these devices have a strong tendency to be as ambiguous as heaven. Many such, especially those connected with religious philosophy, are generally considered to be a great deal less ambiguous than they actually are, when critically analyzed. When read or recited to an audience of the faithful, all nod knowingly in approval, not only of their familiarity with the saying or story and its enigmatic moral or meaning; but also, at the spirit of unanimity which they share, as to the 'true interpretation' of its meaning. It seems odd in the history of Christianity the disciples of the original twelve seem to have been unable to grasp the meanings of the parables and allegories of J.C. As a teaching device, the instructor (in his advance wisdom) can often demonstrate some complex ideas or relationships by creating allegories based upon parallels between the known experience of his students; and the higher experience and knowledge which he wishes to illustrate. But the parallels are not exact, and some are a great deal more ambiguous than others. And when simple allegories lengthen into allegorical parables and stories, their superficial simplicity can make them terribly misleading. At their superficial levels they flow easily, account of their drawing, as they do, from common experience. Upon hearing the allegory, one tends to get a feeling of exhilaration, as though marching in seven-league boots. The feeling, that is, of traversing immense distance with each and every step; seeming as though to comprehend large bites of wisdom. Unfortunately, that feeling is easily delusional. For if one is truly probing for the deeper meanings and implications, then one is required to examine and critically analyze each allegory and parable in detail. Therein lays the difficulty with the allegorical parables through which C.S. Lewis is so wont to communicate. A parable can be rebutted by a counter-parable; just as an argument ought reasonably be answered by counter-argument.

I have read several of his books - some fifteen or twenty years ago (the non-science fiction ones). C.L.S. has a wide reputation as a Christian Apologist; and ever since my last years in high school, the 'zealots' of the faith have been pushing one or another of his books upon me - and to one another. One can hardly escape having to read at least one or more of them - so that one can assure the nice folks that, yes, you have already read him. His books are acclaimed as 'widely read'. Perhaps that is true. It seems to me more certain however, only that there are a great many of them sold. But, I don't need to explain that to you ... RL recently also sent me some copy of a few chapters of a book by C.S.L. In good faith, I read them critically; just as I would like to believe that he too, reads the copy that I send to him. Even on just a quick read through, I find a lot of problems about the things C.S.L. says. I enclose to you some pages of that copy which I have marked and scored by way of analysis. My thought is that RL may be inclined to talk with me about it some time, if interested in my reaction to it. But I didn't write him any comments about the material, since I prefer he focus his time and energy upon his class work. I read the C.S.L. copy that you sent, too.

There are other problems with C.S.L., in addition to the allegories. He himself is a well-read and literate man. His readers, however, are not necessarily well read. I might hazard to guess that his following is somewhat comparable to that of Garner Ted Armstrong. They tend to see him as their intellectual Goliath. He continuously draws forth his straw-men and his backdrop paintings of concepts and ideas - all, presumably, drawn from his vast background of literary acquaintance. Each, in turn, he summarily demolishes with a few neat thrusts from his well-inked lance. Like a barrister, he has his own peculiar line of interrogation, designed to bring forth only such information as he prefers to deal with - but at the same time, intended to not allow his various defendants the opportunity to express themselves freely, nor from another perspective. His manner and attitude in each of these tilts is much the same as that of Don Quixote - except that C.L.S. sets himself up as the perpetual victor in each foray; whereas Don Q. was forever repeatedly tossed to the ground. But what of the sources from which he draws his men of straw? There are phrases such as; "the Germans define justice as …"; "the moral reformer says that good means …"; "the reformer pretends to start with a clean slate …", etc. But specifically who are these vague entities - so that we may question them, to determine if they really said or implied, that with which they are credited? Are their notions really so puny as to be inevitably doomed by the mere specter of this self-styled Goliath? He talks of things such as "a subjective by-product of nature". I can't imagine what that might be. He browbeats his reader with phrases they can not begin to comprehend, such as, "it is impossible to derive from premises in the indicative mood, a conclusion in the imperative". Perhaps he is correct on that point. I don't have that keen an interest in grammar to wade through it. In any case, the straw-man he is propping up with that expression, does not have an identity we can check upon. For the faithful among his readers, of course, it is sufficient that C.S.L. has noticed the peril, and was so quick and able to knock it down, as their champion and lord protector. In his role as apologist, C.S.L. implies that ancient beliefs must not change; when what he means, is that the ancient views to which he subscribes must not change. His reason for this notion that the ancient ought not to change is that (says he) change precludes (moral) progress. Says he with great conviction and authority, "one can't hit a moving target". Do all of his applauding readers buzz by such statements as that, without noticing that it really doesn't square with even their own personal and limited experience?

It is my experience over the years, that fundamentalist Bible study groups occasionally take the bold step of doing a 'book study' on one of these books by C.S.L. When they arrive upon the evening of the discussion, few have even read it, let alone examined it critically. They end up underlining the conclusive sentence, following the demolition of each of the various straw-boys. Nor dare one ask about the validity of (C.L.S.) dogma or the veracity of his scholastic pronouncements and conclusions; for that seems sorely to pain the naive and innocent believers. Comes then the ominous silence, as in the poem, 'Orphan Anne'--"and you can hear the crickets stop". And then one feels sorry for having pained the dear innocents with skepticisms - to no effective purpose. Too late (!) though; for the train is now in motion, and the sequence has already built to some inevitable climax. For the social expectation is now, that they must ask the very question that they wish not to ask, "What do you mean by that?" One's response needs must then clarify. They still don't follow you. Further simplification progresses to blunt and fundamental issues. Despite the psychological chill, all seem to be flushed and warm. The gals head for the kitchen, to ready the pie and coffee. The fellows open some windows. Such is the background of my experience with C.S.L.

I defy you to read a single exposition of C.L.S., from among his Christian apologetics, which do not have nearly all of these little problems - and more, that we have not yet discovered. But, of course, you already know that; and you are just fishing for some sort of reaction from me such as to assure you that I still have at least two Betz cells functioning. By way of post script I might add that the C.S. Lewis's writings have been around quite a few years; and despite being "widely read"; yet I am unaware of anything he has written, which is ever considered for study and discussion in any Humanities or Literature Courses. And so the little anecdote about the fellow seeking a book by C.L.S. in a non-religious bookstore; and having to be directed finally to a Bible Bookstore. That probably tells us something reasonably valid about the types of people to whom the writings of C.S.L. appeal - and why. But I am glad that you and RL saw fit to bring him to my attention again, for in this world of fundamentalists there is always someone tossing out his name to me. And it was time for me to take another reading, in order to analyze the rationality of my previously vague dispassion for his writings.

Concerning Haley's Comet, I enclose a couple pages from my *Astronomy* journal, which speaks of its passage in BC 11; last seen Oct. 21 of that year. The apparent regularity of its transit gives us, perhaps, our best clue for rectifying the historical flaws of the dating system. It is obvious that society of the western world has been toying around with the records concerning the order of the years. Falsification of the record - I suppose - it might be called. I don't know why, except that one of the potential explanations might be, 'accidental'. A question that never previously occurred to me is this: have any other equally primitive societies had the same sort of difficulty - with the players surreptitiously marking the cards?

Concerning the Yakima Herald blurb, pertaining to manic/depressive psychosis as being related to a faulty gene. If the original study and research paper had any validity, certainly the newspaper article seems to have missed that.

Concerning Russia, one must keep in mind that she is not now, nor ever has been, what we might call a 'middle of the road' type culture or nation. Everything, about Russia presses to the extremes, in one sense or another. And her peoples - to paraphrase Handle - are a people of sorrow, and acquainted with grief. As in Alaska, even the brighter days of Russia possess a sort of melancholy dimness. The land itself is harsh and forbidding. Neither Ivan the Terrible, nor any of Russia's subsequent masters has ever dealt kindly with her peoples, though it is said that at least a couple of them had intended to. Since the founding of Moscow, the only people that ever prospered in Russia were the colonists from Germany. They, because they had a special bill of rights, granted them in perpetuity, to induce their arrival; so that they might make the barren steppes agriculturally productive for 'Mother Russia'. Once that was accomplished, of course, the 'perpetual rights' they were promised were revoked. Later, these Germans were then held captive, to labor as slaves. The wealth and material benisons of life in Russia have always accrued to but ten percent, who constitute her elite families. Poverty, sacrifice and misery have accrued to the masses. It might fairly be said that they are not pampered; nor afflicted with materialism. Piety in the masses, in turn, seems somehow enhanced by chronic want and the intermittent brutality they needs must suffer. And while all of that is true on the one hand; it is on the other hand a form of propaganda, too. Life in America has also been brutal. Certainly the natives of America have not been fairly dealt with. Even many of us from among the immigrant stock might not choose to remain, if we could but find some alternative land as prosperous, where the government would tinker less in our private lives and affairs.

Issuing forth from Russia's profound sorrow and misery, comes steadily a flow of profound thinkers, artists, writers, poets ... One wonders how a society so brutal and cold can be the source of these warm streams of humanity. But glaciers, too, of the ever frozen northlands, continue to generate heat from the very weight of that deep ice. And that alone, assures the streams which further erode their glacial icy undersurfaces. I am sure that you have read some philosophy, and I should guess that - like myself - you find it mostly hard to penetrate; and a rather slow task. In general, it is what Uncle Victor Boepple would have designated as, "unbearable". Yet, through the years, one does seem to pick up a little patience for it. It is difficult, of course, because of its abstract nature; but even more - thinks I - from the unsettled state of its semantics. So that to read, for example, Spinoza, it is useful to read first an introduction to his life and times; and pick up some clues as to what he means by this expression, or that. Another writer uses the same expression in a different way etc. Anyhow, I was at first stymied by the throwaways that you sent me pertaining to these Russian philosophers, whose past existence was news to me. I did read through it all; and I had the impression that these summaries were fairly well done. I was especially interested in this Vladmer Soloyov (1853-1900) - mystic and philosopher. If those dates are correct, that means that he died at about forty- seven years of age; yet, in the picture, he looks to be at least age seventy! He appears bent and gnarled, leaning upon a post - or perhaps talking to it. Perhaps he had arthritis - which might help to explain his peculiar choice of life style. His personal acquaintance and friendship with well-known Russian authors undoubtedly had something to do with the force of his own influence - or vice versa. He touches on two ideas, in particular, with which I myself have wrestled. The first, his general concept that all valid fields of study or branches of knowledge must eventually be integrated, if we are to arrive at a balanced and accurate understanding of reality. A-Unitary-Concert-of-That-Which-Is, as it were.

You and I have already gone over that matter between us - so, on to the second idea which he brings forth: <u>that God entered the course</u>

<u>of human history (an assertion), after which there was a qualitative change in humanity.</u>

To begin with, let me make it clear that I certainly do not agree with the way he puts things together - for, in the first place, he has formulated backwards. Secondly, there are elements in his equation, which do not belong there. In order that his statement even be considered, (that is, presented to us in a form that we may analyze) it ought to read the other way around, i.e. "<u>Having noticed a qualitative change in humanity (a supposition), let us consider (jump to the conclusion) this as being the result of the appearance in history of (what he calls)</u> "The Godmanhood". Starting now with the first phrase, concerning the qualitative change in humanity. As I am probing about in search of family history, (Brasseur and Boepple) one of the questions at the back of my mind is this - where is the transition point in our ancestors, from the barbarian condition, into the civilized state (?) of deportment and self-restraint? But, perhaps mere self-restraint is not actually the dividing point. It might instead, for example, be the dawn of intellectual self-discipline that more nearly delineates the onset of the civilized beginnings of the individual; or, perhaps, the day in which he begins first to be aware of his evolving set of values. In point of fact, we need a definition as to what constitutes a civilized state of being. Most probably, we will need to recognize that some people are more civilized than others; that infants are not civilized; children, only a little; and they become so only gradually. That adults may fluctuate, in and out of barbarism from time to time; or that some of the aspects of their being are barbaric, other aspects civilized - or nearly so. Next, then, the same questions and searching's as to what constitutes a civilization, or a civilized nation.

Without knowing the answer to those questions - or even if they are the questions that we should be asking; yet, along with Solovyov, I have the vague impression of 'a qualitative difference' that has gradually become manifest among mankind. However, to date the onset of that incremental progression as subsequent to the "Godmanhood" of J.C. is out of the question. For, obviously, civilizations have existed; and men of some societies have been civilized to some degree from since thousands of years prior to his time. And individuals, as well as nations, are still coming into their first civilized condition; and vacillating in and out of barbaric behavior patterns, etc. Practically - I think - the practice is this; individuals and nations tend to date their 'changed condition' to some dramatic event, or to some ceremonious ritual - coupled (most commonly), in either case, by other changes of their circumstance of life, such as to enhance communion and reciprocity within their group. As for example, the rites of puberty; they are expectantly anticipated, one submits to the ceremony - and thereafter, one enjoys enhanced status, enlarged privileges, and a certain license. Solovyov, I suspect, was overly impressed with the drama of the history of his peoples; and with how the pagan barbarians were baptized in masse, in the Dneiper River at Kiev. But that event was brought about - only - at the command of Prince Vladimir, about 988 AD. Subsequent, in any case, to Vladimir's own - so called - 'conversion' to Christianity from paganism. Vladimir (like putty) in the hands of, and under the influence of a beguiling Byzantine Princess - itself, a dubious process. All of the pagan temples in Kiev were immediately replaced by Christian Churches in the Byzantine Style. The pagan icons were destroyed. A whole new set of rules and moral principles were imposed upon the masses. Long acquainted with the notion of harsh justice, they must now ponder and scratch their heads concerning this new and perplexing business of forgiveness and 'love your enemy'. Almost unnoticed, perhaps, was that it was exclusively applicable only to a new form of guilt into which they must buy, in order to experience its benefit. Thus was Russia launched upon her role of "Holy Russia" - the third Rome.

Just previous to that event, first the barbarian hordes of Bulgars ravaged eastern and central Europe; before themselves, settling down to a 'civilized' and stable agricultural life as a newly converted 'Christian Nation' in Bulgaria, about 960 AD.

They were immediately followed, in the same manner by another similar horde of Tartar Huns, whose chief, 'Vaik' was baptized in mass with his hoard of pagans in the Dneister River 985 AD. Every ignorant soul of this people was likewise converted, we may suppose (?); and this new group immediately became a 'Christian Nation' and settled in Hungary. And so this 'Christianizing' trend of central and Eastern Europe, had slowly progressed, since St. Boniface set out from England in 716 AD, as a missionary to the area. Charlemagne, I guess, was their first politically dramatic spectacle of conversion. Since our history of those times comes to us always through the church, or through one of its organs or agents, we tend to get stuck with interpretations of history that are - or have been - useful to the church's political purposes. The assault of the Roman Church, upon the hearts and minds of mankind has been a rather effective two-pronged approach. On the one hand, the barefoot missionaries of St. Boniface's work at the grass-roots level of humanity. On the other hand, we have the long experience in socio-economics and political methods of Rome and Greece, to which the high Church Hierarchy has fallen heir. Afoot, at all times, before and after 'the fall of the Roman Empire' (476 A.D.), there are hundreds of political intrigues, concerned with the co-mingling of religion, money, power, ideas, trade, economics etc. There weren't computers to keep track of the far-flung goings-on of Europe and the near-cast. None-the-less, it seems a safe bet that the church officials in Rome and in Constantinople were more-or-less regularly updated as to the goings-on of men, tribes, roving bands of nomadic warriors, and the troops of the private armies of hundreds of principalities. Not unlikely, their main preoccupation was this giant 'chess-game', of the making and un-making of rulers and nations: along with the increase of their churchly resources of land, politically useful information, skill of gamesmanship, and booty. Or perhaps like a glass-bead game of pulling the strings of puppets behind the scene.

I enclose to you some random pages from Pyrenne's, *A History of Europe*, to illustrate some of this, by way of example. Warring nomads could be diverted to religiously useful projects, such as the wholesale destruction of large populations labeled as 'heretics', the fall of dynasties not compliant to the holy will, etc. And in the end, the wild barbarians, having acted as agents of the pope - their lust for blood and adventure sated - could be settled down as heroes and converts, in the lands of the peoples thus dispatched. Meanwhile, the hordes of disaffected men from within the Empire (who always pose a potential problem concerning revolution) seem always almost willing, to have their energies and lives expended as heroes in some 'holy cause', in combat against the enemies of the church. Nothing, in these past ages, was more politically powerful than the Roman Religious-Political machine.

And so, one can see how most of Literature and the western world – including Solovyov – might gradually have come to see the progressive civilizing of Europe, as a product of the 'Godmanhood' of J.C. Especially so, if one were to believe in the literal reality of the legend of J.C.; and believe that the Roman Church were primarily concerned with the quest for and preservation of – truths and Truth. Surely, I am not alone in seeing the Roman Church as primarily a political-economic corporation, come to power and sustained in their influence by the manipulation of men, tribes, armies, and nations; through the development and application of empirically derived power plays. They have been enabled in their designs, by access to continuously updated information, material wealth, desperate and greedy rulers susceptible to bribery, intermittent loyalty from widely scattered provincial armies, and the broadcasting of their unified and self-serving concepts and ideas from ten thousand pulpits, by genial saintly barefoot aesthetics whose personal life-style is designed to make them objects of mysterious wonder – among the people of the grass-roots, whom they serve. All of the aforesaid, is not to imply that some culture, civilizing effect, and overall good has not come into the lives of the masses of men in consequence of their connection with the Roman Church – and her various ugly-duckling chicks – for like nearly all religions, these too advocate a goodly number of humanitarian principles. And their regular exhortation to the masses of mankind – which advocates introspection, compassion, and personal peace. That force, to the extent that it remains able to influence lives, is indeed also a civilizing force. Infatuated as religious fanatics have always been, with the 'phantom-of-certitude', they have always been barbaric in other aspects; especially in their often brutal religious in-toleration, and in the studied limits in their capacity or willingness to quest for truths.

It is to be noted that non-Christian peoples and nations also tend to become civilized; and in this, they are in no way inferior, despite their difference from the various Christian Religions. Though I haven't yet dealt with the matter specifically, there is plenty of evidence that tends to suggest, in fact, that it is possible that the civilizing influence has to some degree been retarded and obstructed by the Christian religion through long periods of her history. Ultimately, the secular world became aware of the political-economic nature and devices of the Roman Church. Then, began successfully the counteraction against the church monopoly of ultimate power, through the medium of monarchical nationalism. But, alas, it too became progressively despotic.

But, all governing powers tend to get that way; and we can see it rapidly advancing in that direction even in our own country too, in the past twenty-five or thirty years. Its greatest evil at this time being the machinations of the IRS, which vexes and harasses the citizen continuously. Its main purpose, I expect, is to keep the horses from getting-the-bit-between-their-teeth, as the business of enforcing taxes keeps the common man intimidated even while extorting a continuous steam of cash to those in the seat of power. Those little newspaper blurbs on the IRS, such as you recently sent me, continue to appear from time to time. Perhaps they are intended to prove that the newspaper industry is the guardian of our freedom. So far as I can tell, few pay any attention to these notices. The incidents are merely reported, with no attempt to draw out their drama, or elicit any response from the public at large. Few people earn enough to get into large scrapes with the IRS agents, nor have any possibility of causing the trouble, since the withholding of funds from the paycheck circumvents all of that. Perhaps the average man's general feeling for the 'rich' self-employed, is that they are a different group of people, and are probably deserving of all of their troubles from the IRS. Among the people I have known of, who have had trouble with the IRS, they seem to sense that they are not apt to derive much general sympathy. Nor, do they really seek sympathy - a more or less useless item. Had they any chance of stirring some grass-roots reaction, even of a general nature, then they most would probably be willing to unleash their vexations and contribute some additional energy to the cause the tax-protest cause.

As to the plight of the physicians; only their determined and unified reaction could possibly save their professional income to them now. The mafia does more to forestall tax rebellion, than to expedite the movement. Only a union - and a damn tough one - could loosen the physician from governmental tyranny, at this point.

You wrote a long analysis on investment economics and sent some articles on tax strategy. I read them, but they have no special meaning to me, since I have always been on a subsistence type of income, with never reserve enough for any investment. Whenever some probable nest-egg appeared about to coalesce in my vicinity, it has always been swallowed up, by some one or another necessary business expenditure or family need. That however is not a complaint, for I feel fortunate to have been able to find the resources to meet some of those problems. I still have some various ideas for doing some other things with my life, but none of it requires of me any certainty of financial ease, nor sudden bursts of physical exertion. Rather, it is more of the nature of time consuming and solitary venture, best approached with a quiet and leisurely determination. And on that note, the image of Solovyov returns to my mind. He died a young man of forty-seven; poverty-stricken, as to work experience, family experience, or experience with what is commonly called justice in the courts of the land. It is still possible that I may yet have another twenty or thirty years to gather my ideas into a unity, after the full emergence of fifty years of entanglement with life's troubles, disillusionment's, and dissatisfactions. And so you see, I am still poking about the embers of my soul for clues as to the civilizing or humanizing influences that motivate a man, or drive him into a state of determination to attain or achieve a goal or a proficiency of performance. And those at the same time that arm one with steadfast purpose such as to carry one through the blahs, and icks, and humiliations, and frustrations that are certain to obstruct one's pathway repeatedly - en route to one's personal goals and objectives. It will needs must come down finally, to a set of definitions that will enable us to categorize men into a continuum of degree of civilized attainment; and concomitantly to consider the various aspects of the individual, as to his overall balance of attainment and outlook. Whatever little the status of civilized attainment of the individual, its manifestations are always but a veneer of the primitive 'heavy-bear' within. And a civilized status is dependent upon a reciprocity with other beings. Like paint upon a house, there are always disjunctions through which the primitive can be visualized - and it can be pealed away by accidental crises and specific method.

If you are in no hurry for them, I will hang on to your book, Yvette's notes etc., until I get a chance to get up your way - or you, down to this area.

Your brother
Garner Brasseur

5/13/87

6/29/87

Dear VBB,

I am going to Montana on Wed., July 1st--and won't be back until the 13th or 14th. I have many irons in the fire; and therefore, not time enough right now to write you a proper thoughtful letter. As vacations are dangerous events, it may be that I shan't survive this one. And so I want at least to get you this batch of reprints that I have been accumulating for you. And then there is this letter from Uncle Herman's daughter - Lea - which clears up part of the puzzle of what happened to Uncle Herman. A copy of that letter is enclosed for your records. Also are some copies for you of a couple of death certificates.

Got a letter from EVH about June 8 or 10. He says he runs about four miles per day, and that he has minimal residual numbness and pain. He gardens and studies. And writes - concerning law and the history of law. He 'makes calls' - but I don't know to whom, nor concerning what. The letter has a lot of vague scriptural allusions suggesting that the Jews, perhaps, are the source of much of the world's problems. It may be that some of them, indeed, are rogues, but he hasn't yet sent me any specific information, so as to inform me as to which particular individual Jews are at fault. His method is admittedly more efficient - he implicates them all… with sweeping indictments.

But it is good, and enough for me that he is contentedly pre-occupied, for it spares him from some of his physical pain and suffering.

Your brother
Garner Brasseur

6/29/87

Aug. 15, 1988

Caldwell, Idaho

Dear VBB,

Wife and I; and the children and grandchildren depart Wed. Aug 17th to the Saur family reunion at Broken Arrow Bible Camp, southwest of Livingston. Plan then to be a few days in Billings beginning the 21st, Sunday evening. Always the risk of travel - "as forth we issue, day by day/ death walks companion of our way." Cicero says something to the effect that; a man's body resembles iron, in that to use it, is to wear it out; but that not to do so, is to let it rust into decay.

Now knowing the outcome of the struggle upon the right-of-way, I wanted to be sure to pass on this recently acquired information concerning the Boepples; diagram enclosed. It takes the Boepple lineage back two more generations. I also got some information from Colleen Sieben yesterday - concerning the Brasseurs, but it will take me a few weeks to assimilate that. Colleen is your cousin, Annie (Brasseur) Grimes' youngest child, born in 1936.

Also enclosed is a copy of my recent letter to M.A. All of the references to violence are episodes with which she is acquainted. I believe that a lot of people - especially women - get themselves killed by not being able to control their tongues. And I know that M.A. was a little afraid to walk in some of the sections of town where Yvette seems to walk fearlessly. I want to encourage M.A. to retain some of her fear, for those hot-spots of the city are dangerous - as to probability - though most such episodes of trespass go by without incident. M.A. is also acquainted with the various lines from poems, literature, etc. used in the letter, so that nothing there ought be obscure to her - as to meaning as one might suppose.

And then I used some particular experiences of my own life, to lead her into the thought that all people have episodes of unusual perceptions, and spells of craziness. As in the essay "How Sane is Sane?" (by C.N. Parkinson). And I wanted at the same time - - -
9/3/88 But that trip has now been completed without incident, and I have lost the train of thought that was to have completed the above sentence. And I must get this update, out to you, so that I can get back

to the tangle of my genealogic scraps of notes recently acquired, before they become meaningless and undecipherable to me. And you and I, perhaps, shall get a chance to get together in the mountains of central Idaho - "when the work's all done this fall".

My spouse, M.A., and PM are down in Phoenix to visit EVH's family for a couple of days.

Love (and light)

Your brother,

R. Garner Brasseur

Aug. 15, 1988

February 1990

Caldwell, ID

Dear VBB,

I visited mom, PP, and DFB In January. You were still absent from your home at the time. Nothing exciting happening just now. Trying to overcome the inertia and get back to some writing, reading, and research (genealogy). Had a call from Marcel Brin a few days ago – way up in the northern part of Québec province. Says he will send me some information on the Brin family. He indicates that the family name changed from Brun to Brin, in 1777. Perhaps the information he sends will have more to say about that. On which and other matters, more later.

Me,

RGB

February 1990

24 Oct. 1990

Caldwell, Idaho 93605

Dear VBB,

I had your daughter's copy of Geology notes and your copy of *A Study of History* by Toynbee in the pickup, along with the envelope of assorted articles for your perusal. I intended to leave them with you at the time of our meeting a couple of weeks ago, but my change of plans foiled that scheme. I'll get the other bulkier materials to you when we get together again.

Included in this pack of materials are a couple of articles that have reference to the Hanford contamination, and to the bag-of-worms we call 'nuclear clean-up' – a sweeping of the tschid under the carpet, as it were; and then trying to ignore the reality that it has merely been re-shuffled. Government and private citizens alike, have seemingly retained the ancient practice of, attempting to expiate sin by the lavish expenditure of wealth upon enamel paint and ceremony. The irony of this strange Christian tradition, is that the act would seem to imply that they don't actually believe in the forgiveness of sins. The article by Gould (on the threatened extinction of the Arizona red squirrel) points out that in the long view, the earth can take care of herself; and that our species only has the effect of muddying its own waters for the short period of our existence. It seems to me to be, perhaps, effect enough, that we merely recognize the damage that we have done to ourselves, in the short term; so that we, henceforth, take greater precautions to diminish the contamination of our own environment. It is a thing that we cannot absolutely avoid, for we must eliminate our body wastes, and at least some minimum of industrial tailings; and we must dig at the earth a little - to plant our crop, and to get at the tubers and the mineral wealth. You get the point. The first problem to be resolved is that of assuring that our current and future wastes are, in fact, minimized and contained - far into a distant future. Only then does it make any sense to even consider the possibility of cleaning up of contaminated areas. Adequately concentrated wastes could be secured into the geologically subducting plates at the western edge of the continent, dumped into the maw of an open volcanic crater as in northern Africa, or carried aloft in shuttle cargo - to be ejected into a collision course with the sun. But to cleanse the contaminated geological strata and the ground waters of the earth, would require massive effort at dilution, by pouring water upon the soil and/or pumping rivers of water into the aquifers. Though then, perhaps, diluted; yet the emerging less-toxic solvent and solutes would merely again be concentrated by the flora and fauna of the rivers and oceans that constitute the food-chain. All and all, they are interesting problems; but their ultimate solutions will needs must be heavily tinged with pragmatisms; and the statistically small numbers of induced cancers will be soothed with the cooling poultices of green-backs.

I did send in my forms over to those Hanford area companies; though I don't necessarily have any great hope that I am apt to be summoned forth for interview, nor possible hiring. Especially so, since they haven't actually begun any active decontamination program there at Hanford yet. Still, one never knows just how such a thing is apt to work out. Perhaps if our legislature approves its now long-past-due budget for the current fiscal nonsense, they may get the wheels of these programs a-rollin'; though it may be the case that procrastination would be the best solution - a long procrastination. Of course the subcontracting cliques of companies generally prefer to hire from within their own companies for the filling of positions under the newly won contract work; and from the companies that are their co—conspirators in the cornering of the market for government contracts. Since, however, it is said that they do not have adequately trained personnel for such work as that; therefore, they may be willing to hire some independent outsiders (who also don't know quite how to approach such a bag-of-worms problem) to be readily available as scapegoats; should the mess again, later, become the focus of scathing review at the hands of the news media, 'Responsible professionals', such as you and I could well serve just such a roll as that, providing of course, that an adequate remuneration and some interesting field trips and conversations were in the offing for some reasonable future prospects on the waters of 'golden pond'.

God-knows-what (?) will come of this Iraq confrontation. I expect it might come to a quick end, if Hussein were suddenly to die a <u>natural</u> death; for his people have little to gain whatever the outcome. An internal 'coup' might serve almost as well, perhaps … if it were to come in response to some grass-roots movement of their peoples. Whatever the outcome, it isn't likely that we will ever again see gas selling at anything close to a dollar per gallon. Something more akin to the prices paid in Europe seems more likely to prevail. The volume of auto sales will shift even more toward those that prove to give better gas mileage. That, by no means, an unwholesome trend.

I have enclosed to you a copy of a fine manuscript, of Brasseur genealogy which I recently obtained from Arthur David Brasseur of Penetanguishene, Ontario. It is irreplaceable at the present time. I am hoping that you might still have the copy around in the event that my copy should somehow come to grief from fire or theft. I am adopting his coding system. Between this new manuscript (which covers the F-1 and the F-8 branches) and my own (which covers the F-4 branch), the "F" branch is fairly well begun, though it still needs a lot of fill. But, I have only gotten the very barest beginnings of the "A", "B", "C", "D", "E", and "G" branches of the PM Francois Brasseur/Catherine Pilon and Ursula Pilon family. It begins to appear that the records of most of them may well be found on the Ontario side of the Quebec border - which seems to cut through the Rigaud Settlement. Many, perhaps, are to be found in Montreal, too. Perhaps I shall make another extended trip up into that area this summer, or the next. I expect it to be less troublesome for me than the Quebec trip - since most or all of them are apt to be able to speak English.

As I was composing this letter, I was reconsidering the old questions and the newest information that I have concerning the family of our Great Grandfather, Christoph Boepple, and it became apparent that I would have to reconstruct the chart. I decided to switch the explanation of that, onto a separate and generic form, as I have to send the information out to several of my correspondents. A copy of it is here enclosed to you. It will save me having to rewrite the same thing several times.

Light to you and yours,
Your brother
R. Garner Brasseur

24 Oct. 1990

9 February 1991

Las Vegas, NM

Dear VBB,

I was home for one week – two weeks ago. Then traveled for a week:

- in Billings, saw AL briefly; she looks good!
- In Wolf point, I exchanged information with Cousin Mike Rempfer, and then spent the night at sister Katie's place.
- In Haliday, ND, I met Victor Boepple (son of Reinhold)
- in Dodge, I visited with Clarence Wolf and Elmer Wolf, but missed their sister, Norma.
- in Beulah, I visited with uncle August and aunt Lydia; and with Elmer.
- Spent two days at the genealogy library at NDSU
- visited with some Boepple relatives in Colorado:
  1. Burlington (Arnold Stroebel)
  2. Bethune (Anna Marie Stroebel and her husband, Emil)
- have now worked here in Las Vegas, NM, the past week.
- Have, as of yet, no definite idea how long I shall be here.

Your brother,
Garner

9 February 1991

◄━━◆◆◆━━►

– Addendum Perspective –

[In the intervening and ongoing years (1991-2008) I usually stopped over with VBB and Marg two or three days at a time, a couple of times yearly. Longer, on a few occasions. In 1992 VBB was doing Radiology at the U.S. Public Health Hospital in Gallup, MM - only about 300 miles from my job site. We got together a couple dozen weekends to travel about the state and ponder its geology. And our hours of conversation upon these trips gave us ample opportunity to dialog at length on all manner of philosophical and historical topics. Additionally, through the years, I send them copy of my sometimes lengthy annual summaries, as well as other of my essays for perusal and commentary. And through the years I have received from VBB a considerable number of reprint articles, and sometimes lengthy letters of commentary and discussion - almost none of which is included in this volume.]

RGB

3 February 1993

Las Vegas, NM

(Verse on birthday card to VBB): "You've been buckin' and stompin' all these years, and nothing or nobody has broken you yet". Amazing… amusing… and educational.

Dear VBB,

I got your letter packet. Reading through those materials led me to thinking that this here birthday card is right in keeping with the season – wrangling time. It surely must be the case that all of us itinerant type doctors get caught up into these sorts of political intrigue. Surely not just the Brasseur 'troublemakers'. But, now, you'll get some well deserved 'days-in-the-sun', or upon 'Golden-Pond', in preparation for the next rodeo season.

Perhaps we might put all of our escapades together into a giant tome. We could call it, *Brasseur Traditions*.

Love, brother
R. Garner

3 February 1993

17 February 1994

Las Vegas, NM

Dear VBB,

Late for your birthday of February 11. I bought a new Golden Eagle Card and spent the past 10 days visiting Death Valley (in California) and several other national monuments in Arizona. Also, spent a couple of days in L.V., Nevada to see a couple of their new magnificent casinos. Then stopped at Quartzite, Arizona, to look through the huge collections of gems, rocks, and minerals on display; and bought a few inexpensive nice samples for my own collection.

I am intending to be gone again for two or three weeks beginning mid-March. Would like to attend Elderhostel college programs for retired folks in the province of Québec – but haven't yet heard from them. Alternatively??? – I don't yet know.

I have applied for a Psychiatry three year residency at the UNM, but no word from them yet. Chance of acceptance??... Perhaps, 50/50? If I don't get in, I'll probably get heavily into learning something about computers; or writing ... if some inspiration will settle in upon me. Sent a poem into North American Poetry Contest just after Christmas – no word from them yet.

> Best wishes for your 58th.
> Sincerely, brother,
> R. Garner

17 February 1994

6/1/96

Las Vegas, NM

Dear VBB,

As it was in the beginning; is now; and ever shall be (I suppose) ... trouble seems to prevail. This very earth seems to have come into existence out of chaos and continues unendingly to manifest its ever churning cataclysms of change. We mere mortals are caught up into all of this turmoil. A race of creatures that has originated (amid this turmoil) in total ignorance of the heavenly and earthly processes that continuously threaten our safety, our lives, our well-being, and our few comforts. Slowly, generation-by-generation, some little knowledge and information has accumulated to the human mind; and has been transmitted to subsequent generations of mankind. The accumulating knowledge, information, and wisdom, has not yet progressed nor encompassed the vast proportion of all that is knowable. Knowable, and being potentially useful in averting the dangers of this chaotic world. And yet, some little progress in this direction has come to pass; so that we do avoid some of nature's calamities. Thus, there is reason to hope that man's intelligence and understanding may continue to progress ... so as to enable us ever more - and ever more frequently to elude the natural calamities of this earth and universe.

Slim Odds

Earthquake, deluge, prairie-fire,
Against mere mortal man conspire.
From fate and chance be no appeal,
When mighty wind and wave prevail.

'Twas brute to brute and nail to fang,
On Serengeti's teeming plain.
Though agile youth escape today,
From predator the fate of prey.

Still un-suspect the ranks of men,
By microbe hosts were yearly thinned.
While from the sky and mountains roar,
Fire, ash, and bolts of Thor.

Life stark and brief let each amend,
Eternal pathway to transcend.
And harness skill toward small advance,
In daily life to better chance.

RGB

But still, the brief and controversial history of mankind certainly demonstrates that mankind is as great a danger to itself, as are the natural calamities we would wish to escape. Besides the dangers which confront us, we are troubled with The vague unsteadiness of our truths, rights, wrongs, mores, and legal systems. Yes, besides these, we mere mortals are prone to think, speak, and act in ways that are often decidedly counterproductive to our own best interests. Since we are mere mortals, we needs must try to forgive ourselves of these self-defeating propensities. But there seems little doubt that we also owe it to ourselves and to our kin (and posterity) to rise above our nearsighted 'certitudes-of-belief' which (though comforting to us) are not uncommonly erroneous, and lead us into repetitious error.

I want to thank you, VBB, for all of the sage advice you have so often tendered me. And most especially for all of the time and attention you have given to directing my personal affairs during my recent illness. There is no doubt in my mind but that your interventions and direction of the general course of my medical evaluation and treatment has spelled the difference between life and death as the outcome of that illness. By now, my ashes would surely have been scattered to the winds; whereas in fact, Dr. Ramos tells me that I now have a statistical possibility of 50% - to survive the coming five years. And even "a short time is better than no time your see" (from a ballad by Willie Nelson), since it gives me some hope of finishing up my personal affairs, and an assortment of projects that are dear to my heart.

I seem to be slowly gaining in weight, strength, and exercise tolerance. I can now walk the 1.4 mile perimeter of the state hospital campus … could probably even do it twice if I were to strain my reserve of strength to the limit. I still require a couple of 1½ to 2½ hour naps each day; in addition to a good 8 or 9 hours of sleep at night. When up, I am still beset by a moderate lethargy and inertia - in part related to the only slowly resolving aches and pains in chest and abdomen; and probably in part related to some residual liver deficiency in itself.

In the turmoil of my recent illness I called on both PP and yourself with the intent and hope of getting the ends of my troubled career settled before passing on into the great beyond. My affairs were complex and unsettled due especially to my being in the middle of divorce proceedings.

The looming shortness of my time, along with the progressing delirium of my illness left me unable to be of much assistance to you amid the complexities of those affairs - inadvertently leaving plenty of cause for dispute between the two of you as to how to proceed in the best interests of my 'estate'.

Both you and PP have always been important figures in my life; and both, always supportive and helpful. It troubles me to see that some hostilities have sprung up between the two of you in recent years. It isn't likely that I could do anything to resolve those animosities whose origins are far beyond my poor powers of comprehension. But I do repent at my own recent ambiguous troubles and indirection that has apparently exacerbated some hard feelings between the two of you.

I received your recent pages of manuscript of updated or revised biography; and added them to my copy. Thanks for putting this biographical material together. And I am reminded that I ought soon get back to my own biographical sketch materials - the first draft of which is not yet completed at about a hundred pages.

Meanwhile, time flies; but work accumulates.

Best wishes to you and yours.

Sincerely,

Yer brother,

Garner Brasseur

6/1/96

December 1996

Las Vegas, NM

VBB and M____,

Haven't been in touch with you for several months. Thought you might need a rest from it. I keep track of your movement indirectly via my spies and the grapevine. I am still optimistic (or naïve) enough to believe that my most pressing problems are on the verge of a final settlement. Thanks for your hospitality and assistance.

Sincerely,
R. Garner

December 1996

Feb. 10, 2008

Santa Fe, NM

Dear VBB and M____,

> "Nothing to do but work
> No time to stand beneath the boughs,
> To stare as long as sheep and cows"

> "The nights which once have passed away
> To mingle with the morning ray;
> Return no more; as streams which blend
> With ocean, there, forever end."

On May 11th 2007 I entered into my 75th year. As a youngster I sometimes wondered what it would be like to be an old man. And now I have about forgotten what it was like to be a youngster. I don't recall it being especially easy. Nor is being old. What is this stuff we call time? Perhaps it was invented to keep everything from happening at once, and we mere mortals would not be likely to handle that well. What is this stuff we call space? Perhaps it was invented to keep everything from occurring in the same place, which would also be a confusion and a collision. Einstein supposed that time and space were sort of woven together into a single fabric. There could be no time without space, for time is perhaps only the measurement of the interval required to move from one point to another in space. Without time there could be no space, for there could be no time-consuming movement from ones only point of existence. With neither time nor space, there could be no existence.

Perhaps you were wondering how it is that I go about trying to keep up with what is happening in this world and universe? The constraints of both time and space make that exceedingly difficult. The best that I can do does very little towards even keeping up to speed from my assigned watch-post, let alone giving me access to the other vast quadrants of the universe beside the vastness of the quadrant in which I am standing watch. Never-the-less, I make my time-consuming efforts to observe and comprehend; and then make my puny report back to those who might perchance be interested to hear of it. And this little annual essay is about the best that I can muster. Hello? … Is anybody out there listening? Perhaps not. I continue, never-the-less. And I continue to make my effort to become aware of what others might likewise be reporting back. Through the years I have roamed about the countryside tracking down friends and distant relatives in order to gather what they might have to report. Additionally, I read some magazines such as *Scientific American*, *The Week*, *Discover*, and *Chronicles* … in attempt to stay in tune with current events. And I listen to news commentators such as Rush Limbaugh, and Sean Hannity, since my own personal skepticism of what I hear seems inadequate to the task of ciphering the mass of misinformation with which we are inundated. And on some weekday nights at 11:00 PM, Charley Rose does in-depth interviews into the ideas and thoughts of various politicos, writers, and gurus for our contemplations. I also read some books in my spare time in order to discover what historians and philosophers have had to say on the eternal questions. In truth though, I have done but very little of book reading in the past year or two as I have been preoccupied with a full time job to earn my livelihood and in attempt to prepare for the retirement which the passing of years is apt soon to enforce upon me. And besides the troubles of my family and of our species in this world of crises, I keep finding myself confronted with my own personal problems; and am occasionally called upon to be of assistance to various friends and relatives.

During the past year I have had to wrangle with the manager of the Vision Center where I am employed over a host of issues pertaining to personnel, equipment and supplies, and policies pertaining to our dealing with patients. Though he has been given authority, he does not have the training or experience to enable him to perform up to expectations. Talking to him is rather like talking to a post, as nothing ever comes of it. I am thus forced to get problems settled by going over his head to two or three tiers of personnel above him in the hope of getting action. It requires of me to analyze and study out the issues, and then compose extensive reports to support my views. These reports must be in written form, so as to leave a 'paper trail', if there is to be any hope of action. Otherwise they also have no incentive to respond to merely local situations when they are persons with corporation sized territories and responsibilities. Though they never deign to write me a response, problems are slowly beginning to be resolved.

I get three days off each week in which to contemplate how swiftly that time flies. One must walk an hour of each day, and make the occasional visitation to the homes of the elderly old friends, Dr. Tomlin and Paul and Jackie Lewis.

The local Wall-Mart Vision Center manager has been leaning on me to become a provider to patients covered by vision insurance companies. Compliant to their cryptic rules and agreeable to the seeing of these patients in accordance with a very constrained fee schedule of reimbursement. But I was already staying reasonably busy seeing the many uninsured patients who paid their own way, cash-on-the-barrelhead. So I wanted to stay clear of having to deal with the reduced fees and the squeeze of insurance middlemen. I was then informed that the vision center had now made it a requirement for all of their associated eye care providers to become insurance providers. I suspected this may have been just a bluff, so I told them that if this requirement was a non-negotiable reality, that they could consider me as being retired as of the end of February 2008. I was told a couple of weeks ago that my resignation has been accepted. Well, by then I will have worked about the 2½ additional years more than I had projected, so I wasn't terribly put out by this turn of events. Nevertheless, I was then again to be confronted with the problem of what it was that I was going to do to occupy my spare time. After all, an old geezer has to find something to do to maintain his delusion that he is yet of some use or value in this old world. In anticipation of this eventuality, I began a few months ago to try my hand at the writing of novel - based, of course, on my own blundering experiences of life. That project ought to keep me busy for a couple of years.

The reality, of course, is that Wall-Mart has not actually yet found anyone to replace me, though I am told that they have had a couple inquiries in their quest for a replacement. And so I have agreed to continue to work on a temporary day-by-day basis; as I did for the first half year before they took me on as a full time employee. I actually get paid at a bit better rate in consequence. In point of fact, there are a couple other Wal-Mart stores in the area where they would like for someone to work at least a day or two a week until they can find someone to man them as contractual associates. Instead of working - as now - for 4 days a week, I may end up working 5 or possibly even 6 days a week. Still, 3 days a week here in the Santa Fe store, and the other days in either Bernallio or one of the Albuquerque stores. Whether that is apt to go on for a mere month or two; on continue for up to a year or more is quite unknown. For a time, at least, I can continue to put away a few greenbacks - of declining value - into the barns of posterity. The work might become a little boring, but it isn't as though it were grueling physical labor.

Meanwhile, we have recently refinanced our house at 4.62 percent for a fifteen year term, and our monthly payments are quite reduced, so that it appears we can continue to stay afloat even without the actual necessity of any work income. Who would have thought that I would ever end up into a state of affairs so congenial to a state of retirement?

Spring will soon be upon us, and it is my impression that you might soon be figuring on a seasonal migration to Florida. We look forward to the possibility of your visit.

Birthday greetings and best wishes to you both.

Yours truly,

R. Garner Brasseur

Feb. 10, 2008

July 2009

Santa Fe, NM

Hey VBB, it's me, yer brother, Garner.

I reviewed that short film on "We the people…", and then forwarded it about to a few of my acquaintances. And then a few nights ago I had a now disremembered nightmare about how we are being spent into oblivion and how the house of reps has turned into a circus. And on the Charlie Rose show I heard how this Nancy P. rammed through this 'cap-n-trade' bill. How - knowing they had complete control for more than enough votes to pass the thing - they had the audacity to parcel out to their 'most vulnerable' democrats an 'authorization' to vote against the measure, so that the voters would be less likely then to vote the rascals out.

Sort of mind boggling to me - politics within politics, with utter disregard for what is best in the interests of our sovereign nation. You would think that in my retirement I might be able blissfully to forgetfully or ignore all of this rash and impulsive abuse of politicians and the political system.

But I gather now that they passed this monstrosity of a bill more or less to get themselves off the hook, and then home for their summer vacation. It is said that they well know that it has little chance of even being taken up by the senate? But who **knows** any such thing as that? In any case, it is entirely irresponsible, as well as a potential disaster.

And we hear too of the strife in Iran, with protestors being massacred and imprisoned. And heads soon to roll. It would seem to me to be a prudent thing to openly sympathize with Iranian protestations. Our own electorate may well soon be obliged into open protestations, and in need of sympathetic acknowledgment from Iranians - concerning of high handed treatment being dispensed to American citizens from our own 'rulers'.

I plan to attend the 'All 50's Class Reunion' in Miles City on

September 10th, 11th, and 12th. Perhaps you might be interested in taking it in with me? There will be people of your class involved also. The Fandrich boy and the Minkoffs for example have inquired of me concerning you.

Live well, do good work, and stay in touch.

Brother, Garner

July 2009

July 2010
Santa Fe, NM

Dear VBB,

Well, yes. The UND alumni thanked me for contributing the few brief lines of my progress though life; and they inquired whether I was yet going to send them an electronic e-mail copy of a personal photograph. But my want of facility with these modern gadgets and marvels disbars me from accommodating to anything so intricate as that. If I can find out about any <u>one</u> such day as our med-school classmates might gather, I would then make an effort to attend <u>that</u>. Not that I was much acquainted with any of them. So far as I know, they were generally all good and honest people, but we were all then competitively preoccupied with scholastic matters. It may be that through the years they and I may have stumbled on some matters of mutual interest that may lessen our residual estrangements from one another. And curiosity continues to be a driving force.

Yes, I got the books you sent. I first went through *The Road*, because the print was large and the pages were sparse; and I was in a lazy mood, not wanting to overtax my lethargic synapses. Here is a strange tale to fill some empty pages. What is written is the ending of a story that has no body or beginning (even wanting a conclusion). It reminded me that some twenty or thirty years ago the thought had crossed my mind; that a person might become rich - if only one could figure some way to sell bottled tap-water to the 'huddled masses, yearning to be free'. I ought to have acted on the impulse, but I had not then yet realized what dolts we mere mortals be.

I haven't yet finished the book on the times and tales of *The Badlands* - so all familiar to the experiences of our personal youth's.

As for the Mark Twain collection in the thick pocketbook, I have over the years already read a great deal of what he has written. What an amazing original was Mark Twain. What a remarkable repertoire he owns of adjectives and synonyms; and what a prolific crafter of adjective phrases. I paged through the book and found myself somewhere the middle of *The Mysterious Stranger*. Of course, after reading to its end, I was obliged to finish it from the beginning. What kid would ever abandon a bowl of ice cream still half uneaten?

And last evening after work I found myself in Twain's story of *A Campaign That Failed*. But I couldn't make much headway through it. It was so humanly funny I managed only a few pages. My concentration was repeatedly interrupted into long pauses by my efforts to stifle my spasms of laughter and the rivers of tears that clouded my vision. Perhaps my progress through that tale had best wait until I find myself in some fit of depression.

RGB

July 2010

18 April 2011

Santa Fe, NM

Dear VBB,

It has now been just over forty years that I have been at the keeping of a continuous daily log. It began in about 1969 or 1970 while we lived in Ashland, Oregon. I believe it had its beginnings largely in part due to an intention that originated gradually within me in consequence of my coming across a series of daily log books of such daily entries that was kept by our brother, EVH, during the two years he spent in the Navy. Along with the other small caches of personal possessions acquired by myself and my brothers through our early adult lives, (these caches being mostly of the nature of memorabilia) had a tendency to lodge and accumulate in the basement of our older sister, ALBK, in Miles City, Montana. The residence of she and HK was the closest thing we had to a permanent home and storage place for these accumulations, as we used their home as a sort of refuge and asylum as we came and went about from season to season in our eternal wanderings between our temporary spells of gainful occupation interspersed with semesters of formal college and postgraduate education through those turbulent and sometimes desperate years of uncertainty. My journals chronicle the major events of my day-by-day existence through the months and years. Only rarely has the habit of a daily entry been interrupted through all these years. And in the past twenty years, I have taken to turning out an annual summary of the ideas, activities, and thoughts that have preoccupied me each of those years.

During a few periods of a couple days each year, when I sheltered for brief spells there at my sister's home, I was wont at times to go through the various accumulations of memorabilia that belonged to my four brothers and myself. The sum total of those accumulations amounted perhaps to no more that what might fill the cab of my pickup truck. It was intermingled and scattered in small footlockers, a couple tattered old suitcases, and a few cardboard boxes. A few family photographs and old letters were also there to be found for one's perusal. It was always interesting to scavenge through and ruminate on these little treasures.

Having finished medical school and entered into the practice of medicine during the six or seven years prior to the time we settled in Ashland, I, as a rustic lad of humble origins had been encountering new experiences and situations in a professional career. With no background of family experience on which to ground this business of having become a professional, and in continuously encountering new cultures as we spent a few years in central America, there was a great deal of ever evolving experience for me to wrap my head around. Experiences so novel to me - and curious to my imagination - that I began upon occasion to write some of these things onto paper for my later reconsideration and contemplation. And all of this was now coagulating together with my self-acknowledged intent to investigate and reconsider the truth and realities of what had previously come to be (by default) my fundamental philosophy of the nature of reality and eternal truth.

Thus it was that I at last found the necessity, time, and opportunity to launch out upon this study of the nature of reality and historical truth and began to realign my views according to a new and more objective standard, rather than to continue blindly upon the hand-me-down authoritative and schizophrenic notions which had begun to trouble me in recent years. One might say that these were the two alternatives: Science (and a scientific method); versus authoritative religion (based upon the contradictory assertions of ancient times and manufactured history). There is a large disparity between History - and history. The former, being often manufactured from the later, and fitted up with a great many suppositions and self-serving embellishments of simple error, deceit, and fraud. To what purpose, such deceit and fraud?

And at this time in my personal history, I began to acquire and digest the portable and inexpensive paper-back books such as I might choose in search of answers to the ongoing questions that arose within me as my education progressed. Yes, it progressed - into the philosophical, the scientific, and into the recognition of that divergence of opinion as to what constitutes historical reality. A wide divergence of opinion!

From a vast body of historical documents which presents to one a considerable divergence of opinion and views that are at odds with one another, one must finally arrive at one's own tentative conclusions. Those conclusions best based therefore upon a wide perusal of literature and study; and adequately moderated by one's skepticisms and endowed with a sense of that which is probable. One might come finally to consider oneself somewhat as "sole judge of truth / (though) in endless error hurled / the glory, the jest, the riddle of the world." (Pope)

We had between us previously some discussion of what it is that constitutes wealth, which is what prompted you to send me your recent batch of information about Adam Smith's writings. And I am still trying to come to some more comprehensive understanding of it all. I recently obtained a copy of *The Creature from Jekyll Island* by J. Edward Griffin, concerning the origin, nature of, and workings of 'The Fed'. Informative and interesting. Perhaps, astonishing, is more like it.

While there, 1969-1978 in Ashland, Oregon, I had time and enough of modest income to permit me to delve more extensively into an appreciation for music. The Southern Oregon College Bookstore was importing for sale an ongoing stream of inexpensive off-brand-label 33 1/3 speed platters, at a mere dollar per disc. I accumulated and listened then to a rather large repertoire of mostly classical music. I also began to acquire additional records from Musical Heritage Society. By chance, there in Ashland, I came into possession of three or four records of Folk Music from the area of Bavaria and Southwest Germany. I found it to be charming, and seductive enough that I resorted to it ever more regularly. Then, cassette tape music was soon becoming available and I was able to transcribe this music to my own collection of cassettes, so that I could use it on my automobile trips. With the passage of time I came to use cassettes ever more, and rarely had cause to use the platter recordings that were more cumbersome to deal with. Through the years and through the course of several moves about the country from place to place, I eventually became separated from my record player; then lost track of the original record plates, as I had no further use for them. But it turns out that the cassette tapes have a tendency through repetitious use to distort and to break - become useless. Thus it happened that I eventually had no further access to much of what had become my favorite music. I grieved some at the loss.

But then, a couple months ago, Bayloo got me an I-pod. A compact and handy little device. But it has taken me a lot of frustrating hours to become only gradually familiar with its workings. I have transcribed my CD discs into e-recordings into the I-pod. And recently have gotten access to the I-tunes warehouse, and access to a great much of folk music from which I had become separated through the years. Yes, able to tap into my beloved Bavarian and German Folk Music. And in the past week have acquired a play-list of about 50 pieces of this enchanting music. I find myself sort of enthrall to it. It is sort of intoxicating to hear - infuses me with a great sense of calm and serenity. The music produces a sort of infatuation or euphoria reminiscent of that experienced from a slug of Demerol or Oxycotin such as one has used at some occasional past episode of pre-op or post-op surgical episode.

And so, I have been playing this folk music almost continuously the past few days when I am at home and when not writing, reading, or watching Fox News and TV special programs. Pre-occupied with repetitious use and hearing of the music. As with other comparable euphoric preoccupations with this or that in one's past, I expect that the grip of the music will eventually diminish to more reasonable proportions, so that one need no longer feel deprived when away at work or out on errands.

But, there is this thing called 'taste' and preference in music, just as in foods, dress, artistic enjoyment, etc. And I couldn't help but wonder how wide-spread of appeal might be this Bavarian-German Folk Music to which I am currently enthrall. I thought I might send you a CD copy for your interest, and to find out if it might gain a hold on you anything like the effect is has upon me.

A month or so ago Bayloo got me a Dragon Nuance program for doing dictations directly into typed pages. Of course it also requires of one some certain amount of frustration and a few hours of forbearance to become acquainted with it and learn how to get some use from it. But, I am becoming quite impressed with it. The other day I sat down to about four hours dictation into the device (reading pages of letters composed in cursive) and managed to turn out 16 type written pages in that period of time. It would have taken me, say, six or eight times that to have typed it manually into script.

I thought perhaps you and M___ might come down here to Santa Fe to visit with us a spell. If you still have perhaps some interest in working some of our writings into a joint venture for publication to our family people, we might go over together some of what is now becoming a large body of type-written pages. Discuss what from among those papers we might want to use or eliminate. Come to some definite agreement as to what we might want to put into a joint project, and get on with it. This Dragon Nuance device can greatly facilitate any such intentions we might agree upon.

Love,
Brother,
R. Garner

Enclosed: two CD discs of Bavarian-German Folk Music.
Also some copy of my recently acquired quite good photo copies

of our Great-grandfather, Christoph Boepple (1838 to 1895?) and his second wife, Luise Pohl. Also, a copy of a very nice biography of the Meissel family (the mother of that group being a sister to GF George Boepple) which I obtained from (distant cousin) Wilbert Harsch up in Pick City, ND.

RGB

18 April 2011

2012

- Addendum Perspective -

[Through the middle years of my life until recently I have written a good many letters. Many of them tended to become a bit long. As the extended family continued to enlarge, I slipped into the habit of writing an annual summary, with sometimes an additional long essay each year. These, I would send out to 25 or 35 persons among my relatives and friends - sort of obviating the necessity of writing so many letters. Then, in the past few years, I thought instead that I might just write a book or two, which might be more convenient to my potential readers than a scattered collection of accumulating loose papers from year to year. Those I have written so far are:

A Studied Impression of That Which Is –
  by R. Garner Brasseur, M.D.
  Vantage Press; Copyright 2006
  ISBN: 0-533-15365-4
Inheritors of a Few Years - Second Edition
  by Roosevelt Garner Brasseur, M.D.
  Published by "The Papermill Publisher" in Spokane, WA
  November 2010 No copyright or ISBN: number
Annual summaries - Author House; Copyright 2012
  ISBN:978-1-4685-6168-5 (sc) & 978-1-4685-6167-8 (e)
Impulsive Meditations - Author House; Copyright 2012

ISBN: 978-1-4772-6305-1 (sc) & 978-1-4772-6306-8 (e)

What I am now writing in June 2013 is intended to be my fifth book, and I have tentative plans for at least two more books to follow - time and health permitting.]

RGB

January 2007

To whom it may Concern Re: P.K.

I worked the wards of the state Psychiatric Hospital in Las Vegas several years with Dr. P.K. before I retired from that job seven years ago. Dr. P.K. has recently (2007) contacted me concerning his recent dismissal from the state hospital and has made me aware of some of the allegations against him - upon which his dismissal has been predicated.

As new rules, regulations, and guidelines continuously reshape hospital policy, the official written policy is forever behind and out of date. A policy that is vague and uncertain in many of its aspects. Psychiatry and Psychology themselves incorporate a lot of vagaries and various schools of thought into their practices. There seem to be a continuous stream of complaints from patients, advocates, and various persons of political gravitas that calls forth the not infrequent investigation into this incident, or that. Each investigation must conclude with some sort of corrective action or clear cause for dismissal of allegation. There is blame and finger pointing among the staff, for all are responsible to some degree for patient care. When all are thus involved - then none of course, is wholly responsible. Each staff member has wit enough to strive for personal immunity from castigation. 'Let the onus fall elsewhere', is the principle of survival. Always the search for a scapegoat to bear the every new strain. Better generally to place it upon the 'outsider', than upon one's self or upon one's close ally.

Incident reports (complaints from within one or another of the hospital employees) arise from time-to-time and come to the attention of the medical staff for discussion, enlightenment, and resolution. Such reports are often spontaneous in practice, but can also be solicited (manufactured) to serve internal political purposes. Resolution of such reports is often by discussion of misunderstandings, though they sometimes end in reprimand letter. Letters of reprimand are authored by administrative personnel and may be challenged.

Dr. P.K. has sent me copy of two letters he has received from the state hospital. The first being a letter of dismissal to Dr. P.K. The second letter to him is subsequent to his answering of the charges against him.

First, some general comments. This case is not being presented to what we shall presume to be a civil, unbiased, open court proceeding, but rather to the bureaucracy of a state agency which is most apt to weigh its judgments in its own favor. I don't hold great expectations for a favorable judgment to the accused. If that judgment is then to be considered binding, I would forgo the bureaucratic hearing and spend my efforts rather on a civil hearing with charges of slander and defamation against the individuals who have signed the letters of Dec. 12 2006 and Jan 22, 2007.

I notice secondly that the body of these two letters is almost identical - as though there had been neither oral nor written refutation by Dr. P.K. in response to these charges which have been leveled against him. Were it true that Dr. P.K. had not tendered his well considered response; I do not see that Dr. P.K. would have any cause to pursue this matter through the State Personnel Board Rule. But, I am told by Dr. P.K., that he did present both oral and written refutation to the charges. If he did so, then it seems to me that the second of these two letters is remiss in its failure to acknowledge and respond to his refutations.

As to the hope of Dr. P.K. finding justice to his cause within the policy rules of the state hospital? I am doubtful that that could happen unless he were to have the firm support of at least several of the professional staff. I would think his chances better by an approach through the judicial system of the state.

But Dr. P.K. had been unable to summon up any show of support from his fellow employees towards his self-defense. They were "not wanting to get involved". For they might be next in line, should they incur the wrath of administration. Thus it was that Dr. P.K. asked me to be of assistance to him in this matter. Though I too am reluctant to involve myself in such time-consuming adventures, one must do what one can in the interests of justice. And so I studied the bogus allegations against him; and it appeared to me that an injustice was here in the making. Empathy and a bit of indignation arose within the core of my being. And I resolved at least to make an effort on his behalf.

Having no training in extempory oratory, I was relegated to the necessity of a written exposition to present my views and opinion. An undertaking that left me with mixed feelings knowing that I must finally then give birth to an essay. But that, only after enduring the pains of labor that it shall require. I'll be relieved when I have finally delivered this burden in a healthy condition.

4 March 2007

To whom it may concern:

[Concerning Dr. P.K. and the various charges recently leveled as a pretext for his dismissal from the state hospital medical staff.]

If the state hospital is determined to be rid of Dr. P.K., there is a much less dastardly way to go about it than to put him through this ordeal of manufactured false allegations that slander his personal and professional reputation. Charges that appear to have been manufactured after the fact and appear largely retrospective in nature. Charges which if not proven might subject its signaturers to countercharges of malicious slander to his personal and professional reputation. Charges which put Dr. P.K. in the position of having to defend his medical licensure against suspension and cancellation actions at the hands of State Board of Medical Licensure in each state in which he is licensed to the practice of medicine and surgery.

Dr. P.K. is, after all, age 65 and eligible for both SS and PERA retirement benefits. And it is my understanding that he was already contemplating retirement at the time that this assassination plot was being hatched against him. They might very simply have requested his retirement to obviate the complex necessity of drumming up dubious allegations of fault concerning Dr. P.K. An option of civil decency as opposed to one of malice aforethought.

I write, having myself worked seven or eight years at the state hospital and having worked and been acquainted with Dr. P.K. since those years. From my own experience and recollection it is my impression that Dr. P.K. has been 'on-the-carpet' at the hands of Dr. P.V on a number of occasions for allegations of dubious validity in my view. To put things into their proper perspective, I call to your attention to the tone of the author of these charges against Dr. P.K._ as being insultingly pedantic. The background of medical training and experience of Dr. P.K. is in no wise inferior to that of Dr. P,V. It is my understanding that Dr. P.K. is, himself, a diabetic, and especially in matters pertaining to the management of diabetic patients, I would certainly far prefer to defer to his medical judgment. I also point out that the department head of general Medical Officers was by no means appointed to that position in lieu any outstanding scholastic achievement nor on the basis of having distinguished himself in any way as a clinician. I am aware that the previous head of that department had recommended that Dr. P.V. might be well advised to take some further post-graduate training to better fit himself for his position of general medical officer. The reasons behind his appointment to head of the department were rather a surprise to many of us at the time. There are ethnic and family connections that seem to have been weighed into that appointment.

It is my impression that Dr. P.K. has been subjected to more than his share of adverse actions from the investigation of various allegations over the years. He is an obvious and easy sort of target. A foreigner of East India origins and owning a foreign accent that easily identifies him as an 'outsider'. And it is my impression that the Chief of the general Medicine Department of the state hospital seems to harbor a special animosity towards him. I recall several of those situations where charges were laid at his doorstep; and I have taken the part of Dr. P.K. in at least one such of those major confrontations. Anybody who has lived and worked in Las Vegas, NM would probably agree that it seems a tight community of Hispanic peoples and somewhat centered on their own racial self interests with a certain animosity even towards we 'anglos'.

This seems no less true concerning those of them employed by the state hospital.

Various allegations against the hospital and the staff come to the attention of hospital administration intermittently from commonly oppositional patient allegations, patient guardian representatives, patient advocates of their legal rights, from other members of staff and from political issues originating within the state hospital and in Santa Fe, and about the state from private citizens with complaints. In response to such things there are administrative 'investigations' of a sort, wherein it becomes expedient to fasten some blame upon some one or another staff member, in order to give the impression that some 'remedial action' has been taken and thus to satisfy the blood lust at the heart of the complaint.

I recall some thirty or more various medical doctors and psychiatrists, as well as some psychologists and social workers that have been dismissed or pressured to resign one-by-one through the years of my tenure at the hospital. A surprisingly large number of professional staff to have been fired or resigned in frustration and disgust at the chaos of wrangling accusations since I was hired in 1991.

[This letter lists the names of thirty recalled to my memory:

—————◆◆◆—————

Shall we suppose that all of these now dismissed and pressured-departed professionals are to be considered incompetent or involved in grievous misbehavior? Or might we not well suspect that some sort of politics is here involved? Scapegoats of a sort, in my view. Not a new or unique solution of convenience to the politics of the state hospital: and widely resorted to in all bureaucratic structure of political and economic organizations.

Some ten years ago, a group of we the state hospital professionals agreed to attempt to establish a union, in order to secure ourselves against the secretive and high-handed dictates of the state hospital administration through the state mandated rules pertaining to the abridged rules re: Public Employees. Dr. P.K. and I were both a part of that effort to establish a union. We did succeed in that effort. Again, our involvement in that effort did seem to precipitate upon us some additional animosity from administration. The union's existence was short lived, as the governor of the state absolved the union about a year after its birth. I expect that Dr. P.K._ is probably one of the last of those union members to now have finally been expelled from employment at the state hospital.

Dr. P.K. has contacted me concerning his recent firing from the state hospital and has made me aware of some of the allegations against him - upon which his dismissal has been predicated. It is a matter of record that I myself have tangled with the state hospital administration concerning their bogus allegations to be rid of me back in 1999, following a previously foiled attempt in 1998. It is also a matter or record that I was absolved of those allegations. I was given a letter from the state hospital medical staff which indicated that the medical staff investigation of allegations proved those allegations to be without substance. I was thus absolved of those charges against me, and I was able to use that information to clear myself of suspicion in the eyes of the various state medical boards which would otherwise be seeking to suspend or cancel my medical licensure. Since that time, I have arrived at an agreement with the state hospital that prohibits me from any further discussion of the details and the settlement of the issues between me and them.

In my view, the recent charges against Dr. P.K._ are irresponsible allegations, as they seem not well substantiated. And more especially irresponsible in that they threaten his livelihood, threaten his medical licensure, and threaten his reputation. Those things, in addition to subjecting him to personal unnecessary mental anguish. In short, the whole business seems to have something of the quality of malicious mischief.

I note that one of the of charges against him specifically accuses Dr. P.K. of "lying", when, in fact, they might more judiciously have considered a more charitable interpretation of 'the facts' on which they base their suggestion of a bold-faced lie. A charge which they neglected to moderate even in the face of Dr. P.K.'s quite believable and probable explanation for the basis of the misunderstanding.

Polybius reminds us that it is well to keep in mind a firm distinction between a cause and a pretext. It is my impression that the slate of charges against Dr. P.K. seems to have been drummed up against him as part of a specific concerted action during the period of time that he was absent on a prolonged leave to visit his family abroad. In his absence they seem first to have decided upon a conclusion concerning Dr. P.K.; and then proceeded to manufacture the 'cause' by a superficial search through some fragmented charts. The perpetrators of this injustice seem also to have specifically marched about among the line staff to solicit vague and incomplete 'supportive statements' of innuendo and partial truth by force of their gravitas upon the lesser beings of various ward line staff.

Though charges are specifically leveled against Dr. P.K., there is an implication that the self same instigators of these actions against Dr. P.K. might somehow come off scot-free of any such similar taints against them, where their own performances to undergo similar scrutiny in review under malicious intent by careful examination.

Concerning the patient admitted and known by history to have been treated with thyroid replacement therapy, I wonder that allegations did not immediately fall upon the admitting physician (Dr. A__) who neglected to write orders for Synthyroid at the time of the patient's admission, and who five days later even in the face of high TSH levels, yet failed to write orders for what he knew ought to have been 100, rather than 50 mcg. It appears to be something of a double standard to ignore the initial lapse, in order to detour on to a point further in the chain of events to where there might be a place where Dr. P.K.'s name could be dragged into the chain of events that had its origin with the misadventures of the original admitting physician. The case is further complicated by the switching of the patient to other wards (To ACU and subsequently to Forensic) where other physicians might be easily confused and entangled in the transfer process. I wonder that the patient was not also noted upon admission to be "sluggish and slow", if he had not been actually taking his thyroid medications - as is suggested by admitting TSH reports. Certainly Dr H.G. had no reason or excuse for being unaware of the questionable state of the patient's thyroid status and has both an obligation and right to order testing of thyroid status if there be any cause or source of miscommunication between himself and the general medical officer.

One might wonder if the diagnostic decision of Dr. P.V. as to the possible cause of the patient's being "sluggish and slow" was based upon a hands-on physical examination, or rather just on a visual inspection. How were the deep tendon reflexes; and what does he report about the palpation of the thyroid gland and the texture of the skin. In this context, we are informed again of another situation in which it is implied that Dr. P.K. did not perform an examination appropriate to a patient's problem. A situation imbedded in circumstances well explained by Dr. P.K. An event in which his good judgment and appropriate intervention resulted in a beneficent outcome to the situation. Commendation to Dr. P.K. might rather be conferred, than castigation.

Another issue under consideration is that of Dr. P.K. having written an order for Penicillin, not knowing that the patient had a history of some sort of reaction to Penicillin previously. Dr. P.K. indicates that information from the chart was not readily available so as to inform him of that problem. In any case, the nursing staffs who work continuously with the patients on their wards are generally readily attuned to these allergic problems and are readily available to inform the doctor in order caution him of any relevant allergies - especially to penicillin allergies. Perhaps within thirty minutes of the order having been written, the nurse picked up the penicillin order from the chart order sheet, and called the doctor to get the order changed. And exercised her good judgment in withholding the medication until the doctor was given opportunity to rectify the oversight. Dr. P.K. was paged and responded by phone to make the required change of medication. He is said to have been paged "several times" before he called back to the ward to make the medication change. Do the pagers always work? And is the person carrying the pager always free in an instant to respond? Perhaps he is in consultation by phone on another problem or with another physician. A chapter from Jacobs and Jawetz (Current Medical Diagnosis and Treatment) reminds us that "A history of a penicillin reaction in the past is not reliable; however, if there is a history of a severe reaction (anaphylaxis) the drug should be administered with caution" "or a substitute drug should be given." A bit less restrictive than "absolutely contraindicated".

Concerning the issue of the care of brittle diabetic on the ward, I believe that the retrospective comments made to disparage the approach of Dr. P.K. in the management of his patient are something more of the nature of a matter of opinion and will not find consensus among practitioners of medicine. The nursing staff is constantly upon the ward to monitor her patients, while the doctor is present only relatively briefly to consult with the nurse about the ward patients. In the ongoing daily process of monitoring the ward patients, the nursing staff does accumulate diagnostic acumen which informs them to suspect that a particular patient may be having (for example) a hypoglycemic episode – call it a tentative diagnosis, if you wish. It is at that point, they are most likely to contact the patient's doctor for instructions. There is no reason they may not then first quickly establish or disestablish that impression by doing a very simple and quick finger-stick glucometer test before contacting the doctor, so as to inform him of that useful information. I mean, are they not there to be of some assistance to the doctor in his duties? No reason first to get an order from the doctor to do a glucometer test, and then to have to call the doctor a second time with those results.

As for the assertion that nurses are unable to make diagnoses – that is patent nonsense. When I was at the state hospital, a nurse assistant was hired onto the staff to evaluate, diagnose, and write treatment orders for patients. It was under the supervision, of course, of staff physicians. But so are ward nurses also acting under the supervision of the medical staff.

Such then are my impressions concerning the manufactured pretext for the dismissal of Dr. P.K. from the medical staff of the state hospital.

R. Garner Brasseur, M.D.

Dr. P.K. and I were both relieved when this railroading job came to an abrupt halt. He was then reinstated to his employment and given back-pay for the many months that his case went awaiting arbitration. 2007

December 2007

Santa Fe, NM

Greetings Betty, Kelley, and Jim,

"Ah, if with the dead there slumbered the pain. Or if the hearts that bled, slept with the slain. Or if the grief died. But no. Death will not have it so." - author unremembered at this moment -

I became acquainted with Raymond Horton in the summer of 1944 upon the arrival of our family in Scobey, Montana. We were best of friends during that summer, and in the summer of 1945 when we met again in Miles City, Montana.

From my autobiography-family biography of 1997:

My buddy, Raymond Horton, from Scobey had arrived in Miles City also - they lived a mile or more distant from us. He worked with the newspapers too, as best I can recall. He and I were inseparable. Besides being good friends, we had a sort of defense pact between us. For those few of us young fellows out upon the streets to earn some cash were generally susceptible to some dozen or two bullies in various parts of town that were apt to threaten and intimidate us, and we occasionally lost a couple of our hard earned nickels to them. And I no longer had the looming shadow of my two older brothers, whose previous mere presence gave me a certain immunity from extortion, It became well known that Raymond and I backed up one another, so that we rarely even encountered a face-off situation. As I reflect back upon those days, it seems strange that actually so very few of my peers were out upon the streets to earn some income. I don't actually know what they did with their after school and evening hours. Some, I know, were rural and suburban rural residents who would have had some evening chores, but what of the rest of them (?).

Raymond Horton and I had somehow come to the conclusion that it was prudent for us to keep ourselves in prime physical trim. There was a space of a few weeks where we used to take turns in jumping from the top of a railroad boxcar at the stockyards, to a pile of sand below - to toughen up our legs. It was a punishing bit of foolishness and we soon gave that up ... without either of us having actually confessed that it seemed also to be frighteningly dangerous. We would often take long hikes along the foot of the cliffs on the north side of the Yellowstone River, or out across the Tongue River via the Milwaukee Railroad bridge, to the water pumping plant. In town, we would go swimming once or twice a day, but we had a sort of preoccupation and passion for running, and we would regularly run a few miles each day - mostly back and forth between his home and mine - a little over two miles on the roundtrip. So far as I know, he didn't actually derive any more pleasure from running than I did, but we were both earnestly convinced of its beneficial effect upon our continued health and progressive conditioning.

The sixth grade ended and the ensuing summer of 1946 passed much the same as had the previous summer, except that Raymond Horton had also departed the area. Nor did I ever see nor hear again from him, though in my late 50's I did make a couple unsuccessful attempts to locate him.

———◆◆———

And then, suddenly, in September of 2000, I received from Raymond an E-Mail note. I stopped by to visit with him in Redding a month or two later; and I often since stop by for a couple of days at a time to visit with him and his family. It was astonishing how much we seemed yet to have in common. Perhaps a lad's character becomes fairly well set in about those tender years of age 12 or 13. In any case, our perceptions and general outlook seem always to have been fairly congruous. In the course of our many hours of subsequent conversation I expect that we fairly completely filled one another in on the course of our lives during the hiatus of our friendship from 1946 through those years to Y2K. Besides the reciting of our personal and family experiences, our conversations then ranged widely through subjects such as Geology, Astronomy, History, Natural History, and Philosophy - in which we had common interests. In point of fact, I don't believe that I ever had the opportunity to share more extensive and far ranging discussions with anyone other of my personal acquaintance. But of course, we were already then a couple of old geezers, and such openness of discussion is one of the few benisons that those of our age are apt to fall into - in those declining years. A sort of natural inclination to arriving at a kind of summing-up of our seasoned conclusions. Yes, a sort of debriefing before moving on. Betty and Jim were also about at times to enter into our conversations, and I was astonished at how closely they kept in touch with Kelley by phone.

And so, I am grateful for the hospitality and good fellowship I so much enjoyed in the home of Betty and Raymond in these past seven years. I know you shall greatly miss him and that it will be small consolation to you three; Kelley, Jim, and Betty, that you are not alone in your mourning.

My condolences to you all – and best wishes.

Sincerely,

R. Garner Brasseur, MD

December 2007

10 February 1989

Caldwell, Idaho 83605

Dear PP,

This note to you is but a continuation of "my letter to the world, that never wrote to me …", as Emily Dickinson has put it. The implication of that being, that it is as though I were abruptly awakened one day – some fifty five years ago – to find myself (somehow) marooned upon this strange planet. And in thrall to mighty and, seemingly inexplicable forces; and having been acquired by this strange collection of beings, that were designated as constituting a 'family'. Besides my own creature, this family possessed at one time or another, other strange creatures such as a horse, a cow, a goat, a cat, a dog, and some rabbits, and chickens. Additionally, there were eight other juvenile creatures of the same type as myself, that gradually and imperceptible changed, from juvenile, to adult form – a thing I did not, at first perceive but, only gradually and in retrospect. The two adult and eight other juvenile beings, seemed all to be gifted with a spontaneity of speech and behavior, and interacted among themselves, and in a society of similar beings, as though it were all a part of a something akin to a theatre production, whose actions and lines were preordained - requiring, perhaps, no decisions from them - at to its drama. In essence, it was - as it were - a sort of dramatic production, such as a play, or an opera. I myself was - as it were - a sort of spectator, but not a part of the cast. Much as is an outsider to an inside joke. My presence seemed an irrelevance to the goings-on upon the stage of life and in this family. At times I found myself upon the 'set'. A sort of embarrassment for me - where I was seemingly expected (judging by the context of action and words) to make some sort of reply, or take some sort of action. I was stymied and it seemed unjust, for I had never seen nor been instructed concerning the script, nor the action seemingly now required of me. The cat had it much easier than I, for she could enter and exit the set in complete freedom and silence at her whim, with no apparent expectations of her. A cat seems never to be embarrassed, though I have seen at times a dog that seemed to be. It has been said that no one can own a cat or make requirements of its comings and goings. It seems true though, that most other domestic creatures can be 'mastered', to some degree.

Observing my own creaturely being in the mirror made me aware that I had the humanoid features of that family of ten others. How was that brought about? What was its meaning; and what, its implications? I felt stupidly inadequate and out of place, for the whole world of my experience was inexplicable to me. It began to seem obvious that I must engage in some sort of daily routine and schedule - but what schedule (?), and to what intent or purpose? I was chided, urged, and nudged along. Besides the accidental pains and sufferings that one endures, there was that which seemed at times as though intentional. Censure … apparently sometimes deserved, but often not, in so far as I could discern. Besides the occasional physical pain, one somehow gradually acquires a capacity to suffer psychic pain - another discomfort somehow unjust in that one seemed somehow even to be inflicting it upon oneself. Ones sensitivity to it seemed gradually to increase, so that the circle of those who may inflict it upon one seems gradually to enlarge, until in a world of one's close associates, one can finally be grateful for the anonymous mass of mankind that is not even aware of ones being. First the parent; then the siblings; next, the uniformed civilians; and at last, the schoolmarms – all seem to acquire some dexterity in their ability to cause one some little psychic discomfort. And their methods evolve, so as to become more subtle and applicable at a more remote distance. Aimed in ones direction by a mere glance, a stiffness of posture, a sigh, an excess formality of customary mode of speech. Such things inform one of having been adjudged guilty of something or another. So subtle indeed, that one may upon occasion perceive censure and threat whose existence cannot be precisely confirmed – just as persons may irradiate censure from their subconscious being, at times without being aware of that at a conscious level. The charges of witchcraft, undoubtedly, contain some such things. Almost any act or behavior is unsuitable – by someone, somewhere, under some circumstance or another. Enigmatic as life is, it could hardly fail to excite one's curiosity. And the end of life, so far as anyone knows, deprives one even the opportunity to further satisfy one's curiosity. Each life owns some few pleasures and satisfactions, such as to hearten a man against its rigors. Yet often enough pain, misery, and discouragement as to cause one to wonder at the price. And, death itself seemingly oft acquired through such uncomfortable passages, that it hardly seems inviting, except as a remedy itself, to severe and prolonged pain and misery. Through the years we gradually become aware that those with whom we share our lives are, in reality, quite like ourselves … are also aliens in this curious world; yet own also potentially interesting lives. And, again, so far as anyone can know with certainty, life itself seems the only game in town. One can either play someone else's version of that game, his own private version, or not play it at all. What other options? For all practical purposes, the mass of mankind is aliened and in opposition to one's own life objectives and plans. One's only potential natural allies, are some few relatives and friends. Where one fails to own friends or any certain rights, one can often acquire some, by congenially courting favor – or painfully reforming one's own self. Even the succeeding generation of one's own family seems often sternly set against one. Yet, knowing that they will inevitably need our alliance in some of their own difficult passages of life, therefore we needs must exert our own influence on their behalf … out of concern for their best interests. An obligation of humanitarian concern of one generation to another, and between some few friends, regardless that they may also be relatives.

The natural world itself seems willing enough to slowly surrender to one the evidence of its veracity; and insight into the mechanisms of its method of progressive change and evolution. Yet, the whole of creation seems blithely unconcerned for our individual and collective welfare. Thus, the world and the universe remain to me a thing of wonder and interest, and I am content to abide within it - so long as my pain and misery do not become disproportional to some minimum of joys and satisfactions; or, so long as there seems some reasonable hope thereof.

To also derive some measure of pleasure and satisfaction from the necessity of living out this mortal existence. And that, in voluntary and honorable reciprocity with ones fellow mortals - with whom ones fate has been cast.

My own interests and curiosity are currently centered upon History, Family History (currently attempting to extract such first-hand information as is possible, before those who remember its details, depart forever, into the sunset of the universe). Philosophy, Geology, Weather, and Human Nature - things that you, VBB, and I were discussing, in those few days last fall that we spent together in Idaho County, in the State of Idaho. I was curious to get your views, your opinions, and to hear of your experiences of life - and to delve into your conclusions, and cross-examine your reasons for holding them.

Like yourself, I too am interested in wealth - including gold and coin-of-the-realm. For those things can lubricate and greatly facilitate our access to life, liberty, health, and a general satisfaction with life. I must suspect that you and VBB were humorously exaggerating your true opinion, as to the actual probability of finding some gold in those stream beds. Still, I was surprised at the apparent determination of your efforts. It was as though you actually did expect to uncover gold! Though I too, would gladly have stooped to pick up any stray nuggets I might have spotted, my own interest was merely to discover some interesting rocks, minerals, and observe some geological formations. Of course, there can be no doubt, that we must certainly have passed over, at least, some traces of gold. Yet, its diminutive particle size and peculiar combinations with surrounding minerals made it too elusive for us to discover - given our limited methods, time, and efforts; and given the fact this historically productive area has already been thoroughly worked over at least twice in the past century or more. It may require another ten thousand years of weathering, to loosen any significant number of nuggets, and rich pockets again into the stream beds.

Some fifteen or twenty years ago, the example of our brother, EVH, started me upon the custom of a daily entry of my day's events into a journal. In consequence of that, I have gotten the habit of daily meditation and reflection, concerning the events of each day. To get away from the usual routine of my life (as with the three days we spent in Idaho County) puts me in touch with a great many things to weigh and ponder. What was said, done, and discussed in that time was recorded in my diary day-by-day. Nearly all of that was novel to my experience. Knowing that it might take me a week or two, to consider and record more thoroughly some of my impressions, thoughts, questions, and ideas in consequence of that trip, I seized the opportunity to spend an additional day and a night to travel in solitude, while listening to some soul music in order to facilitate the simmering together of the new, with the old of personal history and experience within my deep caves of thought. I drove as far as Cambridge, and then took Hwy 71 into Hells Canyon, stopping here and there along the way to inspect the rocks and the geological formations. In Hells Canyon later in the afternoon I napped; and I fasted and I read some ancient history. There, I spent the night in the back of my pick-up truck. There, upon this solitary pilgrimage, all of the above mentioned ingredients simmered together in my mind, along with old recollections of family, and of bygone days. Then, they began to merge into a train of loosely associated thoughts and ideas, which preoccupied my attention. Some of which I am now attempting to recapture into the rough draft I made at that time. And as I ponder some of the sorrows, regrets, and satisfactions of the past, I am reminded that mankind seems well to enjoy the tragic play, the tragic opera, the bittersweet country western song … One seems able to take a certain mellow pleasure in the remembrance of a lost love, or a sadly departed member of one's family. It is commonplace to see and to hear of old folks who have become forgetful as they while away their declining years. Some of them have actually developed psychopathology from declining Central Nervous System circulatory perfusion; and some from actual organic structural disease of the CNS, such as Alzheimer's disease.

Another category of the agedly declining however, represents something other than actual CNS problems. They manifest a mere exaggeration of ones natural tendency to focus the attention upon the more satisfying times and experiences of bygone years and better times; and on the memory of loved ones now departed etc. Even while up and about, and occupied with their daily routine, or scanning a newspaper or staring at a TV-set; even while looking directly at someone who is speaking to them - yet, they are catching only occasional snatches of that, for they are not uncommonly preoccupied with some old memory, or fantasy of how thing were - or might have been. Then, of course, they don't remember the experience of this immediate past, for at the time of its occurrence they were focused upon some aspect of the remote past, or a fantasy version thereof. We all have our personal experience of that of course, to some variable degree. It is rather an interesting experience to which I treat myself - upon occasion. It is based upon what I think of as, "the two world problem" of Philosophy. What transpires in the real world, versus the moment-by-moment fragments of perceptions and thoughts that occupy ones attention. Each of us has these two different worlds to negotiate in our everyday lives.

First, the real objective world with which we must forever be grappling. We must establish and maintain for ourselves a niche for our physical and psychological peace in existential reality. It is troublesome to us because it has so many sub-realities for us to negotiate. The reality amid ones siblings at home is one thing; that in the school yard is something different; that in the classroom, something else again. Still different, selling newspapers upon the streets in the evening etc. And we mere mortals must figure out how to switch between our various masks and roles as we run this ever-changing gauntlet from day to day. By the age of perhaps 14 or 20, most can fend for themselves well enough, so as to establish for themselves some sort of precarious peace with the existential world of reality.

Then, there is that second world, which we each inhabit in

solitary confinement - inside our own head. Here, one ponders and weighs the first-hand and second-hand experience of ones life; and the hearsay, legends, and myth, with which we are inundated. One develops a priority and scheme of valuation of things, persons, ideas, and Philosophies. One can be tempted by logic and reason to maintain an internal order and consistency between the various subject matter of ones diverse subjective appraisals. Tempted too, to align ones subjective evaluation towards always a correspondence with the objective reality of the external world. It is probably the case however, that no two persons perceive identically, the unitary reality of that-which-is. And it is most certainly the case that no one has yet attained a perfect grasp on any subject whatever, let alone a comprehensive grasp of all that is knowable. This race of creatures we now designate as 'mankind', seems probably to have evolved in only the past 100,000 to 125,000 years; and probably has now, only a modestly higher level of native intelligence than it possessed at the inception of the race we label as Homo sapiens. The progress of technology, and the accumulation of knowledge have been acquired only slowly. Knowledge builds on knowledge so that the pace of its accumulation tends to accelerate - like the effect of gravity, upon a falling object.

A few cave drawings seem to have originated as early as 35,000 years ago. Perhaps by 25,000 years ago the bow and arrow was an innovation; and the domestication of plants and animals by man was begun perhaps about 10,000 years ago. The first evidence of any writing dates from only about 5,500 years ago.

The organized society of men crowding one another, and clamoring for the limited privileges and honors that accumulate to the elite - that, seems to be a stimulus that encourages thought, technical know-how, self expression, artistic expression, and the rudimentary science of observation and reflection. Learning and some form of teaching have been the basis of all human creaturely survival for millions of years. Mankind has exploited that mechanism, much in advance of any other known creature. Never-the-less, man's progress and exploration of his own potential is only rudimentary, even in our advanced times. Conscious recognition of the concept (of the utility of teaching and learning) is probably the achievement that initiated tribal man on the road to civilization.

Information, arts, technology, and the sciences have advanced the elite in the course of achievement. Misinformation, superstition, and myth, seem forever to have been used as a weapon between the classes of men, whereby a system of more valid (inside information) serves to keep the elite one-up, above the common man. The elite endowed with hubris have some tendency to overreach and to do-themselves-in, by dint of pride, personal vanity, and excess of ease and pleasure. Overly greedy of increased wealth and power, they expose themselves to unnecessary risks of warfare and intrigue. Burdened with vanities and depleted of virtues, their own families play deadly games of intrigue that oft-times bring a family line to an end. Thus, those of humble origin, have often the opportunity to rise somewhat above the ranks of their compatriots. Nor is their native genius inferior to the challenge, once given the opportunity. Should they have the character to remember their humble origins, their powers may benefit by the exercise of prudence.

In any case, the accumulation of accurate information has only seen its beginnings, among mankind. And the process of teaching, and the art of encouragement to learn, are both yet inefficient. It seems probable that the acquisition of information might encourage a people gradually to discard old prejudices and superstitions. Those who live the unsheltered life, upon the frontiers of exploration and battle, are best served by that science which affords them the most accurate facts, and concepts, and truths, with which to fashion tools, weapons, and strategy. It doesn't guarantee them certain success, for the factors of physical advantage, chance, and even occasional opposition by a science superior to their own, will still bring them some proportion of defeat. But an adequate science may bring them a willingness to learn even from defeat. That itself, a powerful tool of instruction to their own benefit - encouraging them to grasp and utilize the newer technology or the greater truth. That, the basis of the instructive and moral value of reality. By degree, we learn from reality; and begin to incorporate the rules and regulations of our general and particular reality into our patterns of behavior and character. But the inertia of old prejudice and belief requires years and generations to dissipate. Thus, an idea whose time has come, has generally been around for some time, before its coming into ones personal awareness.

From our trip to central Idaho, I recall in particular your humorous little suggestion as to how it is that trees might be considered as a detriment to the environment. That led us into a few other mirthful myths and suggestions such as 'the divine elixir', the detrimental effect of gravity on the human form and function, the symbolic cattle-guards, symbolic fences, and symbolic walls. We spoke of 'symbolism-over-substance', and other forms of human folly. [Things I mention specifically in another volume.]

As we travel together, I am reminded of the fastidiousness of your eating habits. Yours being particularly noticeable to me account of their being more demanding than my own. In point of fact, this business of eating and digesting consumes a goodly portion of ones day-by-day existence.

When one looks about it can be seen that dietary fads and food cults are many and diverse. Our simplest, and our most sophisticated of persons alike, follow an erratic course of adherence to and 'certitude-of-belief', in first one …, then another of these food fads and cults. The world seems greatly troubled with digestive ailments, whose symptoms are commonly vague, but sometimes life-threatening. Medications have become available, to curb and mitigate some of the most troublesome of these symptoms. But, there appears to be a great diversity and non-uniformity of digestive systems among the population. Our sometimes helpful medications do not benefit the function of some variant systems unto their owners. Thus, in addition to the sometimes useful medications, people still seem to be constantly in quest of yet another diet that one can tolerate with minimal side-effects, and maximal benefit to ones sense of well-being. What works for one, does not work for another. It would appear then that there is something very real about the digestive complaints of this world - that it is more than a world-class neurosis. Small wonder, too, that folks are attentive to their bowel troubles. For anyone that has been ill with retching or with diarrhea - everyone, thus - can recall how that problem impinged upon his own being. All other matters pale into insignificance when one is in the grips of such necessities as those. Should ones any such acute disorder continue long, the possibility of death looms close at hand - though ones fear of death is apt to diminish as the misery increases. In addition to the signs and symptoms of bowel dysfunction, there are other problems that can arise silently to torment and to shorten ones life. The absorption of too much vitamin; not enough; too much cholesterol and triglycerides; not enough iron; too much alcohol and other drugs; accidental and intentional poisoning; etc.

It may perhaps turn out that the continuous ingestion of foods imperfect for our systems is the thing that nudges men into the ageing process - and towards their demise. Consider too, all of the cancers that arise from the intestine, often hidden away from detection until metastases make death inevitable. Of what use is the appendix? Perhaps it had a use at one time, far back in man's evolutionary history - but none now, so far as anyone can ascertain. Consider the time one wastes in the ritual and acts of eating - perhaps a total six years of one life (says *U.S. News and World Report*). A housewife may, perhaps, spend another 8 or 10 years preparing meals, and putting the table and kitchen back into order after meals.

Just as you have been known upon occasion to ponder the riddle of perpetual motion, I have been inclined at times to wonder at what I might use as ingredients to concoct 'the divine elixir'. Ah, yes ... the nectar of the gods. The perfect nutriment, which is perfectly absorbed. Perhaps 'the divine nectar' will soon have been concocted? Then, free from subservience of ones whole life routine to an impetuous and unpredictable gastrointestinal system, man may finally have the capability of living a long, healthful, and thoughtful life.

People living the contemplative life, do not require as many calories of energy to maintain their being, as do those whose days are spent in physical exertion. In any case, whether or not one is contemplative, his chemical-physical mechanisms of the body require a sort of minimum routine of exercise and exertion, in order to maintain the function of limb as well as of mind. Cicero Says that one might think of the body of a man as being somewhat of the nature of iron. To use it, is gradually to wear it out. But then, not to use it leaves it fated to rust into uselessness. By how much does the bear or the ground-hog extend the span of its years by an annual period of dormancy (?) - Though it would not seem likely that it thereby extends the period of activity of its useful thought. But thought, like physical exertion, is a form of work that requires a will as well as a thorough self-discipline.

Perhaps it is well to rethink the old ideas, beliefs, and prejudices from time to time. The newly discovered realities oft prove quite different from the old, established views. There was a time - not too long past - when men upon the sea dared not venture out of sight of land. Few suspected the existence of the new world of the Americas. The tall mountains of the world were never climbed before the early 1880's. Flight, for man, was long dreamed of, but never commonly thought possible until the first balloon flights of the mid-eighteen hundreds. Few dreamed that epidemic disease was caused by micro-organisms, until the late 1790's or early 1800's - and how much that discovery has gradually changed the world! That was not commonly accepted until less than one hundred years ago. Ben Franklin seems to have been the first to seriously enquire into, and to the study of weather and its causes. Less than hundred years ago no one had any good clue as to what constituted clouds. In England, a man finally began an investigation of that phenomenon by simply categorizing the various shapes and forms of clouds. Skiing is only a recent innovation; scuba diving, only within the span of our own life-times. It has always been considered very dangerous to mess with the sting-ray creatures of the sea; now, in a recent issue of *National Geographic*, I see that scuba divers drop into the shallow waters to feed them, and to hug them - once they have obtained the confidence of the creatures. All of these newly discovered and evolving realities continue to astound our primitive race of creatures. That we are yet a primitive race, one should fix firmly into one's mind - to temper one's perspective. New ideas and new truths arrive into our times at a rate far in excess of our ability to even perceive.

In this month, I am to be working several fourteen hour shifts at one of those Urgent Care Medical Centers in Boise. Beginning at the end of this month and in March I will also work some shifts in Pocatello. I shall have to fly out of Boise in order to get there. I don't really much care for flying as it makes me a little nervous. I thought I had better get caught up on my correspondence before I start taking those risks. My own office practice is rather slow. The Yellow Pages listed my address and phone number as being with the office, and associated with Dr. C. - the way it was listed last year, during the three or four months I was associated with him. That yellow pages error, after I repeatedly called them, to be sure that just that, did not occur! One might as well talk to a post; and send one's correspondence to a rabbit-hole, for all the good it does.

Since I sent that letter to you a week ago, I have examined some additional genealogical Microfilms - of St. Dominique in P.Q. And have gathered some additional information on the Brasseurs. Additionally, I had a windfall of information from an 84 year old Brasseur relative in St. Hyacinthe, Quebec. I enclose to you an updated and corrected version of that chart. It might be best if you simply destroy the first copy I sent you. Otherwise, it might by chance fall into the wrong hands, and at some time in the future end up being thought more accurate because of bearing a slightly earlier date. It is a strange world, as you know.

Through the years, PP, you have been more than helpful and generous to your family. I particularly appreciate the way you took care of so many of the recent problems revolving around the long illness, death, and funeral of our brother EVH. It was the closest thing to a family reunion that the Brasseurs have ever had. You served up a very fine social event and I think that everyone enjoyed it - a fine tribute to his memory, and I guess that he would very much have enjoyed it himself. When we were up in central Idaho, the past fall, I was reminded again, about how very skeptical you are. A fine trait! I wouldn't want you to think that it hasn't been instructive to me through the years. Though you probably were not aware of it, your own example of aloofness from sanctimonious piety has - through the years; and by degree - been useful in helping me to shed a great deal of my own religious superstition. Especially you, Dad, and DFB seem to me, all to have had that same sort of usefully skeptical predisposition. I am tempted to suppose that it is a sort of a culturally transmitted attitude that is passed on from generation to generation along the male line of the family. I know that Uncles Herman and Louis were much the same way. I should like to get a chance to meet some of the more distantly related Brasseurs, such as those in Quebec Province, to see if some of the same trait is present there, too. But, especially the Catholic Church has held a heavy hand upon the French peoples for hundreds of years, and it may be the case that most Frenchmen - having of necessity had to go through ritual formalities under threat of heavy penalty for many generations - have, perhaps, picked up this personal aloofness, as a sort of national trait. I have never known enough French people to enable me to say. The Protestant groups, on the other hand - in the past couple hundred years - have mostly been religiously less heavy handed; having developed instead, a system that encourage them to deal harshly with their individual selves, instead.

Perhaps there is a Deity; and perhaps there is not. I have not seen nor heard from Him. Nor seen the slightest evidence that He gets himself involved in the affairs of men, or of this world. In my view, 'The Word of God' is surly authored by mere mortal man. As R. G. Ingersol puts it:

"Is there a God? I do not know.
Is man immortal? I do not know.
One thing I do know: that neither hope nor fear, belief
nor denial, can change the (yet unknown) fact. It is as
it is; and it will be as it must be.
We must wait. We may hope."

Such evidence as exists, suggests that man has evolved from an ape-like creature, and that his most closely related species is the chimpanzee (among creatures that have not yet become extinct). But, what of man's dignity ... if he be just another creature evolved from those of the tree-tops? Thomas Huxley's response was something to the effect that, it seemed to him that mankind might own a certain rustic pride, in consequence of having lifted himself from the slime; and in consequence of his slowly evolving achievements, enlarging understanding, and determination to improve. I think we do well to consider what he has to say. And Stevenson's essay, *Pulvis Et Umbra*, is a fine reading exercise with which to attune oneself to the very humble nature of the creature - man. It is well, I think, to keep such things in mind, as the pace of progress seems slow in the case of mankind. Yes, well to maintain a little compassion for the bumbling and halting efforts of mankind.

So much then, for how I see things, in general. But can I make anything out of my own problems - or find a way to hold body and soul together for a few more years? I expect I shall be able to find a way, if only I can continue to find enough or interest to make it worth the while. There is little, if anything about the practice of Ophthalmology that is beyond my ability to comprehend, and few ophthalmologic skills that are beyond my capacity to acquire with extra training and experience. The economics and the politics of the practice of Ophthalmology are the limiting parameters in my own case. Money alone, through its influence for advertisement could greatly improve volume of patient flow; regardless of whether one were even a capable physician. Though there is adequate equipment and facilities for the practice of Ophthalmology in my area and across this whole country, one needs must gain access to that by buying one's own equipment and facilities (a minimal cost of say, $600,000), and by the medical-political-economic expedient of continuously flying off to meetings where the elite certify one another, to gain their own access to otherwise public equipment. And at the same time, disbar those whom they do not certify. Another factor in our times, is that the field is a bit overcrowded. And the tide of prejudice in employment runs against the older physician. Especially against those who have not finally established their place in a community by some twenty or thirty years of continuous presence in one locality where - through the years - they have seen a significant proportion of the population native to that area, among whom their name is well known. Another factor still, is that I am not by nature an outgoing personality; rather, a bit reclusive. Nor has my volume of surgery, or economic success been such as to embolden me with any large measure of arrogance, as a form of advertisement.

As I indicated in our recent phone conversation, I will be spending a large part of the month of March, working at an urgent-care-center in Pocatello. I am enclosing to Dot, a copy of some information concerning at least some of the persons that have been buried at Battle Ridge. If I locate anything more, I shall send it later.

Love

Your brother,
R. Garner Brasseur, M.D.

10 February 1989

- <u>Addendum Perspective</u> -

[PP has displayed little predisposition to writing. Since correspondence is generally a matter of reciprocity, my correspondence to him is likewise not extensive. Our dialectic through these many years is largely thus that of conversation. He seems often willing to peruse my essays and the annual summaries I send him regularly. And through these many years I have usually spent two or three days at a time visiting him and Dot at their home in Spokane some two or three times each year. We discuss and exchange a great deal of information and ideas. And he and I have taken a dozen of two or three day trips together into Canada and Idaho. Through the years he has made himself useful to myself and his other sibling in helping them puzzle their way through their various real estate and financial complications. And in the declining years of the lives of our parents, he has been diligent in looking after them in Coeur d'Alene, some thirty five miles from his quarters in Spokane.]

RGB

10 February 1989

29 March 1997

Las Vegas, New Mexico

Dear PM,

Had I known of it, I would have notified you in advance. But, it came about sort of inadvertently and spontaneously on Friday, the 21st of March. I had arrived at Carmen Serdon, in Baja California the night before. In the afternoon on Friday, BC, your sister and I, along with one of the other workers, drove north to Tecote, on the border.

As we often think of you, it isn't surprising that your name came up in the course of our conversation. Our calculations led us to suppose that you would be 41 years of age within a few days. Since I had planned to depart from Mexico the next day, we decided that we would use the occasion of your upcoming birthday to make a bit of a fiesta on this very day - in your honor. And so we stopped to have a Chinese meal there in Tecate ... in remembrance of you. So sorry that you couldn't have been with us, but happy birthday to you anyway. Since you weren't there, I did my best to keep up the conversation on your behalf. BC spoke a couple of words to the Deity on our behalf before we headed out to celebrate your birthday. Judging from his words, I gather that he doesn't have much faith in Mexican drivers or in the roads of Mexico. But he was rather reserved in his words to us, his mortal companions. Prudently testing the wind of words of the conversation, no doubt, so as to be ready with a possible amiable theme for some later conversation — in the event that the well-spring of my monologue themes might eventually go dry. By way of conversation, I wanted to be sure that he had some idea about the many and very serious diseases one is apt to come into contact with in these third world countries such as Mexico. But our time together was so short that I know I didn't do justice to the list of my subject materials. And I know from personal experience that there is a great plenty of disease and illness down there in Baja Mexico, because I got lost down there for about six hours the night I looked them up. I drove 150 miles or more in that general area, looking for the 'orphanatorio' where they were located; and I was astounded to learn that there are <u>many</u> orphanatorios even in just that one general area. "Why should that be (?)" you may be asking myself. Good question. I am still trying to discover some tentative answers unto myself. Part of the reason - besides poverty - must surely be related to rampant disease. Before that evening was over, I had spoken with a dozen Mexican folks in a 75 mile radius, and each of them pointed out some two or three orphanatorios with which he was acquainted. My limited Spanish made those interviews rather complex, but got me by. I stopped at several of the various orphanatorios, each time a-thinking' that this time I had the correct one ... only again to find myself in error. And then I suddenly remembered that I had a phone conversation with your sister in February, in which she had mentioned the name of the village. I looked up the date in my journal. Sure enough, there was the name - Carmen Serdon. And I then easily located the place, about six miles off of the main highway, over a washboard gravel road. In that dark village, when I finally arrived about 11:30 PM, "Everything was sleepin'. /All but the nightingale". And so I climbed into my sleeping bag in the pickup for a quiet night of rest. No noise except the occasional howling of the coyote. Early the next morning when the camp had come back to life I wandered into the orphanatorio campus . Your sister and her spouse are sleeping in a rather small trailer, so I got to sleep in the pickup on the second night also. After breakfast, M.A. showed me around the camp, and then she and I took a little walk. It was latter that day when we celebrated your birthday. I had one other chance to speak with them the following morning when we went to El Cajun to have breakfast together. A diverse subject matter, including:

- tuberculosis
- the Black Death (Plague)
- echinococcus
- hepatitis
- polio
- childhood disease and immunizations.
- My poor experiences with the Subaru car.
- some stories about M.A., and about my brothers, PP and EVH.
- About EVH's 'black box'
- About PP's 'perpetual motion machine'.
- About my own experience of wasted hours in attempt to design a perpetual motion machine.
- About my recent discussion with JRO concerning the same subject.
- About the connection between Cincinnatus and your own passion for war games.
- Relevance of that to a movie, *The Flight of the Phoenix*.
- About flying saucers.
- About the definition of revelation.

- About my recent trip with JRO.
- About PP's swing-bike.
- About the detrimental effect of poisonous oxygen.
- About the detrimental effects **of** gravity.
- About Black-holes.
- About Stephan Hawking.
- About the poisonous aspect of food, and why we need to find a way to concoct 'The Devine Elixir'.
- About man's even current primitive condition.
- The first climbing of mountains - in the 1850s.
- Man's first flight — a hot air balloon - about 1750.
- About the moral corrective effect of 'Reality'.
- About Jean-Luc Piccard's spaceship, 'Enterprise'.
- About what ought to be our primary objective — to align our view ofreality with the actuality of that reality.
- About my current projects; and their relative priorities.

———◆◆◆———

But, as you may already have been suspecting, we ran quite out of time before we ran out of conversational materials. And what we did cover, is mostly yet in need of a great deal of clarification. None of this material is new to your sister, of course, but BC appeared to be a little weary when I finally offered to give their poor souls a rest, and head north about 1:00 PM. I drove up highway 15 toward Las Vegas, stopping at Barstow to get my oil changed at about 201,000 miles. There they offered to service my fuel injector unit for about $135.00, saying that the engine was hitting on only three cylinders and that I would then be able to get better gas mileage. I didn't want to indicate my disbelief at his suggestion, so I promised him that I would get it done the next time I came through - but that right now *I* was 'down-at-the-heel'. As I drove along the high desert just after sundown, I stopped for half an hour to view the comet in the night sky. The first one that I have ever seen. Though interesting, it was a lot less spectacular than what I had anticipated. The traffic was terribly heavy. I guess it must have been 'spring-break' from school. I drove as far a St-George before I finally found a motel room. Then drove the final 300 miles into Salt Lake

City on Sunday. There I attend some post-graduate courses on Monday, Tuesday, and Wednesday. On Thursday I spent the day at the Mormon Genealogical Center. Then, that evening, I went to hear the Mormon Tabernacle Choir practice. I love to hear a great chorus singing great music. The young volunteer 'sisters' who staff the genealogy center are more than happy to assist and supply one with information. They even offered me a free Book of Mormon, but I eluded that by telling them that I am in the process of saving up my money so as to be able to buy for myself the newest and fanciest edition available. But I did take <u>and</u> read, a 17-page tract entitled *The Testimony of Joseph Smith*. It was the story of his personal revelation ... so we are assured. If so, then he certainly had some obligation to follow and live in accordance with that revelation. But to me and everyone else, it needs must be (by definition) mere hearsay. We may give it credence if we wish, but it does not thereby become a revelation to us. We must each await and search out our own personal revelations, which in turn become mere hearsay to all to whom we recite our astonishing insights. I left Salt Lake City 9:00 AM on Friday and arrived back home twelve hours later.

And then, again, a happy birthday to you, PM. And my best regards to the children: Bah, Boo, Belle, Bam-bam and Beans.

Love,

Yer dad

R.Garner Brasseur

29 March 1997

4 March 2007

Santa Fe, New Mexico

Greetings PM,

Bayloo tells me she received an e-mail communication from you the other day. Well now here it is Sunday - my day off, and I have now the opportunity to catch up on some my correspondence and work out the details of some of the other projects to which I find myself committed. This business of living is a time consuming and complex matter. I know that the grim reaper is relentless in his pursuit to catch up with me and is surely closing the gap that separates us, but I have no way of knowing just how soon that fatal meeting will occur. Meanwhile, I chug along as best I can so as not to leave too many of my projects uncompleted.

You mention that you again have some sort of upcoming date with the court to determine the issue of custody of your children. I note that Bah and Boo are now adults and in control their own fates independent of any hold on them from the courts. Surely, no jurisdiction of the courts applies to them in this matter. I note that Belle too, will soon be eighteen and I wonder if she too, as a young adult woman might not also be considered outside of the jurisdiction of the courts on this matter? Meanwhile, Bam-bam is age 15 and Beans is 13. Do not they in their teens have some say in how they wish to be farmed out into the jurisdiction of the parents?

As you know, I am caught up into a full-time schedule of employment with Wal-Mart and am expected to show up for work on a regular basis. Perhaps within a couple of years I may be able to get out from under that necessity and into a final retirement. You will recall that I was in a state of retirement from 1999 until mid-summer of 2005. Were I now retired I would welcome the chance to attend this circus of court proceedings with which you are saddled. A plausible excuse for the making of another adventure into the Northwest. This coming summer it will now be two years since I have had the opportunity to wander about freely upon the open roads in accordance with my vague whims. I miss that freedom and look forward to the hope of re-acquiring that leisure; so as to be able once more to intrude upon and disturb the domestic tranquility of my various relatives and friends. In fact, if my health remains stable, I will be entitled to a week of vacation in the coming summer. Just barely enough time to get briefly re-acquainted with some of my grandchildren and perhaps travel a few miles with a few of them along the roadways of life. But for the summer of 2008, my aspirations are definitely more expansive.

In my view, based upon years of involvement within the courts on a number of various issues, and based on the strange injustices I have witnessed them already to have inflicted on you in their inexplicable machinations, I am inclined to view their intrusions into the domestic affairs of private citizens as merely something of a charade. Their 'decisions' seem to me more or less each a foregone conclusion and heavily biased to the support of the willful designs and the highly vindictive nature of the women of our societies. ("Hell hath no fury like a woman scorned".) It is not all without some usefulness however, for it forms the pretext of a neat sinecure to a viper's nest of lawyers, social workers, psychologists, and judges who might otherwise swell the roles of the unemployed.

It seems like perhaps three or four years ago that you were wanting me to be at hand for matters concerning the judicial decision concerning the custody of your children. The idea was that I would be on hand to give testimony on your behalf to support your claim for custody of the children. But the court is forever in delay and in the process of continuation of the proceedings (more of the nature of non-proceedings). Postponement, you know - until next month etc. I hung about for two or three of those opportunities to testify, but the court never got around to calling for that testimony. I am not surprised by that. If there suddenly were somehow to occur an unexpected excess of time on the court schedule, they might call on me to answer some few abbreviated court-permitted questions. To give at least the appearance of some interest in what a father might be prepared to say in support of his son. A show for appearances sake. But one cannot believe they would put any weight in what a father were to say about his own son … unless it were something of a derogatory nature. And so, I didn't then - and I don't now - believe that my presence at court would serve any actual purpose. Though I would gladly use that pretext for getting out once more upon the open road to enjoy some leisure; and excuse for again imposing upon the hospitality of my people and friends. If I were free to do so.

It is often the case that I find myself wishing and hoping that my opinion is wrong. I hope for it at this time. But the truth is that I believe you need to be preparing yourself for the disappointment of yet another set-back in your often overly optimistic expectations. I am hoping that you will begin now - early - to see around and beyond the disappointment you will have to be facing. It is my view that surely the teen-aged children ought to have some say in how they are distributed out into the custody of their parents and relatives, but so far as I know the courts do not pursue that course. Am I wrong in that?

Next, there is the matter of your now adult children. Surely they are in position to harbor some personal views on how this custody matter would be most equitably arranged. Do you get along with them? Have you had cause or opportunity to discuss with them their views of this matter of custody? Would they be inclined to favor you or their mother in this concern - or willing to support even a joint custody? Will the courts give ear to their views on this matter, since they are adult citizens in a position to have opinion based upon first hand experience of the issues in question? Of course, I have no delusions about any father being able to win a popularity contest against the mother of the children. But for all I know, the children might have at least some rational capacity such as may weight somewhat against the deep emotional overtones that are often want to outweigh all other considerations in their young lives.

Presuming that the custody of the children ends up favoring your ex-spouse, I expect that you will still be able to see them at times? In any case, as time goes by the children will naturally have some hope of at least seeing you from time-to-time. In fact, there is always going to be occasional enough conflict of child with the parent who has custody, that they will each from time-to-time deeply wish they could get free from this parent to hang out with the other.

And so, PM, I urge you to hang onto your equanimity in whatever ordeal you must face in this matter.

Come visit us sometime. Best wishes PM.

Love,

Dad,

R. Garner Brasseur

4 March 2007

July of 2010

Santa Fe, NM

Dear Jim,

The main reason for my recent offering to you somewhat of my writing for your perusal was in the spirit of reciprocity - as you at times send me some of your publications. And I thank you for the time and trouble you have put into your recent return letter. I don't see that you are likely to have been surprised (nor injured) by my few insignificant snippets of writing - nor by this missile, either. Perhaps even a bit invigorated by the challenge? And it gives you and I yet one more opportunity to clear the air between us; and re-establish between us, our pragmatic no-man's-land.

I wasn't surprised at the theme of your response to some of my writings that I recently placed into your hands. I didn't leave them with you to mock you or belittle your preoccupations with your religion or the things you chose to do with your life. Nor do I expect to convert you to my own view of the nature of reality. I merely thought that you - like myself - might be somewhat curious as to the private mental life of an old acquaintance, a relative, or an ancestor. There is a certain element of friendship and affection that has and often still seems to exist between us lo these many years, despite our Philosophical divergence.

Perhaps you might be aware that in the past 25 years I have devoted considerable time and effort in chasing down my genealogical connections and trying to gather some information about their lives within the times and places of their existence. Though I have had some success in gathering their names and places of their lives, there is almost nothing available to give one any insight into their actual individual personal problems and psychological preoccupations. Yet, I am nosey, and such things are of interest to me. Case histories, you know. An interest that may have taken root when I took my first Psychology course - in high school. An interest that continued to grow and eventually found me working eight years in a psychiatric hospital. An interest that inevitably permeates into my interrelationships with friends and family also. What drives this person? With what are they preoccupied? What do they really think, and why? What is it that they do not even recognize within themselves? How do they deal with their psychological injuries and anxieties? To say nothing of the physical barbs and bruises along life's way.

Your experience in social work seems to have left you also with some of this 'clinical' approach to your acquaintances. In my view, your particular view of 'the nature of reality' appears to be highly tainted with religious eschatology. Your recent letter suggests again to me that you have a somewhat dogmatic prescription which you would hope to impose upon each and every person of your acquaintance. As with your prescription, your diagnosis is certainly always the same - to whit, this person needs J.C. As sure as you seem to believe that your notion of eternal truth is correct; so sure also am I - that the notion is mistaken. You are not much astonished that I would tell you that, for you have some acquaintance with me extending over many years. And you might well suspect that I am as ready as are you to give the matter an honest discussion. A private matter between you and me. But to what practical purpose?

On dialectic. The long and the short of it is that I have gradually become ever more obsessed with study, reading, and writing concerning all these things. I find those readings interesting, and the conversations are stimulating. But only by writing can I thoroughly explore and settle unto myself some tentative answers to the problems, complexities, and uncertainties that forever confront me. Dialog. The silent dialog with oneself seems of limited benefit (too fragmented and effervescent) unless it be self enforced by the writing of one's thoughts which one can then scrutinize and compare to one another - for reflection and always possible revision - so as to urge them into a state of reasonable compatibility to one another. **Dialectic** is stated to be the art of reasoning or disputing correctly or soundly. In one's writing, one can reason and dispute with oneself. But -subsequent to that - there does seem to be some advantage in the batting about of concepts and ideas with a thoughtful and analytic correspondent.

Would that I could disabuse you of the notion that I have somehow been 'hurt' as an explanation for why it is that I somehow blame and am angry at your God. But you need not make excuses for what you see as shortcomings within my character. Nor do I perceive within myself an anger or frustrations at anyone's God, or even at our benignly indifferent Universe. But there are aspects of various religions; and the fatuous pretensions of some of their leaders and followers that I find annoying. Some, dangerous. Many, counter-productive of the peace and brotherhood to which they many purport to aspire.

Life, after all, is full of bumps, falls, and all manner of un-pleasantries. I get over mine, and I expect that you get over yours. I tend to regard myself as having been unusually fortunate. Many of my personal disappointments have been what one might label as 'blessings'. That same word is in my vocabulary, also - but with perhaps less of a theological connotation.

On Catharsis

I was somewhat taken aback at your suggestion <u>that I have 'poisoned'</u> my relationships with friends and family. Though I suppose I might have been seen as mild and 'easy-going' in my youth, the harsh realities that have confronted me through the years, have likewise undoubtedly made me somewhat more confrontational - of necessity. Certainly oppositional, upon occasion; but not often defiant (though frequently tempted). It may be necessary for "we the people" to again become defiant. I do sometimes deem it important to make my protests: and do no longer shirk the necessity of going toe-to-toe even with my children and family, when that seems necessary and timely. I regard that necessity as being instructional and informative - not the "poisoning of relationships". One might also regard it as cathartic. "If the urge to kill coincided always with the opportunity to kill, who would escape hanging?" says mark Twain.

Though <u>The Golden Rule</u> is a fine ideal, yet, taken alone, it fails to be applicable to the totality of the life situations with which one must inevitably deal. In coming to terms with our fellow man (and governing institutions), one must oft - in the end - apply <u>The Iron Rule</u> (Do not permit others to do unto you, what you would not do unto them): rather even, than <u>The Silver Rule</u> (Do not do unto others, what you would not have them do onto you).

I remind you of the matter of Socratic Wisdom: Socrates was widely regarded in Ancient Athens as a man of learning. Students and men of knowledge often passed the time of day with him as he haunted the Parthenon and agora engaging sophists, students, and other intellectuals in learned and Philosophical dialogs. Some of his countrymen once stopped at the Oracle of Delphi to ask the priestess there as to 'who was the wisest man in Athens?' After some consideration she informed them that Socrates was the wisest man in Athens. Armed with this new pronouncement, his friends located Socrates and told him of what had happened. He was modestly perplexed by what he had been told. After giving the matter some thought, he attempted to come to some conclusion on the matter and offered his friends an explanation of what this seemed to mean.

Socrates confessed that he did not consider himself to be a knowledgeable man and that he was confused as to what it all meant. Still, he believed in the gods and in the veracity of Oracle, and so he pondered and discussed what might be the hidden meaning of the words of the Oracle. He reminded his friends that he did not purport to be a teacher of wisdom. It was, however, his custom to seek out and engage in dialogue the Sophists and other men of the city who were learned and reputed to be among the wisest men of Athens. He did this because he too aspired to attain wisdom, and it was his intention that by discussing with the experts what they were reputed to know, he would be able to acquire the wisdom which they were supposed to have attained. His experience at this however had left him rather disappointed. For when he closely questioned the reputedly most knowledgeable men of the city, they faltered, became confused, fell into frequent contradictions in their own explanations, and finally always broke off the dialogs with various pretexts for their premature departures.

Socrates finally concluded that the meaning of the Oracle's words must be something like this. That Socrates has the advantage in wisdom, in that he knew nothing, and that he full well knew that he knew nothing. In this sense, perhaps, he had greater wisdom than the most learned men and sophists in Athens. For though they were well educated and learned men, his interrogations of them demonstrated that they did not know what they purported to known. They did not even know or acknowledge that they did not know. They were not aware of their ignorance, which implies that <u>Socrates was the wiser</u>, for in his humility, he was always fully <u>aware of his own ignorance</u>.

The reality, Jim, is that like yourself, I too am somewhat evangelical by nature, so that I too - upon occasion - use that occasional opportunity to say some things that you might not want to hear or read. Some years ago I made a couple of applications to enter a theological seminary (Unitarian), thinking I might thus have access to a pulpit; and an audience. But they declined my offer. Another failure I needs must endure. And so, you have the advantage of me in having a potentially large body of listeners, while my connections are much more narrow - limited to but a few friends and family. A rather sizable extended family. Outside of these, there are but few with whom I have anything approaching an easy regular communication. Of the few that ever come to me for advice, most of them pay cash-on-the-barrelhead. And never have I had an overly demanding practice.

I think I mentioned to you that I did write and publish a book a few years back. Written to summarize my views of what constitutes valid history from ancient times to present. It includes at length, my views of the nature of reality along with what has gradually become my own personal Philosophy. As my incontinence of my studied impressions (that is to say, the publication of said book) would inevitably be offensive to many a person, I don't see that it is helpful to be 'in the face of' those I know who are most likely to be offended by it. Therefore, among my friends and family, I purposefully neglect to present (to some of them) a copy of my book. **Avoid unnecessarily offending you, too.** *A STUDIED IMPRESSION OF THAT WHICH IS*, is the title of my book. Available through Amazon or E-bay, for example. One of my grand-daughters tells me that one can even find the first half of the body of the text which (she says), "is available for reading online at Google books and here is the link: http://books.google.com/books?id=D2RrEJqKtFQC&pg=PA83&dq=r.g.+brasseur&ei=pQQqSujwF4nQkwSt29zzBg#PPP1,M1

But you Jim, would probably not enjoy it. Which is why I have never threatened you with a free copy. You have been able to have your say in the course of your life; and I have had my say. Certainly it is best that we both let it go at that. And continue our long friendship on that less threatening and more superficial basis.

In the long view, of course, we have no ultimate use for the personality, and needs must depart from it - as well as from this mortal flesh. And in departing, the things of consequence are: 1) the amount of truth that we have comprehended and endorsed to those within the sphere of our influence, 2) the inspiration which their memories of us, may have given (imparted) to them - to live a well-proportioned life of self-discipline, so as to enable them to see farther and more clearly than ourselves, and 3) that they continue to sally-forth into the universe of space-time on the wings of scientific advancement.

Such evidence as exists, gives us cause to consider that we are each a fragment of a continuous and ongoing life, on an irreversible course through time and the universe. Though we are physically and physiologically different from our parents, sibling, and descendants, we would nevertheless be individually different even were we clones, because of the inevitability of our various life experience. And our response to that experience. The very fact of history confirms to us that we and all things change under the influence of process and time. There is no reason to suspect that change, process, or time shall cease. There is no science apart from its ongoing change and advancement, based upon observations, experience, reason, and experimentation. Each race of creatures has its supreme gifts and abilities. Those of mankind are curiosity, reason, inventiveness; and a cultural tradition that accumulates, gathers, transmits, and applies knowledge and information to the living of our individual lives and advancement of civilization. So long as the necessary resources and opportunity are available to mankind, there is reason to expect that the frontiers of civilizations shall continue to advance into the universe. And the more so, as there is every reason to expect that there will be both resources and opportunity beyond the confines of planet earth. Since we expect that the universe will continue to show itself as a unity of interrelated parts with cause and effect relationships, we may hope that advancement of science and knowledge might gradually absolve its disjunction from moral Philosophy.

Why does the bear go over the mountain? Why (?), one might ask, do I trouble myself with all of these time consuming projects? Because I have the health, the time, the curiosity and yet enough energy to do so. Because I have not yet learned how to sit quietly nor in blissful peace with myself in the sun. Because even an unwanted and essentially useless life might just as well be lived and endured with some little courage, energy, and hope; just as though it were of some significance.

Because life challenges one to think. Because one must eventually charge oneself with the responsibility for discovering whatever he can of reality. Because a responsible adult being must ultimately define his own worthy agenda of life - even in the very act of living and enduring the agony of one's existence. We - "inheritors of a few years and sorrows." And so I too must sit a spell to contemplate - beneath the Banyan tree.

Sincerely,

R. Garner Brasseur, M.D.

July of 2010

27 July 2011

Santa Fe, New Mexico

Dear Lynn,

The primary purpose of this note is to return to you the set of keys for your apartment. Through the years our occasional get-togethers have been useful and influential to me by virtue of their permitting of open discussion. And by virtue of providing both the venue; and permitting of subjects not commonly allowable with but few of one's contemporaries. Thank you, Lynn, for your always generous hospitality.

Many years ago you sent me pictures of our Washington School 6th grade classes. I review them from time to time, and am always curious to know what has become of those associates of our yesteryears. It is always interesting to me to hear some little detail or incident of their lives. Your letter enclosed with those two pictures implied to me that those lives have all been interesting stories, even though but scant has ever been revealed to us. I am reminded of that ancient curse, "may you live in interesting times", or some such thing. As with you, and each of them, so too do I pause and reflect from time to time upon my personal foibles and the barbs of fate that have plagued me through the years. All, very instructive to me. But to what ultimate purpose? All, beyond my poor powers of comprehension. And my mind turns then to a song I hear from Neil Diamond: "All have sweated beneath the same sun. Looked up in wonder at the same moon. And wept when it was done - for being done too soon."

I had decided to stay over in El Centro that one more day, so that I could visit with you one additional evening, before heading back home. As I sat alone that morning in your apartment just after I arose, I was thinking how an unusual an occurrence this was for me. Unusual, in that I was faced with now an entire day all to myself in the cool comfort of your spacious apartment with nary a chore or an obligation to occupy my time or energy. No need even to venture out into the uncomfortable heat of the day. It occurred to me that I might under this circumstance of fate, do something akin to what Descartes had done, by way of a thought experiment.

Away from my occupation and home for the past few weeks, I had begun to ponder as to what us older specimens of humanity (such as you and I) might decide to do with ourselves if suddenly confronted one day with a state of solitary retirement though, while yet in a state of good health, well housed and clothed, and economically comfortable with pensions and saving into our advancing years; and with no immediate family concerns to bedevil our domestic tranquility. And with advancing years, even our passions seem gradually to wither away into ghost-like apparitions. <u>What then, would one decide to do with oneself?</u> This then, is what was on my mind; and my plan was then to sit there in silence until moved by some existential necessity, or until the answer to my question occurred to me that very morning. Yes, I had hopes that a plan or a cause with some specific and practical objective might begin to dawn upon me that very morning. One to which I might devote my ongoing daily efforts and intentions in the coming years. But that revelation was not forthcoming, and I gave it up as a conscious intention after a few fruitless hours. Decided instead, to settle for a quiet little nap. With my sails already set in the direction of that morning's intention, I had yet some hope that the answer might come to me in my dream state. It didn't.

I was reminded that day in El Centro, of my strange experience of some thirty five years ago on a very quiet Sunday morning when I had slept-in. My wife of those times had dragged my children off to her church - which is why it was so unusually quiet that day. The instant

I awoke to consciousness I became aware that I did not know who I was; nor where I was. My first impulse was to open my eyes, to gather clues from my surroundings as to who and where I was. But I resolved to resist that impulse. Nor was there a sound ("there wasn't a breath in that land of death") available to clue me in. I intended from pure intense effort of recollection, alone - to summon forth to my consciousness the details of my past and present. I supposed that a single clue would then cascade all of that into my accustomed waking state of awareness. I awaited a long while. As best I can recall, that first clue was finally an external faint auditory clue to remind me where I be. And I oped mine eyes to reaffirm my first impression. In the blink of an eye, my accustomed state of consciousness was again cascaded upon me.

In the past few weeks of my odyssey across the countryside, revisiting the various many neighborhoods of my life experience and having many a cause to recollect some of what I thought myself to remember as to the facts of the recollections and ideas in my memory banks, I became again aware that there was many an error harbored amongst them. Humbled, every day, by my having to recognize and reform the errors of my always too vague store of recollections - as when confronted by an obvious conflicting reality in the immediate light of very day. Sometimes even having to endure the ignominy of being corrected by on occasional acquaintance or friend. Yes, I not infrequently find my mere recollections in obvious need of correction by stark reality. Furthermore, it is also the case that one's own immediate perceptions of reality are - at times - in disagreement with what seems logical, and thereby in need of a second look. One must then either ratify or refute one's own observations. Yes, one's perceptions of reality in need of correction by one's own rational faculties. Ones own memory, face to face (vis-à-vis) and opposed to one's own powers of reason.

I arrived home at 1:00 AM on the 16th after a 14 hour drive from El Centro, CA. The next evening we watched a movie, *I'm not Rapport* - a conversation between a couple of old geezers in New York's Central Park. Walter Mathau says something to the effect that "sex is not the main game. The main game is actually romance. The little bit of hot bodies and an itty bit of sex is of rather small consequence, compared to the theme of romanticism." That idea caught my attention and I intended later with the 'playback button' on the TV, to go back for the exact quotation. But, alas, the cancel mechanism had already erased the whole movie. Small matter, however.

Here now was an idea that had never before crossed my mind. The more I think about it, the more profoundly am I impressed with the idea. Romanticism does seem to me as though perhaps merely a culturally derived idea that has overtaken Homo sapiens - alone, among all species. While primitive and unanalyzed, this matter of sexuality is genetically imposed upon man; and all creatures - a primary imperative. It would seem that if a man is not currently more thoroughly dominated by sexually than by the impulse to romanticism, then somehow it can be said that a culturally derived idea or motive has managed to dominate or overshadow a very deeply ingrained and powerful mandate of nature. It doesn't mean that the two ideas are not yet harnessed together like a poorly matched pair of horses in 'a team'. Just that 'the team concept' has placed significant constraint upon one of man's most powerful motivating intentions.

Of course, the slowly progressing civilizing process into which mankind has become progressively entangled - in consequence of the ongoing 'dialectics' (evolving conversation of ever expanding nuance from one generation to the next) has left we individuals of our species in a 'conflicted state' of uncertainty on many a subject. Such as: under what circumstances is it permissible to kill a fellow human being - or even another animal? Under what circumstances is it permissible to take the property of another person, or a neighboring tribe? Etc. The voice of conscience which we imagine ourselves to be hearing - as words and connotations of words evolve into the ever expanding lexicon of our personal, familial, and tribal languages. And, of course, the degree to which we as individuals are thus 'civilly conflicted' varies considerably from one individual to another, and even from one phase to the next of any one individual's progress through the years and vicissitudes of his life's experience.

One might make the case that reproductive sexual activity is the fundamental primary motive and 'purpose' of 'mankind' - in common with every genus and species among 'the higher forms of life' here on earth. Needs must be - in order to maintain the ever ongoing cycle-of-life. All other necessities (for air, food, water, shelter, and rest) of one's individual physiological life are merely supportive of that one objective with which one is genetically imbued. It is not necessary that one perceive that primary purpose and objective for it yet to be generally valid and 'operative'. It being a harsh and cruel world here on the plains of Serengeti, there is many an individual who does not achieve that reproductive mandate. Never-the-less, a great many more individuals are conceived and born than ever survive to adult reproductive status; and even among that few, many - for various reasons - fail in that mandate towards reproduction.

One's sexuality being generated hormonally within one 'in the fullness of time' of one's life, and being strongly reinforced by 'the pleasure principle' serves to ensure that the sexually mature individual will be predisposed to engage in sexual behavior as surely as one is drawn intermittently to a source of drinking water. The 'thirst' for sexual action, just as the thirst for water is intermittent and influenced, due to such phenomena as, thirst, satiation, and hormonal cycles. In the pursuit of sexual pleasure and the intent to achieve satiation, there exist the matters of competition and preference. Among mammals, the female is more heavily influenced into an only periodic sexual receptivity under the influence of her hormonal cycles; and the subtle signals of that receptivity are readily 'sniffed out' by an ever ready and eager male contingency of her society. Though her sexual role is passive, she is commonly selective, exercising her personal preference from among the males in pursuit of her attentions and favors. The males in pursuit, exercise their wiles and physical prowess in competition for 'the smiles and favors' of the eternal maternal being. A primitive reminiscent emotional adoration and an object of quest only perhaps vaguely perceived as somehow related to the satisfactions which preoccupied them previously - in their remote infancy.

Much of the aforesaid applies also to our own species - Homo sapiens - considered by ourselves to be far more intelligent, socially refined in our tastes, better organized as groups, and more civil in deportment and mannerisms. And intellectually a bit advanced above the beasts of the seas, fields, and jungles. Despite that, our species seems yet primarily sexual as to behavior and underlying motivation.

A few thousand recent years of religious-philosophical suppositions, speculations, and contest has brought us to the point that a large part of the populations of mankind are beginning to wonder - and even then to presume - that perhaps we (WE, alone, among the creatures of this earth); that we each possess 'an immortal soul'(?). A comforting delusion, at least.

That we possess a certain ill defined and as yet indemonstrable 'essence' that continues to exist into eternity (?). Intentionally believing this, even though we are intimately acquainted with - and certain of our own physical death and subsequent slow demise and decomposition into the dusts and chemical elements which we know to be then recycled into our earth's ongoing processes.

> "Why, if the soul can fling the dust aside.
> And naked on the air of heaven ride.
> Were it not a shame - were it not a shame for him.
> In this clay carcass crippled to abide?"

> "Strange, is it not?
> That of the myriads who
> Before us passed the door of Darkness through
> Not one returns to tell us of the Road
> Which to discover we must travel too."
>
> Omar Khayyam

This business of sex is a manifold and omnipresent thing in the hearts and minds of mankind. A matter of concern, and a problem among the societies of our species. Yes, this thing called lust tromps at times through every mortal adult breast. At times perchance ideally paired with affection; but oft too, paired up with hate and anger, and intention to vague revenge, insult, and injury. And there is also the misguided, mis-directed, perverted, and scandalous sexual behavior that graces seemingly every news program, and newspaper; and probably a good much of private conversation. I get weary of hearing about it. But it will not go away. Sexual problems and troubles appear to be ubiquitous. Sexual deviancy and pathology would seem to be as common as what we would call 'normal' sexuality. The news media being aware that the subject of sex is so ever upon the minds of the adolescent and adult of our species, would seem to be adequate explanation as to why sexual deviancy is so continuously at the forefront in the news. Only 3.5% of the population is said to be gay or lesbian. Thus, the vast majority are heterosexual.

Perhaps the commonest and most proper place of sex is that which occurs between married couples and in a setting generally intended to be conducive to and productive of each newly founded generation. But even among and between each 'happily married' couple there seems to be cause for considerable tension and dissatisfactions concerning their sexual relationships. Secular and religious 'councilors' are often called upon to mediate and 'save' marriages, and offer vague suggestions for remediation. Marriages, after all, are most commonly founded upon sexual relationships - or are they founded upon unadulterated romantic love (?), (with the necessity of sex thrown into the mix for the inevitable necessity for the release of normal cyclic sexual tensions - and the production of a family and perpetuation-of-the-species). The generally accepted high esteem for family might commonly be supposed to somewhat stabilize the relationship between a married couple as they learn to work together to solve the ever evolving problems of an ever evolving family.

But what has sex got to do with love? The word, 'love', is itself somewhat problematic here. The word 'love' being far much overused, with so many connotations (often as a pretext for duplicity) one might do well to give up the use of the word, in favor of specific labels for other aspects of what is often blithely designated as love. It might truly be said that sex itself is a generally much cherished and pleasurable pass-time among we mere mortals, and that it can be experienced as a sort of 'icing on the cake' of a romantic relationship between a couple with genuine affections for one another. But sex is far from uncommon between persons who neither esteem nor maintain any affection for one another. Enjoyed for pure wonton animal lust ("man's favorite sport"), for money, for political advantage. Enjoyed by one - endured by the other? Used to punish or intentionally to cause pain or embarrassment. Widespread rape is regularly used as a tactic in war to demoralize and strike fear into a population being invaded and conquered. Destined to assure an ongoing animosity between the enemy and one's own troops, for "the perpetrators of an injustice never forgive their victims."

Since 9 or 10 years of age, I have been intermittently attracted romantically at one time or another to one or another of perhaps 15 or 20 girls of my age with whom I have been generally only vaguely acquainted as schoolmates. As I recall, my attraction to them in those pre-pubescent years was purely one of a romantic nature, with no attending element of sexual interest as a component of that attraction (silent and transient infatuations). Most of them were unlikely to have been even aware of my attraction to them, while a few seemed perhaps at least vaguely aware and faintly reciprocated minimal indications of mutual interest. Even into adulthood and advancing years there still occurs from time to time a similar silent transient attraction to one or another female age-mate with whom one becomes acquainted occupationally or socially. To even a 'happily married man' of overly bold or recklessness of spirit, there is always the possibility of one or another of such an acquaintance turning into what is termed, 'an affair'. ("Man is essentially a polygamous animal - and has been, through the eons; except for the slowly progressive civilizing effect of women", says Krouthammer). And as to the female of the species, "Like all women everywhere, her principle conquest was man" as Von Hagen puts it.

For the single man, there seems to be some tendency for these loose social-sexual arrangements to become a pattern of behavior. They too are many destined eventually at last to be tamed - and sometimes cured - by an uncommonly adorable woman of compatible disposition. Call it reciprocity of respect and affection. And when that reciprocity has flown, so has the romance.

Through the ages and the civilizing influences of the evolving societies of mankind, the sexually conflicted personal perceptions of people begins to show signs of <u>a culturally derived motive force</u> within the minds of many <u>that becomes co-equivalent with primitive natural sexual impulses as an enduring attraction between male and female</u>. Its early beginnings perhaps seen in the middle ages of European culture as 'chivalry'; and having perhaps only convolutedly arrived but gradually from the combining influences of Near Eastern religions and philosophies of the previous two or three thousand years. The culturally transmitted influence has been such, that it is as though - in the minds of many - <u>the main game has become one of courtly romance</u>, which has begun to replace that of orgiastic sexuality. Sex is still a part of the game despite the yet conflicted attitudes and perceptions in the minds of the many. But each night's dreams and pillow-talk are dissipate at dawn; while the vagaries of romance linger long in the memory.

And so again, Lynn, thanks for your recent hospitality. Perhaps the occasion of our upcoming 60th high school reunion will get us together again? If not, I'll try to run you down once more at some time within the space of the coming year.

Sincerely,

R. Garner Brasseur

27 July 2011

◆◆◆

- <u>An Anonymous Addendum Perspective </u>-

[I tend to agree with most of these comments as it seems to have been my own experience, as well. Although most people in our society, particularly the male component, of whatever age or health, spend a great deal of their time in idle thought on the sexual aspects of the game, the female seems more interested in the romantic parts, with the sexual part only a by-product - hours of good behavior and courting by the male will eventually elicit a sexual response if the female is 'in the mood'. If not, he may as well go back to his abode, or take a cold shower, or simply try to get some sleep before dawn. There are other girls to pursue if the favored one is seldom receptive, but then it all falls into the same old cycle, eventually. But if the favored one is a good companion and good company and does her share of the heavy lifting of life, then some receptive shortcomings are often understandable and acceptable. And, of fact, the ones who are 'high maintenance' and hot-to-trot can wear one down after awhile, too, as there are other things to do with one's limited time away from work, and certainly many other interests, even aside from one's children. Life is limited, with seldom enough time to accomplish even a fraction of the projects one finds. You, even now in your elder years, find even more to do now without financial, familial or household constraints than when you were a young man and endlessly busy with the necessities of life for yourself and dependents. So, it seems there is little benefit to pursuing old distractions as you know well enough what that road looks like, having been down it too often. If you had it to do all over again, how would you comport yourself to have improved on what of the past you yet clearly recall? One life is all one person can live, and you've been fortunate enough, later illnesses not withstanding, to have come through it so long and so well, and still with most of your faculties and abilities with you. So count your blessings, and don't be concerned with whatever opportunities you may have missed or rewards gone wanting. And keep-on-truckin'.]

21 May 1997

Las Vegas, New Mexico

Dear Nephew GMK.,

Your grandmother is still alive at age 91, though it has been 5 years or more since she has been able to recognize or conceive who I might be, or anyone else of her family, either. She is what one would call demented - a series of small strokes has gradually robbed her of her memory and intellectual powers. It is a difficult predicament, though not a problem, for to call a thing a problem is to suggest that it has a solution.

I am now age 64, just 15 months older than your mother. Brother VBB and I drove over to Marysville to visit with your mother last summer. VBB is just 15 months younger than your mother. She certainly looks well, and was in very good spirits, though I know she has this chronic illness called Lupus Erythematosis, which gives her trouble with easy fatigue-ability and intermittent episodes of severe dizziness. Though she and I have always been on good terms, our paths have not often crossed through these many years. I used to see your family more often back in 1957 and 1958, when I was attending the University, in Missoula. Since that time, I have never again seen your father, Marvin. I understand he lives somewhere in Las Vegas, Nevada. I'll try to get in touch with him the next time I get there

I finished medical school training at age thirty, and then did general practice of medicine for three years before spending three more years of training down in Panama. I then practiced Ophthalmology for about twenty years, in Oregon, Washington, New Mexico, and Idaho. In the past seven years I am employed here in Las Vegas, New Mexico, at the State Psychiatric Hospital. I have long had an interest in psychology and psychiatry, so I have found my work with these patients to be quite interesting. Perhaps you knew that I have been divorced for a few years now. Hardly an unusual situation, since, as you know, half of the marriages in this country end in divorce, and there is no way of knowing how poorly the others are doing. I think that marriage with children is worth doing, for it is an education in itself. If one is fortunate enough to find a mate who is truly compatible it may last a lifetime, but there are plenty of good reasons why it often doesn't work out that way. But I'll duck out on that subject for now because it is long and involved, and because the subject of this letter is only marginally related to it.

Besides my four children (your cousins), I have 12 grandsons and 4 grand-daughters. Though EVH and ALKE are both deceased, I still have 3 brothers and 3 sisters. I usually see most of these on a yearly basis … some of them, 2 or 3 times yearly, even though I am as far from them as are *you,* from your family. Additionally, we frequently communicate by phone and by letter. The letters sometimes resemble manuscripts, by virtue of their length. I also have 35 nephews and 29 nieces, who are now all adults, and whom I see relatively infrequently, though I am reasonably well acquainted with most of them through the years. As with us, of the older generation, some of them get themselves into trouble and encounter various problems on their life's journeys, and that is when they are most apt to hear from me. I know that a couple of them have even spent a little time in prison, but they have served their time and then gone off into more promising directions.

It is no secret, nephew, that you have spent the past few years in self-imposed suffering. Suffering is a part of the human condition. Most folks have but a limited endurance for it, but your personal tolerance for suffering seems to be above average. The moral value of <u>suffering</u>, is that when one has come to the limits of his ability to tolerate it any further, the soil of his being becomes fertile to the possibility of <u>insight</u>. That is to say, that he begins to acknowledge that he has been suffering, and that he is now interested in inquiring as to the cause of his suffering, and that he has some interest in the possibility of rooting out the cause. One then works up enough righteous anger and courage to fortify his will. The empowered will then finally produces the necessary <u>action</u>; and it is only that action that can at last produce <u>change</u>. Let us only then take care that it be reasonable, appropriate, and adequate action and change. Huxley says it more concisely, "There is no alleviation for the sufferings of mankind … except veracity of thought and action; and the resolute facing of the world as it is."

It is important though, for one to recognize that there is an essential difference between <u>problems</u> and <u>predicaments</u>, since the one can and ought to be supplied with remedy, while the other requires of us that we become meaningfully philosophic, so as to be able to endure the burden with equanimity. What Frost would call, moving easily in a comfortable harness. Predicament (?) or problem (?), that is the question. Can one face the question courageously and honestly? Benjamin Franklin says, "As the happiness or real good of men consists in right action, and right action can not be produced without right opinion, it behooves us, above all things in this world, to take care that our opinions of things be according to the nature of things. The foundation of all virtue and happiness is in thinking rightly."

Hobbs brings to our attention that vain conceit of one's own wisdom, which almost all men think they possess in greater degree than others. They may acknowledge others to be more witty, more eloquent, or more learned, yet will hardly believe there may be many so wise as themselves. Every man seems content with his own share of wisdom.

We tend, each, to get hung up on our gradually acquired 'certitudes-of-belief'. They get in the way of our intellectual and moral progress. We need to keep them down-graded at least to the status of 'tentative beliefs', so that they are not constant obstacles to the improvement of our individual understanding.

To my way of thinking, nephew, it seems curious that you have never had recourse to anyone in your family, concerning your problems. For you, too, are mere mortal, just as am I, and all of those in our immediate family. How is it possible that you, alone, have never been in need of consolation, advice nor assistance of any kind? But perhaps you purchase your advice upon the streets of Phoenix, from such professionals as psychologists, psychiatrists, palm-readers or astrology experts who claim to be able to calculate the best advice for you, based upon the position of the planets. Certainly it cannot be the case that you are unaware of your major problems and predicaments. The fact that you flunked a grade in the course of your elementary education seems to me irrelevant, since I know so many bright, excellent, and well educated people that have been through the same thing. Besides myself, in my own family, your mother and a sister, DFB, and AG are a part of that same privileged minority, and seem to have benefited from that insult - as though it were of the nature of a wake-up call.

I say that it is curious you have not consulted your family, because the whole of my experience is densely studded with hundreds of communications between myself and my brothers, sisters, nephews, nieces, children and even a certain number of trusted non-relatives. Such is the nature of my not terribly exclusive inner circle of troubled beings. Persons who find their way to that communion by dint of informal sharing and discussion of the various problems and predicaments in their lives. I have personally required such advice on many issues and occasions; and have often been required to exert myself toward the hope of resolution to the problems of others in return.

Historically, it is the case that people have generally regarded and cherished their nephews and nieces with much the same esteem as if they were their own children. In point of fact (historically), who gives a damn about any child, other than its parents and close relatives? And who has there been to rescue the orphan from his cruel fate except the aunts and uncles, primarily? Don't be deceived by the current situation where there seems to be some actual demand for the child whom fate has torn from the tender mercies of its parents; for that demand is not actually too strong a current, on a world-wide basis. In situations of economic desperation, there is no demand whatsoever for the orphan.

The point of this letter, as you can see, is that I have had strong indications that suggest that you have some serious problems on your hands. We have all been rooting for you here on the sidelines, in the hope that you would soon extricate yourself from your oppression. Yet, no such good news seems to be forthcoming, and it is my understanding that instead of turning to those who should be your natural allies, you have, instead, turned them off. Perhaps you have struck some deal with the Devil, so that you feel yourself to be hopeless, helpless, and useless.

I call your attention to *The Devil and Daniel Webster,* by Stephen Benet:

> (Daniel Webster is in court pleading the case of a man who has sold his soul to the Devil.) "Now here is this man with good and evil in his heart. Do you know him? He is your brother. Will you take the law of the oppressor and bind him down? It is not for him that I speak, it is for all of you. There is a sadness in being a man, but it is a proud thing too. There is failure and despair on the journey - the endless journey of mankind. We are tricked and trapped - we stumble into the pit - but out of the pit we rise again. No demon that was ever foaled can know the inwardness of that. Only men - bewildered men. They have broken freedom with their hands and cast her out from the nations - yet shall she live while man lives. She shall live in the blood and the heart - she shall live in the earth of this country - she shall not be broken. When the whips of the oppressors are broken and their names forgotten and destroyed, I see with you, a mighty, shining, liberty! I

see free men walking and talking under a free star. God save the United States and the men who have made her free! The defense rests. (The Devil has loaded the jury with lost souls who have been residing in Hell. But they haven't quite yet forgotten that they too once knew freedom, and that it was glorious). Says now the jury: "Not guilty!"

You can see, nephew, that we have here even a precedent for pleading your case against the very Devil, if need be. How do I know anything at all about you and the most troublesome problems in your life? After all, it is many years since I have even seen you, and we have never so much as had a conversation together. It has been said truly, that one doesn't have to be a weatherman to know which way the wind is blowing. My information doesn't come from any single piece of evidence, but rather, from a thousand scattered impressions; what I read, what I see, what I hear, what I experience, and what I am led to infer. From among my people, I know of only six that have been even somewhat acquainted with you: your mother, your Uncle EVH, your Uncle PP and your three brothers. Though what I have gleaned from them is meager, it firmly establishes the reality and fundamental nature of the thing that is eating you alive. What I decidedly do not know, concerns your personal mental status. That, I could decide from a conversation with you. A thirty minute, face to face conversation would be adequate to give me some rough idea about that. An hour or two would certainly be better. When I next come through Phoenix, will you make yourself available to a conversation with me? It would be a one to one encounter. It wouldn't cost you anything except the time and the inconvenience. You need make no preparation. I can learn as well from what you don't say, as from what you do say; as well from what you hide, as from what you speak of freely; as well from your anger, as from your geniality. If it turns out that you are a criminal, I won't squeal on you. If you are psychotic, I will make no effort to have you committed. If you are a Christian, I will neither dunk you nor revive you.

If it turns out that you are merely another prodigal son, and not yet ready to return to your people, I will let them know there no is need yet for the slaying of the fatted calf. I'll then be content to let you abide where you chose, though not necessarily with my blessing. Since when(?) does anyone need my blessing?

In short, I bear you no anger or hostility - quite the opposite. If there be some economical method of helping to absolve you of your trouble, I would surely consider that. If you are in need of a fish, I will not supply it to you, rather, as Dr. Laura Schlessinger suggests, I would see to it that you are provided with fishing gear. All I am suggesting is a chance to discover for myself just what is going on with you. For in accordance with Ben Franklin's advice I would prefer that you have a well-founded opinion of the nature of reality.

I propose to you the following scheme - into which various categories we may assign the whole of mankind:

- Organic pathology of the brain such as Dementia.
- Major psychopathology. Commonly treatable to competency with antipsychotic medications, but requiring regular follow-up care and evaluation, (since such conditions tend to relapse). Potentially dangerous to self and others and often incapable of making informed consent. At times requiring institutional care or even permanent custodial care.
- Character disorders. Coping skills are habitually counterproductive to their own best interests. We all own some of these various maladaptive tendencies, of at least minor intensity. Borderline character disorder and Mixed Character Disorder are the most troublesome of the character disorders. They tend to decompensate under even relatively small amounts of stress. When decompensate, these folks may well become a danger to themselves and others - some may actually decompensate into transient episodes of psychosis and require antipsychotic medications and /or temporary hospitalizations. Often require regular follow-up care and evaluation, except when their behavior can be moderated by voluntary ongoing interaction with friends and relatives who are informed as to the nature of patient's psychological instability. The friends and relatives then constitute this patients 'support system'.

My limited information suggests that you, nephew, have become entangled into the web of one these tenacious and always 'needy' Borderline Character Disordered women. They prey upon the resources and sympathies of their victims by manipulating them with high drama. Should they be physically attractive, it serves only to make of them the more of a threat as they cling tenaciously to their bewildered provider. No realistic prospects here for 'the taming of the shrew'. Many of them will be discovered to have spent long sessions upon the therapist's couch, and/or stints of time in psychiatric facilities.

- Character trait, rather than Character disorder. Persons with only minor character problems. Hence, called by the name of traits. Capable of acquiring good insight - which is to say, their psychopathology has not become deeply ingrained and fixed. They are the vast lot of mankind. We all own some of these various maladaptive traits, though only rarely are we apt to briefly decompensate - as when we are in the grip of severe and sustained stress and physical illness.

In April of 1996 I was so ill and weakened with near terminal cancer, and I recognized that my energy and powers of concentration were so compromised that I no longer deemed myself competent to manage my own affairs. Brother VBB agreed to accept those responsibilities on my behalf, and I signed over to him my 'powers of attorney', so that he was legally empowered to act on my behalf.

I am recovered well enough that I am again managing my own affairs, and have returned to working half-time. I am using the rest of my time into putting my affairs in order, and to complete several personal projects to which I have long felt committed.

Nephew, it may be the case that you have already finally resolved your problem by your own initiative. Considering how long it has been going on, I don't think that is likely. Regardless of that, I take this opportunity to remind you of a few things. Things that we all do well to consider, and to keep firmly in mind: This world is a troublesome and dangerous place. Not all of the monkeys are in the zoo. Suffering is inescapable, but we are not obliged to seek it out. No man's error becomes his own law, nor obliges him to persist in it. Our lives are universally shortened by our own ignorance. Those who do not set their own agenda, typically get absorbed into someone else's agenda. Each of one's individual relationships functions on the basis of reciprocity (I supply something to you; and you supply something to me). If that something is not equitable to the perceptions of both parties, those values must either be re-negotiated, or the relationship ends. It is more commonly a subconscious, than a formal process.

"A man is perhaps, morally obligated to evaluate his own life and come to his own conclusions. One is then obligated, if he has the ability, to say and write what he believes. That one should rise against untruth when he meets it, and that he should defend the individual liberty necessary for the progress of conscience." says DuNouy. I agree with him, and towards that end, I am writing a biography-autobiography of the Brasseur family, of which I have now completed only about 160 pages. Included in that volume, will be a sketch of some information concerning the family of my sister - your mother, which I include to you as part of this letter. It is only a tentative version which I expect will require more information than what I so far possess. I include it to you because part of it pertains to your situation. It is only speculative, and is only based on the little that I have been able to deduce up till this time. I hope to have discovered more by the time it comes to the necessary re-writing.

Well, who am I to judge (?), you will be asking yourself. And in reply, I remind you that both you and I make such judgments on a regular basis. This business of living in a crowded, complicated, and dangerous world requires that we do so. We must make our judgments and then apply one of the three great rules (the Golden Rule, the Silver Rule or the Iron Rule) to every person with whom we have dealings, every day ... to everyone that we merely even only encounter, every day. Those judgments are not of the nature of an indictment, but rather, merely a routine approach to one's necessity of avoiding unnecessary dangers and un-pleasantries.

Just yet this brief summary of the three great rules. No one of them seems to me more useful than the others. Each has its own particular application and usefulness. We must apply one or another of them, to our relationships with other people - our tentative judgment as to how we shall deal which each person we encounter on life's journey.

The **Golden Rule**: Do onto others as you would have them do unto you. The **Silver Rule**: Do not do unto others what you would not have them do unto you (Live, and let live). The **Iron Rule**: Do not permit others to do onto you, what you would not do unto them (Defensively enforcing the golden rule).

If you are agreeable to the principle of our getting together sometime, you might even be interested in meeting me somewhere in New Mexico or Arizona, where we might spend a day or two in surveying the fascinating geology of this large area as we come understand one another. Alternatively, we might consider meeting in Las Vegas, Nevada, where we could try to get together with your dad. Otherwise, I can easily enough get down to Phoenix, too.

Best wishes.

Peace attend thee

Your Uncle

R. Garner Brasseur, M.D.

21 May 1997

3-26-81

Hobbs, NM

Dear JRO,

We lead busy lives. And we are surrounded by a sea of problems. We push past one problem, only to recognize another that we hadn't noticed while occupied with the previous one. We sometimes get the illusion that we solve some of those problems - and perhaps we do. But many more of them, we only ride out; and whatever resolution they attain is far beyond our reach. Our attempts to grasp a problem, or come to grips with it, often only bring about to us, a rude shock from some unanticipated quarter of its obtuse being.

Many of our problems, we undoubtedly create for ourselves. These, brought about both by our innate selfishness and by unanticipated ramifications of our good intensions. Selfishness is a more honest and straight forward form of motivation. We can accept its inevitably present reality. We can plan upon it in our interpersonal relationship, and be forever prepared, or at least not surprised at its appearance in whatever guise.

Honest, good intentions are a perfect flower of delight. When offered, they must be accepted graciously, but not necessarily with enthusiasm, and never without a proper reserve of suspicion. Accepted graciously, because on some few occasions, they truly may be honest intent. Even then though, they are prone to bring with them such things as thorns, micro-livestock, itches, and abrasions. And even failing to present with these unhappy omens; of what real value are mere good intentions, and how long can these flowers continue un-withered? ("I sent thee late a rosy wreath/ Not so much honoring thee/ As giving it the hope that there/ It might not withered be")

For the most part, good intentions come to naught, or are a disguise for the more honest forms of selfishness. Nevertheless, the more solid core of our being, is built upon this rare commodity - the honest good intention; and its sibling, goodwill. Thus it is that we build our lives around (and with) people, animals, geographies, economics, etc., that give us cause for hope, and demonstrate to us their relative constancy. A constancy which is specifically favorable to our best personal interests. So that even though good will and good intentions fails elsewhere, or fails others, it still favors us. It is a form of inequality. Honest inequality - a reality of life! One that a person can comprehend and deal with. How fine, when it favors oneself. Consider well, before you abandon your own best interests to those of another.

I met the other day with a group of about 20 of the local preachers and clergymen at the hospital for a luncheon engagement. I was their featured speaker (if you can feature that) and talked to them for about 25 minutes. I was up late the night before trying to decide what to tell them. I was finally left to suppose that they probably hear all manner of standard medical technical talk; and probably they are not any happier about enduring these, than I am about conventional details of hell fire revival sermons. Therefore, I dug through my notebooks to find some of my favorite jokes and anecdotes. I strung about half a dozen of these together, using the pretext of a theme on communication and understanding in a Philosophical rather than a didactic format. They seemed to like the humorous tales and I rather enjoyed them again myself.

None of them got around to talking about religion, or asking me what church I went to. And thus I avoided the possibility of putting my foot into my mouth. I had decided that should I face that question, I might rather quickly be able to change the subject. Failing in that, I might have had to lie (just a little). "A lie is a poor substitute for a truth," says mark Twain "but then, who has ever invented anything that is apt to work any better?"

We are still looking around for a house to buy, or at least your mother is. She has looked at a lot of them, but not many seem much to her liking. I don't care to chase around looking at any except those she might seriously consider to her taste.

The place we are renting is quite adequate, but the rental is high, and we don't like it well enough to purchase it at the price they are asking. (Notice that the old real estate adage to the effect that - never let a potential buyer live in a house before he has signed the purchase contract). We have hung sheets across the windows, rather than curtains. A pleasantly practical touch - in keeping with my currently embarrassing economic status. There are a couple of things I don't like about the rental property. The lawn will soon be needing attention. I don't overly like working even on my own lawn/yard, let alone on someone else's. Also, because we are not settling into the home permanently, all my books and records remain in boxes in the garage. I would prefer to have them out where I can have ready and frequent access to them.

I rather like the clinic group of doctors and rather expect they may offer me a partnership at the end of my first year, provided of course the business picks up well enough so that I am pulling my own weight economically. And the business does seem to be picking up fairly well. I am about the median age among the doctors of this group. There are fifteen of them in all, with three more coming in the next few months and expectations of there being up to a total of about twenty-five within perhaps five years. They are all physically active and seem to be in good health. Some run 4 to 5 miles per day. Some even talk about having done 8 miles per day. But who knows how far to believe such tales? I find that my 2 miles of jogging takes a tremendous volume of energy to say nothing of the time that it requires.

A modest proportion of the people I see speak Spanish and only understand a little English. Therefore, I use what little Spanish I have; but it is not as useful as I would wish. "If wishes were horses, beggars would ride." I look for Spanish to become increasingly important. Perhaps it may even become a second national language, as you suggest.

As for money, we don't seem to have enough of it - but appear not to be unique in that regard. I don't know what is holding up the closing of the sale on our Kennewick house which is supposed to have been completed this very day. As soon as that transaction is completed, we will be out from under some of the current financial stress. If I had extra money, I would put some in silver, as a hedge against economic chaos. But silver isn't moving up right now and no one (except perhaps the Hunts) can predict when it will rise again significantly. That it will rise, however, seems fairly certain. T-bills (not money market certificates) have a steady and predictable rate of return. Land is not as certain and regular as T-bills, yet over the long haul, is said always to have been a better investment. Not, of course, just any land, but land that has some prospects of being used within the foreseeable near future. It takes a combination of money, luck, courage, and wisdom (called foolishness if the venture fails).

Will Reagan accomplish anything? How much can any one man as President accomplish? How many hours are there in a day? How much energy of life has any one man? How dedicated will any man be to any rhetorical cause, once he encounters turbulence? How sensitive to any direction is the ponderous machine of government/bureaucracy? Can any one man grasp any significant proportion of the problems of this country?

Your uncle EVH is betting that Reagan will "straighten out the IRS," but this is news to me, since I had not heard even that he had his sights on that particular instrument of terror. I don't think that there is much doubt, however, that the IRS truly is public enemy number one to the economic aspirations of the common man in this land. And the IRS is deeply enmeshed with public enemy number two, (the political-judicial system) in the production of chaos and intimidation of citizens. Both stand badly in need of a thorough working over.

The days go by, each filled with so many tasks and necessary preparations, that there is always a great backlog of things yet undone. We do what we can do, or must do to meet each deadline. And the many little things we might wish to do (because we enjoy them and to broaden our outlook); these things we rarely get around to. Frustrating, ain't it? I haven't had time to memorize even a small poem in the past couple of months, let alone time to write one.

I was a bit surprised that you had taken the time to write your own little poem. It expresses well the idea of the boy that ought not ever depart from within the man. And of course, the effort (of the organization of the idea, into the poem), bespeaks the evolution of thoughtful maturity, seeking ever to enter and temper the bloom of youth. One must write the poem while the spirit of the inspiration of the thing is upon him. That part cannot be forced (or so it seems to me). Thereafter one can sit down (even in periods of lesser inspiration) to modify and polish the verses. They can be made more memorable (i.e., more easy to memorize) by compressing the ideas and adding devices such as rhythm, cadence, picturesque phrasing, rhyming, and short strings of words and phrases that begin with the similar letters or sounds, etc. All-in-all, I presume that the writing of a poem must be perhaps as difficult to others as to myself, since I notice that even professional poets do not seem to produce a great volume of works. One of the last poems that I attempted was while I was in Chicago in November of 1980. I watched on TV, an astronomy program by Carl Sagan, and was pleased that someone was trying to get the message of that science before a much disinterested public, which seems commonly to prefer to spend their time and money on politics, religion, and magical potions.

<u>The Wanderer</u>

Eternity of years and more,
Comprise a primal dark of night,
Ere first golden beam deployed,

FADING ECHOES

To bath the sky in blaze of light.

We each lonely sphere adrift,
Amid now myriad million stars,
Perched on shoulders deep in space,
Where dreadful darkness overpowers.

Projecting mortal sight afar Strain to
waken, fain discern
In quest of yet another truth
Determined riddle yet to learn

Brief our holidays in heaven
As our orbits coincide.
Pleasantly distracting days,
As we journey side by side.

Each to ponder as to why,
Companion spirits one has known,
All warmly soft and comforting,
Abrupt abide, and soon are flown.

All too soon from each departed Our
solitary paths diverge.
Each to drift the sky, eternal.
Till with Brahma we are merged.

RGB

———◆———

I was alone (and nearly broke) in Chicago about 10 days. I rode the bus an hour each way to get downtown to the professional meetings. I ate but once a day – because food did cost so much. I purchased cheese and crackers to snack upon in my motel room. Though a bit depressing was my circumstance, I still clung to some shreds of optimism. There is a certain satisfaction in being alone for a spell – and it gives one time for a lot of thinking, reading, and writing. I tried another type of writing that goes like this:

> A river ran, (now all ignored) through an occasional patch of trees and shrubs; with leaves enshrined upon its mantle, o'er the earth beneath the golden trees. And I felt a vague deep sorrow; and sympathy for that stream. For it had all been straightened out, with even and parallel banks. And its pace was slowed by the occasional concrete harness that reached across its breadth. I remembered a folk song in the form of a lament, mockingly chanted by the repressed Irish against the British occupational troops - "And we shall all be civilized; and neat; and clean; and well advised."

> Still, that once noble stream flowed, without discernable complaint, silently intending what it would; and waiting for the moment that it might once more rise in revolt from its bonds; against those who torment its noble natural course and dignity. Now and then, its shackled spirit received another insult, yet suffers it to bear - quietly, for now. The ubiquitous old tire, the bottle fragments, cans, and over-shoes - all discarded as though in mock sacrifice of taunt along this stream. A large motel built upon its banks, has split the stream along its length, with a concrete pier; and supports a slab of concrete and asphalt, roofing the stream from bank to bank. Those who park their Lincolns and Cadillacs here, are not even aware of this old stream that flows so placidly beneath this parking lot.

> Upstream, away from Chicago, lay an occasional barren scattered acre. "For sale," (and at your service) - just pay the price; and use it as you will. Tall, woven wire fences enclose those packaged parcels of land. And the

uninviting, plainly printed signs hung thereon explain their meaning for the unimaginative.

It is all quite changed in the past 150 years, though not necessarily improved. Still, it shall change again, and no man can but guess among some of its potential options.

"Boys will be boys," and men will be men. And perhaps no man bears intentional malice towards the rustic beauty of the countryside. It only, sometime appears, that he does so?

A mountain is an inspiration, a thing to behold, and against which playfully to pit one's strength - but not with the intent, seriously to subdue it. A mountain can be terraced or mined and thus become a difficult way to earn a living. Worn down, it can become a fruitful valley. Leveled, a fertile plain. But man must have mountains, or so it seems; for from the plains he once again worshipfully raises them. See the ziggurats of Mesopotamia, the pyramids of Egypt. See their newer versions in New York City or Chicago. Whole new ranges of such mountains have appeared in this "new world." And these man-made cordilleras are growing so formidable, that like nature's own, they affect and alter the very patterns of weather that wander thereabout.

As boys must have their toys and their dreams; so must men. But their proportions change dramatically. As boys evolve into men, and men into spirits; so also does the earth respond and evolve upon occasion to shrug off some of the creations of mankind.

Sand castles crumble. Those of stone survive - perhaps too long, for their interiors seem often to require renovation. Sand writings are ephemeral; those on stone tablets are 'historical', even if not truly accurately so. Of what man constructs of wood, clay, and steel, the larger portion will be seen eventually to crumble. If not timely enough, then at times intentionally razed by man himself. Working from his dreams, and with his building blocks man's passions also fancy works of art, which also do not always satisfy. Always some little imperfection

- often too obtuse. His reach on the one hand, and his grasp on the other hand, needs must be situated on extremities of proportion and length, lest his balance be disturbed.

And always, amid the altars one would build, he finds his progress overly slow. Alters builded up to whom? Many appear to be alters to man himself.

I read a story the other day that did amaze me. A short story by Dorothy M. Johnson (whom I had never heard of). The story, *A man Called Horse* must certainly be a true story. The events ring of truth, and looking through the story, one gains insight into the primitive structure of the psyche of the American Indian as he dwelled upon the prairies. And one can see how the Indian, as an individual, is caught fast into the web of Indian society and tradition. The individual perhaps never finding time to reflect within himself as to who he is, why things are thus and so, why must it continue despite the grief and suffering that it brings? Is there not another way, etc.? Caught up with the imperative of personal heroism, lest his family suffer some vague disgrace, to say nothing of poverty. Native American caught up in the politics of the tribe. His pathway to respect and notice is often through foolishly daring physical feats which maimed and killed them.

have had that story on my mind a great deal the past few days since I read it. Though I grew up with the Indians in Montana and North Dakota always near at hand, I never had an inkling into these aspects of their being. These Indian family and tribal patterns are deeply ingrained and carried forward to each subsequent generation at an often non-verbal cultural level. Being thus deeply patterned and ingrained, the individuals themselves are not perhaps conceptually aware of them. Nor can they therefore bring them verbally into discussion for analysis and consideration. Sort of like living in always, among the trees, and not, therefore, being aware of the concept of forest. Magic and superstition along with mystical belief preoccupied their patterns of thought. We do well to suppose that we (hopefully more enlightened?) are likewise still somewhat overburdened with erroneous concepts.

In any case, the story (*A man Called Horse*) has been made into a movie, which I should like to see. I doubt though, that a movie would portray those aspects of the story which so intrigued me.

Of course, the Indians are now several generations removed from the historical and Native Indian traditions and way of life; and are beginning to mingle with the Whites. And so, are slowly losing their Indian identity. None-the-less, they tend to be sequestered together on reservations and remote areas, so that their traditions fade only slowly. Perhaps, hopefully, at least a small remnant will always remain thoroughly Indians. It would be a shame to see them all 'civilized'.

For that matter, our ancestors and we ourselves are not fully civilized either. Civilization is a good thing, no doubt - up to a certain point. But, in truth, the process is always in need of renovation. Untended, it tends to produce apathy, depression, and loss of hope. And the uncivilized and the uncivilized element within us needs to rise in indignation, and like the French, to tear up the paving stone in the streets of civilization from time to time. To build them into barricades and, let run some blood and chaos. Not all civilizations are of equal benevolence, and there seems a tendency for them to become despotic. Civilization chastised might again proceed - more modestly perhaps, this time, so as to give our poor souls a little rest.

I read a short essay by Mark Twain entitled *Advice to Youth*. He has a way of bringing enlightenment, along with humor, modesty, and cheer. He commonly deals with the serious aspects of life's problems; or with the absurdities of peoples and governments. What he has to say does not solve or cure any of these problems or difficulties. But we all know what he is talking about, and we might agree with the absurdities he points out to us. Then, called upon as we are, to bear up with these problems ourselves (still without much hope of resolution) at least we can bear them a little more easily; seeing the humor from the mark Twain point of view. It seems to me that Henry Mencken and James Thurber, write in that same vein of <u>serious</u> humor. But the greatest of these, is Twain.

It was good to have you home at Christmas. Though it was a busy time for you, as it was for me. Of course, it is not surprising that there is little time for long conversations at such times as that, when so many things are going on, and so many people getting together. Mostly, it is then a time for hearing the news, hashing over the old times, discussing the new plans and for the celebration of the renewal of the old and loved acquaintances. A time for making merry together.

I recall meeting this young woman, Martha. She seems to be of the self-reliant and able tradition. And she seems to come from a family of tradition. Keep in mind the unique importance of good health and do your best to assure healthy ancestors for your children. Good health and healthy children are among the prime determining factors of the quantity of grief one must encounter in life. Not of course to suggest that grief cannot make a better person of one. But, it is altogether too easy to inherit more than what one can use constructively. "But when thou findest sensibility of heart joined with softness of manners, and accomplished mind, with a form agreeable to thy fancy, take her home to thy house; she is worthy to be thy friend, thy companion in life, the wife of thy bosom." I don't intend to rush you into anything – only to indicate that the thing in principal has my approval and I am ready for it, when you think you are. It is not any picnic, and not all romance, yet the experience is a thing not to be avoided under any circumstances. Nothing but family can put you in touch with reality. Pick a gal with spirit enough to try your metal, and compassion enough finally to let an argument end, once you both noticed that it can't be resolved.

Thanks for the loan of your cash on several recent occasions. I would never consider borrowing from you unless I had some cause for confidence in being able to repay it soon. As for economic security, none of us has it, as you can see. And I am not worried about being able to eke out a living under most circumstance, health permitting. I am, however, concerned about the natural tendency to work, perhaps too hard, to acquire overly much security – only to discover it has eluded us once again with false promise and wasted effort.

I have included in this note a page upon which you will find my record of how things stand between us financially. I intend to get the loan repaid to you as soon as possible, so that it is freed up to you in the event that anything happens to me. I hope to have it paid off by the end of this summer, sooner if possible.

As you see, we now live in Southeast New Mexico. It is only a few miles from the Texas border. We are on a high plain country called Llano Estacado (meaning, staked plain). Not long ago, it was the bottom of an ocean, the western edge of which is the Carlsbad Cavern area (80 miles west). It was a shallow sea, and therefore teeming with life that tended to concentrate calcium compounds. The winds and rains brought down large deposits of debris from the mountains and poured them into this basin. And so the entire landscape is one of degenerate limestone materials, locally called 'caliche', (probably implying leached calcium). The closest river is 80 miles away. There are not even any dry stream-beds, for water seems not to run horizontally in this area. The infrequent rains simply dissolve their way straight down through the soluble calcium base rock and hardpan, to end up as an underground types of river, embedded within aquifers of sandstone - there, to await the ingenuity of man; or Nietzsche's 'superman' for use in irrigation.

In Washington, Oregon, or Montana, one can climb a mountain and see for miles around. Here, one can do likewise by simply standing on your tiptoes. Nothing grows here naturally, except mesquite bushes and some undiscriminating forms of cactus. I think a little native grass is available between the bushes seasonally, but the local livestock keep that down pretty well. I rather like the area. There is not much diversity of rock here in the immediate terrain, but in general, New Mexico is considered a rock-hound's paradise. Even here, amid the apparently gray/white continuous 'caliche' there are undoubtedly some interesting local outcrops to break up the uniformity. And certainly, there must be fossils a-plenty. The mountains are only 100 miles to the west, and there are some picturesque old town and remnants of building, there among the arroyos and the mountains themselves.

I am usually up by 7:45 AM and drive M.A. to school before going to the office. I often get 75 minutes to nap over the noon hours. I jog 2 miles, 3 times a week, taking RL's dog along to give her exercise. M.A. feeds the dog. And your mother cares for RL's parrot. When M.A. is playing her flute, the bird often echoes back on the same high notes. Not really too surprising - some of the notes are pitched high enough that even I have to restrain myself against the spontaneous echoes.

Well, I must close this note with best wishes to you for your upcoming 22nd birthday.

Love,

yer dad,

Garner Brasseur

3-26-81

8/24/85

Hobbs, NM

Dear RL,

Even in this country and in this day, many positions of responsibility and importance are held by persons who are poorly informed and exercise only limited responsibility in the performance of their offices and duties. Despite this, many of them have some sort of certificate or credentials that suggest - at least - that they are capable and diligent in the performance of their duties. Not all, however, attain even this. And those certified are by no means, all capable and or productive in their occupation. Some get worse - instead of improving - with practice and experience. Nevertheless, in our day and place, some sorts of credentials are usually prerequisite to employment, except among salesmen and those manually employed.

Diplomas and certificates from certified institutions of education seem all to pass muster as pre-requisite for employment. A few institutions--but very few, actually--have a special status such as to enhance the value of their paper, beyond the actual average and mediocre value. Thus, among universities and collages for example, Harvard, Stanford, Cal Poly-tech (San Luis Obispo), M.I.T., St. John's, and the Ivy League schools are prominent and their documents assure their holders of some enhanced opportunity and likelihood of employment. This, despite the fact that a host of other private and state colleges and universities produce graduates of equal caliber.

Most of the big name schools require megabucks for tuition and are, therefore populated primarily by the children of wealthy parents, who make that sacrifice of expense because of the related "snob appeal" that thereby accrues to themselves, as well as to their children. Also however, their minimal requirement of acceptable effort and achievement for graduation is probably somewhat more demanding than is that of most other private and public institutions. Strangely, despite the trend toward high tuition in the big name and Ivy League schools; you, in fact - qualifying as a California resident - could attend Cal Poly-tech in San

Luis Obispo and pay no tuition cost. It is probable however that it would require advanced registration and a high prerequisite grade point average. So don't bother your head about it, anyway. For neither you, nor myself, nor anyone from our family of late-blooming peasant stock was likely ever to have been acceptable to their admissions committee; with the possible exception of JRO, who alone took the time and effort to prepare himself. Interestingly, he - like Albert Einstein - never earned a high school diploma. Life, indeed, has some strange and interesting twists and turns.

I have listed for you some of the least expensive schools in the states of Oregon, California, and New Mexico. Some are junior colleges and community colleges which offer predominantly courses for the 2nd and 1st years. Some of these you might consider, but only for a semester or a quarter terms; in conjunction with plans for switching into other more advanced and nearby schools. Thus, Weed C.C. or Rogue Valley C.C. might be considered in conjunction with the Ashland school. Or, the Salem Chemeketa Community College might be considered in conjunction with the Monmouth College - in either depending upon the resident status rules that apply to your situation. Obviously - presuming my information is correct - La Grande (Eastern Oregon College of Education) is best suited to your economic and non-resident status. Not only that, but La Grande is a very nice and picturesque town, in every way comparable - if not superior - to Ashland. This, again, presuming only that you are absolutely determined to go to school in Oregon.

To the best of my knowledge, you are in fact qualified to resident status in both California and New Mexico. Cheapest of course is the zero tuition available to you in several of the California schools. Even Humboldt State College at $462.00 per year sound like a likely possibility. Or others, that I have listed. In California you would probably have to act for this fall term, in order to preserve your resident status. The same may - but not necessarily - apply to your resident status for New Mexico, depending perhaps on whether we get the house sold.

In New Mexico, both Las Vegas and Silver City are places that would probably please you - based upon considerations of cost; and your seeming preferences for smaller schools in pretty little mountain towns. Both Portales (100 miles north of Hobbs - in the rolling plains with adjoining farmlands) and Las Cruces are worthy of your consideration, too.

So ponder these pragmatic and economic considerations to see if they do not have meaning for you. All payments that we make are a form of tax or duty that we pay for our own prejudice and ignorance - when that payment exceeds the minimum cost available option to us. Or, alternatively, if we have abundant wealth; then it is a premium we pay for superior quality or simple preference or convenience. This is the case in general, but even more true in regards to undergraduate education since we have nearly equal access to books and literature and information regardless what college we choose; and since the process of education proceeds out of the student - not out of the college.

The choice, of course, is yours; and the action must proceed from you. I would be happy to make the decision easier for you by giving your, say, $500.00 as a subsidy to defray your extra expenditures, should you decide upon a more advantageously economic school to attend than the one in Ashland. You might even use my pick-up to facilitate your move, if you think that advantageous. The logistics of that, (considering the distance in hundreds of miles that separates us) makes that complicated however.

Have courage though, and do whatever you must in the face of honest reality - or do whatever you wish, and accept the duty (tax) payment of that decision should you decide to remain in Ashland. You realize, of course, that my own decision and upcoming move is not less troublesome or difficult for me; than what I am suggesting as a possible alternative, to you. Should you decide to move, get your family to agree democratically - if that be possible. Otherwise then, proceed humbly but with stoical determination.

Your dad,
R. Garner Brasseur

P.S.: RL - you and I had the uncommon good fortune to become acquainted with a volcanic pyroclastic eruptions in the form of Mt.

Ste. Helens in 1980. Most consider it to have been a disaster - not good fortune - but both views are correct.

Enclosed are two articles, each of which astounded me; for I had never considered that either could actually be witnessed by human eyes. I did believe in both, however, even before I read the descriptions. I had thought that they could merely be surmised, from the finding respectively of geology and astronomy.

One article is the eye witness account of the birth of a mountain. The other - more astounding and recent - the eye witness account of the death of a star.

RGB

8/24/85

2 February 1988

Re: Cowboy Brasseur

I saw him again recently, during the Christmas holidays. He is 18 months of age. His body configuration is tall and lanky. He is confident in his ability to walk. He even begins to run a little, but with an awkward gait of long steps and seemingly requiring of him a rather concentrated effort of determination.

He has begun to say a few words, a few of which are even understandable by me. His voice is rather high-pitched. "Eipfe-jewc" seems to be an important part of his life and of his vocabulary. He looks at one intensely and expectantly when he has something to say with his two or three word sentences.

Cowboy seems to have made a definite start at separating his own identity from that of his mother. He is almost as closely connected now with RL, his father. He likes to be tossed about occasionally by his father. He has two kinds of laughter; one of mere joy - the other deeper in tone and with his chin tucked against his chest, giving one the impression that he is expressing his perception of a subtle humorous aspect of his encounter in this particular interaction with one. He is gradually giving up his reluctance to encounter other persons on an individual basis and apart from his parents, though he still confides solely in them, in his natural fits and spells of fatigue, frustration, and in times of injury and hurt feelings. All in all, therefore, it appears to be the case that he is psychologically well situated for the arrival of the second child to RL and TM. An event that is expected in about 5 or 6 weeks.

———◆◆———

At age 21 months Cowboy is a bright and cheerful child. Sings a lot. Knows the entire alphabet, both to recite and to read in capital letters. He occasional confuses U and V - as do some of our public buildings. He does not know the small letters well. He can count to ten. He is often read to. Asked to find spider, he knows in just what book to seek it; and on what page to find it.

R Garner Brasseur

———◆◆———

10 September 1988   Re: Cowboy

RL and TM stopped by at our place in Caldwell a couple of days before we all drove off to the Saur Family reunion in Montana, just after the middle of August. I haven't seen Cowboy since Christmas. He is a little less shy, and ventures out a little further from his parents - and more often, too. After being around him a few hours, he seemed to become quite confident that he need not fear me. But coming alone into the living room where I am alone, he hesitates briefly with the left index finger tucked into the corner of his mouth, and with his head lowered slightly as he scans me and the immediate surroundings with his deep brown and penetrating eyes. He is long and lean; and very quiet. He will come forward, look at me, and make a two or three word statement, or inquiry, with a slight halt between each word. One can usually figure out what he is saying, though his words are still a bit clumsy. He will never present himself to me, in order to sit upon my lap, but upon occasion, he will come to look at me - with finger in the corner of mouth; and will be close enough that I can engage his attention with some words of conversation, and then lift him to my lap for a moment. He will not stay there long however - his general shyness doesn't permit him that comfort yet. When his father instructs him to kiss me goodnight, he will do so. He will play with his cousins of about his same age and size, though he is often but a spectator in the midst of those goings-on. After sharply observing the playing situation for a few moments (index finger in opposite corner of his mouth) he may or may not elect to join in. He will not pick a fight, but if a child should attempt to take a toy from his grasp, he often will hang on for a tugging contest. A youngster that annoys him, may occasionally get bit, but he is regularly reproved for that; and those occasions are declining.

He has a peculiarity of speech that is interesting - a sort of German brogue. "Epfil chuce"; instead of apple juice. "Chump", instead of jump. And "chump" to him, is a big thing. He loves to jump; perhaps it started with the small trampoline. But he works at it intermittently, every day. He will half squat as he says, "chump"; then puts forth a mighty effort to see how high he can jump. He doesn't get off the ground more than and inch; or two, but he seems quite pleased with it; and he is apt to make a half dozen such jumps in a row, before he gives it up for a new interest and then he spontaneously returns to the jump again, a bit later.

His most definitive characteristic is the concentrated effort that he puts forth to observe, to learn, or to acquire a skill. The intensity of his gaze was a striking phenomenon already when he was a mere 2 months of age. That intensity is less conspicuous now - presumably it requires less effort for him now, to abstract the information he seeks; yet, he still does scrutinize and ponder, before he takes action. And he can count, and recite his letters. And he is learning to frame questions, and likes to ask questions. But I fear that his propensity for inquiry may lead him into disappointment and then to disillusionment. For the world is not good at answering good questions, or even in giving them honest consideration. Questions could soon be rewarding him with rebuke, I fear. I expect that the best hope for preserving his inquiring spirit, is to teach him early, to read. And then to accustom him to seek his own answers from books, rather than conversation. For a great deal of conversation is bogus and fraudulent.

R G Brasseur

1988

3 March 2001

Albuquerque, New Mexico

Dear Cowboy,

My grandfather died at age 83 in Minot, North Dakota. I was age 20 at the time and found myself in Chicago that summer, attempting to earn and save enough money to enable me to return to Concordia College to continue my education in the fall. I worked days as a lifeguard on the North Avenue Beach of Lake Michigan; and I worked nights as a hospital orderly. It was an unusually hot summer and I worked 18 hours a day on five days a week. On the other two days I had to work only 8 hours a day, and my oldest brother, EVH kept me preoccupied with various outings during my free hours on those two easy days.

My grandfather George Boepple died 25 July 1953. I knew him as a kindly and often jovial old fellow, but I had seen him only occasionally through the years, and didn't know much about him. Thirty three years later (1986) I launched out upon a self imposed mission to discover something about him. I spent about six weeks traveling about the country in my old pickup to search for information about him. I visited his brothers, and sisters, and nephews, and nieces all over the continent to gather information. I had for a guide only a very sketchy copy of information from my mother, which had been compiled by mother's sister, (Aunt Ann) some years earlier. I got a good start on the project that summer, but my store of information has only gradually accumulated in my ongoing search through these subsequent years.

Briefly, the story is this. His ancestors had left south Germany in 1817 to settle into lands made available to them by the Russian Czar, and located in Bessarabia (known now as Moldavia), situated on the northwest edge of the Black Sea. Grandfather and his siblings were the third generation of their family to have lived there. He seems to have had at least 15 brothers and sisters. As a young man he had to serve 5 years in the Russian Army. There he served in a musical detachment of the army - playing concerts, at holiday and ceremonial occasions, in parades etc. His main instrument was the trumpet, but he also played other brass instruments, woodwinds, and the organ. He finished his military duty and then went back to begin his civilian life in the community where his father lived (Mannsburg, Bessarabia). I presume he went into the grain-buying business at that time. He was living at his father's home soon after his return when his father then died in 1895 at the very young age of about 57 years. A year later grandfather Georg married Christina Gotz and soon had a couple of daughters. But the Russian government was becoming repressive and harsh to these 'foreign' settlers. So grandfather saved his money, and was then able to buy passage to America in 1898. He settled in the Dakota Territory and raised his family there. He was short, energetic, and quite dynamic – sort of like your father's cousin, André Brasseur. In his late fifties he left the grain buying business and became a music teacher in the several public schools there in and near Mercer County.

Grandfather was concerned about his brothers and sisters still living under worsening conditions over there in Russia. He encouraged and helped many of them to escape and settle into this country. You and I are indeed fortunate that his emigration assured us the advantages of being born and raised in this country. Such then is the general outline of the story of my Grandfather George Boepple. Four years ago, after my unlikely escape from cancer I wrote a book, *Inheritors of a Few Years*, which gives the story in greater detail. I have intended that you, and your brothers each have a copy of that book. I have left the copies with your father, and asked him to give a copy to each of you at such time as he feels to be appropriate. In that book, you will also read something of my own life, and you will see that my life has been strongly shaped and influenced by my various brothers. An important influence. I wouldn't say that I have had overly much influence on the life of your father or his brothers and sister, but they do seem to have had some important influence on the lives of one another.

You children of RL's family seem to have not much of economic advantage beyond my own situation as I was growing up. Fortunately, your opportunity to obtain a good education never-the-less lies within your own grasp. As the oldest sons, you and Poco Uno are in the strongest position to influence and encourage your brothers and sister along into fulfilling, interesting, and useful lives. Much will depend upon your example by way of encouragement. I know that all of you enjoy the benefits of having inherited good health and a good native intelligence. What is still required of each of you however, is a personal determination and the self-discipline to prepare yourselves to something of excellence in your lives.

I am impressed already at the physical adeptness and coordination that you have achieved on the skate board and upon the court of athletic game. In so far as I am aware, your progress in learning is also quite satisfactory. But you will have to struggle against yourselves in order to maintain your focus and determination to achieve worthy goals. Do not neglect to set some goals that will try your metal; and some that will require years of effort to achieve.

Aside from the natural lethargy of the mere mortal nature of all men, your greatest distraction will be your own peers and classmates. Keep a <u>clear distinction in your own mind</u> between appearances and reality; between the difficult and the impossible; between what is worthy and what is unworthy; between what is enough and what is too much; between long term and short term benefits and advantages; and between what is healthy and what is unhealthy. Do not call by the name of friend, those who encourage you to anything less than what is excellent. And be prepared to make the effort to recover from each failure that you will inevitably suffer.

Have you read *Men Against the Sea*, that book I left for you a year or two ago, about the journey of Captain Bleigh half way around the world in a row-boat after his crew of the ship *HMS Bounty* mutinied? One of the few books I have read more than once. What a tremendous real life adventure. I have never found anything in fiction that compares to what is available from such real life history as that. I think also of two books by William Prescott where real history is just astounding - *The Conquest of Mexico* and *The Conquest of Peru*. I notice that RL still has copy of those two in his bookcase. An even more astounding adventure is that of the first journey from Peru, in exploration down into the Amazon River basin and led by youngest of the Pizzaro family. The book, *A Crossbowman's Story* I have only ever seen once. Fortunately, I grabbed it and read it then. Perhaps I shall search the web pages to try and find another copy - so I can read it again. *Caesars War Commentary*, and *Xenephon's march Up Country* are yet two other books that rivet ones attention. To read such things as these is at once both interesting and historically informative. I hope that you might have the chance to fall under their spell.

I may get a chance to get up your way in late May or early June. I sure was glad to run into you on Halloween, so that you could put me in touch with RL. It would have been a little cool to have slept in the pickup that night.

I usually travel out to the Dakotas in July to take in the German Convention. I took my sister Kate along with me three years ago but she says she is too feeble to go with me again (she has Multiple Sclerosis). PM and Bam-Bam came with me two years ago. Last summer I tried to talk your dad into going along with me, but he seems to have to keep himself busy and earning to support the family. If I go this summer, perhaps I will try to talk you or Boo or Mich into going along. When I get back into the Dakotas, I generally get a chance to stop off and see a couple old friends and relatives too. And I generally try to get a chance to visit the graves of my grandparents. The Boepple grandparents in Beulah, and the Brasseur grandparents in Dunseith. Both are towns where I have previously lived.

Well then ... on to other projects for me.

Give my best regards to both of your parents - who of course are among my favorite people.

Love,
Your grandfather,
R. Garner Brasseur, M.D.

3 March 2001

8 November 2002

Albuquerque, NM

Dear Cowboy,

Here is a recent Paul Harvey RIDDLE. When asked this riddle,

80% of kindergarten kids got the answer, compared to 17% of Stanford University seniors.

What is greater than God, More evil than the devil, The poor have it, The rich need it, And if you eat it, you'll die?

Here is an older riddle. I wonder if you have heard it. From Plato's writings:

What animal walks on four legs in the morning, on two legs in the afternoon, and three legs in the evening?

But you can figure out the answers to the riddles later, or get your brothers to help you out. I was through Medford recently on the last leg of a six week long trip that took me across country to New England and New France; and then across through Michigan and westward through North Dakota and Montana into Washington and Oregon. I was stopping all along the way at libraries, city halls, and interviewing various distant relatives in order to collect further information on the Brasseur genealogy. I had fairly good success, too. A good part of the time I slept out in the back of the pickup, parked at highway rest areas and occasionally in a Wal-Mart parking lot. I spent some of those nights at the homes of some of those distant relatives and at the homes of near relatives and friends. One night I stayed at a campground, and I even stayed 2 or 3 intermittent nights in different motels - but I don't do that often, as it is a bit too expensive. I saw my sisters in Montana and my brothers in Washington State before arriving in Oregon. I am currently in the process of writing up the details of that trip into a travelogue, and sending it - installment by installment - by E-mail. I have included both your father and mother on the mailing lists, so you could peruse it there if you wished.

I am sorry I missed seeing you in Medford, though I was told that you somehow saw me. How can that be? Naturally I stopped to visit with both your dad and mom - and all your siblings. And I am given to understand that you are sort of on the 'outs' at both places. Family friction of some sort? What family doesn't have that? Well, I must tell you that I am not too surprised. It is just those magical teen-age years in which various contests begin to arise between a lad and the family. Yes, I learned from your parents the nature of some of the issues that have gotten you upon the outs. But, I never heard anything to suggest that any of them didn't love you or weren't concerned about you. And since you were not staying with either your mom or your dad when I was there, that means you were somewhere else. Where?

And so it seems to me of the utmost importance to make you aware of some problematic and even potentially dangerous realities. As you know, I worked with various sorts of insane people at the New Mexico Psychiatric Hospital during the last eight years before I retired. Firstly, about 10% of the population in this country is psychiatrically disturbed, meaning they are, or have been, or will be, or, could be enough disturbed to require psychiatric care. They haven't all been discovered – some of them may never be discovered. Of those that have been discovered, many or most have been placed on psychiatric medication. Some call it 'brain glue' for it keeps their thought patterns coherent enough that they can function 'almost' normally in society; so long as they continue to take the medication. But they mostly don't like to take the medication and very commonly stop taking it. As to the nature of psychotic thought processes for example, ask your dad to show you a copy of letter he recently got from an old acquaintance. By no means can one easily discern that they are 'certifiably' crazy, for at least a small trace of disturbed thinking seems to run through most if not the whole of mankind. Episodes or 'spells' or periods of craziness commonly tend to come and go. When severe and prolonged they end up in the psychiatric hospital for a bit until they can be calmed down with medication. Secondly during these episodes of insanity, many of these people can be dangerous – I mean 'deadly' dangerous – more commonly only sexually and psychologically dangerous. They are especially apt then to take advantage the young, the naive, the compliant, and the frail – or catch a person 'off guard'. If 'confronted' with a strong person or outnumbered, an individual will generally restrain themselves, for as one of them once told me, "I might be crazy, but I am not stupid". Like fish in the ocean, they can have the most astounding of disguises. Don't think for a minute that you won't encounter them even also in churches and schools, and among the ranks of those in the fields of education, ministry, psychology, and psychiatry itself. So, Cowboy, take care of yourself.

Though it is not absolutely true, it is nearly always true that **nobody** (including no church body, no school system, no government agency and no judges nor lawyers) **is more interested in the well being of their children than are the parents.** A person can safely entrust himself into the care and keeping of his parents - and can find help and consolation there as long as they live and are able. Perhaps a dog might be as good a friend to a lad as his parents, but a dog can't provide for you, see to your health and education, engage with you in an intelligent discussion, or give you guidance for your day-by-day living in a complex society and a dangerous world.

Of course you are almost old enough and big enough to get a job and take care of yourself, if that were necessary. But it is not necessary. Nor is it advisable. For the chances of living an interesting, useful, fruitful, and long life are far the best if you continue your preparation for life by furthering your education. Merely attending school however will not provide you with that education. For all learning must eventually be self-learning. Which means that you must have the will and make the effort to learn. Much of that is most apt to occur only if you continue attending adequate school systems. Some of that - perhaps even a lot of it - is best acquired throughout the course of your life, in the years (and after) when you are raising your own family. And so I hope you will ponder this advice and continue to maintain and build your bridges of association with your own immediate and extended family. Is there any practical advice on how to accomplish that? Remember what Garrison Kiehlor (from *A Prairie Home Companion*) says; about "what is the challenge in being able to get along only with folks who are easy to get along with?" Time perhaps to practice and improve upon ones negotiation skills. Or you might try charm - the method of getting the answer "yes" without having necessarily having even clearly asked the question.

I wonder now what will be your personal agenda. As my brother often reminds me, those who do not follow their own agenda generally get swept up into someone else's agenda. Time to think about what you might wish to become - and to get started off in that direction. There is no practical alternative to learning and study that compares to reading - in combination with one's own well reflected experience of reality. It has been said that the person who can read, but does not, has no advantage whatever over the person who cannot read. Give to yourself every advantage of time, background, and preparation, for our world is indeed a competitive one. And the world is so filled with writings that you could not possibly get through any significant portion of what has been written in a hundred lifetimes. And far the largest proportion of what has been written is not worth the reading. Therefore, it is important to read valid and worthy materials. Be selective.

The most influential fact in the world is probably ignorance, and right behind that is personal prejudice, which is also the most detrimental. For prejudice is commonly coupled with 'certitude-of-belief', which makes its influence a mighty obstacle of self-righteous determination to isolate oneself from truth and reality. Among our foremost problems is that of getting free from ignorance and prejudice - to the extent that is possible. "Freeing the mind of bunk"

Upon my trip I stopped to visit and stay the night with your father's cousin, Gordon Huft, in Townsend, Montana. He buys grain upon the local market to sell and ship around the world. He tells me that at any one time, there is only enough grain in the world to feed the populations for not more than three of four months. When Tambora volcano of Indonesia exploded in 1815, it so darkened the skies of the Northern Hemisphere throughout 1816, that there was widespread crop failure across the whole northern hemisphere. Widespread famine and disease followed. That or something akin to it could occur at any time once more, and in this now crowded world, there would be widespread hunger and starvation once again. So, we live on the very edge of disaster at all times. Economic, as well as personal. It has been that way throughout the ages. Don't be lulled into believing that the modern world is immune from that. Large scale disasters leave governments unable to intervene. Friends might then be of some help, but as the scale of disaster enlarges, friends are undependable, and ones only possibility for mutual aid is from among family. I could give you dozens of examples of that from within my very own family. The obvious moral - maintain close ties with your family. "Blood is thicker than water."

"And little orphan Annie says,

That when the sky is blue
And the lamp wick flutters,
And the wind goes W-o-o-o-o

And you can hear the cricket stop,
And the moon is gray.
And the lightn'n bugs and dew
Is all sequenched away.

Well then you better mind your parents
And your teachers fond and dear
And cherish them that loves you,
And dry the orphans tear.

And help the poor and needy ones
That's gathered all about.
Or the gobilins will get you …
If you don't watch out."

Well, Cowboy, I half expect to be down through Medford again perhaps sometime in about the second or third week of December. I look foreword to the possibility of seeing you again at that time. Let me know if there is anything I can do for you. You may recall that I had some hope of taking you along with me this past summer on my trip into the Dakotas. Sorry you couldn't make it. If the old pickup holds up, I may make another such trip this coming summer. It would be good to have you along with me, if that works out.

Love,
Yer grandfather,
R. Garner Brasseur, M.D.

8 November 2002

22 February 2003

Santa Fe. Mew Mexico

Hello Cowboy,

I hear that you have escaped or been paroled from the Sunny Valley area. Seriously though, me and the rest of your family are quite pleased with what you have accomplished in earning your GED certificate during the past year. But life is filled with challenges, and now that you have gotten a little lead on your age peers, I am curious to see which of those challenges you are going to tackle. I know that you have already gotten accustomed to work, and since you were not born with a silver spoon in your mouth (as the saying goes) that you are going to have to work to earn an income. I suppose that you are going to be living at home for at least a year or two yet, so your economic circumstance will not be anything like desperate. "Make hay while the sun shines", as they say; and don't be burning it all in the moonlight. Frugality does not mean simply the habit of not spending your money, but more especially that of spending or investing it wisely. No better place to invest money than in your own education. No better place to invest your time than in honest experience and in education.

A young man in Poland was living at home and had a mediocre job as he was trying to save money so that he could go to college. Each morning he would build his own lunch and take it with him in a brown bag. He came home all out of breath. His mother asked him why. "Well" says he "I was able to save twenty five cents by running home behind a bus". His mother says, "you dummy ... you could just as well have run home behind a taxi and saved $2.00."

As to what will be your chosen occupation in life, you have probably not yet decided. And it will be a few years before that is determined by your choices, the education you have achieved, and by fate. Until then, it seems likely you will be working at lesser paying jobs to get your spending money, and to pay for your education. I recommended to my own children that they get some few years of work experience in one or several of the building trades because of the usefulness of such experience for the remainder of your life. Carpentry would certainly be one of the most valuable, but electrical, plumbing/air conditioning, automotive, and landscaping are also useful. It would be best to hire out as an apprentice - as though you were serious about it as a life's occupation - rather than as a job site laborer. You need not let on that you are going to be a doctor, or an engineer, or a teacher - for that would make your potential employer less apt to hirc you as the apprentice. With a good background of experience in one of those major trades, you would have a backup and alternative way to make a living if you suddenly find yourself unemployed as is happening to many people (in the field of engineering for example) at this time in our economy. As with your Uncle JRO, you may find that you might save yourself many thousands of dollars at a later time in your life by building your own home. Oh, yes, it is good while you are young to have a job to be able to get some income, but so much better to also be working at a job that is giving you valuable training and experience.

After I finished my high school, it took me six years to finish my college education, as I was unable to attend on a full time basis. I worked as a locomotive fireman on the Great Northern Railway in Northern Montana. Even when working full time, I attended college classes on a part time basis. And when business slowed immediately after the New Years Day, they laid me off. I then ran off to take full time class work for a quarter or two before the railroading business picked up again in early summers, and I was called back to work. When I finally left the railroad job for good, I had more than seven years of seniority and was about to be promoted to locomotive engineer. My brother was three years behind me when I finished high school. Like myself and an older brother, he was able to find relatively good paying work on the railroad in the summer season, and my older brother and I were able to lend him just enough money so that he had to miss only one quarter of classes. And he performed so well in studies, that he was accepted into medical school after only three and a half years of college. In fact, he and I entered medical school as classmates and lab partners. One of our classmates was only age 19 - like you he had finished some of his schooling unusually early. Brother VBB was 23, and I was age 26 when we entered medical school.

I am trying in my mind's eye to picture what field you might be well suited to. It seems to me that Cui for example might be particularly well suited to become something like a lawyer, a city manager, or even a politician. Poco Uno, perhaps something like a dentist. Celt, maybe a coach and a teacher. Ribs (rather an introspected guy) a college professor and a writer. Bah - a psychologist? Boo - an engineer. Bam-Bam, a pilot or an astronaught. Belle, a veterinarian. Mich has already decided. JoJo, something like a managing engineer. Stan - something in the health field such as social worker or nurse - or perhaps a pharmacist? But what with Cowboy? Well, you can be whatever you make up your mind to become - I haven't yet got a picture of you. At the present time, one of the best paying professional occupations is that of pharmacy - and there are plenty of available jobs in the field. And there is plenty of opportunity for young and energetic medical doctors.

But I haven't been successful in getting anybody to send me your e-mail address. So I guess I'll have to send this note to you by snail-mail. I'll check with some of your cousins to see if they might have your e-mail address. And so, if this letter finally arrives to you with a 37 cent stamp on it, I hope you might take that as an evidence that I don't yet have your e-mail address and then you might foreword that on to me.

My wife broke her leg a couple months ago and is still having to hobble about on crutches. She is thinking about going back to work in a few weeks despite the crutch. And it looks like she is wanting to leave Albuquerque and move up to Santa Fe - which is just 60 miles north of here. That is where she has been working the past couple years and it would spare her having to travel that long distance to work. And so I will let you know my new address, in case you decide to come down here for a visit or looking around for work or for schooling.

We have gotten almost no precipitation yet this year, so it looks like we might be susceptible to some mighty forest fires this spring and summer. New Mexico is quite an interesting place - and one of the top tourist destinations in the county. And Santa Fe is both its capital city and its cultural center. Located high in the mountains of the Sangre de Christo Mountains at an elevation of more than 7,000 feet, so that it is relatively cool in the summers in spite of being so far south.

I am about finished with the writing of my Philosophy book and am writing a few letters about, and trying to find someone that would be interested in publishing it for me. I haven't yet figured out my travel plans for the summer. I would kind of like to get back to New England and New France, since I didn't get there in the past summer or fall as I usually do in the past 12 or 15 years. A lot of Brasseur people back in that part of the country. I have not quite completed my Brasseur genealogy research and visits to that area. But the pickup is getting on in years, and I wonder how much longer it is going to live. At least it has good tires. And if it quits on me … well, I would just have to find some other way home. Of course, I'll try to get back to Oregon for a summer visit too, though I don't know when. The German meeting of this year is sometime in early September. By then, most of the grandchildren are in school. If so, I may have to go it alone this year.

Well then Cowboy, back now to my self-appointed tasks.

Best wishes to you.

Convey my greetings to your mother, Poco Uno, Cui, Zelt, Ribs, Mijita, and Nombres.

Love,

Gramps,

R. Garner Brasseur, MD

22 February 2003

15 September 2006

Santa Fe, New Mexico

Dear Cowboy,

I spent one summer at age 16 helping a carpenter build a house for my oldest sister, ALBK. He was my sister's brother-in-law and I was a sort of apprentice to him. And that is the limit of my experience with carpentry - just a sort of introduction to a very practical and useful skill. But such work was sort of spotty and seasonal and I never again saw enough demand or had the right inside connections to work at carpentry. Through the years I have been acquainted with enough carpenters to notice that there is a decent sort of living to be made in construction to those who are determined to stay the course and expand their experience.

I was so impressed with the usefulness of carpentry and the benefits of such skills to even a non-professional carpenter that I always encouraged my sons to get some experience in the field before they drifted off into their final professional careers. Each of the three thus worked at construction jobs for a year of more, and seems to have found those skills quite useful through subsequent years. JRO and PM did a large part of the construction on JRO's house in their after hours from their regular jobs. I expect it saved JRO quite a bit of money. And one does not have to pay taxes on what one saves - only on what earns, and again spends.

At age 21 I was determined to hire out as a locomotive fireman, having discovered that it was perhaps the best paying work an inexperienced young man such as myself could hope to find. On the job training and an hourly rate of pay the same as my fellows who had already many years of service at the time. I tell you this because I know that such work still pays well, and that those jobs are still available from time to time. Some 8 or 10 years ago, my nephew hired out on a railroad job. Once hired, he had a guarantee of $60,000.00 per year (more now, I should suppose) and opportunity to do even better when the work became more steady with his increasing seniority.

During those 7 years I worked on the railroad as a locomotive fireman up in Havre, Montana, I noticed that many of the fellows I worked with were working at their own construction projects in their off hours from railroading, as the work hours were seasonal and irregular. Between runs, they might at times be idle for a day or two - more, in slack seasons. Rather than idle that time away into bad habits and pass-times, they were able to remain productive and to benefit their own economic circumstance.

To find my railroad job, I had to travel about the state of Montana to the various railroad terminals to inquire specifically about that work. My brother VBB, later did the same thing to help finance his own education. But it was important to <u>not</u> let them know that we were students with other plans for eventual occupations elsewhere. For the railroads prefer to employ young fellows that will remain in service for their full working years.

I rather liked the railroad job and could just as well have made a career of it - and a good living. But I already had my sights set on other goals. Rather than using my off hours in the building of my own home, I was spending that extra time as a part-time college student, before I finally entered medical school at age 25 - just before I was about to be promoted to locomotive engineer.

By this time, Cowboy, you already have a good background in construction and carpentry at the very tender age of twenty years. You are now one year older than I was when I finished high school. And I hear tell that you have a good reputation as a hard worker. I also know that you have done well in school, finishing your high school equivalent education earlier that those with whom you entered the first grade. I wonder what your thinking is at so tender an age with your whole life stretching out ahead of you for perhaps another 60 years or more. Are you still considering the multitude of options available to you as a life career, or are you perhaps determined to follow out this one course into a career in carpentry and construction work? You know of course that opportunities in that career are constrained by the forces of politics and social connections among those who are already established in the field. All occupations seem to have that in common.

The reality is that in our own current times, it is generally acknowledged that one can not expect to remain in but one occupation for a lifetime. Most end up having worked at several occupations before they finally settle in to a state of retirement. Throughout the course of my life, I have worked at perhaps 25 or 30 different jobs. And the broader one's experience and adaptability to various sorts of work, the more apt is one to be able to find ongoing employment in their mid and later years of life - when a good many suddenly find themselves unemployed. Not a pleasant situation when one has car payments, house payments, mouths to feed, and insurance premiums to pay. Helpful then to be able when necessary to fall back on carpentry and whatever other work experience one has acquired in earlier years.

Other than those with inherited wealth, most young men of your age tend to be hard pressed economically. My own situation at that age was in no way better than yours - worse if anything. But being broke does not disbar one from further education nor from entering into any occupation of profession one might wish. It only requires that one recognize that fact, and that you pursue your intentions energetically.

Hiring into railroad work in current times is different now than when I hired out. I gather that one can probably enquire into such work opportunities on-line at the computer. I enclose to you several papers from the web which you might peruse if such possibilities strike your fancy. And, now-a-days, a man would hire out as a conductor (rather than as a fireman). The conductor rides in the locomotive cab along with the engineer and as a sort of understudy to also learn how to run the engine and later be promoted to the engineer position.

I enclose to you some copy of conductor-engineer jobs that are available in several states for your perusal. You, being young and single, are able to move about to any such place where you might find some such work. Work which would pay you enough to save some money to get on with the business of living your own life and/or getting on into college education. Work which permits you to also do some carpentry work in your spare time.

I don't mean to intrude into your life, but I know that getting a job with good pay is difficult for a young fellow without college education. And so, I merely mention such job possibilities as these which pay well and which I suspect that you might find interesting.

On the other hand, if you were thinking that you are about ready to get directly into college soon without another year or two in the work pool, there are various grants and loans that would make that possible. Your nearby junior colleges could serve you well for the first year or two of full or part-time studies.

Best wishes to you, Cowboy.

Love,
Gramps
R. Garner Brasseur

15 September 2006

22 October 2009

Santa Fe, New Mexico

Dear Grandson Cauxby,

Though you have given me an invitation to your October wedding, it lies yet unfound amid the clutter of materials in my work room. I recall it as being in October – this very month – but the exact date is unremembered. It makes but little difference however, for the necessity of earning a living leaves me unable to get free to attend this fine event. Best wishes to you both. Enclosed please find my check as a donation of some few dollars. A wedding gift.

(I am unable to recall the name of your bride. I will have to pick that up later, to add it to my genealogy books. It starts with a "K", as I recall?)

> Some for the glories of this world; and some
> Sigh for the prophet's paradise to come.
> Ah, take the cash and let the credit go.
> Nor heed the rumble of the distant drums.
>
> From "The Rubaiyet" of Omar
> Kyam

"May the menace of the years yet find us unafraid"
Best wishes and kind regards to you both.

> Love,
> Gramps
> R. Garner Brasseur M.D.

P.S.

Since "art is long and time is fleeting", I use this declining moment to send to you the following observations from my notes: concerning how I saw you as youngster. You continue to be observed ... from a distance.

22 October 2009

9 July 2008

Santa Fe, NM

Dear Grandson Cui,

I recently returned from southern California, where I attended the graduation exercises of Michah from Loma Linda Medical School and spent a few days there with Michah and his parents. I guess you probably know that Michah will then soon be launched out onto a seven year stint of training in Neurosurgery in Milwaukee, Wisconsin. I am given to understand that Stan has finished her basic degree in Architecture and will probability be continuing on into advanced training next year.

And PM tells me that Bam-bam is to spend several weeks of the summer in ground school and basic training with an eye toward becoming a military pilot and the possibility of getting into the Air Force Academy.

And now you too will have to be moving forward into a career. So it is for all these grandchildren who will each have soon to commence with the living of their adult lives. Life can be long, and their is:

> Nothing to do but work
> Nothing to eat but food
> Nothing to wear but clothes
> To keep one from going nude
>
> Nothing to breath but air
> Quick as a flash 'tis gone
> Nowhere to fall but off
> Nowhere to stand but on
>
> Nothing to comb but hair
> Nowhere to sleep but in bed
> Nothing to weep but tears
> No one to bury but dead

Nothing to sing but a song
Ah well, alas and alack
Nowhere to go but out
Nowhere to come but back

Nothing to see but sights
Northing to quench but thirst
Nothing to have but what we've got
Thus through life we are cursed

Nothing to strike but a gait
Everything moves that goes
Nothing at all but common sense
Can ever resolve these woes
                    Ben King

My own life has been a busy process as it rapidly unfolds before me, and I continue to work full time now into my 76th year. Ones life is that of a long preparation followed by the long years of a work career.

Upon Thy Belly, Shalt Not Go

Infinite stars explode through time,
Some random dust becomes a slime,
Natural law does not forbid
From this, arising--man--the Id

Hunger gnaws the stomach,
Lion gnaws the bone,
man without a talent,
Feeds upon a stone.

Swift the prey
In bounding leap
Perused in chase

FADING ECHOES

Through draw and steep

Awed was Adam
At the sight
Of Archaeopteryx
In flight

Strained with envy,
One might guess,
He flapped his arms
Without success

Speed and flight
Seemed much the same,
And came to share
A common name.

Swift the horse,
Nor did he bite,
When man first harnessed
Him to flight.

Onward, upward
Soar man's dreams
Ever onward
So it seems

Wing of sail
Upon a boat,
Hot balloon
In sky afloat.

Jet airplane
Outruns its sound
Of deafening noise,
As props go round.

Moon … and mars
A leap away.
The prints of man
Are there to stay.

Speed of light
Surpasses time.
Star Trek schemes
Not far behind.

And man shall surely rise to heaven.
'Tis urgent we prepare,
To merge "The Force" with "Enterprise".
Be fine in conduct there.

RGB

Congratulations on your high school graduation

Love,

Gramps

R. Garner Brasseur

9 July 2008

18 February 2009

Santa Fe, NM

Greetings Cui.

Yes, I got your letter. I guess you probably have a little spare time on your hands and some time for reading. Since you ask, yes, I would be glad to send you some of my writings to peruse. Enclosed you will find this little manuscript of information. Your picture was enclosed with your letter - your head imbedded in a pile of leaves. It led me to thinking about my experience under the leaves when I worked as a locomotive fireman on the Great Northern Railway in northern Montana when I was just a couple years older than you now are.

"Having once been called to make a trip to Williston, it was best for me to have been called to work in the night hours, so that we arrived in Williston somewhere near sunrise, for then, I could sleep out the warming hours of sunshine in the city park. But that of course, was a matter of pure chance. With the usual layover of eight to sixteen hours, I would then likely be called for the return leg of the trip in the mid-evening and be able again to pass the cold night in the warmth of the locomotive cab. On nights that I was forced to spend in Williston, I might sometime merely dress warmly and hope to catch enough warmth for a couple hours sleep in the park by climbing under a pile of leaves. When it got too cold for that, I one night tried to rest in the public waiting room at the depot, but the benches were segmented by arm-rests, so that one was unable to stretch out any at all. It just didn't work out. There were always a few locomotive engines sitting about the diesel shop, and I would sometimes climb into one of those warm cabs to sleep a few hours in the unoccupied fireman's seat, but I had to be prepared to evacuate in a hurry if it began to move, lest I find myself to be an unpaid passenger upon some outgoing train to which I had not been assigned. On the diesel shop campus was a small storage building in which were kept a pile of clean rags that were for use in cleaning the cabs and engine rooms of the locomotives. There one might burrow into the clean rag pile to find warmth and comfort on a cold night. But that necessity was somewhat unpleasant, in that access to these spots seemed generally to be the prerogatives of the engine maintenance crews - persons of a different occupation cast, to whom I was an unknown outsider of a different tribe of employee.

When they discovered me, I seemed to be owing them at least a brief explanation for what business I have, being in their territory. My little explanation seemed to satisfy the situations, though I could sense a trace of their resentment, account of my being camped in their space. My situational predicament of those economically desperate months brings to mind a parallel to the occasional un-fed and unwanted young dog I noticed to have been abandoned up near the state hospital where I was employed years later. They are meek and shifty-eyed with subservient posture and tail between their legs when one approaches them. They seem sometimes hopeful, but progressively un-expectant of ever finding acceptance into the hearts and territories of the local masters. The older stray has abandoned even its hope of belonging, and adapts, instead, to a rejected self-acceptance. It appropriates the use of a self-appointed territory of large proportion, upon which it forages its own living. A territory to which it seems to claim only usage, rather than ownership. Not uncommonly, several such strays, finding themselves unaccepted and alone, will form their own society and rove about upon the edges of a community."

And now, there you are in Carmen Serdon where I stopped to visit MABC and BC in 1997. Upon that trip, I first took a few days to drive out to California, and drove into Baja California, Mexico, to look up daughter MABC and BC at Carmen Serdon. Later in the year, their son Josiah Israel was born 4 September. But earlier - 2 April - was born the seventh and last child to RL and TM - a lad of many names who I call "Nombres" (Names) for the many names he carries. At that time, I then had 13 grandsons and 4 granddaughters.

From my journal of March 1997:
I drive westward across Hwy 8 to Hwy 94, and then south to Tecate. There I gas up before crossing into

Tecate, Mexico (population about 40,000) about 6:00 PM. Account of rather vague information from the Mexican Border guard, I am under the impression that the mission (where MABC and BC are working) is near the village of Guadalupe. From there, another bum steer leads me further astray into San Anton, Salazar, and even up to La Mission. I then search my own journal pages (this journal - Jan 22, 1997) to discover that I am looking for Carmen Serdon. So I have to back track and find that place, which is about 10 miles north of Guadalupe. The last 6 kilometers are up a washboard road before I finally arrive at Carmen Serdon. The entire village seems to have retired with no lighted windows or street lights to be seen when I arrive at about 11:30 PM. So I just pull off to the side of the road (actually only 2 or 3 blocks from the mission) and bed down for the night in the front of the pickup. I was up about 7:00 AM in the morning. I stop to talk with one of the locals to discover where "the mission de los Orphanatorio" is located. Just where I had guessed, only 2 blocks distant. There I stop for a little breakfast with them and talk about 1½ hours with MABC, and then let her get back to her job while I read a couple of hours and then have a little siesta. About 4:00 PM, MABC, BC, one of their associates and I drive to Tecate. There we eat out at a Chinese restaurant and then drive back to the mission. I had this captive audience in the car and did my best to keep their ears full.

And so I fill them in about the history of 'orphan trains' in the U.S. in the early 1900's; about Tuberculosis, Plague, and Echinoccocus; about Subaru cars; some stories of MABC; about brothers PP's and EVH's 'perpetual motion' machines; about my recent talk with JRO and his family. About the *Flight of the Phoenix;* about flying saucers etc. Later, back at the mission, I catch up on my journal notes while they go to a friend's place for some dessert.

I climb into the sleeping bag in the pickup camper to end my day about 11:00 PM. After a cool night, I was up next day about 7:00 AM. I take a hike for exercise and then wear my jacket while reading in the warming morning sun. Soon MABC and BC arise, and we then drive up through Tecote to El Cajun. There we have breakfast at an IHOP - greatly overpriced because they insist on serving one enough for two breakfasts. Again I end up doing most of the talking. PP's swing bike; about a trip with JRO; on the intensity of PM; on 'poisonous' oxygen; about poisonous foods; on the 'divine elixir'; on gravity; on space travel; on my uncertainty as to the strange things people tell me. How a lie is a poor substitute for a truth; on the certitudes of belief; that I have no answers ... only questions; on our primitive race of mere mortals; on man's first flight in 1750; about the first climbing of mountains about 1850; about the necessity of aligning our opinion of reality with its actual reality; about the moral corrective force of reality; about enterprise; about my escape from the grip of cancer; about the priority of my projects - number one being the writing of my autobiography and then on to various other unspecified projects. We parted about 1:00 PM. And I depart north on Hwy 15 to get an oil change, and then stop at a rest area near Boron, Calif, to watch a comet in the night sky.

A couple of years ago I wrote a book and had it published - *A Studied Impression of that Which Is*. I would be glad to make you a gift of a copy of that when and if you might wish. Also, in 1998 I wrote an Autobiography/ family biography - *Inheritors of a Few Years*. I left copies enough for you and each of your siblings with RL. It could be that he has lost those copies in the process of his moving about from one place to another there in Medford. If so, I would be glad to print out a copy of it for your own. I have other travelogue manuscripts, letters, essays, and poems that I could easily make available to you when and if you ever get time for them.

I took the month of October recently to travel and visit about the country. My summary of that is within this enclosed manuscript. If my health continues well, I will probably be able to take off time again in the summer or fall to visit about and make some trips. Give my some idea of when you might have time and we could plan a little outing.

Nice to hear from you, Cui.

Stay in touch.

Love,

Gramps,

R. Garner Brasseur, MD

18 February 2009

28 April 2009

Santa Fe, NM

Greetings Cui,

The vice president of the United States of America in 1933 was John Nance Garner from the state of Texas. I was the first boy in the country to be named after him - as well as for the president, Roosevelt. The picture of my parents and me was splashed on the front page of the Minneapolis Tribune to announce the fact to an astounded world. Vice president Garner sent a letter of congratulations to my parents. And he sent me a book entitled *The Speaker of the House*, which he hoped I might read one day. I had it in mind to read the book, but somehow, in the process of my family moving about from town to town through the years the book sort of disappeared before I got around to reading it.

I enclose now to you a copy of the book I had published a few years ago - *A Studied Impression of That Which Is*. Which is to say, my personal tentative conclusions as to the nature of reality. Not all of the copies that were published were actually purchased, and the publisher sent the several boxes of unsold books to me to do with as I wished. I thought perhaps you might be interest in having a copy which you might some day wish to peruse, before it becomes lost in the shuffle of your moving about from place to place.

Concerning these books, I thought you might enjoy the irony of what is happening to some of these extra copies that have come into my possession. I know that sometimes people go into stores to grab things off the shelves and then sneak out without paying for them. What I am doing with these extra copies is somewhat the obverse of that. I hide the copies under my jacket to sneak them **into** various used book stores, to place them on the shelf while no one is watching. So far as I am aware, I am the only one ever to conceive of so clever a scheme - ha. I check back with these stores later to see if the books have actually been purchased off the shelves. If so, I steal in with another to replace it. No, I am not pulling your leg. "Well," you might be thinking, "then what is the payoff". In truth, a writer always hopes to be able to earn a few dollars from each of his books, but failing in achieving that, he hopes at least to have someone read what he has to say. In this country, every person is allowed to have his say; but on the other hand, no one is obliged to either listen to or read what he has to say.

In your previous letter you spoke of wisdom and experience. It recalled to mind a source to which I have often referred through the years. "A people who have many proverbs in current use will be less given to talking nonsense." And, what are Proverbs? – "short sentences drawn from long experience". I thought you might find some of the following to be thought provoking:

- "Thought makes the whole dignity of man; and the endeavor to think well is the basic morality." Pascal
- "Thought is life, and strength, and breath;
And the want of thought, is death."
- "No man's error becomes his own law, nor obliges him to persist in it."
- "Error does not become a mistake until you refuse to admit it."
- "The unexamined life is not worth having lived." Socrates

- "The child, too, is father of the man."
- "If a man will begin with certainties, he shall end with doubts. But if content to begin with doubts he may well move toward certainties, i.e. the process of education." Francis Bacon

Metaphysical the honor accrued to patient men.
Endure the worlds absurdities, again and yet again.
To seek and advocate for light with Sisyphusian cheer,
The soul's symbolic blood is wept, for causes oft unclear.
-A poem by RGB-

- "Rhymes the rudders are of verses, by which, like ships they steer their courses."
- "If wanting to know be a sin, it constitutes both our guilt and our innocence." Camus
- "Even great minds can be baffled."
- "An idea is not necessarily true because someone dies for it."
- "Failure is not fatal, and success is not permanent."
- "A goal without a plan is simply a wish."
- "Philosophy has no end in view ... save truth. Faith looks for nothing but obedience and piety." Spinoza
- Knowles's Law--"It is easier to make a commitment or get involved in something than it is to get out of it."
- "Commit in haste, and repent at leisure"
- "Enough is as good as a feast."
- "A maxim - a minimum of sound, and a maximum of sense."
- "Reciprocity - a concise maxim."
- "What is an epigram? A dwarfish whole, its body wisdom, and wit ... its soul."
- The noblest of all occupations is to search for truth.

      "The eye it cannot choose but see.
      We cannot bid the ear be still.
      Our bodies feel where're they be
      Against or with our will."

- "Not all who wander are lost."

- "Eagles do not fly in flocks."
- "Science begins after it has been realized that the world is unknown."
- "There is no alleviation for the sufferings of mankind … except veracity of thought and action; and the resolute facing of the world as it is." T. Huxley
- "This world is a comedy for those who think, and a tragedy for those who feel."
- "Enemies make dangerous friends."
- "Love your enemies - it really gets on their nerves."

Some definitions:

Cabbage - a common vegetable about as large and as wise as a man's head.

Capital - the seat of misgovernment.

Bride - a woman with a fine prospect of happiness behind her.

Alone - in bad company.

Famous - conspicuously miserable.

Experience - the sum total of one's failures.

Hers - his.

Once - enough.

History - an account (mostly false) of events (mostly unimportant) which are brought about by rulers (mostly knaves) and solders (mostly fools).

Freedom - moving easy in the harness. Robert Frost

Will - desire of significant intensity that it is translated into action.

Wisdom - the exercise of judgment, acting on experience, common sense, and available information.

- "Heroism is the shortest career there is … and often fatal."
- "Men must be taught as though you taught them not,
  And things unknown, proposed as things forgot."
- "As wit is the capacity to laugh at others; so humor is the capacity to laugh at oneself."
- "Manners are minor morals."
- "Individuality lifts a person out of the collective authority."

- "It is only during the course of an eventful life that men are differentiated into a full individuality."
- "It is necessary to keep oneself free (to preserve oneself for one's own life) to withdraw from the all too binding obligation to the world's affairs."
- "Waste not; want not."
- "A fool and his money are soon parted."
- "A penny saved is a penny earned ."
- "All that glitters is not gold."
- "Feed a fever; starve a cold."
- "Let sleeping dogs lie."
- "Laws are not a panacea; and are not self-enforcing."
- "Where there are laws, there will be injustice."
- Maimonides; "Custom precedes law; and custom annuls law."
- "A coward dies a thousand deaths; a brave man dies but once."
- "A yawn is a silent shout."

"Live well
Do good work, and
Keep in touch"

Love,
Gramps,
R. Garner Brasseur, MD

28 April 2009

?Autumn of 2001

Albuquerque, NM

Greetings TMBW,

Thank you for your thoughtful recent message. How could I not be flattered at having you so concerned for me? In truth, it seems to me that you and I have always gotten along remarkably well, especially since we struck up a sort of informal truce several years ago concerning religion. And I dare say that we have always managed to be patient with and kind to one another. My impression of that informal truce between us was that you could have whatever religion you preferred, and that I was to be free to follow my own religious-philosophical mandate in my ongoing and relentless pursuit of what is true. And that we wouldn't assault one another with our separate philosophies.

I must say this for you; you are a wonderful source of news. And I recognize in you a real person, in that you are active and that your personal conversation displays an honest ambiguity with even some evidence of honest doubt and humble uncertainty concerning your certitudes-of-belief. I would be more than proud to nominate you for membership among the Unitarians if you ever get a hankering in that direction.

And who among us does not prefer to be loved and admired? To command the love and admiration of others is be invested with at least some little power over them. In this whole world, I can only think of just a few specific individuals whose love and admiration I would prefer not to have. There are few women in this world that I have liked more than I have always liked you. As you know, I always hedge about the word love, because it has become such a cliché word that it retains hardly any specific meaning for me. And even if it did have a specific meaning for me, it would still have only an ambiguous meaning to anyone that heard the word from my lips. And so I only use the L word in its one directional and non-contingent form, as what a parent feels for his children and grandchildren, whether or not they like one in return.

Obviously people have long been accustomed to using the L word in order to manipulate one another through the tether of emotions and feelings. Perhaps I am overly sensitive to that because my feelings are easily touched and I am saturated with emotional ooze account of the many people with whom I have been so closely involved throughout my many years. Look around you on any day and you can see the manipulative forces at work upon you through the guise of the L word. At home, of course; but even impersonally through radio, television, and billboards. But what this world and what individuals really need is self-discipline, self-control, and self-restraint; and to be able to direct their lives upon a coherent and rational course. Need some of the warm and fuzzy L stuff too, to maintain their sense of balance as human beings. But it is always best to keep that coming from the home base, where the manipulation generally always favors the best interests of our children. When it starts oozing out of the mouths of politicians, radio and TV announcer, preachers, and off of the road-signs, it tends easily to serve agendas which are not in the best interests of our descendants.

And to set the record straight, we need to remember that it is not the possession of emotions that makes us human. One can easily observe the effect of those emotions in your ordinary mammals and birds. Though I haven't been a close witness to the presence of emotions in flies, mosquitoes, and cockroaches, I do not doubt but what they too may be ruled by emotions. The quality which truly sets mankind above and apart from other species is the capacity to reason. A quality to which one is predisposed genetically, but which is greatly facilitated by man's advancing culture. One is truly human to the degree that he possesses and uses his powers of reason. There is no reason to suppose that anyone is free of the powerful influence of emotion, though it is true that some are more practiced at disguising their emotion, while others are the more practiced at playing upon the emotions. In general, the subculture of men within our society tends more to favor and encourage the rational capacity and to play down the overly powerful influence of emotion in our lives. Our subculture of women, however, tends generally to take the opposite position. Do you not agree that is the situation?

I recall your previously having mentioned an interest in the possibility of selling Mary Kay Cosmetics as a way to supplement your income. I have no reason to doubt that you might indeed do well at it, providing only that your motivation is constant enough to keep you plugging away at it. You strike me as a rather social sort of person and apt therefore to be able to fulfill some of your requirement for social contacts even while making a few bucks on the side. If you and I continue to remain on good terms, you might even sometime let me drive the pink Cadillac? I certainly hope for you success in that new venture.

Concerning CrossroadChristianMinistry.com, there is a message on my address book that says "this is not a valid e-mail address". And then suppose that I had a valid e-mail address: could I then get my e-mail letters through to Cowboy? And does the arrangement you have with Cowboy's living program permit him to receive mail from his infidel grandfather? If so, to what address would I send it? Is Cowboy getting home schooling or is he attending public schools? Is he participating in any regular sports program? Is he making any plans for education after he completes his high school education? Does he know that he would need a decent grade point average in order to get into college? Does he know that without a scholarship, the costs of a college education might prove almost prohibitive? Does he read any actually good books, or just the routine psycho-babble and goody two-shoes stuff?

I know that you are not surprised that I am a little concerned by the overemphasis of religious influence upon the young mind of Cowboy. But from what little I could see of the situation, it does seem advisable that he get away from the perverse influence of aimless peers in the middle teens of their school years. But will his mind be turned to some analytical thought and honest and questioning introspection, or will he merely be cowed into an apparent submission?

Stay as sweet as you are TM. Greeting to my grandchildren.

Yers trooly,
Dad,
RGB

Autumn 2001

17 Aug 2010

Santa Fe, New Mexico

Dear TMBW,

Through the years, I have written many essays, letters, and (in more recent years) quite a few of the more brief e-mails. Also a couple of books and a couple of what have become voluminous genealogy manuscripts. And in return I have received a modest amount of correspondence. As I have been unemployed and in desperate economic straits from time to time, I have had time to reflect and agonize over all sorts of real and imaginary problems. There seems a natural tendency for the themes of one's thought to 'short-circuit' and become endless loops (like Mobius strips) leading to nowhere. And destitute of any useful or interesting conclusions or ideas - just the sort of thing that is wont then to progress into sleepless nights, for example. Fragments of thought awaiting to be precipitated into either into an action, or at least into a coherent thought on paper - so as to 'get-it-off-ones-chest' and out-of-mind. Yes, requiring some such definitive action to put an end to its continuing to disturb ones night of rest. That, along with my genealogy records tends to keep me preoccupied with various form of writing.

Writing requires a certain determination of effort, and I always find myself reticent to make each new beginning - account of my natural laziness. But it is enough satisfying thus to have thoughtfully dealt with (and put behind me) each burning deed and thought, that it seems well worth the time and effort it costs me. And then, wrapped in pleasing delusions I can sink - and cease to be. Thus, I generally sleep fairly well. And awake rested. Free of yesterday's worrisome theme, and ready to face the inevitable dilemmas of the every new day.

But I digress. What I started out saying, is that in return for the considerable correspondence I produce, I receive not all that much correspondence in return. It would be pleasing to suppose that something of what I write might stimulate some thought; or perhaps even some action. But, probably not much, actually. Of course I have always gotten thoughtful correspondence and good advice from my twin brother, VBB; and some from DFB, too. Apart from them, as much correspondence from you as anybody. And through you - gratefully - some access to, and information concerning my grandchildren.

So the answer is yes, I would greatly appreciate and enjoy another report from the mother of my grandchildren, concerning their individual status; and the trajectory of the course of their lives at this point in time.

In my 78th year I still feel well, and I am still working a few days per week. But on the 11th of September I will head out alone in my little red wagon to wander about into the northwest, to interrupt the domestic tranquility of some of my people and some friends. And back to work again on the 13ᵗʰ of October - hopefully before the ice and snows make driving a hazard.

Well, it would be nice to have the company of one or two of my younger grandchildren on my trip, but surely they will be committed to school attendance at this time of the year? Still, the invitation is open to Nombres to make with me a bit of journey through time and space in the little red wagon sometime next summer. If he has the interest and the time, we could surely work something out.

Best wishes to you and yours, TM.

Yers trooly,

Dad,

R. Garner Brasseur

17 Aug 2010

18 April 2011

Santa Fe, NM

Dear Beaux,

Having received from you a notice to the effect that you have plans for marriage in June, I now have an address to which I can send you a couple of books and things. In the past 15 or 20 years I have been in the process of putting together my memoirs and various writings from years past.

It has now been just over forty years that I have been at the keeping of a continuous daily log. It began in about 1969 or 1970 while we lived in Ashland, Oregon. I believe it had its beginnings largely in part due to an intention that originated gradually within me in consequence of my coming across a series of daily log books of such daily entries that was kept by my brother, EVH, during the two years he spent in the Navy. Along with the other small caches of personal possessions acquired by myself and my brothers through our early adult lives, (these caches being mostly of the nature of memorabilia) had a tendency to lodge and accumulate in the basement of our older sister, ALBK, in Miles City, Montana. The residence of her and HK was the closest thing we had to a permanent home and storage place for these accumulations, as we used their home as a sort of refuge and asylum as we came and went about from season to season in our eternal wanderings between our temporary spells of gainful occupation interspersed with semesters of formal college and postgraduate education through those turbulent and sometimes desperate years of uncertainty. My journals chronicle the major events of my day-by-day existence through the months and years. Only rarely has the habit of a daily entry been interrupted through all these years. And in the past twenty years, I have taken to turning out an annual summary of the ideas, activities, and thoughts that have preoccupied me each of those years. The latest of which I have enclosed to you (Summary of 2010).

During a few periods of a couple days each year, when I sheltered for brief spells there at my sister's home, I was wont at times to go through the various accumulations of memorabilia that belonged to my four brothers and myself. The sum total of those accumulations amounted perhaps to no more that what might fill the cab of my pickup truck. It was intermingled and scattered in small footlockers, a couple tattered old suitcases and a few cardboard boxes. A few family photographs and old letters were also there to be found for one's perusal. It was always interesting to scavenge through and ruminate on these little treasures.

Having finished medical school and entered into the practice of medicine during the six or seven years prior to the time we settled in Ashland, I, as a rustic lad of humble origins had been encountering new experiences and situations in a professional career. With no background of family experience on which to ground this business of having become a professional, and in continuously encountering new cultures as we spent a few years in central America, there was a great deal of ever evolving experience for me to wrap my head around. Experiences so novel to me - and curious to my imagination - that I began upon occasion to write some of these things onto paper for my later reconsideration and contemplation. And all of this was now coagulating together with my self-acknowledged intent to investigate and reconsider the truth and realities of what had previously come to be (by default) my fundamental Philosophy of the nature of reality and eternal truth.

Thus it was that I at last found the necessity, time, and opportunity to launch out upon this study of the nature of reality and historical truth and began to realign my views according to a new and more objective standard, rather than to continue blindly upon the mere authoritative and schizophrenic notions which had begun to trouble me in recent years. Science (and a scientific method) versus authoritative religion based upon the contradictory assertions of ancient times and manufactured history - one might say - in a general sort of way. There is a large disparity between History, and history. The former, being often manufactured from the later, and fitted up with a great many suppositions and self serving embellishments of simple error, deceit, fraud. To what purpose, such deceit and fraud?

And at this time in my personal history, I began to acquire and digest the portable and inexpensive paper-back books such as I might choose in search of answers to the ongoing questions that arose within me as my education progressed. Yes, it progressed, into the philosophical, the scientific, and into the divergence of opinion as to what constitutes historical reality. A wide divergence of opinion.

From a vast body of historical documents and writings which presents to one a divergence of opinion and views that are at odds with one another, one must finally arrive at one's own tentative conclusions. Those conclusions best based therefore upon a wide perusal of literature and study; and adequately moderated by one's skepticisms and endowed with a sense of that which is probable. One must come finally to consider oneself somewhat as "sole judge of truth; in endless error hurled; the glory, the jest, the riddle of the world."

My brother VBB and I had between us some discussion of what it is that constitutes **wealth**. It prompted him recently to send me a batch of information about Adam Smith's *The Wealth of Nations*. And I am still trying to come to some more comprehensive understanding of it all. I recently got a copy of *The Creature from Jekyll Island* by J. Edward Griffin, concerning the origin, nature of, and workings of 'The Fed'. Informative and interesting. Perhaps, astonishing, is more like it.

While there, 1969-1978 in Ashland, Oregon, I had time and enough of modest income to permit me to delve more extensively into an appreciation for music. The Southern Oregon College Bookstore was importing for sale an ongoing stream of inexpensive off-brand-label 33 1/3 speed platters, at a mere dollar per disc. I accumulated and listened then to a rather large repertoire of mostly classical music. I also began to acquire additional records from Musical Heritage Society. By chance, there in Ashland, I came into possession of three or four records of Folk Music from the area of Bavaria and Southwest Germany. I found it to be charming, and so beautiful that I resorted to it ever more regularly. Then, cassette tape music was soon becoming available and I was able to transcribe this music to my own collection of cassettes, so that I could use it in my automobile trips. With the passage of time I came to use cassettes ever more, and rarely had cause to use the platter recordings that were more cumbersome to deal with. Through the years and through the course of several moves about the country from place to place, I eventually became separated from my record player; then lost track of the original record plates, as I had no further use for them. But it turns out that the cassette tapes have a tendency through repetitious use to distort and to break--become useless. Thus it happened that I eventually had no further access to much of what had become my favorite music. I grieved some at the loss.

But, a couple months ago, Bayloo got me an I-pod. A compact and handy little device. But it has taken me a lot of frustrating hours to become only gradually familiar with its workings. I have transcribed my CD discs into e-recordings into the I-pod. And recently have gotten access to the I-tunes warehouse, and access to a great much of folk music from which I had become separated through the years. Yes, able to tap into my beloved Bavarian and German Folk Music. And in the past few weeks I have acquired a play-list of about 50 pieces of this lovely music. I find myself sort of enthrall to it. It is sort of intoxicating to hear - infuses me with a great sense of calm and serenity. Produces a sort of infatuation or euphoria reminiscent of that experienced from a slug of Demerol or Oxycotin such as I have experienced at several occasional past episode of pre-op or post-op surgical episode.

And so, I have been playing this folk music almost continuously the past few days when I am not at work. At home and when not writing, reading, watching Fox News and TV special programs, I am often pre-occupied with the repetitious use and hearing of the music. As with other comparable euphoric preoccupations with this or that in one's past, I expect that the grip of the music will eventually diminish to more reasonable proportions, so that one no longer feels deprived when away at work or out on errands.

But, there is this thing called 'taste' and preference in music, just as in foods, dress, artistic enjoyment, etc. And I couldn't help but wonder how wide-spread of appeal might be this Bavarian-German Folk Music to which I am currently enthrall.

A month or so ago Bayloo got me a Dragon Nuance program for doing dictations directly into typed pages. Of course it also requires of one some certain amount of frustration and a few hours of forbearance to become acquainted with it and learn how to get some use from it. But, I am becoming quite impressed with it. The other day I sat down to about four hours dictation into the device (reading pages of letters composed in cursive) and managed to turn out 16 type written pages in that period of time. It would have taken me, say, six or eight times that to have typed it manually into script.

So that is what is going on currently down here in Santa Fe - in case you wanted to know.

Love,
Gramps
R. Garner Brasseur

18 April 2011

11 May 2011

Santa Fe, NM

Dear Ribs

I received your nicely written and thoughtful letter. You write a more coherent essay than I would anticipate from an eighteen year old fellow. Happy birthday. I find it always inspirational that one can

FADING ECHOES

both perceive <u>and</u> acknowledge personal fault within oneself. And that one can resolve to the necessity of personal responsibility; and a determination to make an effort toward self-improvement. I had indeed heard faint rumors to the effect that you had taken up some bad habits in the form of MJ. You are not the first within my family to have given it a try. It would be a comforting delusion for me to suppose that you are the last. But error does not become a mistake unless one refuses to correct it. And the various substance abuses have been the ruination of many a life. They become overly expensive in many ways, and one becomes desperate for ever 'more'. About how honest can a desperate man then be?

What is will power? Will is desire of sufficient intensity as to translate into individual motivation and action. It must surely have its inception within one's own mental life. One thing for sure, bad habits seem always easier to acquire than good habits - and a lot harder to shed. Having summoned up one's will power, one must then conceive a goal towards which might aspire. But a goal without a plan cannot be well focused. And so one must labor against mighty odds as one speculates and begins to evolve a workable plan. The goal and the plan then gradually merge into one's 'personal agenda'.

One of the more humorous little stories that I have read is by mark Twain, *A Campaign That Failed*. I mention this both because it illustrates the foolishness of involving oneself in someone else's agenda (campaign), AND because he points out that making a retreat from an ill-advised action is a difficult maneuver - one that is worthy of deep consideration. Not to be resorted to rashly in haste. If you, Ribs, are now determined to make changes in your life, be careful not to be overly ambitious as you go about it. For Knowles's Law informs us that: "It is easier to make a commitment or get involved in something than it is to get our of it". "Commit in haste: repent at leisure", as the expression goes.

And at this point as you are set to make some changes in your life, you would seem to be at risk. Among the strongest forces that constitute one's being are those of <u>emotion</u> and <u>reason</u>. Along with Ethan Allen, it is my opinion that "reason is man's only valid oracle". Historically, however, the inescapable power of emotion seems generally always to have held the upper hand; and it is through the power of emotion that one is so always easily guided (or misguided) and led (or misled) by one's fellow beings into actions and beliefs that are generally the less advantageous to one's own best interests. It is generally well worth one's while to keep his emotions in check by the exercise of one's reason. Especially for we of the male gender. For we must navigate and earn our livelihood in the real and unforgiving world of natural (and man-made) laws, rules, and regulations; in competition with our fellow man for the always limited (and sometimes scarce) necessities required to the sustaining of our own lives - and those of our families. In that melee, one is well advised to be well grounded with valid information, knowledge, and wisdom; and prepared to exercise reason to avert the ever present possibility of being scammed and defrauded of one's few comforts and hard earned assets. Meanwhile, of course, it is well that one have acquired skills and abilities to make an honest living - so as to avoid the temptation to mislead and defraud one's compatriots and fellow citizens. Personal integrity will allow one to maintain his self-respect - and sleep better at night.

Though the probability is only remote that you will find yourself ever able to support yourself by the playing of a guitar it is a art well worth while, for your own edification and enjoyment. Next to that of the human voice, guitar music is probably my favorite. I have been hoping to acquire for my I-pod, a copy of a beautiful piece of three or four minutes, by Handel, entitled *The Harmonious Blacksmith* which I have heard only a few times on the radio as I drive the 60 miles back and forth between my work and home. Played, I believe by either John Williams or Elliot Fisk.

Look about yourself, Ribs. Glenn Beck perceives 'agendas' everywhere he looks; and is roundly criticized for voicing his suspicions on FOX News and on his talk radio show. It is as though the whole of society were either blind to - or in denial of - the reality of agendas. Visible to the discerning mind, though not to the eye. Granted, that they are not tangible or easily visible to the unpracticed mind, yet they are there - in abundance and at all times. And the agenda is a species of what we might call 'an idea', but compounded with 'intent'. Though most ideas be either 'stillborn' or 'hare-brained', yet the occasional idea can indeed be a powerful force in the course of history. As Victor Hugo puts it, "Greater than the marching of armies, is an idea whose time has come". If one does not set a personal agenda, then one's time and energies are certain to somehow be incorporated and siphoned off into someone else's agenda.

Aside from earning an honest living, what might we consider to be a reasonable agenda? To perhaps free oneself from the superstition and ignorance which are obstacles to one's rational purpose; and an obstruction to one's view of reality. As one commences to advance in wisdom and stature, and in the making of one's personal life, it is well to maintain an interest in a diversity of skills and subject materials. For just as balance and proportion are at the heart of physical beauty - so too, are they at the heart of inner beauty (strength of character).

Like you, Ribs, I too sometimes ponder deep and weighty thoughts. I recall having had a couple of dreams, wherein I was instantly enlightened; and all things were suddenly crystal clear to my perceptions. So clear and certain that I could not conceive of the possibility that it could ever be forgotten - and I drifted off pleasantly into ongoing dreams and ruminations of my newfound wisdom. But, alas, when I arose to dawn's early light, all had vanished, except the recollection that I had briefly attained enlightenment. And that I had permitted it to slip through my fingers. I resolved that if ever again this mighty enlightenment were to visit into my dreams, I would rise immediately to set it to paper for posterity - as a benison to self and mankind. Lo, and behold - it did again visit my dreams one cold dark night. With a mighty effort of will power, I managed to escape the warmth and comfort of my bed and the euphoria of my vision (a sort of 'high', we might call it) and scrambled to my desk to set it down on paper, lest it elude me once again. But I was mistaken! Just part way into the second or third sentence, as I approached the nub of this golden nugget of wisdom, I discovered that it was receding before me - like a mirage or a ghost - and it slipped like sand, through my mere mortal mental fingers. Fool's gold, we might call it. Sorrowfully disappointed, I was able at least to return to the comfort of my still warm bed; and to the possibility of yet another happy dream.

"The heights by wise men sought and kept

Was not attained by sudden flight
But they, while their companions slept,
Were climbing upward in the night."
H.W. Longfellow

———•◆•———

Did I request this mortal frame?
Upon this ageless rock I pout.
Enslaved within this land of shame,
Beset by certitudes I doubt.

Why do we tread this beaten path?
Why yet to sing and dance and spin?
Why do we brave this threat of death?
Why yet pursue in love to win?

With patience yet to stay the course,
Not full contentedly, be sure.
Though filled with outrage and remorse,
Resigned a while yet to endure.
by RGB

———•◆•———

We no longer maintain shelter care for Native American Indian girls. Bayloo has now gone out of her way to outfit me into one of the two spare bedrooms to be used as a 'den'. There, I can be 'out-from-under-foot', when on my off-days and leisure hours. To paraphrase a poem:

Panger Ban the Cat

'Tis a merry thing to see
At our tasks how glad are we
When at home we sit and find
Entertainment to the mind.

So in peace our tasks we ply
She finds make-work as do I
In these arts we find our bliss
Mine ... and whatsoever she may wish

Better far than praise of men
'Tis to sit with book and pen
With spouse that bears me no ill will
As she plies her arts and skills

Practice every day has made
For us, contentment at this trade
Where I seek wisdom day and night
To turn my darkness into light.
                    RGB

———◆———

"If wanting to know be a sin, it constitutes both our guilt and our innocence." says Albert Camus.

My views on this matter of religion and philosophy have gradually changed. I have gradually come to see that it is not my responsibility to remain true to my native beliefs. Rather, it is my obligation to inquire into their dubious validity on the basis of my reading, my conversations, my experience of life and reality, and my long considered meditations.

"An endless sleep may close our eyes,
A sleep with neither dreams nor sighs.
And yet we question, dream, and guess,
But knowledge we do not possess."
                    R. G. Ingersol

"Is there a God? I do not know.
Is man immortal? I do not know.
One thing I do know: that neither hope nor fear, belief

nor denial, can change the (yet unknown) fact. It is as
it is; and it will be as it must be.
We must wait. We may hope."

R. G. Ingersol

———◆◆◆———

Yet another reality is that even we, 'the have-nots' are mostly all
of adequate intellectual potential and mostly physically able enough
that we might each aim and aspire higher than we do. Yes, might
become somewhat 'more equal', if only we had given the matter more
consideration, and focused on the more distant - rather than on the
more immediate satisfactions. Most get swept up into someone else's
agenda, rather than thoughtfully evolving their own. We are well
advised to take note of whether any such agenda has merit - and to
whose benefit. Yes, there is something to be said for giving heed to the
advice and agenda of the thoughtful friend or relative - such as might
be concerned and willingly to trouble himself to be of benefit to one's
best interests.

Explanation to a child

Mine to prepare for you the way.
In a world disposed to lead astray.
Mine to hold you to the task.
When over-inclined in the sun to bask.

Mine to object to the hopelessness plea.
However great discouragement be.
To obstruct the urge to uselessness.
To inspire insistently unto success.

Personal faults and demons to face.
Nor linger long in lethargic embrace.
Cast thou from life all influence malign.
Transcend by degree onto the sublime.

FADING ECHOES

Flattering world would seduce with applause,
Of intent be thou cautious, such dubious cause.
As to vague future, nor fearfully heed,
Meaningless garble of myriad creed.

From certitudes glib of hereafter resign.
Cling yet to life with the rational mind.
Justly confounding the trials of each day.
Nor dread the unknowable Deity's way.

RGB

Where will you be staying when you arrive in Medford? You might give me an address and a telephone number so that I can contact you if I find myself arrived there. When in Medford, I usually camp out in the Wal-Mart parking lot - the one out towards White City, so that if you get a voice-message from me, you will know where to look for me. They have a very good pizza place right near by to there.

I received a card from Beaux suggesting that he is planning to get married on June 25th, but it doesn't say where, or at what hour. I suppose that your mother and the rest of your family might be there also? I hear tell that grandson Michah is getting married just a few days earlier - on the 19th - way out in Milwaukee, Wisconsin?

Well, of course, Ribs, if you have the time and inclination to stop over with us for a spell on your way back to Florida at summer's end, we would be glad to see you. If I know in advance when that might be, I am sure I can get some time off of work - to permit of us having some travel time together in the old pickup, frugally camping and exploring our way through New Mexico and along The Gulf Coast into Florida.

Convey my greetings to your mother and the family.

Love,

Gramps,

R. Garner Brasseur

11 May 2011

18 May 2012

Santa Fe, NM

Greetings Nombres,

Many a day seems interminable long, but the years swiftly pass. And so I have launched out into my 80th year. It has been said that the first 50 or 60 years of one's life gives one the text, and that those whatever subsequent years give one time for commentary. That is where I am currently lodged. And so I have just completed the publication of my third book, and expect to have published my fourth book within the next couple of months. A copy of each is reserved for you. Why do I write so much, you might wonder? It is a long habit that I have acquired from my brothers and from my medical training.

The world and what goes on in one's mind tends to be somewhat chaotic. To write an analytic essay seems to me to be a useful approach for putting order into that chaos. It has been said that the unexamined life is not worth the trouble of having lived it. An element of truth in that – thinks I.

As the years pass, one hopes to advance in wisdom, as in stature. Both are in need of thoughtful consideration, and of effort. It is always well to have some generally good rules to guide one in one's day-by-day ventures into life. I expect that you are acquainted with what is called the Golden Rule. It is one of three rules which one does well to keep in mind. The other two are, the Silver Rule and the Iron Rule. The Iron Rule is - do not permit others to do onto you, that which you would not do want to them.

I spent January, February, and March of this year in Fargo, North Dakota, where I worked 32 hours per week. Lived there alone in a small apartment, and spent most of the rest of my hours doing the thinking and the writing that has gone into my most recent book - and the up-coming book.

I then visited and collected some genealogy information as I traveled westward through North Dakota and Montana into Washington state. There I visited my brothers PP, DFB, and VBB. I'm concerned mostly about DFB, who at age 83, is spiraling downward into a state of forgetful dementia, and has now been lodged into a nursing home, as he can no longer fully care for himself. I tried for an hour to visit with him, but it was an exercise in futility, as his memory is in a state of near complete disarray. A sad state, for a life that has been lived so intensely and vigorously. "So we the beaten path must tread - on which our sires of yore have led. Since none can nature's course elude, why, o'er they doom, in sorrow brood?" - as the poet puts it.

Having now arrived back home to Santa Fe, I am currently working one or two days per week, but beginning in June, I expect to be working four or five days per week. Health and whether permitting, I shall find my way into Oregon, for Cui's wedding in mid-July. And I look forward to seeing you there, where we can hold hands and hop three times into the air.

Greetings to all of your people there in Florida.

Love,
Gramps.
R. Garner Brasseur

18 May 2012

3/31/88

Caldwell, Idaho

Dear M.A.,

Your mother tells me she talked with you last night - and that you have changed your plans; and will not be coming home this weekend. On the one hand, I am sorry to miss the opportunity to see you; but on the other hand, it pleases me that you have the courage and self-discipline to decide against a trip that I know you did want to take. It suggests that the seed of wisdom has begun to take root in your being - a thing separate from mere knowledge, though often enhanced by knowledge.

There were a couple of books that I wanted you to have, for I think they might help to give one insight into the philosophical problems that you and I must face. This one by Mortimer Adler is done in an Ann Landers type of format. That is to say, the question-answer type of dialog. Most of the questions are practical and good questions. Good questions are of the essence in communication. Keep in mind though, that not all questions are good ones; and even this book may have questions that need improvement. The answers he gives (for those questions) seem also quite good - though we must each decide that for ourselves, finally. It, at least, does give you some idea as to how to go about answering this good question, or that one. This is the sort of book one might keep in the bathroom, where one can ponder its wisdom in the solitude of private meditations. Thus, one never really has to take time to read the book at all, for it only occupies a few - often, otherwise wasted minutes of one's time intermittently. Then, behold! One day you find that it has been accomplished. I'll send you also a couple of reprint essays for your consideration. Most of them will eventually be going into a couple of books that I am compiling; and hope some day to publish - should I live long enough yet to accomplish that. The first is already nearly complete - *Cannon: A More Recent Testament*. The second - *Think on These Things* - was mandated because the first has already become too voluminous. Some of the essays in each, will be written by myself, but the majority are to be merely excellent essays that I have read, and validated because of their excellence and because of the importance of subject matter with which they concern themselves.

I understand that you are taking a course in Philosophy this quarter. I presume it is a general introductory course to the subject - in which case it is going to deal more with the History of Philosophy, rather than with philosophy per se. That is to say, it is apt to cover a little information about each of quite a number of Philosophers. You may find that your religious background will be of little use to you in this course - if anything, perhaps a detriment. Keep that in mind during your class discussions; and especially when you write exams in the course. Philosophy 101 was among the more difficult courses that I took in college - difficult for me, at least. The reasons, I think, because I was poorly read, at that stage of my life; and, because I was rather opinionated in my religious views at that time. Since then, I have given up a large part of my religious certainty, in favor of a philosophical openness to the great 'ultimate questions' which confront mankind. So, while I look for you to have some trouble the course; still, I think that you are better prepared than I was, at your age. If you find the time, you might let me know what questions come up in that course - both on the exams, and in the daily rhetoric. For, when good questions come up, I like to wrestle with them too.

FADING ECHOES

I am a bit behind on my correspondence. I need to write to PM and my mom (whose birthdays have already slipped by) to JRO, whose birthday is forthcoming; and to brother VBB who is still out of the country (which gives me a plausible excuse, since his address is constantly changing). So I am writing you, since you have already been out of the home for seven months. And I like to keep in touch with the youth, particularly - to remind them who they are; and where they come from; and to remind them of the incompletely defined reality of 'that-which-is'. And of their moral obligation (to themselves, to their ancestors, and to their descendants) to align their opinions of that reality with the actuality of 'that-which-is'. Not an urgent thing which one can 'get over' and accomplish in a month, say; or even a year or a decade. But something that one must constantly be chipping away at.

I wrote to Mike Rempfer, in Santa Fe, and he responded with some information that tells me more about my (and your) Boepple ancestors. So I am gradually accumulating more information. I called Emil Boepple in Boise to arrange to get together with him to exchange some of the new findings. Emil is about 65 or 70 years of age. He was rather depressed - for his only son, Norman, was recently killed in a 15 foot fall at work. On the other hand, his 90 year mother-in-law, on the verge of death has endured two recent operations and is now recovering. Emil didn't say anything about the wisdom of divine judgment that this implies, but I get the distinct impression that the thought, or the rudiments of that thought were beginning to take shape inside of his head.

Your mother's mother - has been here visiting the past couple weeks. Her oldest brother (Henry) died in January of this year. One of her younger brothers (Albert) lives in Buhl, Idaho - not far from here. Emile and Albert were at the funeral in Billings. One of Albert's two sons (Randy) was returning to Buhl on Feb 7th, when the airplane he was flying crashed into a mountain near Yellowstone Park; killing Randy (age 33) and his two (non-related) companions. Albert, of course, is disturbed by that - now he has only one son left. It is the sort of problem that would bother any of us, but it seems like it may be more of problem to folks that have those small families. I was able to squeeze a little more information from your grandmother's memory, concerning her ancestors, but the details are still minimal and sketchy. It is a great wonder to me, as to how so little family history is remembered and transmitted from generation to generation. Of course, I do have some ideas as to how that state of affairs comes about, but that will be the subject of a whole additional essay at a later time. Of course, as I accumulate this information, I get it out, bit-by-bit, to your brothers too. I have copies of all of the same information for you, too. I have it set aside for you in envelopes and notebooks that are designated under your name, and which I will send out to you at a later time. Should anything happen to me in the meantime, you will know where to get your hands on that information. Your mother says that her family reunion will be in August this summer - and at a different location than usual - up by Flathead Lake in western Montana.

But I must get on to my other projects. Even working only three or two days weekly, I never seem to get them caught up. It seems odd that ones projects continue to multiply, even as ones residual years decline. Where will it end? Quien sabe?

More love; and more light
Your dad,
R. Garner Brasseur

3/31/88

5/24/88

Caldwell, Idaho

Dear Tzing,

"Time drinketh the virtue of good intentions" -so I once read. I know that I seem always short of my goal. I presume that it could be the same with you, also. A certain poet gets us off the hook by assuring us that "One's reach should always exceed one's grasp; or what's a heaven for?"

Enclosed to you are the various letters and essays - each with a certain massage - food for thought. Concepts and ideas, of course, require of one the effort of digestion. Therefore, it is not surprising that no one is ever known to have gained weight from too much of them.

Your brother, JRO called my attention to the fact that AIDs seems not to be getting the honest and reasonable respect that it warrants. I agree that that is the case, after studying the evidence. I wrote to California and to Washington D.C., hoping to get some vocalization of that fact. The enclosed letter I have written to Rev. Johnson is my response to his letter, requesting why I am so much more concerned about the problem than is the Public Health Dept. I do not say that AIDS definitely is bringing doom and gloom. I do say that it definitely has the potential to do so.

But, M.A., I must a get this out to you before time drinketh the essence etc.

Love and Light
Dad
Garner Brasseur

5-28-1988

8/7/88

Caldwell, Idaho

Dear Tzing,

Several weeks ago, your Uncle PP and Aunt D. went out to the Twin Cities (Minneapolis/St. Paul) to help my Aunt Leah (my dad's sister) get moved from a regular apartment, into a retirement home where she could get some minimal nursing assistance in the routine of her life. She is over ninety years of age, and is beginning to get a little fragile and feeble; and has no one to check in on her to see that she hasn't fallen and injured herself, or is not ill nor unable to get out of bed. That sort of thing. They came across a few old letters; one written by dad, another by Uncle Louis, and a third one written by my dad's sister Annie - in 1942. Knowing that I am interested in that sort of material for my source of genealogic source he sent the letters to me, but sent me only a copy of the letter that Annie had written, as he wanted to put the original into the hands of her own children. The letter by Aunt Annie, is an especially good one; for in it, she mentions each of her fourteen children, and how old they are at that time, and what they are doing, and where they live. A rich and documentary source for a genealogist. But PP didn't know the people personally, having never actually met them - though they are his cousins - and he wasn't just certain as to how to get in touch with them. As it happens, I had written to Colleen Siben (the youngest of Aunt Annie's children) about ten weeks ago; so I told PP that I would let him know her address, should I happen to get a response. Shazam! Yesterday I got a phone call from Colleen; she lives way up in Saskatoon, Saskatchewan, Canada. She is the same age as your Uncle VBB. I had met her only once, at the funeral of Aunt Leah's husband, in about 1964, up in Dunseith, North Dakota. Colleen says that she had just gotten my letter, the previous day. Of those fourteen children, only seven are yet living. They are planning to have a family reunion next weekend; and she wanted me to know that I was welcome to come, if I could manage to get there on such short notice. For there, with all those people, we would have a great source of information concerning matters pertaining to family history. But, alas; however interesting the idea, the distance - 1600 or 1700 miles - is altogether just too forbidding. But, I told her that PP had her mother's letter, which he wanted her to have; and that I would send her copies of whatever family history information was in my possession. And lo ... these things were arranged, even as I had suggested.

In regards to my recent illness, the truth of the matter is that I had no fear of death when I was writhing in agony and misery. As of this time, my recovery seems to be progressing well. About ninety years ago, my great-grandfather died when he just about my present age; though I have no idea what he died from - for **all** things must have a cause, you know. If he had a ruptured appendix or gall-bladder, there was no treatment available to offer him any realistic hope of recovery. Ninety years is not a long interval of time - just to give you some idea of how primitive and backward a place this world was and still is, for that matter. While I was in the hospital, I had a fever part of the time, and part of the time I was under heavy medication for pain, and to help me rest. In consequence, I experienced some strangely vivid and realistic dream states; and had a few delusions and hallucinations. In other words, I was delirious. The brain is highly susceptible to this sort of malfunction, from all manner of causes: fever, concussion, abnormal build-up of body wastes which accumulate in consequence of heart, liver, or kidney failure, abnormally low or high blood sugar levels, and with a great many drugs as well as with high levels of stress, fatigue, and exhaustion. It is a strangely confusing situation to one's only partially conscious mind. You have experienced it yourself, from time to time, if you will think back on it. Both you and JRO, in fact, are occasionally in that sort of state of confusion transiently, when suddenly awakened in the middle of the night. I should suppose that nearly everyone has experienced that upon some occasion or another, but you and JRO appear to experience it more than anyone of the few people with whom I am closely enough associated, to have observed. In any case, things that we see, hear, experience, and believe in one of those weird states of delirium, are commonly disturbing and somewhat unbelievable to us; for we are vaguely aware that something about their detail is amiss, and they are commonly out of context with the general experience of our day-to-day waking lives. And so we are apt to sit up, blink our eyes, shake our heads and look all around - in attempt to put our perceptions in order; and to try to figure out if we are dreaming, or if this is for real. On occasion, I have gotten out of bed, gone into the bathroom, turned on the lights and splashed cold water upon my face, in order to bring my perceptions into order. Some such action as these, will commonly serve to get our dream state disentangled from our reality. In my experience that has always been a great relief; but my personal experience in this is limited, for I have never had a prolonged serious illness, nor organ failure, nor heavy intoxications with drugs, nor any concussion. As a physician, I have occasionally noted these states of patient delirium to continue for prolonged periods of time. I have no reason to suppose these prolonged states of delirium are any more pleasant to them, than my occasional short periods of delirium have been to me.

As you may recall, there is a bit of a philosophical problem concerning the dream state of our existence, versus the waking state of being. You have heard of the Chinese Philosopher who once dreamed that he was a dragon; and then upon awakening, he felt he could no longer be sure whether he was actually a Chinese Philosopher who had only dreamed that he was a dragon; or, if he was really a dragon that was now dreaming itself to be a Chinese Philosopher. And then there is Berkeley's Philosophy, which argues that all of what one commonly regards as external reality, is actually only a figment of ones imagination; and that the whole world - the whole universe - is only an imaginary thing within my consciousness. If so, then when I close my eyes and fall into a dreamless sleep, then the whole universe and everything in it disappears. Well, they are interesting little conundrums that one can argue from either side; and in toying with them, one can exercise his mental apparatus; and exercise the muscular strength which it gives to one's jaw.

But, what I started out to say, was that the dreaming state seems to be as natural a function of the brain, as is the waking state. And however complex the rhetorical arguments seem to get; yet even your common man, woman, or child, seems to have no difficulty whatsoever, in distinguishing between the two states as he experiences them in his own personal life. And that it is commonly recognized - but, only in the past century - that when some occasional individual here and there does have difficulty in keeping his dream state and his waking state disentangled, it signifies the presence of some underlying illness or toxicity. Even the uneducated citizen is apt to recognize such a problem, by asking, "What's the problem with that guy? Is he drunk or something?" It is well to keep in mind what Thomas Hobbs has said, "Waking, I often observe the absurdity of my dreams, but never dream of the absurdities of my waking life thoughts." I am sure that you are aware, that throughout the history of mankind, there have always been people who are intentionally seeking strange and exotic experiences, by inhaling fumes and ingesting drugs and chemicals which are known by reputation to produce these vivid delirium-like states-of-mind. It is a common notion that in achieving that delusional state, that they have had an encounter with - or a cryptic personal message from the Deity. And it not uncommonly gives them a certain sense of self-righteousness, and enhancement of status within the tribe. The history of the American Indians suggests that they were accustomed to achieve these 'states of bliss' by submitting to sleep deprivation, hunger, and self-inflicted pain. Many of them also used various drugs for that purpose. Drugs such as the Night-Shade Plant, poisonous mushrooms, the Jimson Weed, and Peyote buttons. Many aspects of most religions seem to have centered around such mystic delirium-states; and even where the practice has been covered over or de-emphasized, one can still find its continuation in some of their rituals, and in some of the cults and sects that are still attached to those religions. Thus we can still find the whirling dervish, the flagellates, the cloistered monk or nun, Marti Gras revelry, painful pilgrimages, fast days, night-long prayer-vigils, and other such. So the question is; what does the dream state, and the related states of delirium have to do with religion or with communion with the Deity, or to the great beyond? What is the significance of dreams; and do they bring us prophetic messages? Or is it only the more vivid trances and dream states that bear us religious, spiritual, and prophetic information? Is there any body of proof to support these notions? I do not speak of dreams in the sense of their being distant goals and objectives, to which we may aspire; but rather, in the sense of their being fragmented mental experiences which nearly all people seem to experience - during their non-waking hours. I have long been interested in dreams and dream-like states; and in addition to my formal studies and reading on that subject, I have also recorded some of the common and the more unusual dream experience of my own being; and have reflected and meditated upon that experience in my attempt to learn more about it. During the past fifteen years in which I have been keeping a journal, there are a good many entries concerning dreams that I have had; and scattered notes pertaining to the insights, thoughts, and conclusions I have come to - concerning dreams. Those dreams can be vivid and realistic events while we are in the throws of their experience; though more often, perhaps, dreams are phantoms of amorphous psychic chaos, of which we have essentially no recollection beyond the moment we open our eyes. And one must soon discover that even the more vivid of the species tend to be non-cohesive fragments as we attempt to hurriedly set them to paper, before they completely evaporate from our labors of recollection. When once awakened from an especially pleasant dream, only rarely are we ever able intentionally to re-enter into the same happy dream-trail. There are a few dreams which we tend to have recurrently, at intervals; invariably unpleasant ones, from which we are glad to waken. And here now is an example of a particularly vivid dream, with which I took some particular pains. In order to learn from it as much as I possibly could, I awoke at 7:15 A.M. on 18 Dec. 1986, having dreamed this excellent and ingenious mystery story; and which at the same time, seemed to endow me with an enlightened perception of the whole universe. It seemed to me so blissful and unforgettable that I hardly wanted to rouse myself. And so I sat there at the edge of the bed in the darkness for a minute, debating myself as to whether I should arise now, to sketch down the details and outline of my story - and my 'enlightenment'. Though it seemed so remarkably clear and distinct; and though I wanted to dive right back into that same dream-trail - to gather some additional pearls of wisdom, before the trail got cold. Yet I feared (from past experience) that there was a good chance that I might not recover the threads of my story upon re-awakening in the morning. Therefore, I arose; and set myself to the task. For I had missed enlightenment on several similar previous occasions, from just that same careless sort of procrastination. But, I was greatly disappointed in my effort. Though I truly believed in the exquisite excellence of this story and its enlightening information; and though I had complete confidence in my grasp of its details, its course, and the moral of its message: yet, I could hardly have been more wrong! I was pleased only in this: that I had made an appropriate and honest effort to capture the essence of my enlightenment to the written page. Otherwise, I might now be unjustly reviling myself for my neglect, in failing to preserve this treasure to mankind.

The waking state is one of continuous moment-by-moment activity within one's central nervous system. And one of a continuous readiness of input/output interaction with our environment, world, and universe. A perceptive state of being in which one can note the interaction between the objects of our surrounding world and universe. Even in the waking state, the microcircuits of ones brain seem not to require large amounts of electrical-chemical energy sources. Never-the-less, its vital fuel of chemicals can be accumulated at only a certain maximal rate; and are expended at only a certain minimal rate, even in the basal, non-waking state. Thus, apparently, we needs must regularly return to sleep, to re-accumulate those vital neuro-chemicals; and to dissipate the excess neuro-heat and neuro-chemical waste products which interfere with the efficient function of the CNS. And then - but apparently, only at a certain depth of that unconscious state - the random bits and bytes of our experience, hope, and expectation drift in some now unordered sequence, across the display terminal of our restfully suppressed semi-consciousness. And we then may perceive the after-image ghosts-of-thought and ideas; which our scheme of judgment - in its lethargy - neglects to censor. Thus, the illusional impression - as though of a bone-fide and certified experience. But, as I have done in the above example; you too, I think, are safe in setting aside the certitude of your belief, concerning your unevaluated dream. Yes, do; just try setting some of those dreams to paper; and then scrutinize them in your waking state. Seeing now some of my experience, thoughts, and ideas concerning dreams, you can readily perceive that I do not attach any spiritual or intellectual merit to dreams. No, not even to one's most vivid dreams. And concerning the illness and disturbed metabolism that underlies the state of delirium, there seems even less reason to accord faith in, nor status to that disordered imagery.

As it happens, we are also subject to delusions in the waking hours of our existence. Interestingly, in fact, delusions are not uncommonly experienced and shared among the members of a group - sometimes, accidentally. At the other extreme, some groups of people meet regularly, to intentionally reinforce a particular delusion to one another. From my own experience on this subject, I refer you to my essay, *The genesis of a Delusion*, which I sent to you a month or two ago. And I came across this interesting epigram by Joseph Campbell: "Myths are public dreams; dreams are private myths." And "What is an epigram? A dwarfish whole. Its body, brevity. And wit, its soul."

To my mind, the meaning of the word, delusion, is closely related to that of myth. As to my essay, I think it points to some of the probable causes, and pre-disposing circumstances that contribute to our delusions. Undoubtedly, we could examine other similar experiences, and find additional causative factors.

I'11 put aside my intention of saying more about illusions, magic, and magicians: to tell you instead about a particular interesting experience that I had in Mexico about ten years ago. It disturbed and confused me for about three months, before I finally uncovered its elusive answer. Your mother and I flew to Mexico, to tour some of its archeological marvels - and they are many, in that strange land. While upon a Mexico

City bus tour, the second day of our stay, I suddenly became ill – one of those gastrointestinal ailments commonly called 'Montezuma's Revenge'. The name, a sort of joke; but there is nothing at all humorous about the illness. I had your mother stay with the tour group and, myself, took a taxi back to our hotel room; arriving there not a minute too soon; for, like Hoover Dam, one's intestinal outlet can withstand only a limited amount of pressure. I barely avoided making a mess of myself in public. Besides the 'trots', I had generalized aching, malaise, and intermittent fever for several days; in other words, a more severe illness than a simple short term viral diarrhea.

I already possessed the necessary medications – antibiotics and a narcotic – and I got started upon them immediately. The medications took hold wonderfully well, and I was already on a slow course of recovery within the first 12 or 18 hours; though it was necessary to continue the medications for a week or ten days to avoid recurrence. Two days after the onset of the illness, we were in Meridia, on the Yucatan Peninsula; and I was feeling a whole lot better, though by no means yet entirely well; and I was still using my medications regularly. We had toured some of the ancient pyramids in the area during the day, and arrived back at our hotel room late in the afternoon. I laid down to rest, and soon fell into a deep sleep. Your mother had gone out to shop the town. An hour and a half later I awoke – or, at least I thought I did – and I discovered that I was paralyzed. The daylight was already beginning to fade, and the room was in a darkening condition. As I lay there on my left side, I faced the entry and the bathroom doors. Though I could open my eyes, I was unable to move my body, my limbs, or my head; and I was disturbed about my predicament. And I had the feeling of another presence within that room, though I could see none. Perhaps, behind me … where I was unable to see. I heard the muffled traffic in the street below; and I thought of it as life going round and around … forevermore. But still, I could not move. Was I dreaming? I drifted back to sleep, only to reawaken again and again, to that same unpleasant circumstance. The room each time being somewhat darker. At length, I saw your mother arrive, and slip into the bathroom. A bit of light came into the room once more, from beneath the bathroom door. I expected that she would presently come to touch and awaken me, for it was time that we should dine. Then, I did feel one hand … and then another, make firm pressure upon my right flank, and my right lateral chest wall. But I could not move. And in the next moment, the bathroom door opened; and there was light. Your mother came and stood before, me and touched my shoulder to awaken me. And I arose - as simply as that - but I was puzzled, as I looked about the room. No one was there, but we two. That strange experience I had just finished, must have been a sort of dream; and yet, I could not truly accept that tentative conclusion - for it had been far too real an experience. It was the first such experience I had known, in which I was unable to decide the question,

Was it real? Or, was it a dream? Or, perhaps, was it more of the nature of a delirium? In any case, in the subsequent weeks I had several very similar experiences, and was still unable to decide if they were real, or delusions. Then, one Sunday afternoon, I did find the clue which enabled me to decide the question. Once again I awoke from a nap to discover that I was paralyzed; and there was a pillow across my face, which disturbed my breathing. With a huge effort I was finally able to barely move one arm sufficiently to grasp the lower edge of the pillow and drag the pillow from my face. Then drifted back to sleep. Shortly thereafter, I awoke to arise, but the pillow was still across my face! It was obvious therefore, that the paralysis episode was not a part of my waking experience; for it was tied to the difficult task of removing the pillow from my face - an event that had not, in fact, occurred. Not real, nor not a dream; it was therefore of the nature of delusion of delirium. Since discovering that, I have had no recurrent similar spells.

There are, of course, other kinds of delusions than those of delirium. They are, in fact so common-place, that they must surely be considered an essentially normal phenomena in the individual lives of people. You and I, like everyone else, each possess a great many of them. John Dewey says that the educational process is a matter of "freeing the mind of bunk". What he calls bunk, are the various delusions to which we each cling. In other words, delusions are composed of such things as bias, prejudice, misunderstandings, inaccuracies, and outright untruths. It is widely held that people can become educated; that many do in fact become educated. Each community, and each of the United

States spends perhaps, something like ninety percent of its budget upon education; and the federal government spends perhaps, a sum comparable to that spent locally and at the state level, though a much smaller percent of its total budget on education. So there seems to be a rather widespread belief that, surely, people can become free from - at least some of - their delusions; and that there seems to be some sort of an advantage in that accomplishment. Perhaps that belief is valid; and I believe that it is. But on the other hand, beliefs, like emotions, are often translated into actions without ever having been thoroughly evaluated by the faculty of reason; and reason … often deficient for want of experience. Does the excessive spending on public education in this state or in this nation, prove that the taxpayers overwhelmingly approve of that expenditure? Or is private education in any way inferior to public education? And is there no such thing as self education? The schools themselves are, to some variable extent, perpetrators of a great many American delusions and contradictions - along with popular rhetoric, and the news media. As Jack Matthews puts it in his short story, *Bitter Knowledge* — of which you have a copy - "Sometimes I think that cynicism is a kind of disease in our family". It is unlikely, that you have failed to notice the streak of cynicism that seems to run throughout the various branches of the Brasseur family? All are skeptical of what they read and hear. A well-justified and healthy predisposition - so thinks I. Now, naive gullibility is, perhaps, the opposite extreme of skepticism; and those whose nature and predisposition places them toward that extreme often give the appearance of Pollyannaism in a social setting - a not unpleasant demeanor, in some social gatherings. The skeptic, however, may appear to show himself as being sarcastic, and sometimes unnecessarily unpleasant in social gathering, for he tends to put people on edge - seeing that there is some possibility they may be challenged as to content of what they are saying. Aware of his social liability, the skeptic will commonly clothe his speech and conversation in wit and humor; though few enjoy any great success at this ploy. For wit and humor are difficult of attainment. Among one's family and friends, that humor and wit are often entirely satisfactory, for ones own family are often well enough acquainted with one's style and mannerisms so as to enable them to discern the subtitles of his speech and pronouncements.

FADING ECHOES

One of the younger girls once asked your Uncle EVH a question, to which he responded with a cryptic bit of wit which I thought interesting and humorous. But the poor girl - taking his instruction literally - in consequence, did something or another in the kitchen that got her into difficulty with her mother. When she informed her mother that her dad had put her up to it, Betty marched to query him. Uncle EVH was surprised that the girl had taken him seriously. Betty took him to task about always giving these children his smart-alec answers, so that they were often unable to tell whether he was being serious, or only kidding. In defense, says EVH, "Well, sometimes I can't tell, myself." And that is the way it often is, with sarcastic humor; for skeptics are often very serious minded people, and tend to say precisely what they mean, except clothing what they say with ambiguity and wit. Sometimes both interpretations are correct; sometimes only one; and at times, neither.

Anyone who has ever kept a daily journal, can tell you from experience, just how poor and fragile an instrument is the human memory. Should one neglect his daily log, even only a day or two, how difficult it is to accurately recover that information from one's recollection. To memorize a list of names, or even a poem is troublesome and time-consuming. We are often given to believe that people of previous generations and past centuries were much more adept at feats of memory than are those of our own times. If, by that, they mean to imply only that their education in previous times was such that there was far greater emphasis on the faculty of memory - then, I have no reason to doubt it. But there is no reason to suspect that the potential ability for feats of memory is in any way diminished in the species as a whole. For a certain small proportion of individuals, even in our times, demonstrate prodigious faculty of memory. All skills of body and of mind require exercise, method, and practice, in order for the individual to convert his potential ability into an actual attainment. It may be the case that memory skills should be considered a part of the fundamental components of ones elementary education - along with 'the three R's'. Though I have seen books and essays concerning a methodology for acquiring memory skills, I have never known of any such courses offered to grade-school or high school students. Since you are majoring in Business Administration, I am certain that you have at least a general sort of awareness of the importance of maintaining accurate and up-to-date records on all business and financial transactions in which you are involved. On the other hand, it is highly characteristic our species to somehow fall short, in practice, of what they know and believe. And so if you are - as Daniel puts it - "Mene, mene, tekel upharsin", then this is the time to put your accounting into order. A separate account, you know, for each individual or organization with which you have dealings - including brothers and friends. Though that undertaking already has, or shall cause you some trouble and grief; in the long view, it will spare you more grief than it gives you. But you already know that. And yet, there was another point that I wanted to make. It hardly seems worthwhile to take a touring trip, if one doesn't trouble himself to look at the sights along the way; and to give those sights and experiences rein to work upon one's imagination - to learn from them what one can. I dare say, that our day-by-day lives by comparison, are a similar excursion; and that we are most apt to derive some value from that experience if we will trouble ourselves to make objective notations concerning what we see and hear; and then to take the time to reflect upon that experience. But where in the business of one's busy life will he daily find the time to recollect, ponder, and make even brief notations of each day? I agree that it presents some difficulties; but on the other hand, perhaps the question is irrelevant. A better question may be: is the unconsidered life worth living? Can one take a trip without considering where one is going; or without evaluating ones course and progress; or without a certain willingness to alter one's course - even one's objectives - in the face of newly perceived circumstances?

This world, as you know, is a dangerous place. Just the other day a middle-aged Hispanic man was gunned down on a street corner, here in Caldwell. No arrests have yet been made; and we have no clue yet as to the motive. Perhaps related to drugs or other underworld activity; perhaps an accidental discharge of gun; perhaps a case of mistaken identity. Quien sabe? You may recall that earlier, a middle-aged man and wife were both shot in the head one early Sunday morning, as they were folding newspapers before distributing them on their paper route. They seem to have in custody the fellow that did it, but the incident is rather bizarre and, not too surprisingly, the suspect manifests evidence of being bizarre, too.

And I think you may recall our local story of Dr. S__'s daughter, seventeen years of age, who was recently stabbed to death in College of Idaho's dormitory - by the son of one of her father's best friends. The high school principle and the teachers were astounded, for the lad seemed to them to have been one of the kindest and most polite students of their acquaintance. The evidence was abundant, and he was indicted for murder. And yet he pleaded innocent. Perhaps he is innocent, for all we know - for as in the case of Roger Rabbit, people are 'framed' from time to time; and we haven't heard the testimony of any of the witnesses. All we have heard are the news media reports - such evidence as that falls into the category of 'hearsay'. But perhaps the young man only claims to be 'innocent, as charged'. In other words he may have been charged with first-degree murder; whereas he claims instead that he is guilty only of third—degree murder. For the motive and circumstances concerning any crime have a bearing on the actual culpability of the accused. There is even such a thing as justifiable homicide - a situation in which the killer may even be considered as being somewhat of a hero. But, in any case, one must not presume that the hundreds and thousands of people, whom one can encounter upon the streets in any given day, are fully alert and attuned to the same reality as oneself. For all minds are disturbed and delusional from time to time - at some time or another in the course of their lives. Some to a greater degree and much more often than others. Many circumstances and life situations - not to mentions intoxications and disease states - can disorder the most stable of minds. One is relatively safe in proportion to his caution, alertness, and personal physical strength; more so, when well armed; and in strength of numbers. One encounters more risk in times of chaos (political unrest; civil disorder; and after dark - especially on Friday and on Saturday nights). Certain sections of any community are more dangerous than others.

Disagreements have a tendency to escalate into arguments, and from there into warfare, both, as regards person to person; as well as nation to nation. Misunderstandings and harsh words commonly precede physical violence. Anyone who has ever been involved in an intense argument can, undoubtedly, recall some of that stepwise progression, by which an argument becomes heated. Even the coward, and the peace-maker, has been - at least tempted - to violence upon occasion. As mark Twain puts it, "If the urge to kill, and the opportunity to kill, came always at the same time; who would escape hanging?" These little lover's-quarrels, and triangular un-pleasantries are very predisposed to lead to violence; and in a certain proportion, even to death. Unhappily, that seems to have been the case at our local college, recently. Upon occasion, it is the young man that ends up dead. Especially the Italian, the Spanish, and the Mexican ladies have some tendency towards violence in these affairs. They have been known to carry razor-blades and stilettos, with which they suddenly wreak their vengeance at a certain point in a 'discussion'. In our recent local case, it may be that the young man came with premeditated plans for murder; but that is not likely, and the preliminary indications suggest that the fatal outcome was in consequence of an escalating discussion. If true, she did undoubtedly perceive some of that stepwise escalation; without recognizing its deadly potential. She then might easily have averted that fate, had she been more circumspect in her speech. And with, perhaps 98 or 99 out of one hundred men, she might not have precipitated violence, even as far as she did vent her - whatever - invective. But there is no certain method for predicting accurately, which one or two percent is most apt to be tongue-lashed into physical violence. Now I do not say that the girl was at fault, concerning whatever they were discussing. But she is responsible to protect herself from physical violence, by exercising good judgment, prudent behavior, and judicial speech. Each mature individual must be his own first line of defense against a hostile world. For beneath that thin veneer of civilized appearance - of each person - resides "The heavy bear who goes with me/ Dragging me with him in his mouthing care, / Amid the hundred million of his kind, / The scrimmage of appetite everywhere."

Among the old letters which your Uncle PP recently sent me was one written by my Uncle Louis to his sister, my Aunt Leah, in about 1975. He mentions that she - Aunt Leah - first started her teaching career at Gackle, in Logan County of North Dakota, in 1915. That is in the general area where your mother's people settled, when they first came to this country (from southern Russia). Uncle Louis, himself, taught for a few years - first in Strasburg, N.D., then in Beulah, N.D. (at least, that is what his letter says). Anyhow, in the letter, he reminds Aunt Leah of her own experience with these strange people - the 'Russians' - as they referred to them. It would appear that she did have experience with these 'Russians'; and took amusement at the folly of some of their rustic customs and ideas. I am not sure that Uncle Louis and Aunt Leah ever truly realized that these people were not Russians; but, rather, Germans. It reminded me that when I was about age 12, my parents moved our family up to Scobey, Montana. There was always a certain excitement of anticipation in moving. How big a town was it (?), what was that area of the country like (?), what was there for one 'to do' there, etc? And, we overheard the conversation of our parents with some interest, hoping to get some clues about these things. On several occasions, I heard these people referred to as 'Russians'; and Scobey was said to be a 'Russian town'. I envisioned a backward people in strange clothing and speaking some undecipherable tongue; and a town with onion-domes upon their buildings. Once arrived there, I was puzzled to find nothing of what I had anticipated. I found a few buddies with whom to while away the remainder of those summer days; and then became immersed with the routine of school. My preconceptions of the town and the people just sort of dissipated and were forgotten; without ever having been weighed in the balance of any rational thought process. Years later (1965-1966), your mother and I moved back to that general area from which her ancestors had come - and the area where Aunt Leah had taught among the 'Russians'. There, at Jamestown, N.D., I first practiced medicine. Some sixty or seventy miles to the south, my cousin, Gordon Neuberger was a Lutheran Pastor in (was it Gackle, or Wishek?) - he still delivered his sermons in the German Language, to these people. The exact area in which your mother's ancestors had lived. Undoubtedly, a number of the people still living in the area are related to her. You may remember that cousin Gordon and his wife Erma visited and stayed a night or two with us in Kennewick, when we lived in that large white stucco elephant. His parents - August and Lydia Neuberger - were with them on that trip. Lydia Neuberger was my mother's sister. The year that we left Jamestown, we moved to the

Panama Canal Zone; and my brother, EVH moved his family into Jamestown, from Texas. EVH often expressed some amusement at that backward little community where Cousin Gordon lived; and what he called, its 'little people'. They are, in general, a rather short and stocky people. About fifteen years ago it began to dawn upon me, that these, so-called, Russians, were actually a German people. I mean all of these people throughout this whole North Dakota and Montana area. None of them are Russian people. My very own ancestors - and yours - are derived from these Germans. They did live in Russia for some three generations before immigrating into the Dakotas. It is a strange turn of events, to my mind, that these foreigners should turn out to be my own people. It is an elementary fact that you would think I should have discovered long before, for the evidence was all around us. And even a part of our own family life was of that same culture. And I was 'an educated person', long before I discovered it. That tells us something, I suspect, about the degree of education possessed by even educated people. It is mostly a state of ignorance about the universe, the world, history, and what goes on in the world. It means that while one does know something, at least; yet it assures a knowledge of only a certain narrow field in which one is specifically educated. Nor is that education a mere small accomplishment, when one considers the methods, tools, and skills one acquires as a by-product, while acquiring a degree in one's narrow field of study. For those things are, in fact, the true essence of his education; the rest of it is more of the nature of job training. Thereby is one enabled to acquire a remarkably broad education in his leisure time, should he ever wish to do so. But that is more or less uncommon. That being the case, it might be said that our standard of education is rather prolonged and expensive, but that few have actually much use for it. And it is well to remember that most education - even that acquired in and through our school systems - is of the nature of self-education. Thus, the schools serve mainly the functions of organizing and standardizing curriculum, guiding the students through each course at a certain minimum pace, and testing the students as to accomplishments. The teaching personnel strive also for some measure of accomplishment in the art of motivation of the pupils - to make 'students' of them, to some variable degree.

And, as previously suggested, the schools serve a national political purpose in the distribution of propaganda and maintenance of group delusions which are politically useful to the state. There exists the need; and we have the right to question the educational system. So also, the political system; and the various national delusions by which the common throng is led, for better or for worse. The reason for our questioning of the system, is that there is no 'divine right' of one man to rule another; nor of one group, to control another. None of our educational or political systems comes to us without a cost; it is always paid for by the common man, the taxpayer. In both, at the present time, it does appear that the tail is wagging the dog, as it were. Our individual lives go on this way - upon a course set and determined by government and an entrenched educational system. Just as though our bureaucracies knew our specific individual aims and objectives; and as though we each consented to those. But, do they; and do we? Is there any consensus of opinion, as to how we should live our lives; and to what purpose? There is another notion of government - not a new one - which holds that the function of government ought more properly, merely assure a certain minimum of protection against coercion and physical violence, so that we can individually decide upon our own private objectives, and be in charge of our own values and lives. It would require a reversal of our present, highly centralized system of government.

Within historical times, the arrangement of societies has been such that the majority of men and women have found it necessary to occupy most of their waking lives at labor. In this country, since the turn of the century, the number of weekly hours required for labor has declined from about 72, to sometimes only 40. Man has been a beast of burden, though his own burden was somewhat mitigated by the aid of domestic animals. Then came the age of mechanical engines, and now robots and automated equipment are progressively involved in agriculture and the production of goods and services. One wonders, in fact, how so large a population is able to find, each, 40 hours of work each week; especially since so few employ any domestic service. The answer seems to be that an ever enlarging proportion is involved in 'make-work'. The various government employees must represent at least forty percent of the 'working force' of the nation - perhaps more.

Do they produce anything (?) or do any useful work (?) or provide any service to the consuming nation (?). It seems, in general, that they shuffle papers; and devise obstacles of paperwork with which the private sector must struggle in their effort to produce the goods and services for the consumer. Obviously, that must greatly increase the cost of those commodities, since the private sector must hire another task force of paper-shufflers to deal with the government obstructionists. Concerning the administration of the IRS, for example, it would be economical to the nation if the govt. would just send their agents to the private citizen's office; and let IRS agent answer all of his own questionnaires; thereby sparing himself the trouble (and sparing the govt. the expense) of doubting all of the replies. Or they might go even a step further, and simply eliminate all of the unnecessary complexities of the entire tax system. That would eliminate both the private and the government task-forces of taxation. But what I am driving at is this: if automated equipment and robots are producing most of the goods and the services to the economy; and if most of the jobs are merely imaginary and make-work; then why not simply abandon the unnecessary jobs, so as to require the work force to do only the necessary productive work; and reduce the required hours of work for all. Then, the question is; would the majority of people be willing and able to use this new found free time in a constructive way (?), or even simply while it away innocently? Or would the result be mere chaos and wanton trouble and destruction within the communities? But you are a Business Administration major; and you no doubt could speak to some of these ideas, though they are as much related to Philosophy as to Business and Political Theory.

You are well aware of the concept of protest. And in your own family, there is a great deal of discussion that is of the nature of protest. Neither change nor improvement in social, economic, or philosophical conditions and ideas ever comes into being apart from some form of protest. Protest is a great deal more ancient than written history itself. For there has never been a time when people did not take it upon themselves to vote with their legs - if nothing else. Our own ancestors were not deficient in that characteristic. When the Romans intended to invade and to conquer Germany, they discovered that to be impossible. In the Roman Catholic attempt to control and repress them with religion, the Germans became warriors of the mind; and their protest was aptly called, Protestantism. They have continuously protested even from that. A part of the reason our ancestors left Wurttemberg, Germany in 1817 was to be free of the now established Lutheran Religion; so that they could establish a new congregation, based upon their own more recent ideas. In fact, that community from which your mother's ancestors have come was a 'Separatist' community. More recently I have discovered that the Boepples, too, were separatists - a minority group - from the Lutheran Church, which then predominated among those who immigrated into Russia. After Jesus failed to materialize for the newly anticipated and proclaimed 'Second Coming' in 1856, the separatist movement lost some of its momentum; and some of their congregations rejoined the Lutheran groups. When the Russian government began to repress these transplanted Germans in 1871, many among them began to consider the need to once more 'vote with their legs'. Fortunately, our own direct ancestors voted for the Dakotas; some of their kinfolk went to places such as the Trans-caucus and Dobruja, which were hardly any improvement over what they were leaving behind. Still, even there, some of them have survived, and are involved in the settlement of Russia's new frontier the Ural Mountains and southern Siberia. And the grass-roots protest even there shows some evidence of being heard; and of having some effect upon the ears of Moscow, toward the beginnings of a humanitarian policy towards even those people derived from German stock.

We look forward to seeing you before long. Yes, your grades came. They looked good.

Light to you,
and love
dad
R. Garner Brasseur, M.D.

8-7-1988

9/26/1988

Caldwell, Idaho

Dear M.A.,

I thought of you a couple of weeks ago when your mother had a narrow escape - in her walk-in closet. She survived the incident, however; and then related to me the details. She wondered how the preying-mantis got into the closet. It was a mere rhetorical question, of course; to which I have no answer. In any case, it reminded me of your own encounter with these alien creatures, a few years ago. Concerning that, I enclose to you a short essay which I wrote on the subject, at that time (9/13/84). The preying-mantis is a unique creature. Who can say (?), perhaps they are a form of intelligent life from another planet, or another galaxy?

The enclosed obituary of Dr. S____ probably dropped into your lap as you opened this letter. You are already acquainted with a part of the story. I wanted to remind you of an ancient expression, "one thing leads to another"; some regard it as 'a trite expression', but in my mind it seems more like a fundamental law of nature. Reading the notice, one gets the impression that this young doctor has probably never had to face any economic difficulties of significance. I met him, and have spoken with him on a couple of occasion. He seemed like a nice guy (he even drove a pick-up). But why this suicide? We don't really know. From reading the article, we get the impression that everything was just fine in his life - except, of course, for the recent tragic death of one of his three children. But most men survive the death of a daughter, or a son - however unwillingly. And so it appears that the daughter's death was more of the nature of a 'precipitating event', or a pre-disposing factor in the death of the doctor. I was reminded of a poem, *Richard Cory* which you have heard before.

Richard Cory

Whenever Richard Cory came to town
We people on the pavement looked at him.
He was a gentleman from head to crown,

FADING ECHOES

Clean favored, and imperially slim

And he was always quietly arrayed.
And he was always human when he spoke.
But still, he fluttered pulses when he said, "good morning"
And he (sort of) glistened when he walked.

And he was rich - yes, richer than a king.
And admirably schooled in every grace.
In fine, we thought that he was everything,
To make us wish that we were in hi place.

So, we labored on … and waited for the light.
And went without the meat; and cursed the bread.
And Richard Cory, one calm summer night,
Went home and put a bullet through his head.

Some fifteen or twenty years ago I heard a song which quite enchanted me with its poignant simplicity, pathos, and beauty. From time-to-time, through the years, I would hear it again. Perhaps I heard it as many as a dozen times intermittently, through the years. I intended (through the years) to get a copy of it, so that I could hear it more often. The past weekend, the memory of that song recurred to me. So, I went and bought a tape recording of the song:

Deportees

The crops are in; and the peaches are rott'n
The oranges are piled; and the grapes are all done
You'r flying them back to the Mexican border
To pay all their money, to wade back again.
---Chorus:
      Good-by to my Juan; good-by Roselita
      Adios, mis amigos, Jesus and Maria

You won't have a name, when you ride the big
airplane
All they will call you will be, De-port-tees.
--ETC.--

Having purchased the tape, I treated myself to the pleasure of hearing it several times. In fact, I listened to it repeatedly - in order to catch all the words, and abstract them into my notebook. There is a certain mellow pleasure in the drama of human pathos - a theme (and a reality) as old as the species of mankind. I don't claim to fully understand why, but few will dispute its reality. Much of poetry, too, revolves upon that theme; and music, of course, when well adapted to that theme of the particular poem greatly enhances its power to touch our sentiments. Through the years I have collected quite a number of these songs - 'soul music'. There are many others I wish eventually to accumulate. I may do something more with them - but what? - other than listening to them repeatedly. Perhaps they will become the basis of some particular inspiration to me? The ideas are sifting about in my head.

AG Brasseur plans to arrive here in Caldwell on Wednesday, the 28th. He will be here a few days to read and prepare himself to take an aviation examination in Boise on the first of October - a Saturday. I guess he plans and hopes to get a job flying up in Alaska.

I will drive up to Pullman, Washington on Friday the 30th, in order to take a Law School Admission Test on Saturday. Then, at the middle of the month, perhaps your Uncle VBB, Uncle PP, and I shall spend a few days away out on the mountain, in central Idaho.

Take care of yourself, M.A. Don't let your supply of green-backs trickle down to nothing. Trouble often comes from that. I'll have your mother send a bit more to you. Give me some rough idea of what you may need.

Don't forget the importance of light - and love.

Dad,

R. Garner Brasseur

9-26-1988

FADING ECHOES

9-27-1988

Yesterday I mailed a letter to M.A. I sent her a copy of the obituary of Dr. S___; and I included a little written discussion, to indicate that there must be some ancillary problems that were troubling his life; for none of the information available to me seemed adequate to explain his suicide. To my surprise, the West Valley medical Center Hospital journal Club spent 75 minutes discussing that event - this very day. Here are some of the hidden causes behind that suicide:

-- The anniversary of a tragedy is an ominous time for a suicide.
-- The day before the event, Dr. S___ learned that the young man who murdered his daughter would probably get off after serving a mere ten years of a life-sentence, since the county attorney was not going to recommend the death sentence. Dr. S___ was upset by that, for he felt the killer should definitely get the death sentence.
-- It wasn't said, specifically, but I get the distinct impression that Dr. S___'s wife was overly active in the 'forgiving business'. Reaching-out, you know, to forgive the suffering parents of the 17 year old lad that did the killing. The families were close friends, you may recall, before the murder. Nothing seems (to me) more likely than that Dr. S___ would have been very angry at his wife over this issue. Yet, she had a psychological arm-lock on Dr. S___ in this issue. Dr. S. would have been aware that in the eyes of a 'Christian Society', and in the eyes of the psycho-therapist, she would gain plaudits for her prim and proper attitude. And Dr. S. would earn additional demerits for opposing his wife in this matter. In a sense, she was using the situation to gain personal admiration for her charitable and forgiving spirit. He was the champion of his daughter's cause, and had a right to his anger. An anger which time might eventually soften anyway, if the heat were allowed to dissipate slowly and naturally. He might have endured it if his wife had at least been silent. To publicly oppose him was to strip him of a mechanism for venting his anger either in public or at home. And it generated a second

399

fire-storm of anger towards his wife. I think we would find that to be the situation, if we were to probe the family situation more closely. Besides the grief for a lost daughter, there was undoubtedly a lot of anger. And the anger of the suicide was largely directed at the wife.

-- It is also the case that the day before the suicide, Dr. S___ was served with some legal papers, charging him in a malpractice case. That, alone, is oppressive enough to nearly dement a man. He is quoted as having said, "The shit never quits". One of the staff physicians says that one of every four anesthesiologists that get slapped with a malpractice suit, ends up committing suicide. I have not yet ever been served with papers on malpractice issues, but I have been served with papers on other issues. I can assure you that even that, is very dispiriting.

It is said that Dr. S___ sat down and wrote a note before his suicide. He directed the affairs of his estate and gave instructions concerning his children. He even called his sister in Kansas to leave some instructions with her. What, if anything, else was spoken of in the note, was not disclosed to us today. A very interesting and informative meeting. It comes as no surprise that other matters (in addition to the murder of his daughter) of disorder and discontent were present in his life, such as to give additional explanation as to his suicide.

I recall also, that Dr. S___ has had to contend with some harassment from the medical staff in the past six months or more. For a year and a half, the medical staff has been wrestling with the idea of establishing a no-smoking policy in the hospital. There was a lot of wrangling among the staff on that issue; and the issue seemed to come up at every monthly medical staff meeting. One month, the policy seemed nearly ready for implementation; and the next month it would be placed on hold, while some new objections were to be considered; and then, again, there was delay concerning the stringency with which those rules should be enforced. Should there be total banning of smoking? Should the nurses and doctors be exempted from the policy, etc? Some of the doctors are smokers … some are not. There are some extreme opinions among both groups. Finally, a policy was adopted, and voted into existence. There was negative feed-back, and the policy was adjusted. Some of the physicians themselves, seemed unable or unwilling to comply with the rule. Their non-compliance was overlooked; i.e. the policy was not enforced upon one particular physician. Among the non-smoking physicians, those most adamant in their opinions were angered by this privileged non-compliance. Then arose the issue of a mechanism of enforcement. We are not surprised to learn that Dr. S___ was rather much attached to this unhealthy habit of cigarettes. In any case, Dr. S___ was a hospital E.R. physician, and spent his entire daily work hours in the hospital. Can we expect him to have to go an entire day without a cigarette? So the question arose, specifically, concerning Dr. S___ - who continued to defy the policy. The thing became a contest of wills, between Dr. S___ and those who most radically opposed his non-compliance. I expect that the contest was still at a stalemate when Dr. S___ ended his own career. Undoubtedly, the smoking issue was a part of "the shit that never quits".

RGB

9/27/88

- <u>Additional discoveries from 10/4/88</u> -

Subsequent to WVMC Journal Club meeting today, I encountered Dr. K___ (his office, next to my own) and we chatted as we returned to our offices. I commented upon my interest in Dr. S___'s suicide; and on the interesting information that came forth at last week's meeting - concerning that suicide. "For", says I, "beneath the appearances of such a thing, there needs must always be relevant causes and situations to adequately explain the thing." I pointed out that the obituary left one uninformed - actually glossed over and hid the underlying reality that brought about the suicide. As it happened, Dr. K___ was the author of the obituary. Though I hadn't known that, in retrospect, I ought perhaps have suspected that he might have been the author of the piece. Dr. K___ was a little flustered at my comments, not knowing just how to accept them. I didn't mean to imply that the author had erred in failing to bring to light the incriminating (and personal) details of the private life of Dr. S___. In fact, a very proper obituary ought, undoubtedly, to be euphemistic - as was this one.

I learned a few other interesting details from Dr. K___. As it happens, the economic circumstances of Dr. S___'s life were nowhere as favorable as one might suppose. For it turns out that the S___ Farms Inc. have been on the verge of economic collapse, and being kept afloat only by the excellent and regular income which Dr. S___ pumped into it from his regular Emergency Room job. So, in addition to his daughter's death and his own mortal death (troublesome enough in their own right), we now can see that that 'economic death' was yet about to make its appearance in the family affairs. Is it possible that Dr. S___ - in rage, grief, and despair - failed to be cognizant of the fact that life insurance benefits will be denied to his family? For, it seems elementary, that death benefits are not payable in the event of suicide. The insurance company could not last long, were it not for that clause in the contract.

RGB
10/4/88

10-4-1988

1/18/89

Caldwell, Idaho

Dear M.A.,

During a recent weekend, while your mother was in Portland and Monmouth, I spent the day working for hourly wages in Boise. After work, I went over to Skipper's, to have a bowl of clam-chowder for my supper. I don't know why it should taste so good, and yet, it does. It may be the case that there are certain emotional overtones locked up in my own psyche, which are released within my central nervous system, whenever I eat clam-chowder; and that these emotional overtones color and flavor my perceptions of the taste of clam-chowder. It must have been in 1978 that I tasted my first portion of that concoction. Your Uncle EVH and I were driving down the street, when he saw this Skipper's sign. "Hey!" says he, "let's have a bowl of clam-chowder!" Accustomed as I was to his sometimes odd impulses like that, I took it in stride without demur; for clam chowder seemed to be almost a part of his religion, you know - like borscht soup, or oatmeal mush, or classical music. And somehow, then, it did taste good, though I had not necessarily expected that it would. Now, it has become a sort of sacred thing to my own experience along with borscht soup, too - and a great many other things that I'll try to list at another time (for my own enlightenment). Where was I? Oh yeah. So having been sanctified with the bowl of clam-chowder after having worked the day in Boise, I drove on over to the park, which is contiguous upon the same property with the little round theatre building, where I planned to see *Look Homeward, Angel.* I was early, by a couple of hours, for the performance; so, I climbed into my sleeping-bag upon the five-legged cot, in the back of the pick-up - a much cherished ritual and pass-time. There I dozed, and wrestled with a few ideas and memories, for an hour of more. But the play I saw, was just awful. Naturally, the cast were amateurs - but one's opinion allows for that. The play itself, was just poor script - about the worst that I have seen. Or perhaps it had a more transcendent message which I failed to grasp (?). On the previous evening, I had seen, *King of Hearts*, at the C. of I., in Caldwell. It was produced by the National Theatre of the Deaf; and it was more than excellent.

I remember that last year, you, your mother, and I went to see a musical production at the C. of I. Some of the songs performed were taken from the musical production, *Tom Sawyer.* A woman sang a solo reciting some of her departed past. You were not favorably impressed by the lyrics - perhaps even a little confused, that we should all be burdened by this history of various personal disappointments of this one character. Yet, it is the case that a large part of musical drama and theatre centers itself on tragedy. In a sense, in fact, it is strange that it should be so - and yet ... it is. Why should people find tragedy to be entertaining? Largely, perhaps, because we all have personal problems, and problems in our families - most of which we try to ignore and suffer through, thinking that it is only temporary. And hopeful of some spontaneous resolution of these various problems. For the most part, the depressed individual does not much care to hear about the reforms which you or I might suggest for his character or behavior. Nor care to hear and seek to commiserate therapeutically with ones own problems. "Laugh and the world laughs with you/ but weep, and you cry alone. / For the world would share in your pleasures, / but has troubles enough of its own." In truth, many of our problems <u>are</u> but temporary; and many are self-resolving as we proceed with the necessary routine of our day-by-day living. But, pragmatically, there is another portion of our disaffection with 'the-way-things-are', that is fixed and inevitable. It remains for us to accept and adjust to that as best we can; for the world - like ourselves - owns a certain resistance to reform. We must learn to confront that philosophically and artistically; and often struggle to reform our own impatience, prejudice, and intolerance. As Sancho Panza says, towards the end of the book, as they near the end of their journey, "Open thine eyes, longed-for home, and see how thy son Sancho Panza comes back to thee; if not very rich, very well whipped! Open thine eyes and receive, too, thy son Don Quixote, who, if he comes vanquished by the arm of another, comes victor over himself, which, as he himself has told me, is the greatest victory any one can desire." And still, one must be alert to yet a third portion of our personal misery, owned simply because we neglect to consider it analytically - and fail to approach it forthrightly. Folks have a tendency to wallow in their emotions … for minutes; for days; for weeks, without taking the time or making the effort to comprehend the mechanisms and true source of their private emotional state. To be sure, there is some certain satisfaction and peculiar pleasure to be had in the mental re-living of emotionally charged past experience; where-in the streams of image and emotion co-mingle, and streams of thought-fragments flow upon some spontaneous and meandering course through one's mind. Ourselves as audience and spectator, at times, takes a melancholy enjoyment in that; with no personal risk, nor effort of exertion being required. Thus we can taste and savor, a thrill or a sorrow repeatedly. The thrills of remembered pleasantries we can enjoy directly; while the replay of remembered un-pleasantries, we can enjoy, perhaps, by consoling ourselves with sympathetic understanding ("There, there, self. Peace be unto thee.") Perhaps consoling ourselves that the thing was unavoidable; or, inevitable; or, due to one of the natural human defects common to man; etc. And one can take some pleasure in the knowing that he has survived the simulated tragic experience of the play production, which he shall be wise enough personally to henceforth avoid in the reality of ones life. That, certainly a satisfaction. Undoubtedly, we edit these acts of recollection onto ourselves, so that that 'the re-runs' tend to be enhanced to suit our personal tastes - and their negative aspects diminished unto ourselves. It must be the case that we all thus interact with our own past experience from time to time. No doubt therefore, the phenomenon itself is 'normal'. And we are certainly entitled to the taking of some such intermittent little satisfaction onto ourselves. For, who are we as mere mortals, that we should begrudge ourselves some simple satisfactions in life? Or, that we should begrudge it to other poor souls? The good or the evil that comes to ourselves from the psychodynamics of these remembrances, has to do with the balance and proportion that we give to them, in the ordering of our lives. Undoubtedly, we might all be well advised to store and savor some of our pleasing remembrances, to which we might intermittently return, for rest and rehabilitation (a military expression - of the front-line soldier from the battleground) in the living of our daily lives, in the work-a-day world. On the other hand, there are those who so lose their sense of proportion in this matter, that they withdraw completely into the land of their much altered schizophrenic remembrances; or, those that do so only intermittently, in bouts, as manic-depressives (perhaps their self-edited recollections are less all-encompassing than that of a schizophrenic). And there are those, whose real-world is so destitute of any hope for achieving or accomplishment, as to almost entitle them to be wrapped in pleasing delusions.

But, getting back to the matter of tragedy in musical and theatrical productions. It is probably the case that an artistic production affords us (as individuals) the opportunity of being charmed, or seduced from preoccupation with our own personal drama, by compelling our attention to the well-laid plot of the staged production. We thereby gain some relief from the narrower problems of the preoccupied self. Perhaps too, one there may gain some insight into the nature of 'my problem', from the unfolding of the plot in the staged drama, and it's generally more broad and thorough treatment of human dilemma. We have nothing to gain, when we wallow in the supposed emotion of the actors (nor, of the actors of the real world), and must deal objectively with any such problems portrayed, switching our point-of-view from that of one actor, to that of another. And reminding ourselves thereby, that we ought look at our own problems, too, from more than one point of view ... if we expect to master them.

I have enclosed to you five pages of additional information of more recent developments, concerning the case of Dr. S___ and their family problems. I am sure you recall their misfortunes which appeared in our local newspaper the past summer. It is only by chance that I have acquired all of this additional information, for it is not available to the public at large. It is an excellent example of that which we already know, but often tend to forget - that gossip and the news media generally give us very incomplete information; information that is often quite misleading. To read the newspaper could be more enlightening, if we could depend upon it eventually to publish to us the final details of each blurb that they explode with such sensation into the eyes of the public. When you and I begin to practice our private skepticism, we soon discover that - almost invariably - even our own doubts have been inadequate to give us anything like a valid picture of the subject in question. Almost never, are we too thorough-going in in our skepticism.

The same problems arise in our attempt to acquire an accurate view of history. Among the earliest of historians of whom there are extant records, were those of Herodotus (b. 484 BC) and Thucydides (b. 471 BC) - both of them Greek, and writing of events in or near to their own historical times. Considering that their works seem to have been without precedent, these first steps seem commendably objective, and thorough. Besides their own view of events, they seem to have inquired into the viewpoint of others who lived with them in this same age. Inquiry and discussion with their contemporaries - a good beginning for the science of History. There was little available to them from any other source. They gave us a great deal of objective information, with little attempt of selling to us 'an official' view of the state politic or religion. Later, by the time of the early Roman Empire, historians were somewhat less objective; and seemingly under some pressure of necessity (political - and of their own prejudice) to portray facts in such a manner as to support specific preconceptions; and to delete information and interpretations which did not fit the 'politically correct' thesis at the hour of composition. A trend perhaps not always intentionally perverse; and some of these writers still managed to write good history. One must merely be aware of their limitations. Later, a great deal of historically useful text seems - curiously - to have become 'lost'; and such information as has been left to us seems to have the quality of specific and narrow point-of-view. A writer such as Gregory of Tours (*The History of the Franks*) or Eusibus of Caesarea, for example, list references to a number of source books, the copies of which have all disappeared early in history. Their writings are useful only especially to the extent that none other are available for our perusal.

The great shortcoming of the various histories produced and transmitted to us under the auspices of the Roman Church of the Dark Ages, is that the facts and details of what they narrate is inevitably fitted up with only such cause and agency as that permitted by the church. In their view, the whole natural world (the only world of which we mortals have experience) and its historical sequence of events is, and always has been, controlled and manipulated from the outside, by <u>their supposition and preoccupation with the myth of a supernatural world and beings</u>. It isn't likely that all (or even many) of those who owned and controlled the power of the church; that they, actually believed <u>that</u>, themselves - though undoubtedly, some of them did. For, those in control of that power were, themselves, manipulating those controls on a daily basis - to bring about such continued subjection of the masses as served their own interests; in maintaining their own status, power and wealth. They were well aware that explanations based upon the natural causes within the real world posed continuous threat to their own factitious churchly view of the world in the dark ages and medieval times. Against that threat, they were obliged to confabulate such deceit and policy as to keep in effect their own self-serving mythical supernatural world-view - useful unto their own best interests.

We hear tell of the Greek Classic Writings, and of how fortunate it is that some of it has survived to us. Yet, how many people do you know of - or I - who have read any significant portion of it? And, in what sense, is any of that writing remarkable? In what way has it subsequently been useful in the history of the world? To begin with, it is remarkable, that any of it has survived; for once the Roman Church came into power (at the time of Constantine - about 312 AD), they spent many centuries seeking out - for repression - all literature (and all peoples, and persons) that represented anything controversial to their own very narrow views, and authoritative pronouncements. A remarkably thorough effort. In Greece however, and in the eastern half of the divided Roman Empire, some of the ancient Greek texts did survive. The 'Dark Ages' were dark, because of church repression, war, famine, widespread disease, and obstruction to commerce. But, there remained a stream of commerce between Constantinople and Venice. The citizens of Venice had founded their city upon a nearly impregnable position, in the swamps and marshes at the mouth of the Po River. Their livelihood was based upon commerce; and there, they were able to fend off the threat of barbarian invasion, and resist the heavy hand of the pope. Along with the usual commerce in merchandise and goods; thoughts, ideas, and copies of ancient manuscripts undoubtedly trickled into northern Italy, via Venice and across the trade routes up the Po to Florence, to spark the Renaissance of thought and culture in 14th century of Europe. And a small spark of skepticism would undoubtedly have been adequate. For among the multitudes (of common people, soldiers and merchants who were daily obliged to negotiate their livelihood in the harsh realities of a stifled world) we may reasonably suppose that many owned a decided tendency - in their private lives of thought - to arrive at a point of cynicism, regarding monks, priests, and popes.

In particular, the city of Athens is to be credited for the innovative spirit that gave rise to the evolving customs of individual freedom and liberty for her citizens. That evolving spirit is the probable essential ingredient to that city's wealth, power, and cultural attainments. Athens was said to have been a school to all of Greece. Sparta was the antithesis, rival, and nemesis of Athens. Sparta eventually defeated Athens, in consequence of military action; assisted by a great plague, that weakened Athens. And in consequence of a great superstition that brought about the destruction of the fleet of Athens - at Syracuse, in Sicily. Sparta produced great military forces, but made <u>no</u> significant cultural contributions to the world - thereby leaving itself open to later comparison with Nazi Germany. The Macedonian, Alexander the Great, conquered most of the known world prior to B.C. 300. He received his military machine from the hand of his father; but his education was at the hands of Aristotle of Athens. Not only did Alexander conquer the then known world; he had the vision to imprint upon it the rudiments of Athenian culture.

He seems also to have had some notions of a sense of brotherhood among men - which seems favorably to have affected his dealings with the peoples whom he conquered. Greece was also a major source of culture and arts for Rome, whose own main talent was for war, diplomacy, and law. Thus, is manifest a theme that we see commonly in history - the military conquerors, being made captive to the culture of the conquered. But, the truly grand theme in history … is that of the development and general progress of individual freedom, to ordinary citizens. A slow progress, with frequent setback. For freedom to abide among men, there seems necessary some reciprocity of decency of one citizen towards another - a sort of brotherhood such as to command some minimal respect from one another. But, upon what basis? Equality before the law, or based upon religious dogma? That is the other part of the problem of freedom, which is only slowly being worked out, in the history of our species.

We see that Athens had an ideal of freedom that was building among her citizens. The citizen need not fear speaking his mind to the king, or the ruling body of authority. The same sort of tradition developed among the Jewish people - whose prophets, not infrequently, rebuked their own kings. It was <u>not</u> a strong tendency in the Roman Republic; and less so, in the Roman Empire. Later, to their everlasting credit, the early Christians also seized upon this ideal of freedom - a limit, after all, in the extent to which they would allow themselves to be subjugated by the state. They paid dearly for that stubborn assertion through intermittent persecution; sometimes, including torture and death. By the fifth century A.D., the church was beginning to fall heir to jurisdiction and power in the provinces; and by 590 A.D., had become the established 3rd power, in the Roman Empire. Somewhere in the sixth century, the confessional had been established. It proved a useful source of 'inside information'; and probably produced information more reliable than even exquisite torture. "By the most violent means, she (the Catholic Church) set up as absolute truth, a doctrine that she had distorted in the interest of her own omnipotence." says Burckhardt. The power of the church had been consolidated by A.D. 800; and by A.D. 875, she was launched out into a continuous and full-time program of prosecution into extinction of dissenting religious philosophies within the boundaries of her domain. Having once acquired its own Christian freedom, the church was by no means willing to grant individual freedom of conscience to any non-Christians. For that matter, very little latitude even to their own Christian laity or clerical populations. No religion had been less generous than the Christian movement, in allowing their neighbors a spiritual freedom. In this regard, the liberality of the Greeks transcended them all; for among them, not only were individuals allowed to think and own their own minds, but citizens could call into question even the national Parthenon of established deities. And the beautiful ... the magnificent custom of the Greeks - perhaps merely an arbitrary custom - was that each spoke what he had to say, on behalf of himself. And he was ready to discuss and to debate his view. None made claim or pretense at being spokesman of the Deity, in what they said. Instead of "thus saith the Lord"; we hear, rather, something equivalent to, "here is the way it seems to me". The open question has the potential to move outward, and to explore. The deceitful rhetorical question is a device of the sophists; it flatters the speaker, in that it tends to delude the hearer that he - also - knows, what the speaker knows; a circular device that goes not outward, such as to inquire nor explore. The uppermost idea of Hellenism is to see things as they really are; that of Hebrism, is the control of conduct and obedience to an ever evolving but bogus version of reason. Confucius and Buddha, also spoke for themselves, making no pretense of being mediators of any divine revelation; nor any claim themselves, of having divine credentials. There has always been a great deal of error and misrepresentation that has been injected into history. Intentionally - and in addition to the error which it acquires by innocent ignorance, misunderstanding, and the narrow-mindedness of various groups of vested interests. But it is doubtful that any violence has been done to historical veracity, as great as that perpetrated by the Catholic Church ... up until well beyond the time of the renaissance. For six-hundred years, the Benedictine Order was entrusted with virtually all of the training and education of European mankind. A regressive period of shameful and willful ignorance. They lost and destroyed a large portion of such texts as were then extant. And, yet, we are often advised to be grateful to them for 'preserving' what materials have survived to us from Ancient History? Concerning that, we are ignorant, even of our ignorance - the worst kind of ignorance. For all we know however, it could actually be the case, that there still are - hidden away - great treasures of historical manuscript yet unknown; or known to but a few ecclesiastical persons. Where, would one be likely to discover such a cache? Perhaps, in ancient Vatican City; or in the old monasteries of the Benedictine Order; or in some such place as where 'The-Dead-Sea-Scrolls' were found. In any case, a new historical source has gradually become available in the past couple hundred years - Archeology. It continues to bring forth a great deal of information that was lost or in limbo; and has often been able to corroborate various dubious points of history. And often too, to disestablish corrupted notions, of previously 'established' historical dogma.

And there is yet a third approach to history, which has had, and continues to have a powerful effect upon the information that we can derive from raw historical documents. Namely, the method of intense scrutiny and analysis of history and historical documents - the method typified, by Classical German Scholasticism of the past two hundred years, more or less. Exemplified by such scholars as: Albert Schweitzer, Jacob Burckhardt, Benedetto Croce, Arnold Toynbee, Hans Zinsser, Franz Cumont, Moses Hadas, Friedrich Heer, Pastel de Coulanges etc. They were undoubtedly inspired by a few such early and courageously honest historians of a new bent, such as Voltaire and Gibbons.

Voltaire (1694-1778) points out that History had devoted itself to the chronology of the church; of kings, prelates, and princes; and of principalities, kingdoms, and empires. But Voltaire indicates that in some real sense, this was not History, for it did not give one any information about the plain and average beings of history. Rather, only of those who by fate were born to wealth and power. They had their public lives of ritual and appearances - for which inconveniences, they were amply rewarded. But their private lives were much like yours or mine, perhaps. Official history is still very much that way in our own times, too. You and I know somewhat about the life of the average person in our life and times, because we have lived it. But the 'Official History' still deals with official government, and focuses upon the central figures in that drama. Now, Voltaire is a sort of phenomenon, and the first of the modern great Historians. His approach to history was made possible subsequent and in consequence to the Renaissance and the Reformation - the continuing trend toward liberty in the history of the world. Even so, he was not well received; and spent his share of time in the pokey, and in exile. He would take no hand in the atrocities of the French Revolution, though his thought and writings were, undoubtedly, a contributing factor in that upheaval. Voltaire speaks of his intent to discover the history of the human mind - an amazing subject. He says it was necessary "to emancipate History from Theology, moving the center of history from heaven, to earth; from kings, to humanity." Yes, the history of the human mind - that, is the very subject that has often preoccupied my own interests, over the past fifteen years. My interest in Family History and genealogy is largely an outgrowth of that. An interest which has perhaps become for me somewhat of an obsession.

Information accumulates to me so slowly that I fear I may not discover all that I should wish, before my days are done. How curious it seems, that we should be required to study American History, European History, Ancient History, History of the Dark Ages, and various mythical histories; but, that there is no requirement that we study our own personal history - nor our own family history, of which it is a continuation. "Know then thyself". Yes, let us do that; but we needs must transcend the obstructions to that process. The main obstruction is not that of mere ignorance (darkness), but that of continued intentional prejudice against a seeking of the light. A jamming of the airwaves of communication with endless repetitions of bunk. It is a culturally transmitted bias, which is only slowly and sporadically being relieved.

I don't believe that, in general, one gets much of a sense of personal and independent being until one has acquired enough physical, economic, and social independence - or realistic promise thereof - to enable that as a possibility. As in a game of chess, the various 'pieces' has each a limited and variable value; and each, a limited potential of moves. Their moves are strictly limited by unseen powers, hidden from their world of the flat checker-board. So, in a sense our lives, too, are constrained to some variable extent by forces hidden from our view. And we, the playing-pieces, play out our roles within the limits set for us by fate and circumstance. One can imagine that the carved playing-pieces might be dispensed of, so that the game is actually played with live beings (though it seems likely that the actual sequence of development was the other way around). In man's slow progress toward individual freedom and liberty - generation after generation - he seems slowly to begin to recognize his potential for independence, and a certain chaos develops upon the board when he begins to exercise that power. Some have begun to see that we might be well advised to recognize and attempt to influence those hidden forces behind the scene which control our destinies. The 'Wizard-of-Oz' is one anthropomorphic characterization of those hidden forces. You might think of others. To date, however, the most powerful and productive conception of that hidden force, is that it is a complex of various forces, interrelated by an underlying and unifying law of nature - from which the lives of men can in nowise completely escape. The relationship between cause and effect, has enabled the dim wit of man - slowly and progressively - to surmise with some effect as to the probable nature of some of those forces which seemingly operate as causes. I encourage you to take an occasional hour to consider - and to make your own estimate, of how primitive yet is the human condition in this world - even in our country, and in our enlightened age. Human progress has been slow, though it now begins to gather some momentum. Man has been a beast of burden forever, and far the majority has always lived out their lives with little need of any meaningful organization of his mental potential. But "think of the day - that's coming fast - when we shall all be civilized; and neat;

and clean; and well advised…" There won't be any more jobs for mere brute men - there are hardly many left now. The primitive state of our system of education will have to improve. I think of all the garbage I have learned through the years, only later to learn it isn't true; and how now shall we get rid of all this rot (?). "Leave it at the curb", you say. But first we have to sort through the whole house, article by article. It would have been better if we had foreseen the problem; and if we had been more frugal and selective in what we carry away to our own supposed utility.

About the time that you were born, the 'age of belief' was coming to an end in my own life - though I only recognize that in retrospect. What I had learned about history, for example, was <u>not</u> a great deal; but, however little that was, I certainly did believe it. And you were about eight months old, when I first had the opportunity and took the time to begin to read history. That book was *The Conquest of Mexico*, by Prescott. I was simply amazed and dumb, at first, to think that some six hundred Spaniards could enter a populous and organized civilization, such as Mexico; and make of it a subject nation. I passed on to Prescott's second book, *The Conquest of Peru*; and my amazement began to turn to wonder and curiosity, at how such a thing could come to pass. I could not doubt the fact of those two conquests; though, to my mind, the motive was suspect from the beginning. But, there must be something wrong with the implied and alleged mechanism of that conquest.

Thus, was I launched upon one of the interests that have occupied a part of my mind and my time, through the intervening years. It gradually occurred to me that the American Indian peoples were conquered more by epidemic disease - not, entirely by a few rusty armaments of a handful of Spanish solders. The Spaniards - unbenounced to themselves - were also the transmitters of epidemic disease. Germ warfare, as it were. I have been seeking and accumulating the evidence for that, through the years. But, ideas too, are infectious; and tend to spread. Not only is the history of the conquests in the Americas in need of a revised writing, but the history of Europe as commonly put forth is flawed by the same deficiency - and other deficiencies, as well.

As I was looking through the listing of the courses being offered at the College of Idaho, here in Caldwell, I noticed this course, *Plagues and*

Peoples; the same title as that of a book written by William H. McNeill in about 1975, and which I happened to come across a few years ago. I signed up for the course, meeting for an hour, five days weekly. For I was interested to learn what impact - if any - that this evolving concept is having on History as taught by the History Depts. of our schools. I am pleased to discover that it is not being ignored.

To his disciples, Buddha said something to the effect, 'Go ye therefore into the world, out of compassion for the world'. And then, like Sancho and Don Quixote, we too may come back well whipped; but having - to some degree - made conquest upon ourselves. Having let in a little more light - to enlighten one's own dim wit.

Light to you

> And love
> Your protestant father
> R. Garner Brasseur, M.D.

1-18-1989

13 Oct. 1991

[From my journal: I am in Boise, and preparing to return to my job in New Mexico after a few days absence]

I presumed that my wife and M.A. would be getting up early to attend church. Instead, I awoke at 10:30 a.m. to discover my spouse still abed, and M.A._ and Christine having only just now gotten up. "What is the point of this rare exception to their normal Sunday routine", thinks I.

I work at gathering my gear and loading it into the pickup, an arduous task, requiring memory, concentration, time, and energy. I have a root-beer float about 1:00 p.m. I respond to some of M.A.'s casual remarks to let her know that I disagree with what she is saying. That, in fact, in our twenty-four years, she has but rarely ever taken the time to talk with me. That, in fact, she has oft asked me to desist from a song, or the recitation of a poem, or from some little rant that I have aimed at her. Having put her on the spot with that reality, she seemed now to feel obligated to say the something she was leading up towards. Seemingly obligated - although in dread - to speak out about some subterranean conflict now a-brew within her head. And thus she broached the subject of her newly conceived intent to attend a Bible-School. She took pains to assure me of these truths (which I heartily doubt): that this decision is entirely her own, and that her mother is in no way connected to this idea and plan. She 'reminded me' of my 'prejudice against my son JRO'? News to me. But I am aware that JRO was visiting here last week, while I was absent to NM. It dawns on me that it is not unlikely that JRO has been influential here, in his tacit encouragement to her in this frivolous, 'pie-in-the-sky' notion of now enrolling in a local Bible School. No, not at all unlikely that these direct, subtle, and continuous encouragements are the major precipitating influences in 'her decision'.

M.A.'s 'discussion' with me this day, is much the same as what it has always been; in effect, to assert her right of having no obligation to any discussion with me. A right to which she is certainly entitled - at her twenty-four years of age. But, as an interested, sane, and concerned parent, it is my obligation to override this 'right' of hers - if that be possible - in attempt to align her view of pragmatic reality as closely as possible to the veracity of that reality. And so I did what I could and must (by discussion) to counter this decision to which she has seemingly now already committed herself. It isn't likely that my effort was successful to any significant extent. She refused to put forth any effort at concrete logic in this matter. All that she had to say was mere vague idealism. "How strange", thinks I "that mere mortal creatures should so adamantly presume to dubious certainties" (concerning the arbitrary, vague pronouncements of dogmatic, and ambiguous 'scripture'). "While yet abandoning all of tangible materials, and the potential for evidence that exists in the social, the physical, and the physiological reality in which they have their only certain 'being' and existence!"

I am again audience to this standard Christian fundamentalist line ... that 'the answer' to all of life is simple. Belief and emotion in triumph over reason. The refusal to exercise, develop, and use the human potential for thought, and to facilitate ones own being. Always, the adamant assertion of things that are both unseen and imperceptible - as well as dubious. The apparent certainty, that what-so-ever religious and philosophical concepts her father has acquired are, out-of-hand in error; and can be presumed to be so without even the necessity of knowing what they are. Failure to recognize the implied ego-mania of their own certitudes-of-belief in things unknown and unknowable. Her belief that the Bible is 'a history book' (?). Her notion that science refuses to give-up, or even to reformulate its old theories ... much as though to say, that science is not science ... or that 'X' is not 'X'. I spoke to her of Sophism - the practice of rhetoric whose main purpose is to win one's whatever argument; rather than a more honorable intent, such as arriving at a truth. She denounces the evils of wealth and power; as though poverty were somehow a worthy virtue. Almost as though to suggest that perhaps I owned one or the other, or both of these things (wealth or power). Yet, in truth, she has never borne any significant poverty. Nor is she threatening to give up her nice clothing, or her new car. I spoke to her of fiscal folly, and pointed out the corrective moral influence of the reality of consequences. How the moral lesson of that is transformed into monetary equivalence that man must finally suffer in order to recognize its truth. For, why did the 'iron curtain' finally fall (?), and then even communist Russia, too. Only, perhaps, by allowing time for the effects of their fiscal folly to become transformed into natural monetary equivalents (deficits), and then allowing those deficits to reek havoc upon their creators.

As to the church and religion to which she would dedicate herself: it possesses, and long has had wealth and power as its foremost objective and vital force. But that 'religious missionary agents', in our times, cannot easily gain entrance into a foreign country, except that they come armed with something useful or constructive such as the ability to teach or to dig wells. Perhaps the world is getting better as dogmatic ideological forces are obliged to reign-in, and become civil in deportment.

I was neither pleased nor optimistic about the issues with which we had wrestled that day, as I headed back toward New Mexico. I had a pretty good idea as to the fundamental source and essential adversary in this entire ongoing contest, and there was still hope of freeing myself of this spiteful sabotage as I began to ponder those possibilities.

To my surprise, M.A. did give up her plans for attending a Bible College. She eventually delivered me the defeat she owed me by marrying a 'preacher type' young man.

In all of this butting of heads, I have at least achieved some intermediary gains - which is better than nothing. I certainly didn't want to have my daughter end up as an old maid. And it is inevitable that she is and shall be learning a great deal, at first hand, in her union to a 'Billie Sundae' type of spouse. One might suppose that she might eventually have her fill of kow-towing. Some heat is sure to arise from that ... possibly even some light, along with the heat.

But as I ponder all of this, I must eventually concede that whether the spouse be secular or non-secular tells one not much about his strength of character and his ability to support a family. And it is not uncommon for radical views to moderate with time and experience of the 'ever-present-reality' in which we are all adrift.

As to my son, I had some concern that he may have been planning to haul his family into the interior of Russia's 'mission fields' - from whence our German-Russian ancestors have recently spent three generations in bondage. Hoping at least that he might then figure it out quickly enough, while he still had some money and option at his disposal - to buy his way out.

But subsequently, JRO went on to do something technical and useful with his life. Has been more successful at that and seems to have evolved to himself a much wider diversity of interests than ever he or I had thought likely. That, while he and his wife have shepherded a generation of talented and well-disciplined youngsters into adulthood. Thus, have JRO and his personal Zorasto (reference to *The Magic Flute*) eventually arrived at a détente, and come to be more accommodating to one another.

Well, predictions about the future are enigmatic. It just may be that these things will all work themselves out into happy endings. And "all's well that ends well".

R. Garner Brasseur, M.D

10-13-1991

4/22/92

Las Vegas, NM

Dear M.A.,

Enclosed herewith is a bank form for your signature. Sign in three places. It is a joint account in your name and mine. It is intended to assure funds for the completion of your college loan in the event that anything happens to me before I get that paid off. Besides myself, you are the only one that has access to the funds. In the event of my demise, the entire account is automatically yours. Enclosed is a blank check, which you should keep in case you need to withdraw funds. I think they will send you a few more blank checks later. Actually, I shall continue to send in your monthly repayments as I have been doing, from my regular income source; and allow the money in the joint account to grow from interest accumulation. Once I have paid off your loan, I shall merely then use this joint account money that has accumulated for a part of my retirement funds - keeping you as a co-administrator of the account so that it will not have to pass into probate when I journey to the great beyond. Send the forms back to the bank. Write in black ink. The address is to be found on the check blank.

As to what I will be doing, and where? That has not yet been decided. Though I have work applications in at several other places, it is possible that I might just decide to stay on right here. It all depends on the political climate of the place. Las Vegas is my favorite town - has been, for six or seven years. And I enjoy the work, which gives me the opportunity to probe into the fascinating psyche and histories of mentally disturbed patients; and participate in the guidance and treatment of their problems.

Happy to hear that you are holding up under the strain - and that you notice that it is a strain. And that you have yourself attuned to the possibility of other work, when that becomes available. You would do well to go through the ads of your trade journals regularly. And make application - even though they look unlikely. Even though the work is not actually something you have previous experience of.

Nice talking with you. See you in a couple of months.

Love,
Dad,
R. Garner Brasseur

4-22-1992

30 Nov. 1992

M.A. -

I wrote a couple poems for you, in honor of this day;

But - both, amiss and wanting
I'll send another day.
Cryptic may I answer,
This verse from days of yore;
You wrote and left appended
To refrigerator door.
"Do you love me (?) …
Or do you not(?)."
It isn't likely
You've forgot.

Happy birthday
Dad
R, Garner Brasseur

M.A. -

Traveling in Canada at summer's end one day,
Northward on that journey, a passion came to play.
I was firmly in its grip, when sun began to set;
Enchanted by the notion - that I might reach Miette.

But paucity of time and funds,
And the early frost and snow,
Deferred fulfillment of that quest,
Launched out upon, so long ago.

Winter drafts inclined me south; to Panama I stray.
This former destination, was born a child, one day!
Elusive her attention, in years since we have met;
It hardly seems a likelihood I'll ever reach Miette.

Perhaps another time, neath Northern Lights at play.
To tramp thru Jasper's winter snow some February day?
Ease my pain, by labors strain and ambiguously forget,
in my dotage, quite the sense, in which - in truth -
I finally reached Miette.

RGB

1992

The Orphanatorio

From my journal of March 1997:

I drive westward across Hwy 8 to Hwy 94, and then south to Tecate. There I gas up before crossing into Tecate, Mexico (population about 40,000) about 6:00 PM. Account of rather vague information from the Mexican Border guard, I am under the impression that the mission (where MABC and BC are working) is near the village of Guadalupe. From there, another bum steer leads me further astray into San Anton, Salazar, and even up to La Mission. I then search my own journal pages (this journal - Jan 22, 1997) to discover that I am looking for Carmen Serdon. So I have to back track and find that place, which is about 10 miles north of Guadalupe. The last 6 kilometers are up a washboard road before I finally arrive at Carmen Serdon. The entire village seems to have retired with no lighted windows or street lights to be seen when I arrive at about 11:30 PM. So I just pull off to the side of the road (actually only 2 or 3 blocks from the mission) and bed down for the night in the front of the pickup. I was up about 7:00 AM in the morning. I stop to talk with one of the locals to discover where 'the Mission de Los Orphanatorio' is located – just where I had guessed – only 2 blocks distant. There I stop for a little breakfast with them and talk about 1½ hours with MABC. Then let her get back to her job while I read a couple of hours, and then have a little siesta. About 4:00 p.m. MABC, BC, one of their associates and I drive to Tecate. There we eat out at a Chinese restaurant and then drive back to the mission. I had this captive audience in the car and did my best to keep their ears full. About the source of all the orphans; the history of 'orphan trains' in the U.S. in the early 1900's; about Tuberculosis, Plague, and Echinoccocus; about Subaru cars; some stories of M.A.; about brothers PP's and EVH's 'perpetual motion' machines; about my recent talk with JRO and his family. About the *Flight of the Phoenix* movie; about flying saucers etc. I then catch up on my journal notes while they go to a friend's apartment for some dessert.

I climb into the sleeping bag in the pickup camper to end my day about 11:00 PM. After a cool night, I was up next day about 7:00 AM. I take a hike for exercise and then wear my jacket while reading in the warming morning sun. Soon MABC and BC appear, and we then drive up through Tecote to El Cajun. There we have breakfast at an I-HOP – greatly overpriced because they insist on serving one enough for two breakfasts. Again I end up doing most of the talking. PP's swing bike; about a trip with JRO; on the intensity of PM; on 'poisonous' oxygen; about poisonous foods; on the 'divine elixir'; on gravity; on space travel; on my uncertainty as to the strange things people tell me. How a lie is a poor substitute for a truth; on the certitudes of belief; that I have no answers … only questions; on our primitive race of mere mortals; on man's first flight in 1750; about the first climbing of mountains about 1850; about the necessity of aligning our opinion of reality with its actual reality; about the moral corrective force of reality; about enterprise; about my escape from the grip of cancer; about the priority of my projects – number one being the writing of my autobiography and then on to various other unspecified projects. We parted about 1:00

PM. I depart north on Hwy 15 to get an oil change, and then stop at a rest area near Boron, Calif., to watch a comet in the night sky.

RGB

1997

25 November 1999

Albuquerque, NM

Dear M.A.,

I often think of you. Since I last actually saw you, I have stopped twice by your home without actually finding conditions conducive to a visit. But the days to come may well bring me more fortuitous opportunities for that. Who knows when that will be? It being soon your birthday, I thought I had best at least drop you a line. Yes, happy birthday! And best wishes for many more. The past couple weeks we have been temporarily settled into an apartment here in Albuquerque and are looking about for something a bit more suitable, even though my long-term plans are as yet by no means settled. There are so many places across this country that appeal to me that I have difficulty in choosing. Ideally, I guess, I would rather like to move about from place to place every six months or so - so as to get a chance to become reasonably well acquainted with quite a number of places. Perhaps yet I shall just do that. I don't know just how practical that is, since the moving process is always quite a struggle, even with as little of this world's goods as I possess.

Since I retired the first of May, I have put many thousands of miles on the old pickup. The odometer now reads above 285,000 miles. There seems to be some reasonable question as to which of us will outlast the other - the pickup, or myself. The past six months I have made the rounds in visiting many of my various relatives and friends all across both Canada and the United States. In fact have been with many of them twice in that period of time - some, even more often.

I spent some two or three weeks at the home of my brother, VBB. I suppose you know that YB got 'island fever', and quit her job over on Hawaii. I saw her three or four weeks ago. She is looking about for a job in the Seattle area. While I was at VBB's place I was occupied in putting the lists of the Brasseur genealogy into my computer which I had set up in his basement. This, while he was preoccupied in working on some tile mosaics for entrance into the county fair in Yakima. I finally finished my genealogy project, and then printed it all out into three volumes - about 1200 pages. I then had three sets of copy made and bound. I hand delivered one copy to The Library of Congress in Washington, D.C., in September. It cost me thirty dollars to get a copy-write on it. I don't know just when I shall get around to re-doing the Boepple genealogy similarly. I am sending you a copy of another letter that was given me - written by Grandfather Georg to the folks back in Mannsburg, Bessarabia about eighty years ago. It is the third such letter that has come into my possession. He seemed always to keep in pretty close touch with all his people. Trying, I suppose, to lure the rest of them over to this country. He had already gotten seven of them to make that emigration.

PM, Bam-bam, and I attended the German Convention in Aberdeen this past summer. While there I discovered in the literature the names of three additional siblings of George Boepple, which brings the total up to about fifteen of them. There may well have others yet.

VB and I drove out to western Massachusetts to take a week long course in Philosophy at the end of July. The drive was leisurely, so that we were gone for 2 weeks. After that I made another swing through Oregon. I discovered that RL has not yet been successful in arranging for the purchase of the house as he as intended. I was pleased that his appearance and mannerisms seem much more positive and animated now that he is working and earning his way along with more success. I was astounded to see him even spontaneously pick up a couple plants from the store for planting! One need not be a weatherman, to see which way the wind is blowing - as the expression goes. In recent years I have often taken the occasion of your birthday in order to require myself to make an attempt to write a poem. Enclosed is a copy of this year's effort. I am not well pleased with it, but that is how it came out. The best I could do at the time. I plan to hole-up in solitude at X-mas, and make another such effort - another custom that I have taken to in the past several years. And "what's the point of it?" you say. It is just a challenge that I enjoy, and an occasion that makes it possible. Perhaps too, a sort of turning away from X-mas Past, a sort of reversal of the well-know story by Charles Dickens.

Also enclosed is a copy of a letter to DFB from a few years past. A few things there that might be of interest to you. Also, best wishes to BC and the two sons.

Love, Dad

R. Garner Brasseur

11-25-1999

January 2001

To M.A. -

MILLENNIUM

The new millennium soon shall be.
Pray tell me what you then foresee.
Expectantly this juggernaut,
They say may change the world to naught.

Search the writs ... the sky ... within.
Consult the oracles ... omens ... Zen.
Plainly say what shall have been,
When soon we pass millennium.

Doubtful what magicians say,
I see a century pass away.
And standing with descendants tall,
M.A. enshrined upon the wall.

Like mine their years shall transit fast.
And what has been, shall come to pass.

Offspring join ancestral halls,
Of bygone lives upon the wall.

Portraits frozen in past time,
Remind to distant kith and kind,
The legacy of those depart,
Who lent them useful thought and art.

Perhaps in silence and enlight,
We merely hope we led aright.
Upon the nature of reality,
That was, and is, an e'er shall be.

RGB

I was retired and unemployed this year - but hoped yet to get free
from the entanglements of divorce so as to find the economic separation
that would make it worth my while to return to work. Her intention,
I suppose, to continue her court authorized permission for economic
punishment - regardless of its pointlessness - apart from her vindictive
satisfaction.

I arrived in the Portland Oregon area about the 27th of December in
1999 and spent a few days there. It happened that I was at JRO's place on
New Year's Day. It being a nice day JRO, Mich, Joe-joe, Norg, Bobby,
Daniel, and I played touch football in their front yard. The game ended
when I strained my ankle - the first time in my life that I have had that
problem. I spent the next day with PM and his family; and we also
stopped in to see nephew Mal Brasseur and his girl friend. Mal seems
to have made an amazing turn-around this year. He has been sober,
working regularly, and is even thinking of getting married.

On January 3rd I drove down to Reedsport with the hope of seeing
M.A. and her family. I took a motel room there and then stopped in
to see them on the following day for a while. We all napped in the
afternoon. I then brought in a pizza for supper so that they could be
gone early to a church meeting as I returned to my motel room. They
all seemed to be content and well.

The next morning I drive on to Medford. There I visited Bill and Idris W____ for a couple of hours, before driving over to see RL, TM, and the kids. Quite a noisy bunch, and filled with antics and all sorts of enthusiasms. I slept there upon a mattress on the floor in Cowboy's room, and stayed there another two days before heading home. They are still making vague plans for buying the house that they are living in, though their progress in that direction seems slow. My last night there, TMBW was having a card party while RL, I, and the kids watched *Joan of Arc* on the video.

On Saturday the 9th, I watched Cowboy play a basketball game at a local school gym. I talked then briefly with RL and loaned him a thousand dollars to keep his bills paid so as not to ruin his credit rating if he planned to buy the house. About noon I headed out Hwy 140 through Klamath Falls, over the Albert Rim Fault, into Nevada and on to Carson City. I located my old friend, Bob Brown at work in the emergency room at the Fallon Hospital and had a chance to talk with him about fifteen minutes before I retired to a motel. The following morning I headed south through Nevada and stopped over for the night at a casino motel just south of Boulder City. Yes, indulged myself with a big steak dinner and a plush bed in which I sank deeply into a death-like slumber. A rare deviation from my general rule of Spartan frugality. And I arrived home in Albuquerque the following evening.

On January 13th I straightened out the accounts between Bayloo and me in accordance with our pre-nuptial financial agreements. I re-initiated my daily walks of about two miles and continued them throughout the year. We immediately set up the computer and the word processor and I spend progressively more time with it each day. A lot about that required plenty of fumbling about before I got the knack of the various uses I may put it to. Bayloo seems to have the knack and patience for getting various programs on line and for the getting systems back on line as it was doing its frequent nose-dives. Far too many nose-dives. I finally decided to add more memory - an additional 64 Mb, bringing the total up to 80 Mb. It functioned more reliably after that.

Bayloo is working four-day shifts in Santa Fe. On her return trip from Montana in early January, she hit a deer and put some little wrinkles into the fender, breaking the right headlight. I was able to install a new headlight on 14 January. She indicated that her car has been using a little oil and the clutch has had to be re-adjusted. With her car now 17 years old and her having to drive to work in Santa Fe, I suggested the possibility of getting her a replacement vehicle. So we looked at comparative costs and quality of cars in Kiplinger's magazine, and then proceeded to check out some local used cars. Evaluating those costs suggests that the low to medium price cars cost $14,000.00 to $15,000.00 new. And that those selling such similar (but) used cars are asking prices that follow a consistent sort of pattern. The asking price is generally about $1,000.00 less per one year of age of the vehicle, regardless of the age. So, if on the average each car costs about $1,000.00 per year of usage, then we might just as well buy a brand new car to begin with, knowing that either a used or a new car is going to cost one the same $1,000.00 per year. Hence, we would seem to be well advised just to proceed to the purchase of a new car. And we did so. On 25 February we stopped at Garcia Motor on Central Ave., and picked out a new 2000 model Honda Civic four-door white auto with air conditioning, CD player/radio, electronic locks etc. at a cost of _____. As I was thinking of risking some capital into the venture stock market, I thought it might be wise first to invest some of that cash into the cost of the new car, so that even if I were to end up losing out at the pig-trough, I would have at least something to show for my money. And so, I put $5,000.00 cash into the down payment of the car. The remainder to be paid in monthly payments at 4.9% over three years.

I then proceeded upon a program of stock investment by opening an account with Ameritrade.Com, and made my first stock purchase on-line on 2/18/2000. For the past couple of months, and then upon an ongoing basis I was reading some books and magazine information in an effort to grasp the basics of investing. But there seem to be various notions of how one should invest, and where. For the past couple years I had noticed that there were significant week-to-week variations in prices of some of the stocks. Volatile wide fluctuations that seemed to be ongoing already over several months. It seemed to me as though obvious that if a trend such as that were so regular and so ongoing for so long a time, one could just purchase a ticket and ride the ups and downs to one's financial advantage. Buy cheap, and sell dear – how tidy. And even while thus cycling up and down, some companies such as Intel and Microsoft seemed to have a general upward trend that historically progressed to 'splits' such as to enhance their potential value. Still it was my intention to pick out a few stocks that seemed upward bound and ride them upward. But, as things happened, I ended up riding the gyrations of price change. However, just as I was getting invested in the NASDAQ tech boom, the market experienced a minor crash and I was involved in buying and selling in order to try and make up for the 30% loss I accumulated in March and April. I seemed to be doing fairly well at first and was a little euphoric with the action. In order to make it work the better, I was using progressively a large portion of Margin loan funds. Of course, I was aware of that as being risky. But the market had just made a bit of a crash, and was now recovering. And so, I thought I might continue using this Margin allowance for only yet a teensy little while in order to get a bit of a toehold of financial assets of my own. Then, I would back away from the risks of Margin leverage and rely principally on my own enlarged nest egg. By mid-July I was holding stock purchase investments of up to nearly $120,000.00 – though half of that was Margin financed. Still, from my original total investment of just over $43,000.00, my equity was up to about $60,000.00 at times. And then (of course) the whole fabric of my financial hope began to fall apart – "All at once and nothing first. / Just as bubbles do when the burst" – though rather in a sort of slow motion of that scene. But the net result of the bursting bubble was the same whether it came about all of sudden and all at once, or if it came about in slow invincible certainty.

RGB

January 2001

30 November 2010

Santa Fe, New Mexico

Dear M.A.,

I recently came across this entry in an old diary. April 9th, 1980: "While half awake this morning at 8:30 AM, I heard a clomp, clomp, clomp, clomp, clomp, outside the bedroom door. Back and forth, again and again. I wakened more, and puzzled on it. There seemed to be a message in the clomp, clomp, clomping. I sensed an anguish and a torment in those metered pacings. The steps sounded as though from a big pair of shoes. I thought it must be PM. He tends to pace like that when he is nervous or upset. Perhaps his car has broken down and he needs for me to lend him a hand? So I quickly arose and came out to investigate."

"It was M.A., not PM. She was in her night-gown. She had on a large pair of PM's shoes, and was pacing deliberately back and forth in front of my bedroom door. Her message was for her mother - to the effect that it was time to be up so they two could meet Tandy and her mother for breakfast at McDonalds."

RGB

━━━●◆●━━━

And the following poem was one that you and I worked upon together as I was helping you with some of your homework in Hobbs, NM, in 1987. We modeled it upon a poem by Robert Frost. I never heard as to whether or not it sufficed to give you a passing grade for the assignment. Perhaps you didn't even turn it in?

"Whose sock is this I think I know,
Its mate is in the laundry though.
My brother's wrath I need not fear,
My guilt is never apt to show.

My little dog must think it queer,
I don't regard my life more dear.
The dangling sock I then forsake,
And toss it on the carpet near.

She gives her floppy ears a shake,
To question, "Is it hers to take?"

She'd rather tug with foot and teeth,
To earn instead a stalemate.

In truth I'd rather count my sheep,
But there are deadlines I must meet.
And lines to rhyme before I sleep,
This final line before I sleep."
                              14 April 1987

And as a part of your assignments, we wrestled out what seemed to be the meaning of a few poems. One such was *The Heavy Bear Who Goes With Me* by Delmore Schwartz.

"The heavy bear who goes with me,
A manifold honey to smear his face,
Clumsy and lumbering here and there,
The central ton of every place,
The hungry beating brutish one
In love with candy, anger, and sleep,
Crazy factotum, disheveling all,
Climbs the building, kicks the football,
Boxes his brother in the hate-ridden city."

"Stumbles, flounders, and strives to be fed
Dragging me with him in his mouthing care,
Amid the hundred million of his kind,
The scrimmage of appetite everywhere."

Here was another--
Ecce Puer by James Joyce

Of the dark past
A child is born;

With joy and grief
My heart is torn.

Calm in his cradle
The living lies.
may love and mercy
Unclose his eyes!

Young life is breathed
On the glass;
The world that was not
Comes to pass.

A child is sleeping:
An old man gone.
O, father forsaken,
Forgive your son!

———◆◆———

And here is one that you liked and decided to share with me, only to discover as you read it to me that I already had it memorized.

"You are old, Father William," the young man said,
"And your hair has become very white;
And yet you incessantly stand on your head
Do you think, at your age, it is right?

"In my youth," Father William replied to his son,
"I feared it might injure the brain;
But now that I'm perfectly sure I have none,
Why, I do it again and again."

"You are old," said the youth, "as I mentioned before,
And you have grown most uncommonly fat;
Yet you turned back a somersault in at the door
Pray, what is the reason of that?"

"In my youth," said the sage, as he shook his gray locks,
"I keep all my limbs very supple
By the use of this ointment - one shilling a box
Allow me to sell you a couple."

"You are old," said the youth, "and your jaws are too weak
For anything tougher than suet; Yet
you finished the goose, with the bones and the beak
Pray, how did you manage to do it?"

"In my youth," said his father, "I took to the law,
And argued each case with my wife;
And the muscular strength, which it gave to my jaw,
Has lasted the rest of my life."

"You are old," said the youth, "one would hardly suppose
That your eyes was as steady as ever;
Yet you balanced an eel on the end of your nose
What made you so awfully clever?"

"I have answered three questions, and that is enough,"
Said his father; "don't give yourself airs!
Do you think I can listen all day to such stuff?
Be off, or I'll kick you downstairs!"

———◆———

Recollections of the above things returned to my mind as I came across the newspaper picture (enclosed here to you) of you playing tennis as a high school student in Hobbs.

———◆———

I am given to understand that some half-dozen years preceding my earliest recollections, I came into this world as "a quivering lump of clay - not far removed from a beast that day". Not much advantaged above the station of the lowly earthworm, but equipped with compulsions even as these are. Not exempted from the necessities which are visited upon every creature of earth: the necessity to eat and breathe; and the necessity to beget. The urge to explore and inquire. These things being so, then - like the earthworm - I stirred and wriggled in my perceptive dark earth-bound mortality, and set forth presently on the great adventure of existence, where even just to see the obvious requires of one a constant struggle. [paraphrase from Alan Devoe's essay, *Life and Death of a Worm*]

———◆———

In the beginning I was engulfed in an amorphous totality with no detail whatever to impinge upon my obtunded natal consciousness. None of this into which I had been precipitated was of my choosing. I was not a volunteer. Was but "a quivering lump of clay - not far removed from a beast that day". The functioning machinery of my existence had been turned out in the fullness of time; as is the engine of a motor vehicle, from a lump of metal. Precipitated into a family, a neighborhood, a community, a nation, a world of millions. There to be shaped and nurtured into some one or more of a host of potential possibilities and uses, by the times and circumstances of my being; and by the society of similar creatures with whom I have gradually come to recognize as having a great deal in common with myself and with one another.

As the seed of an acorn becomes an oak in the presence of a nutritious soil, atmospheric gases, a favorable climate, water, and sunlight (and circumstance); so also had I gradually attained a form and being, in accordance with the possibilities and limitations of my genetic inheritance. There was much for me to learn in my first few busy years, just to enable me to establish rudimentary communications with those few about me. I wouldn't have survived, if they had not treated me kindly. And through the years I have gradually become half-civilized, and neat, and clean … and well-advised. But in a few years, I found myself outside the nest, with no tangible assets, and having to make my own way in the world. Being broke, cold, hungry, and without a home is a lonesome business - and depressing. As I had strength, good health, and coordination; and had acquired a general sort of education, and a modest capacity for communication and understanding, it seemed like there might ought to be some way that I could put those things to some use, so as to acquire the bare essentials of sustaining a living. Since I was not yet quite desperate enough to beg, and my limited education left me aware that thievery and robbery might leave me in even further difficulty, I needs must give consideration to the possibilities of somehow earning my way along. Endowed as I was with no inheritance, I allowed as how I perhaps myself ought give consideration to the necessity of the alternative of work. It was a hard and desperate business, this work, yet there seemed to be a great many who managed to sustain themselves with little or no apparent labor. How did they manage to get by without that necessity? At least until I might figure that out and emulate that achievement, I needs must 'get to crackin'.

Though there seemed generally to be a lot of work that needed doing; yet there seemed to be a good many people who had an aversion to work: but were so desperate to have it done, that they paid the able and willing in 'coin of the realm', in order not to have to do the work themselves. And so I enquired about, to learn from my fellow laboring wretches, just where and how one might find some such work for which the more well-to-do might pay a man. Fate always enters into to these arrangements, and I did then begin to find enough income to sustain myself. But the work was fatiguing, and increased my appetite, so that I ended up having to do more work that what I had supposed, to satisfy my increasing caloric needs. And once then enabled by work to sustain myself with my basic needs, I then began to acquire additional appetites. I was no longer content just to eat the bread and go without the meat. I was lured by music, theatre, and the dance. Entertaining companions became an additional expense. Soon I was living beyond my means as this cultural inheritance was making its demands upon me - in addition to the demands of genetic inheritance. Expenses were rising.

Physical work proved to be hard and tiring, and I was becoming ever more aware that I did not actually enjoy the work itself by which I was sustained. Confronted as I was with the realities of this world, questions began to arise into my consciousness. Though I had been gifted with the machinery that constitutes this body - and 'a being' - I had never had access to the instruction manual pertaining to the design, operation, and maintenance of this 'being', and its equipment. This business of 'being' had gotten to the point of making a lot of demands upon me. And I was beginning noticeably to have to exert myself to keep up with these demands. Evolved from work and demands and from appetites was also now this matter of 'concerns' that was beginning to weigh in upon me. Was I irrevocably now economically enslaved? Was there no possibility whatever of escape from the burdens of doing the will of others? Perhaps there are alternatives? Perhaps another way to go about this so as not to be so overly encumbered with the necessity of quite so much labor. Perhaps one could find work that was not so physically demanding. Work that was not so repetitive and boring. Work that was not so intellectually taxing, for thinking, too, turns out to be laborious and tiring. Might one find some type of work that was 'enjoyable'? Perhaps one might find a job with a higher rate of pay, so as to require of one less of his time and effort. Perhaps one might find what is called a 'sinecure' - a well paying 'position' with a comfortable office and a staff of underlings - such as a government 'appointment'. Preferably an appointment such as might accord one with a sense of importance; such that one might be treated deferentially just everywhere one might wish to wander at his leisure.

Is everyone - or even anyone - enamored with this business of working for a living? If so, why do we so look forward to the ever next holiday; why hanker in anticipation for the upcoming vacation period and sabbatical; why the dangling carrot to keep one focused on retirement in the by-and-by?

I ask myself, "Do I enjoy doing this troublesome work of writing?". One might aspire to be paid for writing - that could be satisfying. I do like to have completed each of my writing tasks. And I like to read what I have written. But I don't actually much enjoy the work of writing. "Something attempted, something done,/ Has earned a night's repose."

Well, economic reality is an ever present factor that confronts we mere mortals. The earth is not abundantly fruitful apart from the sweat of man's brow that ensues in consequence of his endless toil and endeavor. Shelter from the elements is a necessity to man's survival and comfort, and none such exists in nature. And the clothing necessary to obviate the nakedness of man needs must be garnered by ones own inventiveness and time-consuming effort. No, nothing at all but common sense can ever resolve these woes!

⬤◆⬤

Even a lone shipwrecked sailor (with something near equivalent to a high school education, say) washed up onto a desert isle of sufficient natural shelter and supply of food and water, would end up considering what he might do with himself in his spare time. (Exclude the possibility of rescue or escape in this thought experiment.) Inevitably, he would eventually take some steps to make himself more comfortable, but what then after that (?). Though he has never taken an interest in books, this marooned fellow might now read some … if he had them. If he had some paper, he might write one. Would we say he has absolute freedom - or that he is imprisoned? As with you or I, in the here and now … neither - and both. His situation excludes him from much of that to which he is ordinarily inclined. Would he be driven to madness in his solitude? Or might he preoccupy his mind with reading, study, writing, local observations of day and of nightly phenomena, Philosophy … Might it eventually occur to him, that though a castaway by fate, he might at least leave behind him:

"Footprints in the sands of time;

Footprints, that perhaps another,
Sailing o'er life's solemn main,
A forlorn and shipwrecked brother,
Seeing, may take heart again."

Might he "then, be up and doing,
With a heart for any fate;
Still achieving, still pursuing,
Learn to labor and to wait."

The general nature of one's existence has the possibility of leading one into the most common and ordinary employment in physical labor or a trade, though there is also some possibility of finding one's way into one of many specialties, professional and non-professional. But, one must spend long years in maturing and in learning something from which one can earn a living.

And one must finally not only realize, but also accept that one will not be able to intellectually encompass all of 'that-which-is', within in his limited time for study; nor develop all of the many possibilities to which he has been genetically endowed. Nor drink to the dregs all of even just one field of knowledge. Never time enough for that.

But the history of the universe, the world, the evolution of man and the murk of his unrecorded and controversial versions of his more recent history is an immense tome through which even a dedicated bookwork is not likely ever far to penetrate in the brief span of a single lifetime. The life of the adult mayfly is but a single day; the span of a man's life is scarcely more. But just because I have not taken nor had sufficient time to comprehend 'the all', does not absolve me from the duty of putting forth at least some little symbolic effort at so grand a conquest. A goodwill gesture to my fellow mortals; and perhaps a moral obligation? And thus, my fitful and discombobulated efforts proceed next to the following.

I am inclined to suppose that no man - reviewing his past life from some whatever 'hereafter' - would be pleased to suddenly then become aware that he had frittered away his life devoted to the study and learning of mistaken ideas, erroneous concepts, and groundless religious systems.

Say, for example that there were such a thing as 'a final judgment' in 'a hereafter'. There, the Hindu would be confronted with that now obvious fact (that their beliefs had been based on nothing more than mythical tales and mistaken legends). Called upon then to explain himself, to 'The Grand Inquisitor' what might one reply in the way of mitigating circumstances to get oneself 'off the hook'? Well, there is always the plea of "innocent by virtue of insanity". After all, some 10% of the population is mentally unstable with psychosis or severe characterological defects. Some such plea perhaps as "I was born and raised with that system of belief"; or, "my life was so preoccupied with the desperate business of the earning of a living, that it left me no time to study and ponder concerning the beliefs into which I was born"; or, "it was dangerous, or made life difficult to go against the grain of our common beliefs".

Innocence by virtue of ignorance would seem to be the most logical and probable of 'explanations' one might offer to any such 'grand inquisitor'. And - surely a 'valid' explanation. Though it is true that valid information and knowledge have been gradually increasing for several hundred years, most of what is potentially knowable has not yet yielded to investigative research. Thus, ignorance and misinformation prevail (only slightly diluted) not only among we of the 'unwashed masses' but still holds sway among even the 'the best and brightest' of minds whose authoritative investigations are narrowly focused into specific fields of knowledge. For the expertise and knowledgability of even the minds of bright, well-intended, and honorable men does not extend widely outside of their specific fields of expertise. And they too can plea, that they are at least putting forth an effort to break free of 'the all prevailing ignorance'.

At the back of the mind, one may wish eventually to have done something of value - something perhaps even ennobling. Would like to know what is the nature of the game going on behind the scenes of our 'being', existing, and individual actions.

> "Thus at the flaming forge of life
> Our fortunes must be wrought.
> Thus at the sounding anvil shaped,
> Each burning deed and thought."

What would I think perhaps a worthy 'mission'? The signs of the times suggest that the peace and freedoms with which we in this nation have been blessed are being squandered by the misguided ideologies and misgovernment of our representative government. In my declining years, it hardly seems likely that I would have the time and energy personally to conceive and execute a plan to acquire and have a voice at the seat of government.

Far more likely - and more practical - that you and BC (or a grandchild) might 'save the world' by making a career of that sort of thing? One can make a living - a career - at it, and I see no reason why one might not well be able to take up the challenge in the years of ones youth and vitality. Do our country a favor. "Ask not what your country can do for you etc." You already have connections all over southwestern Oregon as a base. RL already has connections with one the most powerful of unions. You could enter as new age purists, along with Sarah Palen. Work something out with Mike Huckabee in his upcoming campaign to get your feet wet. Get used to doing some public speaking, and the reading and research which that requires would gradually soon bring one up to speed on topics and issues of political significance.

Mexico is going down in flames over the control of drugs by rival cartels and gangs, and the problem is spilling over into the USA. At the heart of the problem is what has become an enormous appetite by gringos for 'substances'. I had no idea how big a problem that might be until we catch news of the tons of illegal substances coming across the borders. And hundreds of murders and of those killed in the cross-fires by and between the rival gangs.

Even when I lived in Southern Oregon in the late 1960's there was already a drug problem there, which seemed to be centered around the Cave Junction area and radiated to all the surrounding area. As I have never had any personal experience with either alcohol, MJ, or other illegal substances, I was only remotely aware of it all. That whole area between Hwy 5 and Hwy 101, from Roseburg down to Redding is rather of the nature of a wilderness which seems to have been used increasingly for the illegal growing of MJ. As the lumber industry was going out, people from all over the country were moving in to grow

MJ along with those now unemployed lumber industry people. MJ began to sell at a thousand dollars a pound. Mendocino County became then the heart of the problem. There was a helicopter crackdown on this illegal substance farming in the 1980's, and the price rose to $5,000 per pound. It became a good living if one didn't get caught. Many of these 'farmers' became wealthy - strong income on which no taxes were being paid. Some enterprising high school students were raking in fifty thousand or a hundred thousand dollars in their summer vacations. People began to be able to live in comfort with this new income source. The illegal growing persists. In some towns MJ is the only major business, and what other businesses there are, can offer no comparable wage. One Humboldt County resident is quoted as saying that of 300 families in her community, only five were not growing MJ. (These figures and details gathered from *THE WEEK* news magazine, December 3, 2010)

Alcohol had caused a great deal of social difficulties throughout the ages, but when it became illegal, the associated problems became a great deal more troublesome. MJ and possibly other substances may end up in needing to be legalized similarly. Along with alcohol, it may continue to ruin health and lives, but the government will never be big enough to protect people from the detrimental results of their own indiscretions and folly.

I believe you ought to give serious thought to the health and well-being of your nephews and nieces. These youngsters moving back and forth across our southern borders to spend time at Carmen Serdon, are very much at risk of getting caught up into the massive traffic in drugs and arms that is resulting in the deaths of thousands, whose bodies are turning up in mass graves in Northern Mexico. In the first place, some of these youngsters (your nephews and nieces) are said already to have succumbed to minor economic infractions and get-rich schemes. My experience is that some of them have a marked predisposition to fritter away whatever valuable coin comes to within their grasp. The drug cartel outlaws find these young naïve innocents to be ideal tools for the transport of illegal contraband, at low cost and low risk to themselves, and have no qualms about disposing of their lifeless bodies once they have served their purpose to them. The occasional young girl you send them could end up at an involuntary career in what they call 'white slavery'.

The flood waters were rising along the Mississippi and folks were being rescued and evacuated. A man climbed on to the roof of his house as the waters continued to rise. Along came a man with a boat and offered to take him to safety. He declined the assistance, saying, "God will save me". And the boat motored on over the horizon. The water continued to rise. A short time later a helicopter came by and threw a line down to him, instructing him to grab hold and be pulled up to safety. "God will save me" he told the airlift. And the helicopter went away to continue its mission. The waters continued to rise, and eventually washed the house away – and the man drowned.

The man got past the pearly gates to confront God. "I am surprised to see you here", says God. "I was waiting for you to save me", says the man. God says, "But I sent you a boat … and then I even sent you a helicopter."

In the past few years I have had cause to communicate with a particular woman from among my many acquaintances. She was in some sort of financial distress to the extent that she contacted me for a loan to tide her over. She assured me that she would definitely pay me back within a few months, and even went to the trouble of laying out for me the details of how she would be able to accomplish that. I have always liked the woman and was sympathetic to her request. I told her I wasn't interested in going over her list of figures as to how she might pay me back – as these vague and speculative accounting things are rather boring. I would just send her what she needed and that she could pay me back as best she could and when. As I was working at the time, I was not hard pressed to send her what she requested. But, knowing something of her economic circumstances, I did not deem it as being realistic that she would be able to return to me the payments with as much ease and regularity as what she had suggested. But then, to who else she going to turn to get her through this tight spot? And besides, I was long accustomed through the years to the throwing away of similar sums of money on various persons of my acquaintance. The next I heard from her was that she was needing actually a little more money, for this other problem that had slipped up on her unexpectedly. "In for a penny, in for a pound". Being in a rush to get to work that day, and recognizing myself as being an easy mark, I turned her over to Bayloo, who would be able look into our accounts to see if we had enough available to send it out to her this very day. And she did.

Now the game had changed. That evening Bayloo told me that she didn't want to be in the middle of this thing. I had to explain to her that it was necessary. For she would be losing as much money on these loans as was I. And the borrower was now in the situation of having to recognize that she was actually borrowing from both Bayloo and I, and that she was now having to make any further requests through someone not quite so much 'an easy touch', as was I.

That was two or three years ago, and none of the money has yet been repaid. I didn't really expect that it would be, but as I told Bayloo, at least we seem now to be off the hook for any further such 'loans'. The borrower has contacted me a couple times since then to assure me that she now has another plan by which she might soon be able to begin making payments. She and I both seem to sense that some coolness has worked its way into our once closer relationship. Well, I still like this woman, but I am reminded that "a promise made, is a debt unpaid" and that any such situation tends to put a strain on a relationship. Not that I much care whether or not she ever repays the loan. But one can presume that she is now at least a little bit cool toward me, account of the money she still owes. The warmth of it tends to radiate away. I ought just to have given her the money and let it go that way. It is money that I am able to get along without, anyway.

I wondered then how this woman and spouse were figuring on a possible retirement about twenty years down the road from now. I made a wild guess that if they were able to put away a thousand dollars a month regularly, that they could probably retire in twenty years. But a quick calculation indicated that would come to only 240,000.00. With 480,000.00 the possibility of retirement might be a little more realistic (along, of course with some modest social security benefit). That would require putting away two thousand a month. Even so, invested money seems to me as apt to be lost, as to be earning any significant interest on investment.

Well, since you have some education in things like mathematics and accounting, you are probably more aware of matters such as this than ever I was. Perhaps you are putting away two or three thousand dollars a month? Though I have no information on the matter, I don't actually expect that you are. It would please me to be wrong on this matter. Certainly I was never able to give any consideration to retirement funds and pension when I was your age.

My brothers all seem to be retired in reasonable comfort at the present time. But all of them had wives that worked and contributed to the family income through the years. I am currently working only about five or six days a month, as the economy is slow, but expect to get a little busier if the economy picks up after the first of the year. At my age, I could probably get by without working any at all, but then what would I do to occupy my time?

I hear that Fluff and her girls are now living up in Everett, Washington, where she has had to take some refresher courses to get started back to working for a living. From the sound of things, I suppose that she is either divorced or in the process of divorce. I guess that (her mother) BJJB is probably handling most of the household necessities.

Dolly called PP to get his ideas on what to do about their living arrangements as they are what you call 'upside down' on the home they were buying. I guess they are doing as PP advised; just no longer paying the mortgage payments. Saving that money to get a new start on a less costly place, once housing has fallen back down to more realistic and sustainable prices. In the meantime, there are so very many places in default across this nation, that it may well be a couple years or more before the bank gets around to the foreclosure process and getting one out of the place.

Well, M.A., I am supposing that you too could be 'upside down' on the house that you are buying, for all I know. Which is why I passed on the above little piece of news to you. Do what you need to do to stay economically afloat. And pay attention to the tsunami warnings down there on the coastal lowlands.

I haven't heard for sure, but I suspect that Dolly as well as Fluff may have gone back to work in the face of the new economic stringencies. And as far as I know, their sister has continued to work through the years. Until and unless the economics of this country returns to a state of promise and stability, one needs must do what is necessary. And that recovery can happen only if the voters are able and willing to rid themselves of the 'progressive socialists', the frank Marxist Communists, One-Worlders, and 'the anointed one'.

And don't dismiss out of hand the possibility that you too may have to consider finding a way to earn a paycheck to help your family along, as have many of the women in our family of peasant folks.

Greeting to BC, Josh, Izzie, and Moriah.

Love,

Dad,

R. Garner Brasseur

11-30-2010

30 November 2011

Santa Fe, New Mexico

Dear M.A.,

"Everyone wants to save the world; no one wants to help mom do the dishes."

In my childhood and early youth my parents and siblings directly and indirectly swept me into the current of daily routine and activities. I bobbed along sort of treading water in that current of daily routine with no plans or agenda of my own and with only the vaguest perception that perhaps in some distant future day I might be what was called 'an adult' with the liberty and freedom to own an independent life and perhaps be in charge of directing the ongoing goals and objectives of my own little batch of children. As best I could discern, that seemed to be the way things were headed for all of us youngsters - 'in the fullness of time', as the expression goes. And that somewhere 'in the by-and-by', even that would come to an end, and I would probably go to heaven - wherever that was.

Well, I stopped over to see Paul and Jackie Lewis the other day. He was a high school classmate of my brother, EVH. And Jackie is a sister to one of my high-school pals, Jim Phalen. She tells me that EVH once proposed to her. She seems to have turned him down because he wasn't religious enough. So she married Paul and they were attached to an arm of a missionary organization in Brazil for about thirty years, where his main assignment was to maintain and repair airplanes for various bush pilots who shuttled the grass-roots missionaries and supplies into the outback jungle clearings. Then, about 1986, he had a heart attack and had to have coronary artery bypass surgery. At that point (about 25 years ago) they retired and moved here to Santa Fe; because their oldest daughter is married to a local doctor here. When Bayloo and I moved here to Santa Fe (8 or 9 years ago) I ran into them again and discovered that they lived less than two miles from us. And so I stop by to visit them a couple hours every two or few weeks. Paul is about 85 years old now, but still alert and active. Jackie is my age and seems to get along cheerfully despite her several disabilities. So I am well acquainted with them since I was about ten years of age, and we talk of old times and fellow acquaintances. But every once in a while Paul gets a hankering to attempt to put a halter on me and drag me into his heavenly fold. And it sometimes takes a little ingenuity to get him back to some subject less potentially troublesome to our nearly lifelong friendship.

Eluding his intentions once again, I managed to wrangle him back to some superficial talk of politics and economics. And so he was telling me what has happened in Brazil through the years. Some of their children and grandchildren still live there, and Paul and Jackie usually fly back to visit for a spell once or twice a year. As the American dollar seems on the verge of faltering in the past few years, I was interested to learn from Paul that the Brazilian currency had gone into default FIVE times, through the years of his experience. Each time, they moved the decimal point three positions to the left, so that a thousand cruzeros then becomes one cruzero. (A total of 15 zeros had thus gradually been lopped off) - and they now call it a 'Real', rather than a cruzero. You would think that would cause more than just a little disruption in their economic system. I am having a hard time wrapping my head around what would ensue from that sort of devaluation of the American dollar.

And yet, in reality, the Brazilian economy is said currently to be one of the strongest economies in the world. I was thinking that since my daughter has either a minor (or is it a major?) in Economics, I thought she might some day explain this all to me? I am just then beginning to perceive and suppose to myself some rudimentary theory as to what has been going on behind the scenes in American economics. I guess it will be easier for me to grasp once the dollar falls, (perhaps to be replaced by the Nu-dollar?) and I get some first-hand experience of the thing.

Doolittle Economics:

UNEMPLOYMENT BENEFITS ARE IN the news again. Congressional Republicans have proposed a bill that would allow states to redirect federal unemployment funds away from paying cash benefits and toward rebuilding depleted state unemployment-insurance funds.

Democrats object strenuously, saying the idea is neither fair nor effective. The White House lists such cash benefits as "one of the best measures for jump-starting growth and job creation." But House Minority Leader Nancy Pelosi of California declares that curbing cash benefits "could destroy as many as 300,000 jobs over the next year," and that "every dollar invested in unemployment insurance yields a 'return' of $1.60 in economic growth." The Economic Policy Institute says that such benefits put "cash in the hands of needy families that would spend it", and, therefore cash benefits have a high multiplier effect.

The economic reasoning of the Democrats has been consistent (erroneous). Last year, the then 'Speaker Pelosi' told us that extending unemployment cash benefits "injects demand into the economy" because the benefits are "spent quickly". She tells us that alternative policies that cut taxes for 'wealthy people' are judged less effective by economist Paul Krugman because "they're not going to spend very much of it." *Barron's* readers who noticed her little opinion probably chuckled. A few perhaps joked that the same sort of reasoning has put Greece and Zimbabwe on the 'sound fiscal footing' (?) they enjoy to this day. That is to say, ruination.

Literary readers could trace such economic reasoning to Alfred P. Doolittle, George Bernard Shaw's delightful character in *Pygmalion,* one of London's 'common dustmen'. Doolittle could be said to hold

'Keynesian' economic views regarding spending and jobs and the proper rate for the creation of demand from any spare change he could scare up.

Pelosi's views thus bring to mind this character, Alfred Doolittle, from the musical, *My Fair Lady* (based on G.B. Shaw's play, *Pygmalion)*. Doolittle learns that his daughter Eliza has moved in with Professor Henry Higgins to take elocution and grammar lessons. Based on the idea that this constitutes a loss to himself, Doolittle goes to see Higgins and friend Pickering to try to get some 'benefits' out of them - specifically a five-pound note. He assures the two men that he understands their intentions are honorable, for if they weren't he'd ask fifty. When asked whether he has any morals whatsoever, he tells the two gentlemen he "can't afford 'em."

Alfred Doolittle frames his final argument by focusing on the value of his daughter, "what he's brought up, he's fed, he's clothed by the sweat of his brow...until she growed big enough...to be interesting to you two gentlemen? Well, is five pounds unreasonable? I puts it to ya and I leaves it to ya."

Higgins: "Pickering, here. Shall we give him a fiver?"

Pickering: "He'll make bad use of it,"

Doolittle: "No, no. So help me, guvnor. I shan't save it, spare it or live idle on it. There won't be a penny of it left on Monday. Just one good spree for myself and the missus … givin' pleasure to ourselves and employment to others."

Higgins: "This is irresistible. Let's give him ten."

Doolittle: "No. The missus wouldn't have the heart to spend ten. Ten pounds is a lot of money. makes a man feel prudent-like. And then, good-bye to happiness."

This is not to equate the spending of unemployment benefits with the particular spending that the bibulous Mr. Doolittle had in mind, but to point out that Alfred P. Doolittle was by nature, sort of an economic theorist.

Doolittle isn't merely bargaining with Higgins; he is advancing a broader, societal justification for a financial outlay. Doolittle assures Higgins he would inject those five pounds into the economy - and quickly. His comments suggest that something about prudence and thrift has detrimental effects on the health of the economy. Doolittle self-righteously predicts that the effect of his prompt outlay will prove to be a stimulus to employment. He doesn't need the help of dozens of computer-trained dustmen at the Economic Policy Institute to apprise him of what seems to him to be obvious.

Shaw arranges a grand ending for Alfred P. Doolittle. Shortly after his first encounter with Doolittle, Professor Higgins answers a letter from an American millionaire, one Ezra Wallingford, who is interested in starting moral-reform society. Wallingford asks Higgins to recommend a moral instructor. Higgins writes back to suggest Alfred P Doolittle, is "one of the most original moralists in England." Wallingford dies soon afterward, leaving a pot of money for Doolittle to use to lecture and to live on.

Alfred tells his daughter, Eliza that, in so doing, Henry Higgins has gotten his revenge and ruined his previously easy life-style, delivering him up "into the hands of middle-class morality." So situated, Alfred P. Doolittle's position is barely distinguishable from that of (a seeming majority) of tenured 'ivy-league' university economists, who are fattened by wealthy donors and contemptuous of the trappings of middle-class life.

The economic reasoning of the Democrats draws much from the same strain that animated Alfred P. Doolittle. They - like Doolittle - associate prudence and saving with idleness and unhappiness and the sterile image of money stacked up in bank vaults, while supposing that spirited spending leads to happiness and the employment of others.

The arguments in support of unemployment benefits are versatile, and can be used to support countless other programs as well: 'shovel-ready jobs', a 'green economy', and 'infrastructure investments', to name a few. They are expected (by democrats) to liberate capital from the capitalists and put some spending money into the hands of working folks, and thereby keep an ailing economy from producing more unemployment and unhappiness. The variations are many, limited only by the imaginations of public officials anxious to spend other peoples' money.

So the next time you hear another such official or economist trot out one of these arguments, think of Alfred P. Doolittle and his economic policy, and remember that the money will all be happily gone by Monday.

When all is said and done, one must come to recognize that each life is faced with its own particular difficulties. And that all are not equal in any sense, though in this nation there has generally been some intent and some effort to put us on an equal par before the law. An ideal that undoubtedly is destined never to be fully accomplished. Nor will any political system ever succeed in equalizing our economic circumstances. We certainly wouldn't want to be equally destitute. And were we all equally wealthy, where would we find anyone to serve our interests? Whatever the prevailing political climate, there is but little we individually can do to effect much change in it. About the best we can do is to make an effort to recognize the realities in which we are personally immersed, and make what adjustments we can to get by as we must.

A reasonable agenda? To perhaps free oneself from the superstition and ignorance which are obstacles to one's rational purpose; and an obstruction to one's view of reality.

Best wishes M.A. to you in your 45th year now that you are past your 44th birthday. My regards to BC, Josh, Izzy, and Moriah.

Love,
Dad,
R. Garner Brasseur

11-30-2011

January 2013

Santa Fe, NM

Dear Grand Girls,

The evening of Dec. 15th after visiting with Michah and his family, I attended the opening performance of Lolli Brasseur's Christmas Cantata. Their whole family participated in the performance. As it seemed to me that the JRO family might be feeling cramped for space at Michah's place, I arranged to stop over for the night at the home of nephew in Everett. And as my vacation days were hastening on, I drove all the way down to Medford the following day.

Following the performance of Lolli's Cantata, I gathered with those good folks a while that evening before turning in for the night. Grandniece Lolli had written me a week or two earlier, and as we two had little time for any one-to-one conversation, she made me promise to write her. Knowles's Law says that it is easier to make a commitment or get involved in something than it is to get our of it. And so it was that I wrote her - sort of flattered that she might be interested in anything I might have to say. Firstly, of course to congratulate her on what she had achieved in her musical career. Extending herself beyond her mastery of her Harp, and then onward to be numbered among the ranks of composers of music. And beyond that … to actually bring her composition into production. Her genius, energy, and efforts seem well deserving of the recognition she achieved.

As with my grandniece, so also with you - my granddaughter - not much time for any much one-to-one leisurely conversation. As you remind me in your recent note, I am left to suppose that this business of 'jet lag' is a very real thing, though I have never done enough flying to have any personal experience of that.

By now presumably you are all pretty much settled back in China with even enough spare time to honor me with some of your attention. And so I had better now get out a response to you before I get started on the composition of my annual summary - a time consuming habit I have acquired through the years.

Though I am accustomed to being with and around people, I am not much accustomed to social interaction situations. Shy, you might say. I think of myself primarily as an observer when in group situations - somewhat removed from participation. An observer of group dynamics. I lack the proficiency and self confidence in the art of 'small talk' as I mingle with others in the routine of daily life. I tend to feel out of place in the presence of strangers, and even among much of my extended family, unless I have been appointed or self-appointed to serve some specific function whilst I am with or among them. As when I can play the role of a physician, or actively engaged with them is some sport or game, or in the process of collecting information from them, as when obtaining genealogy information.

Quote from DFB:

> "We are all of us essentially isolated and alone, even from those we love most and feel closest to, when we are sick or in pain. We are like prisoners in a large jailhouse, each confined to his own little cell. There is no way to pass a hand through the wall to touch another in a meaningful way nor to see through it to share a common point of view on the nature of our confinement. At best we can rattle the bars or bang a tin cup against the wall to call attention to our plight, our isolation. We can but recognize the one common thread of humanity, and that is our mortality."

One's personal pain, anguish, and angst; as well as one's personal sense of joy and pleasure can never be shared out at anything approaching totality.

Through the years I have had perhaps a dozen or more good friends with whom I am able easily to converse on a one-to-one basis. Likewise, with some of those of my immediate and extended family. I expect I might have encountered more with whom I might have developed closer conversational ease, had I had more time for such leisurely occasions. But life is a busy business.

I note that in our society, most social get-togethers are accompanied by the use of some form of alcohol or drug, and at age 48 I first permitted myself to imbibe a little alcohol on one of those occasions. I noted immediately how much more easily and comfortably the small-talk and socializing then progressed for me. I had expected that might be the case, but with only rare occasion for social get together with persons of only remote acquaintance, and with a dislike for the taste of beer, I had never before gotten around to giving it a try. That first alcoholic drink was a Margarita, and I found the taste and the euphoric effect to be pleasant. The occasion was precipitated upon me by my first get together with professional peers in a community in New Mexico where I had recently associated with a group of fellow physicians. It then became my practice to have a Margarita at each of the monthly medical society meetings, to take the edge off of my social discomfiture. Subsequently, on special social occasions, I have been offered and tried a few different wines - none of which was so pleasing to my palate as to encourage me to wish to sample it again - or to prefer any such wine to a Margarita.

And so, in any case, my first-hand experience has led me to conclude that a bit of 'spirits' eases one's natural discomfiture in the inevitable social gatherings to which one is obliged from time-to-time. It seems to facilitate the generally intended good will of such gatherings by easing one's natural inhibitions and 'loosening the tongue', while also producing a noticeable mild euphoria that somewhat facilitates a spirit of companionship. For while our species is numbered among those with a 'herd' or social instinct, and that instinct is generally always more manifest among those to whom we are more closely related; family first and tribe secondarily. But even among those to whom we are more closely related, there is also yet that stark and ever present awareness of one's individuality and essentials aloneness, so that one is always also a bit at odds with even those to whom one is closest. Hence, there is always a 'pecking order', even within the family, tribe, and herd. In the depths of one's inner thought and being, one can always detect that essential aloneness.

It is obvious that the female of our species is much more inclined to social interaction and conversation then are we fellows. Their role as mothers to each subsequent generation would seem to require that, as they must first to some degree tame the residual beast within the spouse they select: and then with patience, rear and civilize their own offspring. Somewhat by patient example, and by a great deal of rhetoric - much of it, 'small talk' … as one might expect, as they deal so much with small people (the children). And with our ever slow cultural evolution, eventually - perhaps - "We shall all be civilized. And neat. And clean. And well advised. And won't mother nature be surprised."

There is something that is attention-getting about a smile. To encounter one, puts one somewhat at ease from his customary guardedness and suspiciousness. A smile can be inviting – even seductive. But … caution. What appears to be a smile may easily be an intentional deception and a useful ploy. But always an asset to the extent that one can own such a smile. As for example, the seemingly ever present smile of a politician such as Reagan or Obama – disarming. What seems to be a smile may rather, be a smirk or even a question mark. Some fortunate persons have a natural configuration of the mouth that resembles a perpetual smile, which – unknowing to themselves – facilitates their passage in social settings and in business transactions. A short upper lip which keeps the upper teeth always somewhat exposed gives always the faint impression of a smile. Common enough, especially among the female sex, that it seems to me to be a generally feminine trait, just as is the natural curvaceousness of the feminine form. And with just the slightest effort, that 'natural smile' can be easily advantageously enhanced to suit one's purposes. But when the dog, or the lion, or the shark bares its teeth at us, we readily perceive that as something other than a friendly smile.

As we observe the mass of mankind we note that along with all the mammalian beasts of the field and the sea, we seem primarily as though intended to be short-lived individual reproductive units, generally intended and destined primarily to pass our inherited genes on to yet one more generation – ad infinitum. "Constrained by the wonders of dying and birth" to that primary function. And yet, as social creatures and as a part of the herd, our species (Homo sapiens) appears to have within its nature the latent capacity to rise above that primary function. Somewhere – somehow – the herd instincts of our species has gradually evolved into what would eventually become a primitive 'culture'. A culture that has and continues haltingly to evolve within the family and the tribe – generation by generation. Oh, yes … evolved.

But our days are numbered (see 'Mayfly' pp.68-72 of *Impulsive Meditations*); and each day we have energies enough for only a limited number of hours of wakefulness and achievement. We needs must then repair to a dormant state of rest. And yet, even at rest our basal rate of metabolism continues along with a residual chaos of loosely held thought. Thoughts that disentangle – and recombine into other shapes and forms to produce what we call by the name of dreams. Dreams which are shaped by the same hopes, fears, and wishes of our waking hours (but there, constrained and frustrated by the ever present realities of each evolving day). Some of these fragments of thought do seem to have something of a sexual nature about them – in that there in dreamland such fragments of thought meet and mate (electro-physiologically), so that they reproduce and occasionally give 'life' to an entirely new idea. Thesis and antithesis produce the occasional synthesis. And as we slowly awaken to consciousness, most of our dream state images and thought tend to fade, as do mirages in the landscapes of our waking hours of reality. But every once in a while, one of those newborn idea fragments escapes from dreamland into our conscious world. There to lead or inspire onto an innovative action or something of use in the world of reality. From Neil Diamond's *Jonathan Livingston Seagull*, the following: "We sleep ... so (that) we may dream, one more night." "We dream ... for we may wake, one more day" (informed or inspired to new achievement). By increments, our tools and methods evolve to permit us to become less of the nature of mere beasts of burden, and more of the nature of civilized rational beings, with interests and aptitudes for the literature, the arts, sciences, and philosophy. Perhaps even one day peace may settle in among us?

And you, Lolly and Stan - like myself - have been very much influenced by the particular cultural motives and forces of your family. Basically, all that one can have is one's life. What will ... what ought one to do with it? We are all at least somewhat enslaved. Enslaved to the earning of one's living, at least. Enslavement to taxation. Enslaved in reality by one's own misconceptions of reality, and each, limited and enslaved by an ignorance of almost the entirety of the world and universe in which we live. And yet, we in this nation still have some little liberty, opportunity, and time to have a hand in the shaping of our own lives and destinies – and always the possibility of making a positive contribution to perhaps some few of one's friends and relatives - and posterity. I think especially of music, literature, and poetry – which contribute so much to my limited satisfactions with life.

From my manuscript of "Brasseur genealogy":

In the passing of one's life, the self-concept which one owns tends to bump along upon an erratic course: changing, along with historical circumstances of the outcome of the "challenge and response" of Life (Toynbee's theory of history). The challenge and response, cuts in both directions. Encountering challenge, our own response - and its effect - alters the course of one's life. And in our challenging of society in quest of new opportunity we needs must be prepared to exert and concentrate our efforts, to make and sustain our challenge. Our efforts, along with omnipresent fate, always weigh heavily into the equation. Thus, there is always that - in each life - which is of great potential interest, in the telling and hearing. And the history of our ancestors, the more so, since it is relevant to the fates and opportunities that impinge upon one's own life: and since one can so naturally identify with those lives of our very own people.

We each own a personal history of our own changing and evolving existence: which is largely based upon our personal experience, and the recollection of that experience. Based also, upon one's own attitude and interpretation of that experience ... an eminently more subtle influence. And one that is more suitable to the retrospective and evolving history of our immediate family. In turn, how that relates to the history of the tribe, school, region, and nation. No doubt each individual mental existence is based upon the tangible, physical reality of one's individual being. In good health and under favorable circumstance, the essential and fundamental needs of the body and its instincts can be met with efficiency such as may permit to one the requisite time and energy for the flowering of the intangible mental aspect of being. From the mental ... issues forth the possibility of progressively incisive thought. Thought, in turn, may progress to ideas and concepts. These, tempered by the moral influence of reality and a valid experience of reality, form the basis of advancing civilization. This, seems to be what Voltaire has in mind, when he speaks of his intent to discover the history of the human mind. Marx said it well… "Ideas are to history; as thought is to human action".

"Let us remember all we owe to the past as a spiritual continuum which forms part of our supreme spiritual heritage", says Jacob Burckhardt, in his *Reflections on History*. "Anything which can in the remotest way serve our knowledge of it, must be collected, whatever toil it may cost." Now, having acquired some rudimentary facts and progressions of our family history, we are enabled to refer and compare it to the documented history of the place and times to which it belongs - to verify and adjust its probable accuracy. Next, then, is the task of deciding for ourselves, its meaning and relevance to our own lives. Which, places us into the realm of "conjecture and refutation" - Karl Popper's idea, as to the meaning of history. Karl Roth points out that our entire being and doing is dependent on those who preceded us, but that never-the-less, tradition ought not be inflexibility; but rather, creative transmittal.

———◆◆———

Aside from the fundamental necessities of life (air to breathe, food to eat, water, shelter, a place to rest and opportunity for sleep): there seem to me to be two additional motives that drive the individual human being – both of which appear to be driving forces that have the onset of their being early in life, and seem commonly to persist long years into an adult life. One would be the notion of romantic love between a boy and a girl, which I first noticed in my own being at perhaps the age of nine or 10 years. It, perhaps, is a modified version of the love an infant has - especially for the mother upon whom the infant is so nearly entirely dependent.

The other, a sexual interest which has its hormonal beginnings at perhaps age 13 or 14. Somewhat beyond the age of - say 14 - these two impulses seem generally to begin to fuse and predispose to notions of marriage. And yet they seem in some, to remain distinct and separate. Thus love and sex may or may not be vitally linked. Or, may become so only later, in more mature years. Having once fused into a unity the intensity of the romantic aspect seems not uncommonly through the years to fade - as do the colors in the fabric of one's clothing. We note that young love is more physically demonstrative than a mature and aging love. Even so, the ecstasy of sex along with mutual economic interests and mutual interest and affection for the offspring seems generally to continue to hold a marriage together. And yet, the ubiquity of extramarital sex suggests that the two entities (love object and sex object) not uncommonly become detached – and predispose to some marital difficulty, or to the possibility of divorce, where that is socially and economically feasible. And especially where the objectives in life between husband and wife tend to diverge.

Through the years since about age 10, I suppose that I have been infatuated with some two or three dozen or more girls or women at one time or another. Most of them perhaps never so much as suspected that. Others I suppose, would have had more promising prospects than myself. A couple of early promising minor attachments failed from obvious incompatibilities. The sparks and embers of some of those failed infatuations tend to linger in one's psyche. There is always the possibility of those mostly forgotten potential infatuations to flare up in chance meetings, as when one returns to 'the old stomping grounds', or a reunion of some kind. I've seen and heard of it happening on a number of occasions. And so it can be said that there are a number of women that I have loved and do love in one sense or another - yourself included - but my current contentment and circumstance of age make it highly improbable that anything could ever make of any of them anything other then calm and quiet distant admirations, whose recollection occasionally strays across one's mind. Remembering too, of course, there are other varieties of 'love' than romantic love.

What is more intellectually interesting, is the fact that one is attracted to so very few of those with whom one has contact - even among physically attractive, civil, and talented persons. Even among persons with whom one is friendly, one considers but few of them as 'good friends'. The hours of each day, and the days of each life, are all too few to permit of anything more.

Best wishes to you for yet another interesting and productive year. "May the menace of the years yet find us unafraid."

Love,
Gramps
R. Garner Brasseur, M.D.

January 2013